POWER AND PROTEST

POWER AND PROTEST

GLOBAL REVOLUTION AND THE RISE OF DETENTE

JEREMI SURI

HARVARD UNIVERSITY PRESS

CAMBRIDGE, MASSACHUSETTS, AND LONDON, ENGLAND

First Harvard University Press paperback edition, 2005

Library of Congress Cataloging-in-Publication Data

Suri, Jeremi.
   Power and protest : global revolution and the rise of detente / Jeremi Suri.
      p. cm.
   Includes bibliographical references and index.
   ISBN 0-674-01031-0 (cloth)
   ISBN 0-674-01763-3 (pbk.)
      1. Detente.   2. World politics—1965–1975.
   3. Student movements—History—20th century.
   4. United States—Social conditions—1960—1980.
   5. China—Social conditions—1949–   6. Soviet Union—Social conditions—1945–1991.
   7. Europe—Social conditions—20th century.   8. Protest movements—United States.
   9. Protest movements—Europe.   I. Title.

D849 .S83 2003
909.82′6—dc21   2002038812

To Alison

ACKNOWLEDGMENTS

This book received support from many institutions. I wish to thank the University of Wisconsin Graduate School; the U.S. Institute of Peace; the Smith Richardson Foundation; the Center for International and Area Studies at Yale University; the Seeley G. Mudd Manuscript Library at Princeton University; and the Dwight D. Eisenhower, John F. Kennedy, Lyndon B. Johnson, and Gerald R. Ford Presidential Libraries for funding much of my research. Individuals at each of these institutions provided me with encouragement, expert assistance, and good cheer. I must also express my appreciation to the many archivists in Germany, France, Russia, Hungary, Great Britain, and the United States who facilitated my work. Without the skill of such professionals, historians could never make meaningful claims.

I must single out International Security Studies (ISS) at Yale and the Center for International Security and Cooperation (CISAC) at Stanford for allowing me to share in two extraordinary communities of learning. Both institutions sponsored a series of programs that enriched my intellectual vision, provided extensive resources for research and writing, and exposed me to exciting ideas and fascinating people.

The scholars and friends who have offered advice and encouragement are really too numerous to name, but I want to express special gratitude to two individuals—Jeremy Fielding and Jay Geller—who shared lodgings and meals with me during extensive archival expeditions. Their companionship away from home made the long months of foreign research tolerable.

I have been blessed with extraordinary mentors throughout my academic career. While I was a Stanford undergraduate, David M. Kennedy, Barton Bernstein, and Jack Rakove taught me what it meant to be a historian. At Ohio University, Steven Miner and Chester Pach broadened my historical vision. At Yale, Paul Kennedy and Jonathan Spence guided me in conceptualizing, researching, and writing rigorous international history.

Most of all, I have benefited from the consistent support of John Lewis Gaddis. I have known John for more than ten years, and he has always provided a model of academic integrity. He encouraged me to see the value in a broad international study, but he also required me to strive for the very highest standards in accuracy, clarity, and elegance. John read some chapters in twelve successive drafts, demanding that I rewrite errant sentences and rethink unpersuasive arguments. Though possessing strong opinions of his own, John never tried to coerce me to his personal perspective. He held me to the same high standards to which he holds himself. I am profoundly grateful.

The final version of this book reflects the insightful and detailed suggestions of my editor, Kathleen McDermott. Her penciled comments on virtually every page of the manuscript showed me how to write a clearer and more engaging narrative. Her faith in my work has inspired me. My research assistant, Sean Gillen, helped me to follow through on Kathleen's advice. Laura Gottlieb crafted an outstanding index.

I have also found inspiration in my new hometown of Madison and its great university. As one of the youngest members of the faculty, I have received encouragement from many wiser colleagues. Most important, I have drawn energy from a remarkable community of scholars who combine academic breadth, pedagogical passion, and community service. Yes, the "Wisconsin Idea" is alive and well. This is my first contribution.

I have dedicated this book to the most amazing person I know, my wife, Alison Alter. Her creativity and devotion inspired me to think broadly. Her commitment to make the world a better place drove me to ask important questions. Above all, Alison's love gave me the confidence to undertake this project, and also the inclination to finish it and move on to other things.

CONTENTS

INTRODUCTION   1

1
THE STRAINS OF NUCLEAR DESTRUCTION   7

2
POLITICAL CONSTRAINTS AND PERSONAL CHARISMA   44

3
THE LANGUAGE OF DISSENT   88

4
THE ILLIBERAL CONSEQUENCES OF LIBERAL EMPIRE   131

5
THE GLOBAL DISRUPTION OF 1968   164

6
THE DIPLOMACY AND DOMESTIC POLITICS OF DETENTE   213

CONCLUSION   260

APPENDIX: TABLES AND FIGURES   269

NOTES   273

SOURCES   335

INDEX   341

ILLUSTRATIONS FOLLOW P. 130

POWER AND PROTEST

INTRODUCTION

The 1960s were years of unrest: students demonstrated in streets across the United States and Western Europe, dissidents agitated for more freedom in the Soviet Union, and—most astonishing of all—young "Red Guards" created chaos throughout China as part of a "Cultural Revolution." Events in China were certainly unique, especially in that the chairman of the ruling Communist Party, Mao Zedong, manipulated the masses who attacked established authorities. No Western or Soviet leader served as an equivalent inspiration for protesting citizens.

China and the other great powers did, however, share one important similarity in their respective domestic upheavals. Leaders in each state had to accommodate themselves to a stalemated Cold War world that restricted policy flexibility. Protests during the 1960s—controlled from above in China, more independent in Europe and America—attempted to escape the limits of the post-1945 "long peace" between the largest communist and capitalist states.[1]

The mechanisms of dissent differed in each society, but internal unrest threatened the leadership in nearly every country—including China. In July 1967 Mao had to depart in haste from the industrial city of Wuhan, fearful that the domestic upheaval he had unleashed imperiled his personal security. Soon thereafter the chairman began to warn against "extreme anarchism."[2]

Like Mao less than a year earlier, in late May 1968 French President Charles de Gaulle whisked his wife away from turmoil in Paris. After an unplanned helicopter trip across the West German border, de Gaulle lamented the "total paralysis" of his government. Popular protests throughout France left the president confounded by the evidence that he was, by his own admission, "not in charge of anything any more."[3]

In West Germany, where de Gaulle had sought temporary haven, popular unrest in 1968 created similar difficulties for leaders. Foreign Minister Willy Brandt—who became chancellor a year later—despaired that "young people in many of our countries do not understand why we, the older ones, cannot cope with the problems of [our] age." Brandt called for a period of "reason" to control "dangerous tensions" within society.[4]

1

Surveying the unrest abroad and widespread protests within the United States, the Central Intelligence Agency (CIA) reported to President Lyndon Johnson that "dissidence, involving students and non-students alike, is a world-wide phenomenon." On all continents organized "militants" were challenging leaders. Protesters of the sort described by the CIA even placed the White House under siege. One aide remembers that the president "could not go anywhere . . . that was disastrous."[5]

Johnson's successor, Richard Nixon, labeled these conditions a "war at home." He spoke in his inaugural address of a "long night" for the "American spirit." During the wee hours of 9 May 1970 this "long night" produced a bizarre moment. Accompanied only by his valet, Nixon confronted a group of antiwar protesters encamped around the Lincoln Memorial. He attempted to convince the skeptical audience that he shared their ideals but could not avoid "extremely unpopular" policies. The president's late-night efforts proved futile; protests continued across the nation.[6]

Despite severe Soviet restrictions on dissent, leaders in Moscow also confronted a domestic struggle during the late 1960s. General Secretary Leonid Brezhnev received a KGB (Komitet Gosudartsvennoi Bezopasnosti) report in November 1968 concerning "negative processes" and "harmful developments among our youth." The word "opposition" had become "something students find appealing." A young soldier's failed attempt to shoot Brezhnev in January 1969 made the threat of internal violence tangible for the Soviet leader.[7]

The widespread unrest of the 1960s had a direct effect on each state's foreign policy. The reverse was also true: relations among the most powerful nations inflamed domestic contention. Social movements and diplomacy during this period interacted with one another across a broad international terrain. This book narrates and explains these important interactions between peoples, cultures, and governments.

The period of "detente" at the end of the 1960s reflected traditional balance of power considerations, as other authors have argued.[8] The following chapters describe how it also grew from a common urge for stability among leaders under attack at home. The diplomatic compromises and domestic repressions that accompanied detente reflected the deepening anxieties of government officials. Detente, in this sense, had a social origin that scholars have largely neglected. It was a convergent response to disorder among the great powers.

I begin by describing what I call the "strains of nuclear destruction." Thermonuclear warheads and intercontinental missiles greatly expanded the destructive capabilities of the United States and the Soviet Union in the late 1950s. In fact these weapons were so powerful that they were useless. During a series of crises involving Berlin, the Taiwan Strait, and Cuba, leaders recognized that they had to accept permanent stalemate rather than risk a mutually suicidal nuclear exchange. Strategic balance stabilized American-Soviet relations, but it created noticeable discomfort for those who suffered from enforced Cold War divisions—particularly the citizens of Europe. West German Chancellor Konrad Adenauer began in the early 1960s to seek mechanisms for breaking the nuclear logjam through arms control agreements, increased East-West trade, and more frequent cultural exchanges across the Berlin Wall. Domestic groups in the United States and Western Europe also agitated for disarmament measures during this period.

Charles de Gaulle and Mao Zedong expanded on Adenauer's efforts to transcend Cold War divisions. The two men cultivated "charismatic" power by departing from existing routines, institutions, and alliances. In January 1964 they opened official relations between their states, symbolizing a decisive break with the bipolar structure of great-power competition. In their rhetoric de Gaulle and Mao drew on a shared image of revolution that attracted popular support from its promises of independence and national greatness. The energies the two leaders mobilized in their respective societies contributed to dramatic programs—French and Chinese nuclear development and the Chinese Great Leap Forward—but they ultimately produced rising expectations that neither leader could fulfill. The popular hopes encouraged by charismatic figures in France and China contributed to disillusion, anger, and confusion among citizens in the 1960s.

Popular expectations coalesced around what I call an "international language of dissent." As a consequence of the post–World War II baby boom, each of the great powers experienced a large growth in its young population. Expanded institutions of higher education, designed to nurture more productive and loyal citizens, empowered a sizable group of potential dissidents. A series of authors—including John Kenneth Galbraith, Aleksandr Solzhenitsyn, Wu Han, and Herbert Marcuse—provided literate and disillusioned citizens with new ways of expressing their discontent. These writers did not create the unrest of the 1960s. They offered simple arguments and appealing slogans that readers could understand and organize around. Mao Zedong was unique among political leaders in his attempt to kidnap dissident language for his own purposes through a self-proclaimed Cultural Revolution.

Dissident activities—especially the American civil rights movement—preceded the Vietnam War. Ironically, public unrest during the early 1960s motivated policymakers in Washington to pursue a more aggressive program of

foreign intervention. Presidents John Kennedy and Lyndon Johnson attempted to build popular support for their leadership by increasing the nation's commitment to industrial development and communist containment
overseas. Kennedy's calls for a "new frontier" extolled the virtues and glories
of meddling in faraway lands.

Indochina, in particular, appeared to be a safe showcase for America's economic and political capabilities. It was distant from the most dangerous areas
of Cold War conflict—Europe, the Caribbean, and the Taiwan Strait. From
the American perspective, impoverished villagers wanted tutelage in developing a modern economy and a democratic society. Nationalist resistance,
corruption in South Vietnam, and communist assistance to local forces undermined these aims. Evidence of American brutalities and recurrent military setbacks triggered a rapid rise in antiwar protests. Those inspired by the
"new frontier" were now horrified at the destruction it had wrought. Escalating warfare in Southeast Asia deepened domestic turmoil in the United
States and Western Europe.

Attempts to quell domestic discontent through foreign intervention were
profoundly self-defeating. As a consequence of the Vietnam War, President
Johnson lost control of his political agenda. He became isolated from an agitated American public. Johnson painfully reconsidered his mistaken commitment to Indochina at the end of his term in office, but this long-awaited
turnabout came after he had profoundly weakened the moral authority of
the presidency.

The dissident impulses of the early 1960s and the public outrage against
the Vietnam War contributed to a truly "global disruption" in 1968. Domestic violence convulsed urban communities in each of the great powers as
men and women revolted against state institutions. Besieged and physically
threatened, leaders turned their attention away from foreign affairs to more
pressing difficulties at home. Events in 1968 precipitated a crisis of political
authority for the most powerful national figures.

Governments could no longer assume that they commanded legitimacy in
the eyes of their citizens. Local and national authorities frequently resorted
to force against protesters. Police power assured regime continuity, but it
also deepened resentment among many domestic groups. Politics became
noticeably more contentious for the leaders of the largest states.

This was the point, after 1968, when detente among the great powers
took shape. Willy Brandt used his position as West German foreign minister,
and later chancellor, to push for new agreements among leaders that would
replace Cold War competition with economic and social collaboration. This
was Brandt's "Ostpolitik." He accepted the political status quo in Europe,

and worked to use communist authority in the East for his own purposes. Through increased trade and human contact across the Berlin Wall, Brandt sought to make national division appear more "normal." In the process, Brandt condemned domestic critics for jeopardizing East-West cooperation.

President Richard Nixon applied similar techniques for broader purposes. He offered both the Soviet Union and China cooperative overtures in trade and political recognition. In return he sought their assistance in bringing the Vietnam War to an end. Like Brandt, Nixon used the prospects of great-power cooperation to argue that his opponents threatened international peace. The president and his national security adviser, Henry Kissinger, made secrecy a central organizing principle for their leadership, isolating their deliberations from intrusion by the enemies they feared most—domestic bureaucrats, journalists, and critics.

Nixon deserves praise for intelligently playing the Soviet Union and China against each other to America's gain. His "triangular diplomacy" opened new avenues for policy flexibility in what had become a stalemated bipolar world. In this sense, Nixon learned a lot from de Gaulle and Mao. Unfortunately, he lacked their charisma. The secrecy and maneuvering of his administration isolated domestic opponents, without ever reintegrating them into the political system. Many protesters turned away from politics entirely in the next decade.

As detente alienated citizens, it offered communist leaders what they craved most: Western recognition of their legitimacy. Regimes that did not possess a popular base at home exploited connections with the United States, West Germany, and France to bolster their domestic standing. Summit conferences made government officials look strong and powerful. Brezhnev and Mao used detente to condemn their internal critics for threatening international peace and the dignity of the state.

Across North America, Europe, and Asia, detente was a profoundly conservative response to internal disorder. It sacrificed domestic reform for the sake of international stability. Leaders abandoned their hopes for political change in order to smother the challenges they faced at home. The Cold War became less volatile as a consequence of detente, but it also grew more permanent. Although domestic critics posed fewer immediate threats to established authority after the 1960s, they became more isolated from government than before. International collaboration among leaders furthered international disillusion among citizens. To this day, large segments of each nation's population remain politically alienated as a consequence of detente.

This is a story of Cold War stalemate in the early 1960s, a crescendo of global protest, and conservative reaction at the end of the decade. Although events varied greatly across societies, they followed a general pattern that I explain in the following chapters. International history of this sort not only crosses national boundaries; it also connects the world of politics and diplomacy with social and cultural experiences. Institutions and inherited conditions created global difficulties that elicited a series of comparable responses. The 1960s were filled with colorful and tragic personalities who, as Karl Marx predicted, made history, but not as they wished.

1

THE STRAINS OF NUCLEAR DESTRUCTION

Nuclear weapons changed the military landscape after World War II. Their explosive power could destroy cities, and even entire countries, in short order. Amidst widespread nuclear destruction, human civilization might not survive another total war between the great powers. War, in this sense, had become more nearly "absolute" than ever before.[1]

As they embodied the potential future consequences of war, nuclear weapons also bolstered the prestige of the two dominant countries after World War II—the United States and the Soviet Union. The leaders of these governments exercised military influence across the globe. They could threaten, if they so desired, to destroy entire nations unilaterally. More significant, the rapid deployment of nuclear power in the late 1940s and early 1950s gave an indication of the extraordinary accomplishments the United States and the Soviet Union could produce when they mobilized their respective scientific, military, and human resources. Nuclear weapons were indeed symbols of national greatness.

Threats of destruction and promises of greatness went hand in hand. They constituted the central contradiction of the nuclear revolution. Nuclear arsenals made the United States and the Soviet Union "superpowers" in the 1950s, but they did not enhance the usable strength of either nation. Leaders soon recognized that they could not exploit their nuclear power to secure political dominance of distant territories. Land conquered by nuclear force would not serve anyone's purposes, contaminating occupier and occupied alike. The destructive power of nuclear weapons exceeded any proportional definition of political aims. As a consequence, the most powerful states after World War II quickly lost the will to use armed conflict against each other for the "pursuit of policy by other means."[2]

The years 1958–1963 stand as a critical juncture in the history of the nuclear world. The United States and the Soviet Union struggled to reconcile their political aims with the risks posed by developments in thermonuclear weapons and delivery systems. A series of dangerous crises reflected tensions not only between the superpowers but also within their societies. Dwight D. Eisenhower, John F. Kennedy, and Nikita Khrushchev attempted to maintain various external commitments in Europe, Asia, and Latin America by issuing nuclear threats that they were ever more afraid to carry through. By the end of 1963 diplomacy had become incredibly dangerous for its predominant participants. A precarious "peace" emerged from the Cuban missile crisis, but not as the result of victory or defeat or even compromise. Instead, it reflected the threat that nuclear weapons posed to each side. The United States and the Soviet Union accepted stalemate over the prospect of mutual destruction.[3]

The strongest Cold War states approximated overmuscled wrestlers. Through ever-increasing thermonuclear deployments each added mass for the destruction of its adversary. But the continuous addition of mass reduced superpower flexibility. Warily eyeing each other across a broad terrain, the international giants faced an undesirable choice between stalemate and mutual annihilation.

As nuclear stalemate perpetuated divisions in Europe and fears about the future, smaller, less muscular states gained initiative. West German chancellor Konrad Adenauer set an important precedent for others—especially Charles de Gaulle, Mao Zedong, and later Willy Brandt—when he attacked the shallowness of the superpower "peace." Political leaders and ordinary citizens alike turned their attention to arms control, cultural exchanges, and a general redirection of Cold War politics.

▪ Eisenhower and the Nuclear Revolution

No commander-in-chief had better schooling in the dilemmas of nuclear power than Dwight D. Eisenhower. After leading Allied forces in Europe during World War II, he served from 1946 to 1952 as U.S. Army chief of staff, temporary chairman of the Joint Chiefs of Staff, and the first NATO supreme allied commander. Each of these positions provided Eisenhower with intimate knowledge of American nuclear stockpiles and war plans. After his inauguration as president in 1953, he devoted considerable attention to the intricacies of nuclear strategy.

Eisenhower frequently reflected on the horrors of nuclear war. Speaking before the United Nations General Assembly in December 1953, he explained that a conflict involving recently developed thermonuclear capabilities would mean "the probability of civilization destroyed—the annihilation of the irreplaceable heritage of mankind handed down to us generation from generation—and the condemnation of mankind to begin all over again the age-old struggle upward from savagery toward decency, and right, and justice."[4]

The largest American thermonuclear explosion ever—the "BRAVO" test of 1 March 1954—reinforced Eisenhower's fears of nuclear conflict. The detonation at Bikini Atoll, in the Pacific Ocean, produced a colossal fifteen-megaton blast. It left a 250-foot deep crater where there had been an island. The force of the explosion reverberated nearly 200 miles away, with radioactive fallout contaminating areas far downwind. In waters an apparently safe distance away, the crew of the Japanese boat *Lucky Dragon* suffered exposure to the airborne residue from the blast.[5]

The new thermonuclear bombs had become so powerful that even testing them posed grave hazards. Like many other informed observers around the world, Eisenhower quickly realized that the realities of nuclear power made a mockery of any hopes for "victory" through the use of these weapons in war. Days after the BRAVO test he expressed doubt as to "whether any nations as we know them would continue to exist at the conclusion" of hostilities. The prospect of continued growth in nuclear arsenals, he wrote British prime minister Winston Churchill, was "truly appalling."[6]

Eisenhower hoped to use the very horror of nuclear conflict to deter the destructive potential demonstrated in the test at Bikini. Effective war deterrence, he believed, required the assurance that any act of aggression would incur the harshest penalties. Before entering office Eisenhower had observed that the "possibility of total destruction, terrible though it is, could be a blessing." "Confronted by that outcome to another world war, all of us, East and West, are in the same boat." Soviet leaders were rational, not reckless, he explained. They would not "engage in global war because nobody would win it." During his years in the White House, Eisenhower never wavered from this assessment.[7]

Reliance on nuclear deterrence did not, however, extinguish growing concerns about the harmful effects of these weapons on human civilization. The ecological effects of a thermonuclear explosion—as demonstrated by the BRAVO test—were profound and irreversible. In the mid-1950s scientists in Europe and North America began to observe rising levels of radiation in rain, soil, milk, and even human bones. The entire infrastructure of life on Earth was jeopardized in a way inconceivable only a few years earlier. Radioactive fallout knew no boundaries.[8]

Limits on thermonuclear development—including tests—received growing support among citizens, intellectuals, and policymakers around the world. Influential figures such as Albert Einstein, Bertrand Russell, Albert

Schweitzer, and Linus Pauling gave strong public testimony on the need for immediate nuclear arms control.[9] In response to these pressures Eisenhower considered an international moratorium on nuclear explosions during the second half of 1954. Secretary of State John Foster Dulles explained to the president's closest advisers that we cannot "sit here in Washington and develop bigger bombs without any regard for the impact of these developments on world opinion. In the long run it isn't only bombs that win wars, but having public opinion on your side."[10]

In this context of rising thermonuclear fear, Eisenhower made a number of attempts to reduce the dangers of conflict arising from miscalculation, accident, or a simple misreading of intentions. He believed that the time had come for agreed limits on the growth of destructive arsenals. Meeting with the Soviet leadership in Geneva in July 1955, Eisenhower made his intentions clear. "It is essential," the president explained to the Kremlin's delegation, "that we find some way of controlling the threat of the thermonuclear bomb. You know we both have enough weapons to wipe out the entire northern hemisphere from fallout alone. No spot would escape the fallout from an exchange of nuclear stockpiles."[11]

A few days later Eisenhower offered something more concrete: a simple plan for "open skies" that would limit worries about hidden military production and war preparation. He proposed that the United States and the Soviet Union "give to each other a complete blueprint of our military establishments, from beginning to end, from one end of our countries to the other." In addition, each state would provide its counterpart with "facilities for aerial photography" of military installations.[12]

The Soviet leadership summarily rejected this call for greater transparency on the grounds that it disproportionately served the interests of the more open American society. Eisenhower's first foray into arms control provided little immediate return, but it did reveal his deep concern for stabilizing what one writer later called the "delicate balance" of nuclear terror. While he continued to suspect the motives of the Soviet leadership, the president believed that cooperation—even of a very wary and limited kind—was necessary in a world of multiplying nuclear dangers. "Open skies" was a first attempt at building confidence between rivals through arms control rather than arms escalation.[13]

Despite his commitment to controlling the risks of thermonuclear war, Eisenhower continued to rely upon explicit nuclear threats, especially during acute international crises. The president wanted the United States to fight from its particular strengths, rather than react to every enemy move in kind. Instead of raising a huge conventional army that would match those of the

Soviet Union and Communist China in size and cost, the Eisenhower administration relied on nuclear forces to respond quickly, conclusively, and perhaps even preemptively against the resources of adversaries. America prepared for conflict over the "long haul," emphasizing effective but economical striking power with thermonuclear warheads, long-range bombers, and soon missiles as well.[14]

Arms control, in this context, promised to stabilize dangerous military trends by reinforcing the evidence that conflict was unwinnable. The nuclear powers would limit their arsenals, according to Eisenhower's logic, when both recognized that their spending produced new dangers rather than accomplishments at home or abroad. During his second term in office the president displayed growing hope that the Soviet leadership had come to share this perspective. Negotiations among arms control experts and the unprecedented visit of Soviet premier Nikita Khrushchev to the United States in 1959 implied the recognition of an uneasy international equilibrium. Uncertainty about intentions and trustworthiness, however, fed continued pressures for arms races.[15]

The president relied on nuclear retaliatory capabilities not just as a deterrent, but also as an inducement to domestic self-restraint. A secure nuclear force would limit what Eisenhower perceived as a dangerous public tendency to overreact in the face of threat. Without firm ceilings on military expenditures, the president feared that the Cold War would produce what he frequently called a "garrison state" in place of the liberal free-market society that the nation sought to protect. The American "way of life," according to Eisenhower, precluded a bloated and intrusive central government. National security required *both* Washington's preparation to defend the state's critical interests *and* restraint against excessive government interference in society at large.[16]

The "New Look" revision in American strategy, commissioned by Eisenhower, emphasized the economy of nuclear weapons. An arsenal of bombs, aircraft, and later missiles proved far less burdensome for domestic society than large standing armies. The president believed that secure nuclear power would allow for the maintenance of free markets, consumer abundance, and individual rights. More regimented forms of military preparedness would not. Controlled deployment of nuclear weapons, despite all the associated dangers, promised a reliable and cheap American defense.[17]

Nuclear weapons stabilized the international system, as Eisenhower expected, through much of the 1950s. Crises continued to flare around disputed areas—especially the island of Taiwan and the Suez Canal—but these confrontations did not escalate. The two largest nuclear states studiously avoided direct military challenges to each other.

In the summer of 1957, though, the pace of military innovation began to shake the foundations of international stability. A Soviet intercontinental ballistic missile test in August, followed by the launch of the first artificial Earth satellite—"Sputnik I"—on 4 October, forced Eisenhower to reconsider the reliability of peace through nuclear strength. Intercontinental missiles greatly increased the speed and breadth of thermonuclear destruction. Each superpower would soon possess the capacity to destroy its counterpart in a matter of minutes—perhaps without sufficient time for retaliation.

The advent of missile technology undermined the sense of security that the continental United States had previously derived from its ocean frontiers. Fast-moving rockets loaded with thermonuclear warheads made a devastating "bolt from the blue" feasible, with destructive capabilities far beyond those of conventional aerial bombardment in World War II. Most significant, the speed of the new missiles allowed the Soviet Union to contemplate a surprise attack that could annihilate U.S. retaliatory capabilities in one fell swoop. The nation would, according to this nightmare scenario, lie prostrate before the enemy.[18]

The destructive potential of thermonuclear weapons had already inspired questions about the reliability of U.S. defense commitments overseas. With advances in missile capabilities the worries of Washington's allies only deepened. Any attempts at an American defense of West Berlin or Paris now raised the prospect of immediate Soviet nuclear attacks on New York or Chicago. Would the United States sacrifice its own survival to protect allies in Europe and elsewhere? In early 1958 Eisenhower's special assistant for national security affairs, Robert Cutler, wrote a secret letter to Dulles explaining that "doubt is growing in many areas whether U.S. retaliatory power would be used except against attack on the U.S. and U.S. forces." America's nuclear arsenal, Cutler continued, did not provide "usable strength for stable deterrence of, or reply to, minor aggression."[19]

Within months Communist China threatened American-supported Taiwan, and the Soviet Union mounted a new challenge to American interests in West Berlin. At home the Eisenhower administration confronted growing criticism for allowing an alleged "missile gap." In hindsight, it is clear that the United States enjoyed a vast strategic advantage during this period, but policymakers did not have access to such detailed information in the late 1950s. Critics such as former secretary of state Dean Acheson contended that the president's strategy of using nuclear force for purposes of deterrence was in a shambles.[20]

Eisenhower understood that effective deterrence required confidence among both citizens and allies. He grudgingly approved increases in America's nuclear arsenal for "psychological" reasons. The creation of what one historian calls nuclear "overkill" in the late 1950s was, in this sense, largely directed at an audience *within* the United States and NATO. Nuclear warheads and missiles were symbols of national strength and resolve. Most observers did not know the precise contents of America's military arsenal, but the Eisenhower administration embarked on a series of "crash" programs—particularly in missile technology—to allay public insecurities. The U.S. government used displays of nuclear strength to show resolve for those who questioned the nation's commitment to deter communist advances. The White House also emphasized the stability of nuclear deterrence for those who feared the harmful consequences of nuclear testing and superpower arms races. The president remained confident that a strategic buildup was unnecessary, but he could not resist pressures to display additional muscle, far in excess of all challengers.[21]

Even with a considerable expansion in its nuclear forces, the United States found itself in a largely reactive international position. In 1958 the American government responded with strong words to communist threats in West Berlin and around Taiwan. Eisenhower prepared for serious, even suicidal nuclear war, assured that his unblinking resolve would deter adversaries. After the crisis in Berlin temporarily died down, he commented—as he had many times before—that "we must be ready to throw the book at the Russians should they jump us." The Soviet Union and Communist China did indeed curtail their challenges to West Berlin and Taiwan. Eisenhower's cold-blooded willingness to threaten enemies appeared to induce caution.[22]

The effectiveness of nuclear deterrence notwithstanding, Eisenhower understood that the stakes had now risen too high. Bloated nuclear arsenals and enhanced delivery capabilities brought the prospect of annihilation too close. A spiral of threats and counterthreats could produce a deadly conflict that no one wanted. In a climate of mounting international tensions, a state might be tempted to launch its nuclear forces first in order to avoid the perils of a late response to enemy aggression.[23]

The overabundance of thermonuclear capabilities, especially in the United States and Western Europe, lay at the root of this dangerous situation. Intercontinental ballistic missiles and long-range aircraft made a devastating nuclear first strike conceivable. In these circumstances the logic of deterrence would not work. Like the German and French military planners before World War I, leaders in Moscow and Washington might undertake risky offensive military operations for fear that the adversary would otherwise beat them to the punch. Strategic analyst Albert Wohlstetter described this situation as one in which the superpowers faced off like gunslingers, each tempted to fire his weapon first.[24]

Limits on the growth of nuclear arsenals, combined with enhanced international openness, offered an alternative to this dangerous scenario. Eisenhower hoped to use agreed political controls on military technology to make nuclear deterrence more stable, predictable, and reliable. During one particular set of negotiations between East and West in late 1958—"the Surprise Attack Conference"—the United States and its closest European allies formulated a broad array of procedures for eliminating risks of miscalculation, sources of misperception, and incentives for a first nuclear strike. While the Soviet Union wanted to discuss reductions in areas of American strategic superiority (especially long-range aircraft), Eisenhower's representatives emphasized international openness. The president did not expect agreement on immediate arms reductions. Instead, he intended to use inspections and other confidence-building measures to limit the exploitation of new technological capabilities for increasingly destructive purposes. Reduced fears of "surprise attack" would, according to Eisenhower, allow for more stable nuclear deterrence.[25]

To the president's deep chagrin, American attempts to manage the nuclear arms race came to very little in the late 1950s. The United States failed to find effective points of restraint in the military competition between West and East. Washington and Moscow could not even agree on some basic measures to reduce the risks of nuclear miscalculation. Eisenhower did not convince the American public, foreign allies, or perhaps even himself that a limited and relatively inexpensive nuclear deterrent could cover America's broad military commitments. Instead, the U.S. nuclear arsenal continued to grow along with the nation's insecurity.

The president's "Farewell Address" on the harmful consequences of the emerging "military-industrial complex" was, in large part, a testament to the failure of his nuclear strategy. During the years of Eisenhower's leadership the American nuclear stockpile increased from 1,436 warheads in 1953 to a mind-boggling total of 24,173 warheads in 1961. American military expenditures remained abnormally high in comparison with early post–World War II levels. Although nuclear deterrence may have proven the best alternative among a number of bad choices, America's military posture clearly failed to achieve many of the nation's most important political goals. Nuclear threats helped prevent full-scale war, but a growing number of observers doubted the future success of this strategy.[26]

In the eyes of many critics, attempts to ensure stability through nuclear deterrence failed to justify the required sacrifices. Threats of horrific warfare did not alleviate international tensions, but instead made them more permanent. George Kennan and other influential figures criticized Eisenhower's strategy in the late 1950s for prolonging divisions, sufferings, and injustices in Europe and Asia. Kennan argued that "the weapon of mass destruction is a sterile and hopeless weapon which may for a time serve as an answer of sorts to itself and as an uncertain sort of shield against utter cataclysm, but which cannot in any way serve the purposes of a constructive and hopeful foreign policy." The "multiplication" of nuclear dangers, according to this argument, became a self-defeating "substitute for negotiation" among the great powers.[27]

Contrary to these criticisms and the fiscal conservatism of the White House, pressures for ever-greater military preparedness threatened to upset what Eisenhower called, in his Farewell Address, the domestic "balance between the clearly necessary and the comfortably desirable." Instead of protecting the nation's inherited "way of life," Washington's reliance on expanded defense programs contributed, by the president's own admission, to "an immense military establishment and a large arms industry [that] is new in the American experience. The total influence—economic, political, and even spiritual—is felt in every city, every state house, every office of the federal government."[28]

Nuclear weapons had forestalled war among the great powers. In their absence, the American "military-industrial complex" might have grown much larger to contain Soviet advances. Despite these accomplishments, by 1961 nuclear deterrence had become a source of perceived insecurity for the United States and its allies. Eisenhower's successor felt compelled to formulate new strategic initiatives.

▪ Kennedy and the New Frontier

The style and substance of American policy changed radically with the inauguration of John F. Kennedy. He appealed to what one historian has called the "liberal anxiety" festering among citizens and intellectuals during the late 1950s. Confronted by what he admitted were "the authentic problems of our times," Kennedy pledged to "demonstrate anew to the world the superior vitality and the strength of the free society." Image and policy were inseparable. The new president searched for ways to display his energy and activism, in contrast to Eisenhower's perceived conservatism.[29]

Kennedy understood the social and cultural sides of power. America had to do more, he argued, than simply contain communism through nuclear deterrence. The nation's "way of life" required additional accomplishments in economic development and political democratization. At home and abroad, the Kennedy administration committed America to a new Wilsonianism that went hand in hand with a willingness to make "realistic" compromises where necessary.[30]

This was the essence of what Arthur Schlesinger Jr. years earlier had called "tough-minded" liberalism—a renewed commitment to national ideals through pragmatic means. Franklin Roosevelt's leadership during the Depression and World War II provided the new administration with a model. In a frank discussion with an old Roosevelt admirer, Supreme Court justice Felix Frankfurter, Kennedy spoke of his desire to connect his policies with what Frankfurter called the "fundamental purposes of the American democracy." The new president hoped to combine toughness with an abiding faith in international progress. He would avoid the apparent moral shallowness of Eisenhower's foreign policy, especially with regard to nuclear strategy.[31]

After his predecessor's long tenure, Kennedy became, in the words of one adviser, the "executor and repository of all the accumulated wisdom and reflection of this society in the 1950s." The "best and the brightest" who joined the new administration hoped to focus on "the things that were not being done, [and] ought to be done."[32] Roger Hilsman, an influential member of the State Department during the Kennedy years, described the ambitious idealism of those days: "we were activists. We thought the world could be changed. We thought one man could make a difference. You know, this is the Kennedy thesis. We believed that individual effort could change the world; that one man's efforts did make a difference. Pragmatic, idealistic, activist. This was an interventionist administration."[33]

Kennedy denied what Frederick Jackson Turner had proclaimed more than a half-century earlier: that the American frontier had reached its point of closure. During his presidential campaign, Kennedy announced that the nation stood "on the edge of a new frontier—the frontier of the 1960s, a frontier of unknown opportunities and perils, a frontier of unfulfilled hopes and threats." In contrast to Eisenhower's well-informed caution, the new president turned his youth, vigor, and determination into alluringly simple—and perhaps naive—antidotes for the difficulties of policymaking amidst thermonuclear stalemate. Through energy and determination he pledged to transcend the restraints of the nuclear world. He would, in the words of Arthur Schlesinger Jr., provide "a new sense of vision and a new sense of resolution," converting external dangers into creative opportunities.[34]

Kennedy promised to increase the stockpile of American nuclear forces, prohibiting the Soviet Union from attaining any strategic advantage. He called for a wider range of nuclear weapons, allowing for options other than full-scale war and abject surrender in a time of crisis. Most significant, Kennedy pledged to mobilize American will for a more aggressive struggle against communist regimes. The connections that Kennedy drew between changes in nuclear strategy and the new frontier were central to his appeal among Americans yearning for adventure and accomplishment after the stalemated 1950s. Many citizens did not agree with the new president's policies, but during his short time in office he used the rhetoric of the "space race," "flexible response," and the "new economics" to build a strong public following.

Kennedy's earliest initiatives in space exploration and military policy appealed to the new frontier imagery. Delivering a special message to the U.S. Congress on "urgent national needs" in May 1961, Kennedy demanded "a major national commitment of scientific and technical man-power" to land a man on the moon before the end of the decade. The United States had to prevent the Soviet Union from establishing a permanent lead in space exploration. The president recognized that American competition with the Soviets in this area would not contribute to an immediate improvement in the nation's security. It would, however, symbolize the technological capability and personal determination that he wished to associate with his leadership.[35]

The United States sought "a clearly leading role in space achievement," but, Kennedy proclaimed, "Our aims do not prepare for war." "They are," he explained, "efforts to discourage and resist the adventures of others that could end in war." Kennedy asserted that through action, commitment, and collective sacrifice the United States would force the Soviet Union to accept peaceful international change. A moon landing would display America's material and spiritual superiority, convincing adversaries to choose cooperation over conflict.[36]

The "space race" captured the energy and activism that Kennedy hoped to harness as an escape from present dangers. In all his exuberant speeches about rocket launchings and moon landings he never reflected on their specific benefits. Rather, space exploration served as a national exercise in mountain climbing—a search for accomplishment and fulfillment through exertion in itself. Outer space would reopen a frontier that terrestrial space had long since closed. Speaking at Rice University in September 1962, Kennedy made this point explicit, arguing that a "new frontier of science and space" would succeed the old frontier of the American West. "This country of the United States was not built," the president insisted, "by those who waited and rested and wished to look behind them. This country was conquered by those who moved forward." The race to the moon would rekindle the nation's best inherited attributes: "We choose to go to the moon in this decade and do the other things, not because they are easy, but because they are hard, because that goal will serve to organize and measure the best of our energies and skills, because that challenge is one that we are willing to accept, one that we are unwilling to postpone, and one which we intend to win."[37]

The surprise appointment of Robert S. McNamara as secretary of defense brought the new frontier to military planning. The president of the Ford Motor Company and an expert in corporate management, McNamara had no experience with issues of national security. This was his greatest virtue in Kennedy's eyes. When initially approached for the position, McNamara was incredulous. "This is absurd," he exclaimed, "I'm not qualified."[38]

Kennedy, however, wanted an intelligent and energetic man *without* defense expertise in the Pentagon. Although the new president had lambasted the previous administration for tolerating an alleged "missile gap" with the Soviet Union, he understood that an arms buildup alone could hardly solve the difficulties arising from the destructiveness of nuclear weapons. By the summer of 1961, in fact, American satellite reconnaissance confirmed that the "missile gap" favored the United States. Still, America was vulnerable to a Soviet nuclear attack and stalemated in its strategic options. Kennedy hoped that McNamara's injection into the defense community would provide an impetus for the government to rethink basic military doctrine.[39]

The new secretary of defense began by reevaluating inherited nuclear strategy. He replaced the Eisenhower administration's reliance upon "massive retaliation" with a doctrine vaguely labeled "flexible response." McNamara called for a proliferation of military options—a spectrum of conventional and limited nuclear capabilities for a variety of conflicts short of full-scale war. In one of his first reports to the president, he recommended "increased non-nuclear firepower—providing to decision-makers a wider range of alternatives and an improved capability to apply measured force without threatening nuclear devastation." The objective was to avoid the unsatisfactory alternatives of nuclear war or abject surrender.[40]

Paul Nitze—serving as assistant secretary of defense for international security affairs—echoed this call for flexible military capabilities. Nitze advised McNamara and Kennedy that the United States could pursue a more energetic foreign policy only if it developed more diverse instruments for the projection of force. Otherwise, he argued, the nuclear stalemate threatened to paralyze political leadership. "Man has succeeded," Nitze wrote, "in creating an acceleration in technology which has strained to the utmost his ability to direct and control it . . . The critical question for the future is whether man can develop his political and social potential sufficiently to enable him to make technology his servant and not his master. We live in a complex, multi-dimensional world which cannot be viewed in the absolutes of black and white."[41]

Nitze had long advocated a broader mobilization of American resources against the Soviet Union. In 1950 he had been the primary author of a National Security Council strategy paper (NSC 68) that endorsed a "rapid and concerted build-up of the actual strength of both the United States and the other nations of the free world" against the threatening expansion of the Soviet "slave society." In addition to external containment, NSC 68 recommended a "positive program" that would "project" American strength "into the Soviet world in such a way as to bring about an internal change in the Soviet system." Superior military power and moral principles would, according to this strategy, assure "victory" in the Cold War.[42]

Nitze's judgment of the Kremlin's intentions did not change in the 1960s. He now recognized, however, that American strength alone could not promote the nation's security. The United States required superior military power as before, but policymakers had to find more careful applications of force in a thermonuclear world. The assistant secretary of defense warned against aggressive assertions of military strength. "Even as we must be firm, determined and willing to take risks," he advised in late 1961, "we must also avoid the pitfalls of rash actions which could involve the sacrifice of millions of lives, not only in America but elsewhere in the world." "Flexible response" called for a reorganization of military capabilities, providing the American leadership with new initiatives during an extended period "between peace and war."[43]

Despite his spendthrift image, Kennedy did *not* authorize a significant increase in the proportion of government resources at the military's disposal. The growth in American strategic nuclear capabilities during the early 1960s resulted primarily from programs—such as the development of the Polaris submarine-launched missile—initially authorized by Eisenhower. Disciplined by McNamara's cost-benefit accounting methods in the Pentagon, the Kennedy administration redirected previous financial outlays for the procurement of "general purpose" and "counterinsurgency" forces that had received little attention in prior years. More flexible capabilities would, according to this thinking, make power more usable and efficient.[44]

Behind the muscular rhetoric of the "space race" and "flexible response," the Kennedy administration was filled with number-crunchers—including the commander-in-chief. Looking back upon his service as chairman of the president's Council of Economic Advisers, Walter Heller recounted his boss's deep interest in economic affairs. Despite all his other responsibilities, the president apparently read over 300 economic memoranda during the 1,000 days he occupied the White House. Heller described Kennedy and his successor, Lyndon Johnson, as the "first modern economists in the American Presidency."[45]

They rejected Eisenhower's "wrong-headed" emphasis on small government and laissez-faire markets, according to Heller. Full employment and expansion of the nation's productive output became dominant White House priorities. The Kennedy administration, in particular, focused American policy on "realizing the economy's great and growing potential." Speaking at Yale University in June 1962, the president announced that his administration would depart from inherited orthodoxies about limited federal intervention in the economy. The fiscal inhibitions against activist government "sound like old records, long-playing, left over from the middle thirties," Kennedy explained. He called upon Americans to support more "practical management" from Washington that would keep the "great economic machinery moving ahead." Kennedy asserted that the strength of the nation required "sophisticated and technical" intervention in markets to assure "high employment," "steady expansion of output," "stable prices," and a "strong dollar."[46]

This was the essence of the "new economics," heavily influenced by the theories of John Maynard Keynes. Kennedy never rejected the importance of balanced budgets and sound credit, but he embraced the Keynesian idea that the government must use its fiscal resources to stimulate the economy during a period of apparent stagnation. Through increased spending and tax cuts Washington would assure the highest material return from America's agricultural and industrial resources.[47]

The Kennedy administration devised a series of targeted tax reductions and spending increases that, when fully enacted in the second half of 1965, added 48 billion dollars to the economy. This was the capital for building the new frontier. Expanding the nation's activities in technical research and industrial production, the White House aimed to create additional domestic wealth and international strength. A more robust economy provided the tools to change the Cold War status quo, while reinforcing basic political stability.[48]

The president and his advisers believed that faster economic growth in the United States would finance advances against the Soviet Union. A special task force on foreign economic policy, chaired by future undersecretary of state George Ball, argued that a consolidated and better-funded international aid program would channel the "forces of nationalism into constructive nation-building activities." "Soviet economic penetration" in the "third world" made increased American spending on foreign assistance imperative. The task force report advised that Washington should "build up the less-developed nations so they can prosper and grow with free societies."[49]

Kennedy pumped resources into programs designed to foster international "development." One scholar observes that references to U.S.-sponsored economic growth in poor areas acquired prominence as the White House "court vernacular."[50] Policymakers assumed that they could contribute to what Walt Rostow called the universal "stages of economic growth." Identifying countries such as South Vietnam and India as nations ready— in Rostow's words—for economic "take-off," Washington used Keynesian stimuli to sponsor industrialization and turn back Soviet interference in these areas. American financial assistance overseas served as an inoculation against the alleged communist "disease" that would continue to spread if the United States was too passive.[51]

Anxious to find recipients for its aid, the White House expanded its fiscal contributions to anticommunist leaders in poor countries. South Vietnam stands out as perhaps the most important example. In May 1961 the president's interdepartmental task force on this area proposed "A Program of Action to Prevent Communist Domination." Applying Rostow's model for extensive assistance during the critical "take-off" transition, the task force asserted that "the most effective means of establishing Vietnamese confidence in the political and economic future of their country would be for the U.S. to commit itself to a long range economic development program." South Vietnam, and its authoritarian leader Ngo Dinh Diem, required "a minimum of $50 million," according to this analysis. Washington would target the money for industrial investments, improvements in infrastructure, and public administration (including the South Vietnamese military.)[52]

Foreign assistance fitted perfectly with the larger vision of the new frontier. Kennedy used the promise of international "development" and the challenge of the "space race" to popularize the energetic spirit of his administration. He increased American aid programs and implemented "flexible response" to create new tools for overseas action in the context of nuclear stalemate. The "new economics" financed these programs, making a virtue of the very trends Eisenhower had deplored in his Farewell Address. An expansionary fiscal policy increased the size of the "military-industrial complex," but Kennedy championed the ways in which this growth would contribute to American security and initiative. Although the United States could not completely escape the nuclear stalemate, Eisenhower's successor promised that the nation would improve its international position with concerted effort and enlightened leadership.

Despite Kennedy's optimistic words, the thermonuclear stalemate quickly forced him to accept the same unsatisfying strategic status quo he had inherited upon entering office. His calls for political change did not eliminate the frightening risks that accompanied *both* challenges and concessions to Soviet power. Even as the president championed government activism, members of his administration privately planned for more conservative compromises. The image of the new frontier continued to acquire a strong public following, but it was tempered by accumulating evidence of U.S. caution. Kennedy's differences from Eisenhower became more rhetorical than substantive.

Behind the façade of his muscular rhetoric, the president was horrified by the escalating dangers of military conflict. Referring to the technology of nuclear war, he observed that "these guns . . . shoot several generations."[53] Kennedy was dismayed to learn, during his first months in office, that if the U.S. military received warning of a possible Soviet nuclear attack he would have only a few minutes to decide whether he wished to annihilate the enemy or risk unprecedented American suffering.[54]

The president and his closest advisers never wanted to confront this terrible choice. Before the 3–4 June 1961 Vienna summit meeting with Soviet premier Nikita Khrushchev, White House planning documents emphasized international stability rather than positive change. For the sake of survival the United States and the Soviet Union had to reach some "implicit acceptance . . . of certain restraints upon their action." This required a continuation of the nuclear stalemate. Members of the administration asserted that protection of "a more stable world order" must become the central aim of

American foreign policy. As early as 1961 the Kennedy White House was beginning to pull back from its new frontier commitments, even as it sustained this rhetoric in public.[55]

At the Vienna summit Kennedy sought to outline clear limits on potential superpower conflict. The president admitted that the situation in Europe, as well as in Asia, "is not a satisfactory one." "However," he warned with regard to Central Europe, "it is not the right time now to change the situation in Berlin and the balance in general." Around the divided city, where the risk of nuclear war appeared most threatening, the American government desired a stable long-term status quo. The "right time" for geopolitical changes—including the reunification of the two Germanys—would not arrive "for a long time."[56]

Khrushchev, not Kennedy, was the leader who displayed the most bombast in Vienna. He recognized the new administration's attempts to reformulate nuclear policy. This was a potential moment for expanding Moscow's influence. Khrushchev accordingly used the summit to threaten America's access to West Berlin, as he had two years earlier. The Soviet leader hoped to convince his counterpart that he could best achieve his political reforms by withdrawing from inherited points of nuclear conflict. Kennedy's response during the next few months provided the clearest evidence of his firm but cautious turn away from the bold hopes of the new frontier.

Threatened with nuclear conflict over American, British, and French access to West Berlin—guaranteed de facto at the end of World War II—Kennedy determined that he would use force to protect allied rights. He would not, however, risk war for West German reunification with the Soviet-dominated eastern half of the nation. The U.S. government hoped, according to one prominent planning document, to deter Soviet-sponsored aggression in Central Europe and to "maintain the state of political suspension" regarding the future of the two divided Germanys. German reunification remained desirable, but the status quo was far less risky.[57]

Kennedy expressed relief when, on 13 August 1961, East German authorities constructed a barbed-wire barrier—soon replaced by a concrete wall and an army of border guards—firmly dividing the two halves of Berlin. Despite widespread anguish in Europe and pressures for American condemnation of this act, the president did not publicly comment on the construction of the "Berlin Wall" for eight days. In private Kennedy remarked, "It's not a very nice solution, but a wall is a hell of a lot better than a war."[58]

Limited conflict over the official status of West Berlin continued for another few years. Despite occasional difficulties, both Washington and Moscow worked between August 1961 and late 1963 to reinforce German divisions rather than risk nuclear war. The Kennedy administration went so far as to discourage domestic unrest in East Germany, fearful that, in the words of one analyst, "it would reduce the ability of the allies to keep the course of developments under control and might provoke the Soviet leadership to take considerable risks." Seeking to avoid a new crisis in Central Europe, the United States held to "limited objectives." "The disadvantages of an upris- ing" in the East "would outweigh the advantages" for Western interests.[59]

Instead of pursuing new frontiers, the American government clung to the status quo in Central Europe as a favorable alternative to risky conflict with the Soviet Union. Both Washington and Moscow sought to enforce a stable division of Berlin, the two Germanys, and Europe in general. This served as the basis for what one scholar calls the tacit "settlement" between the super- powers in what had been the most dangerous area of the early Cold War. The nuclear arms race continued, but through the rest of the 1960s neither side again threatened war over Berlin.[60]

Historians have noted the geopolitical stability created by the Berlin Wall.[61] They often neglect, however, the social ramifications that made Au- gust 1961 a turning point not only in U.S.-Soviet diplomacy but also in American relations with the West German public. The division of the two postwar Germanys had grown firm in the 1950s. Before the construction of the Wall, however, West Berlin remained a special borderland community— a unique "meeting point" where families, workers, and students separated by Cold War antagonisms came together in relative freedom. It was an island of East-West intermixing within a sea of tightening East German authority. Like other border communities, it was also a haven for spies who sought to infiltrate unnoticed across frontiers.[62]

In a single stroke, the construction of the Berlin Wall smothered this vi- brant and cosmopolitan community that had survived precariously through the first decade and a half of the Cold War. East German citizens who had frequently traveled to West Berlin for employment, education, and scarce goods became prisoners within their own society. East German families could no longer meet their West German relatives in Berlin. The communist regime used an army of border guards to enforce a concrete separation of husbands from wives, children from parents.[63]

The severing of East-West connections in Berlin contributed to a precipi- tous decline in West German public morale. Citizens of the Federal Republic felt powerless in the face of East German and Soviet brutality. The acquies- cence of the United States also nurtured a common sense of abandonment. Egon Bahr, a close adviser and press spokesman for West Berlin mayor Willy Brandt, described the "brutality" of the Wall and the need for new political initiatives to raise falling public spirits. Bahr warned that the "price" of the geopolitical status quo had risen too high. He predicted that West Germans would deeply resent "cutting off 1.1 million people and surrendering Berlin's status as a city open to all intents and purposes, as it was before the 13th of August."[64]

From Washington's perspective, nuclear weapons made stable walls preferable to open frontiers. Despite Bahr's warnings, the American government remained firmly committed to a long-term division in Central Europe after 1961. The Kennedy administration sought a "modus vivendi" with Moscow that would assure the avoidance of war even at the cost of continued human suffering. The president now confined his promises of American activism— symbolized most clearly by the "space race" and the "new economics"—to areas outside Europe.[65]

Protecting the status quo around dangerous points of conflict made sense, but when would the "right time" arise for a change in unsatisfactory conditions? When would the United States exercise its power for the achievement of liberal democratic and capitalist purposes in Europe? How would Washington use its impressive capabilities to secure the promises of universal freedom at the core of the new frontier?

The risks of thermonuclear conflict left the Kennedy administration with few good answers to these questions. The omnipotence associated with nuclear weapons inspired broad promises that the horrors of prospective nuclear warfare summarily extinguished. Bombs and rockets could intimidate, but they could not recreate a united Berlin, Germany, or Europe.

▪ Adenauer and the Early Vision of Detente

International circumstances in the early 1960s foretold a painful future for the Federal Republic of (West) Germany. Nuclear stalemate appeared to assure the permanent separation of the state from its eastern counterpart. If one of the superpowers decided to challenge the other's influence in Central Europe—as Khrushchev did between 1958 and 1961—West Germans had good reason to fear that they would suffer directly in the likely military (possibly nuclear) clashes. With stability they suffered national division; with conflict they risked far-reaching destruction.

Following the construction of the Berlin Wall, citizens of the Federal Republic began to search for new alternatives and reasons for hope. The most prominent West German politician, Chancellor Konrad Adenauer, quickly abandoned his long-standing call for reunification through strength and his attempts to isolate the East German state. Walter Ulbricht's regime had now done that for itself. Opinion polls conducted by the West German Foreign Ministry showed rising public demand for overtures to the East rather than hardened division.[66] Adenauer recognized these sentiments as early as September 1961. He used a national election and a new governing coalition with the Free Democratic Party (FDP) to convert himself into a "peace chancellor." Adenauer's activities in the early 1960s provided the initial architecture for detente among the great powers.[67]

The chancellor shared in the public anguish regarding national division. He lamented what he called the "most important problem of our epoch"—the "inner political" weakness and superficiality of daily life in West Germany. East-West rivalries and the nuclear arms race encouraged an empty "materialism." As an antidote to these circumstances, Adenauer wanted to connect his political activities with a deeper reservoir of religious belief. Breaking out of the Cold War stalemate symbolized by the Berlin Wall, he longed to reawaken public interest in what he described as the "Christian" vision of a simple devout life, free from military tensions and centralized institutions. In place of growing state power, Adenauer hoped to invigorate the freedom and entrepreneurship of local communities. Associations for work and worship provided the foundation for what he perceived as the traditional bourgeois life of German citizens, especially those residing in the rich territories adjacent to the Rhine River. The Christian lifestyle of the Rhine was, in this sense, the antipathy of fascism, communism, and Cold War politics.[68]

The prospect of nuclear war was the most immediate threat to Adenauer's Christian vision in the early 1960s. The crises around Berlin strengthened his determination to rescue Western civilization from the conflicts that smothered its historic accomplishments. The first half of the twentieth century, he explained, had destroyed the best of Europe's inheritance. Adenauer wanted to reverse this trend, creating new ground for unity—or at least cooperation—across the entire continent. The "moment appears to have come," he wrote Soviet premier Nikita Khrushchev in 1960, for "working together" regardless of ideology. Despite his curmudgeonly demeanor and his frequent condemnations of "atheistic, dictatorial communism," Adenauer contemplated wide-ranging ideas for cooperation with the Soviet Union and other East European states.[69]

After months of cryptic public comments at the end of 1961, the chancellor spent much of the next year lobbying for arms control and closer relations among the European governments, East and West. In March 1962 he told the French newspaper *Le Monde* that any future war in Europe "would be a nuclear war . . . without any profit for the survivors." Under these circumstances all the great powers, including the Soviet Union, had an interest in cooperating for basic international stability and crisis avoidance. Characteristically, Adenauer affirmed that "the epoch in which we live is characterized by the contradiction between communism and anticommunism," but, he argued, the risks of nuclear war required work to limit armed conflict. Instead of pressuring Moscow, West Germany and its allies now had to stabilize the balance of power.[70]

More surprisingly, Adenauer devoted considerable attention—probably more than any other Western leader at the time—to the evidence of rising tensions between the Soviet Union and the People's Republic of China. He argued in his March 1962 interview with *Le Monde* that Mao Zedong's government posed the "greatest danger" to Khrushchev. China had a population of approximately 700 million people, compared with the Soviet Union's 200 million. During the Korean War, the various crises in the Taiwan Strait, and the Great Leap Forward, China had shown many signs of what Adenauer called "aggressive" behavior. According to this analysis, Mao's regime was more of a rival than an ally for Soviet leaders in the early 1960s.[71]

Recognizing the importance of the Sino-Soviet split so early, Adenauer anticipated the triangular politics that would emerge at the end of the decade. He also predicted how the German people could exploit the Moscow-Beijing rivalry. "This contradiction between the Soviet Union and China," Adenauer explained, "is a factor for securing world peace." Khrushchev had to strengthen himself against his neighbor to the East, the chancellor argued, and that would make him more accommodating toward the West.[72]

During a series of meetings in 1962 and 1963 with French president Charles de Gaulle, Adenauer and his counterpart frequently discussed Sino-Soviet tensions and debated how they could exploit these developments. De Gaulle's overtures to China in the next two years were one means of pushing the Soviet Union to adopt a more amicable foreign policy. Adenauer's appeals for Soviet-American agreement on arms control and reduced tensions in Central Europe were another.[73]

As Paris and Bonn worked to build a strong bilateral relationship—cemented by their Treaty of Friendship, signed on 22 January 1963—they also attempted to provide a united Western front in negotiations for peace and cooperation on the European continent. Adenauer ignored the criticisms voiced by his own advisers and his allies in the United States who feared de Gaulle's nationalist aims. Instead, he attached his hopes for improved living conditions in the two Germanys to the French president's dream of building a single European community extending from Paris to the Ural Mountains.[74]

Adenauer even considered negotiating an agreement on "Basic Principles" between East and West for the purpose of stability and reduced Cold War tensions. Through his representatives in Washington, the chancellor floated the idea of a ten-year freeze in the status quo around Central Europe. According to his plan, the great powers would pledge not to threaten each other in this area for a whole decade. During this period they would experiment with various arms control measures, trade concessions, and expanded human contacts. Karl Carstens, the West German state secretary for foreign affairs, argued that a "calm and relaxed atmosphere" around the two Germanys would allow for the most promising progress toward improved conditions on both sides of the Berlin Wall.[75]

Adenauer's proposal matched the thoughts of many policymakers in Washington, especially President Kennedy.[76] Some of the president's rhetoric, however, proved deceptive. During his visit to West Berlin in June 1963 the American leader condemned the division of the city and expressed solidarity with those struggling for freedom against communist tyranny. Kennedy closed this forceful speech with one of his most memorable lines: "All free men, wherever they may live, are citizens of Berlin, and therefore, as a free man, I take pride in the words 'Ich bin ein Berliner.'" Kennedy echoed more of Adenauer's caution in his speech hours later at the Free University. The president called upon citizens to "deal with the realities as they actually are, not as they might have been, and not as we wish they were." "I am not impressed by the opportunities open to popular fronts throughout the world," he explained. "I do not believe that any democrat can successfully ride that tiger. But I do believe in the necessity of great powers working together to preserve the human race, or otherwise we can be destroyed."[77]

The nuclear dangers of the early 1960s encouraged many foreign leaders to give Adenauer's calls for arms control and cautious diplomacy a serious hearing.[78] Kennedy recognized the importance of East-West cooperation, but he failed to accept the broader purpose in Adenauer's proposals. The chancellor wanted to use short-term strategic stability to initiate long-term political change, especially in Central Europe. This motive explains why he coupled his overtures to the Soviet Union with the Franco-German Friendship Treaty, discussions of the Sino-Soviet split, and calls for more trade and interaction across the Berlin Wall.

Despite his advanced age—he turned eighty-seven in 1963—Adenauer believed that time was on his side. He expected that a ten-year freeze in the status quo around West Berlin would encourage deterioration of the Soviet bloc. A more unified Western Europe, a stronger China, and increased contacts between East and West would force Moscow to make concessions without another war-threatening crisis. The chancellor did not advocate stability for stability's sake, but instead a dynamic Eastern policy—"Ostpolitik"—that would improve long-term conditions in the two Germanys, and maybe even foster reunification.

The United States failed to implement this vision in full. Obsessed with nuclear dangers, Kennedy simply accepted the status quo in Europe without serious hopes or plans for constructive change. Policymakers in Washington shared Adenauer's anxieties about military conflict, but they lacked his instinct for imagining a better future. German reunification, in the eyes of American officials, remained desirable but impossible.[79] This emphasis on order and division *without* the change that the chancellor advocated inspired some of Adenauer's harshest words. He accused the United States of practicing cowardly "appeasement," like the British before World War II. Kennedy seemed all too content, he believed, to seal current boundaries in Europe against any alteration—even through peaceful means.[80]

Adenauer had offered a practical, if inchoate, plan that balanced power, threats, and expectations to satisfy German demands for improved interpersonal connections across Cold War divisions. His proposals became the kernel of Ostpolitik and West European–sponsored detente in the late 1960s, often working against the aims of *both* the Soviet Union and the United States. Frustrated by the shallowness of Washington's policies, during his last years in office Adenauer adopted much of Charles de Gaulle's long-standing distrust of American hegemony.[81]

Speaking before an audience of German politicians, scholars, and religious figures assembled at the Tutzing Christian Academy in July 1963, the chancellor called upon the "world powers"—the United States, the Soviet Union, and China—to develop a concert among nations that not only stabilized the dangerous international environment but also provided a moral—in Adenauer's terms, "Christian"—foundation for daily life. He praised the United States for its commitment to democracy and economic growth, but he also indicated that this was not enough. Adenauer emphasized the "great role" that the states of Western Europe would have to play in the future development of the international system. They now carried the main burden, he argued, for resisting and reversing the "pressures" from the Soviet bloc. Only through continentwide cooperation and continued commitment to democracy could West Germany and its neighbors improve life in Europe for future generations.[82]

Adenauer offered this vision—in contrast to Kennedy's empty new frontier—for anxious listeners in the Federal Republic, the rest of the Western alliance, and even the Soviet Union. The elderly leader was ahead of his time. "Change through reconciliation" would become a popular idea among a new generation of politicians, especially future chancellor Willy Brandt. The concept, however, remained in tension with the conservative pressures of the nuclear stalemate. In Moscow, Adenauer's determination to pursue political change had the perverse effect of encouraging *additional* Soviet attempts to reinforce the status quo.

▪ Khrushchev and the Nuclear Economy

Nikita Khrushchev—the child of peasants, trained as a mechanic in the coal mines of Ukraine's Donbass region—shared Kennedy's ambition to create power through force of will. Recording his memoirs in the late 1960s, Khrushchev identified himself with a spirit of spontaneous energy and unsystematic reform that ran against the inhibitions of rigid ideologies and detailed strategies. "I'm a man of the earth, a man of action, a miner," he explained. "I'm used to working with metal and chemicals. I have a constitutional block against clerical work—it's completely alien to me. I hate having to look over a stack of forms and files to see the flesh-and-blood."[83]

Khrushchev was drawn to Marxism for untheoretical reasons. He joined the Communist Party because it appeared to offer the most viable mechanism for rapid and far-reaching social change. Theory served as a tool for shaping a more equitable and secure society. Khrushchev recalled the particular influence of the French socialist Emile Zola in his own political development. "When I read Emile Zola's *Germinal*," Khrushchev recounted, "I thought that he was writing not about France, but about the mine in which my father and I worked. The worker's lot was the same both in France and in Russia." The language of Marxism came second to what Khrushchev later described as his determination to build a society that would "provide uninterrupted growth in the standard of living of the population."[84]

If Josef Stalin developed what his biographer calls an "idealized image of himself" as the mythic Caucasian warrior named "Koba," Khrushchev's memoirs reveal a similar identification with Zola's mechanic-hero, Etienne Lantier.[85] Zola anticipated Khrushchev's approach to leadership in his description of the simple, charismatic personality of his nineteenth-century protagonist:

> Etienne began talking again. The old order was breaking up and could not last longer than a few months, he confidently affirmed. When it came to ways and means he was vaguer, jumbling odd bits of reading; and, with such an ignorant audience, not hesitating to embark on explanations that he could not follow himself, into which he threw all the different systems,

tempered by his certain knowledge of an easy triumph, a universal kiss of peace that would put an end to class misunderstandings . . . Etienne's influence spread far and wide and gradually he was revolutionizing the village. His unobtrusive propaganda was made all the more telling by his increasing popularity.[86]

Khrushchev fashioned himself as a Soviet incarnation of Etienne Lantier. He contrasted his work in the Donbass mines, the Moscow city government, and the Ukrainian party leadership with the more adventurous but impractical activities of "loafers" and "good-for-nothings" in distinguished party circles. Josef Stalin did not appeal to Khrushchev for his fearless use of ruthless force in the 1920s —like the mythic "Koba"—but instead for his evident "simplicity and compassion" toward the suffering people of the Soviet Union.[87]

For all his criticisms after the dictator's death in 1953, Khrushchev never abandoned this attachment to the untheoretical, approachable, and pragmatic Stalin of the early Soviet years. Things went wrong, according to Khrushchev, during the party purges and collectivization drives of the 1930s, when Stalin sought industrial mobilization and ideological purity at the cost of countless human lives. "Koba" fought with unceasing energy and all-consuming power, but his actions terrorized the diligent workers who followed the path of Etienne Lantier. Speaking before the Polish Workers' Party in March 1956, Khrushchev explained that "Stalin himself was a convinced Marxist, and he was convinced that society in particular must become a communist society, and he served this society with all his body and soul. Of this, I have no doubt." The "tragedy" began when the destructive power accumulated in the leader's hands eclipsed his creative endeavors. "In protecting the revolution," Khrushchev argued, Stalin "got to the point where, as they say, the artillery fired on its own army . . . Stalin is Stalin. He's a very complex figure. He had a lot of good and a lot, a great lot, of bad. Now we're trying to deal with the bad so that we can strengthen the party's correct path of action."[88]

Khrushchev's denunciations of Stalin served his political interests in the succession struggle after the dictator's death. These words also carried broader implications for the conceptualization of Soviet power in the 1960s. "Strengthening the party's correct path of action" meant little for Khrushchev in theoretical terms. It referred instead to the new leader's ambition to make the Soviet Union's military capabilities more reliable, and ultimately more useful than they had proven during Stalin's dictatorship. The "abuse of power" in earlier years—including frequent purges of distinguished military figures, productive workers, and creative thinkers—had, in Khrushchev's view, "caused untold harm to our party" at home and abroad.[89]

The new leader's attack on the Stalin "cult" proposed an alternative path for Soviet power. Like Kennedy's new frontier, Khrushchev's vision promised a more effective use of state capabilities. He offered a program that would convert military power into increased security and prosperity. Stalin, Khrushchev explained, had become "a serious obstacle in the path of Soviet social development." But "in the last years, when we managed to free ourselves of the harmful practice of the cult of the individual and took several proper steps in the sphere of internal and external policies, everyone saw how activity grew before their very eyes, how the creative activity of the broad working masses developed, how favorably all this acted upon the development of economy and culture."[90]

Khrushchev's revelations of Stalin's crimes required rethinking Soviet power. Instead of the wasted resources, internal turmoil, and international conflict elicited by earlier abuses of state authority, the new program would organize society's military and economic capabilities for the purpose of improving the Soviet Union's political standing. Employing the boisterous Marxist rhetoric for which he became notorious, Khrushchev announced in 1961 that the first socialist state would now create a truly communist society. Moscow's policies would "erase the essential distinctions between town and country and later on between mental and physical labor." Nuclear capabilities played a central role in Khrushchev's plans for rapid "communist construction." Bombs and rockets would guarantee international security and prestige for Soviet society.[91]

Khrushchev's rhetoric frequently resembled Kennedy's in relation to the new frontier. His military policies, however, shared notable similarities with Eisenhower's fiscally conservative nuclear strategy (the "new look"). An overwhelming accumulation of power in the military forces, and of course the Kremlin itself, had proven self-defeating. The Soviet Union would now, through its new technology, provide the basis for both security and increased economic production.

"What country or group of countries in Europe would dare to attack us," Khrushchev asked, "when we can virtually erase these countries from the face of the Earth by our atomic and hydrogen weapons and by launching our rockets to every point of the globe?" Despite his seemingly inconsistent mix of threats and peace overtures, the Soviet leader sought to harness the destructive power of nuclear weapons in order to free other resources for development at home. "For the first time in history," Khrushchev promised, "want will have been fully and finally eliminated. This will be an imposing achievement by the new society. No capitalist country can set itself this task."[92]

These words from what was arguably Khrushchev's most exultant speech—delivered to the Twenty-second Congress of the Communist Party in October 1961—reveal the intimate connection between nuclear strength and domestic prosperity in the Soviet leader's thinking. The international power provided by the Soviet Union's growing arsenal of nuclear warheads and missiles would allow, at least in theory, for the same sorts of domestic savings that Eisenhower had anticipated years earlier. By purchasing international security on the cheap, Khrushchev hoped to divert resources to unprecedented, and in retrospect overambitious, advances in industry and agriculture.[93]

The Soviet leader pushed for immediate savings through non-nuclear disarmament. Having already reduced his nation's conventional forces by more than 1.5 million after Stalin's death, Khrushchev planned to demobilize another 1.2 million troops during the early 1960s. If carried through, these combined reductions would cut the number of armed Soviet personnel nearly in half from their postwar high of approximately 5.4 million. Even without American reciprocity, Khrushchev explained to his military subordinates, "this step would not in any way cause damage to our defenses, but would give us major political, moral, and economic advantages." "If we fail to do this," he warned, "it would mean failing to make a full use of the powerful capital our socialist policy and our socialist economy have accumulated."[94]

This was the essence of Soviet nuclear economy. Despite Khrushchev's knowledge that his state possessed only four intercontinental ballistic missiles in early 1960, he believed that future rocket production would allow a much greater allocation of labor and capital to domestic priorities. The defense of Soviet and East European territory—always a source of anxiety—would become cheaper and more reliable with nuclear parity. Mobilized labor, industry, and science in the Soviet Union—freed from the burdens of Stalin's dictatorship—would support a safer, more prosperous, and more equitable society.[95]

The reliability of Soviet nuclear defense was simple to describe but difficult to ensure. Khrushchev recognized that even with the resource savings promised by nuclear weapons, the Kremlin suffered from "overreaching" strategic commitments in Europe and Asia. In particular, Soviet allies in East Germany and China demanded that Khrushchev use his missile capabilities to defend aggressive behavior that stiffened international resistance. Moscow's promises of expanded nuclear power inspired weaker communist states to take actions that increased the likelihood of war rather than stability. Like Eisenhower and Kennedy, Khrushchev soon realized that the most powerful military forces created new insecurities.[96]

Confronted by a flood of citizens fleeing the oppressive German Democratic Republic for the freer and more prosperous West, East German party secretary Walter Ulbricht called in 1961 for the Soviet Union to close "the open borders" in Central Europe. Ulbricht demanded more forceful Soviet threats to deter what he called "the aggressive forces in West Germany and the Western powers." Emboldened by Khrushchev's claims about the Kremlin's nuclear power, the East German leader contended that the Eastern-bloc states should no longer tolerate geopolitical compromises with the North Atlantic Treaty Organization (NATO). In addition, Ulbricht hoped that Soviet nuclear capabilities would force other countries and international institutions—especially the UN—to abandon their policy of refusing East Germany official recognition as a "normal state."[97]

East Germany was the prime mover during the Berlin crisis of 1961. Ulbricht pushed Khrushchev to challenge the American-led alliance. He also suggested the construction of the Berlin Wall. Khrushchev initially thought that Soviet nuclear capabilities might convince the United States and its allies to give up their access to West Berlin. When threatened by NATO retaliation against any obstruction of Western transport to the city, the Soviet leader used the construction of the Wall as a mechanism for quick retreat. Khrushchev recognized that even his new missile forces could not compel desired behavior from adversaries.[98]

The Soviet Union, in fact, suffered from nuclear weakness in comparison with the United States. On 21 October 1961 the American government announced—Soviet claims to the contrary—that it possessed a significant nuclear advantage over its adversary.[99] Khrushchev, as a consequence, became noticeably more cautious in his public rhetoric. Nuclear threats in Europe, especially when taken seriously by allies, did more damage than good for the Kremlin's security. Khrushchev also recognized, as most observers did at the time, that a significant political and economic asymmetry existed between the two postwar Germanys. By the end of the 1950s the Federal Republic of Germany had the most prosperous economy on the European continent, a stable political system, and a powerful military force with potential access to nuclear weapons. Adenauer's calls for political change in Europe rested on a solid domestic foundation. The German Democratic Republic, in contrast, had grown increasingly dependent upon economic, military, and political aid from the Soviet Union for its basic sustenance.[100]

Soviet nuclear capabilities, if brandished aggressively by allies in Eastern Europe, could elicit independent West German nuclear development outside the stabilizing structure of NATO. Obsessed with what he frequently called—in reference to World War II—West German "revanchism," this was Khrushchev's worst nightmare.[101] The government in Bonn clearly possessed the economic and technological capacity to build its own nuclear force. On a number of occasions, in fact, both Adenauer and his minister of defense, Franz-Josef Strauss, flirted with the idea of an independent West German nuclear capability. President Eisenhower also considered allowing Bonn access to nuclear weapons for the purpose of relieving the American defense burden in Europe.[102]

The Soviet leader reportedly commented that "Berlin is the testicles of the West," but when he self-consciously "squeezed" this exposed position in the early 1960s he quickly realized that he might produce a more threatening West German response. After 1961 Khrushchev sought cooperation, rather than unilateral assertions of military power, in Central Europe. He wrote to the American president in late 1962, emphasizing his desire to avoid a "hotbed of collision." The Soviet leader proposed a series of strong restraints on the two German governments. Khrushchev feared that if uncontrolled, Ulbricht and Adenauer would create "overreaching" commitments for the superpowers, pulling them into an unwanted nuclear war.[103]

Khrushchev harbored similar anxieties about the aggressive behavior of the government in Beijing. Although the Soviet Union and the People's Republic of China enjoyed uneasy but close relations through the mid-1950s, the growth of independent Chinese Communist power created a dangerous split in the Sino-Soviet alliance. Instead of coordinating their military activities with Moscow—as they had done during the Korean War—China's leaders launched a threatening round of attacks on enemy-held territories in the Taiwan Strait during late August 1958 without consulting the "elder brother."[104]

On a visit to Beijing only weeks earlier, Khrushchev had received no indication of Mao Zedong's plans to risk nuclear confrontation with the United States. Soon after Beijing initiated the crisis, it curtailed its attacks across the strait, pledging to shell the Taiwanese-held islands only on alternate days. Mao's government also made this move without Moscow's prior knowledge.

Chinese aims during this period remain difficult to discern, but they surely involved an assertion of independence from *both* superpowers.[105]

Exactly one year later, in late August 1959, the Chinese again acted aggressively without consulting the Soviet Union. This time military conflict occurred around the long-disputed Sino-Indian border, in the plateaus of Tibet. The Chinese Communist government had controlled the region since the first months after victory in the mainland civil war. During the 1950s Beijing constructed a road for communications and military maneuvers from the Xinjiang region into western Tibet. Despite relatively amicable Sino-Indian relations at the time, the Chinese road crossed about 100 miles of Indian-claimed territory without the latter government's consent.

Following the Tibetan rebellion against Chinese rule in the spring of 1959 and the Dalai Lama's consequent flight to northern India, New Delhi challenged Beijing's forces at the border. India claimed the right to defend its territory against Chinese incursions. In August the two states exchanged shots, and clashes quickly spread across the disputed area. China condemned India for its alleged militancy. Beijing also criticized the Soviet Union for failing to support Chinese activities.[106]

Moscow found itself running to catch up with its "little brother," fearful of the damage that Chinese aggression would create for Soviet hopes of increasing the Kremlin's influence in Asia. During Khrushchev's last visit to China, in October 1959, he attempted to moderate Beijing's behavior. He emphasized that the disputes over Taiwan and India had opened new opportunities for the Americans. At the very time when Khrushchev was working hardest to stabilize Soviet security interests in Europe and Asia, Mao Zedong's government was unilaterally inflaming new conflicts. Moscow wished to maintain friendly relations with both Beijing and New Delhi, but Chinese activities threatened to implicate the Soviet Union in extended hostilities between the two states.[107]

Khrushchev's exasperation raised tensions at the 1959 Sino-Soviet summit to unprecedented heights. Mikhail Suslov, a member of the Soviet Central Committee, later summarized his leader's comments in Beijing:

> Comrade Khrushchev told the Chinese comrades that we do not completely understand their foreign policy, particularly with regard to India, and on the issue of Taiwan . . . One cannot regard as normal the situation, when we, China's ally, do not know what the Chinese comrades may undertake tomorrow in the area of foreign policy. Indeed, all countries of the socialist camp are linked not only by common ideas and goals, but also by alliance commitments. Incorrect actions of one country may hurt [the] international situation of the whole socialist camp.[108]

In Khrushchev's eyes, Beijing's belligerence was a more virulent form of risky East German behavior. Soviet nuclear weapons remained pledged to Communist China's defense by the terms of the alliance treaty the two states had signed in 1950. After 1958, however, the Kremlin grew increasingly uneasy with the possible implications of this commitment.[109]

The Soviet leadership suffered from its own overblown rhetoric. Khrushchev understood that Soviet missile capabilities were more limited than public claims indicated. Leaders in Communist China, like those in East Germany, did not get this message. Mao Zedong acted as if increased Soviet military power provided new opportunities to solve long-standing disputes around the Taiwan Strait and the Sino-Indian border. Conversing with the Soviet leader beside a Chinese swimming pool in August 1958, Mao reflected on the apparent strength of the communist world: "Comrade Khrushchev, what do you think? If we compare the military might of the capitalist world with that of the socialist world, you'll see that we obviously have the advantage over our enemies. Think of how many divisions China, the [Soviet Union], and the other socialist countries could raise." Hearing his most effusive public claims parroted with apparent seriousness, Khrushchev quickly backtracked, emphasizing the limits on Soviet nuclear power: "Comrade Mao Zedong, nowadays that sort of thinking is out of date. You can no longer calculate the alignment of forces on the basis of who has the most men . . . with the atomic bomb, the number of troops on each side makes practically no difference to the alignment of real power and the outcome of a war. The more troops on a side, the more bomb fodder."[110]

Khrushchev's prudent attempts to restrain his allies ran against his public calls for communist expansion. When the Soviet leader accepted compromises with adversaries in Asia and Europe, his comrades in Beijing and East Berlin perceived weakness of Kremlin will, not capability. The growth in Soviet military power created rising expectations among allies that Khrushchev could not meet without jeopardizing the security of his own state. Superior American thermonuclear forces made the risks of aggressive Soviet-bloc behavior exceed potential benefits for Moscow. Trapped in his own rhetoric, the Soviet leader sought to curtail his difficulties by controlling the passions of his allies. In an age of nuclear power, Kremlin policy resembled self-containment rather than international revolution.[111]

Khrushchev took decisive action to relieve his strategic unease in Asia. In July 1960 the Soviet Union withdrew its experts who had worked in China since the mid-1950s to build Mao's government a nuclear bomb. Moscow cited the "unfriendly" attitudes of the Beijing leadership during recent years. Khrushchev never revoked his pledge to protect China against direct enemy attack, but Soviet policy split from Mao's international ambitions. When large border skirmishes erupted between China and India again, in October 1962, the Kremlin steered away from any significant public support for Beijing's activities.[112]

Allies in the expansion of Soviet influence now posed difficult challenges for Moscow. Khrushchev could not simply ignore the claims of his alleged ideological partners around Berlin, the Taiwan Strait, and the Sino-Indian border. The independent and reckless behavior of East Germany and mainland China made these international communist associations increasingly burdensome for Khrushchev. His attempts to ensure Soviet security and concentrate resources on domestic development encountered recurring resistance from allies. Like earlier empires, the Soviet Union found in the early 1960s that its broad expansion of international influence multiplied its sources of insecurity.[113]

Khrushchev famously proclaimed that his state would produce nuclear-armed rockets "like sausages." In private, however, he recognized that the United States had much more military beef (and pork!).[114] By late 1961 the imbalance in nuclear power had grown so great that Kennedy ruminated with his closest advisers about a possible attack upon the Soviet Union, eliminating the Kremlin's capability for threatening the United States with nuclear weapons. The president hypothesized that "information from a closely guarded source [could cause] me to conclude that the U.S. should launch an immediate strike against the Soviet bloc."[115]

American discussions about a first strike were not entirely new. During the previous decade members of the Eisenhower administration had suggested that the United States should destroy Soviet nuclear facilities before Moscow could build sufficient forces to challenge Washington's military predominance. The speed and accuracy of intercontinental ballistic missiles made a successful U.S. attack particularly feasible in 1961 and 1962.[116]

America's nuclear predominance was very real at the time. The United States had enough bombers and rockets to wipe out virtually all Soviet strategic nuclear forces. This advantage was, however, a "wasting asset." Washington's capacity to launch a decisive first strike would evaporate once the Soviet Union possessed a large number of nuclear-armed missiles to retaliate against an attack before its own destruction.[117]

Khrushchev surely recognized all of this. He only had to look at the numbers. Fairly accurate information on the size of the American nuclear arsenal was in the public record, and Khrushchev had privileged knowledge about limited Soviet capabilities. While he exaggerated Soviet strength in public,

Khrushchev endeavored to close the real "missile gap" that contradicted Moscow's assertions of nuclear superiority.[118]

In April 1961 the American-sponsored invasion of the Bay of Pigs, in Cuba, provided evidence for the limits of Soviet nuclear deterrence. Fidel Castro's forces defeated the Cuban émigrés attacking the island, but the obvious role of the United States in the operation indicated that Moscow's alleged strength had failed to alter Washington's activities. Cuba had become a Soviet ally in 1960, but American military superiority allowed the U.S. government to disregard the Kremlin's support for Castro. In contrast, neither Khrushchev nor Mao could act without attention to American retaliatory power around Berlin and the Taiwan Strait.

After the Bay of Pigs invasion Khrushchev worried, with reason, that the United States would attack Cuba again. Echoing the "domino theory" that guided America's foreign policy planning, particularly in Southeast Asia, the Soviet leader feared that a successful invasion of Cuba would undermine the credibility of the Kremlin's pledges to defend other states. In particular, the overthrow of Castro's government would contribute to growing criticisms voiced among Soviet allies—especially China—that Moscow failed to meet its explicit promises of protection. Cuban defeat threatened to inflame the already dangerously belligerent tendencies in Beijing and East Berlin. In his memoirs, Khrushchev reflected upon these tensions: "The fate of Cuba and the maintenance of Soviet prestige in that part of the world preoccupied me even when I was busy conducting the affairs of state in Moscow and traveling to other fraternal countries . . . one thought kept hammering away at my brain: what will happen if we lose Cuba? I knew it would have been a terrible blow to Marxism-Leninism. It would gravely diminish our stature throughout the world."[119]

American activities threatened Soviet prestige. In 1962 the White House planned for a number of covert efforts—"Operation Mongoose"—to eliminate the Cuban leader. Exploding cigars and assassination attempts accounted for only a small subset of the U.S. Central Intelligence Agency's nefarious schemes. More immediately, a series of American amphibious maneuvers in the spring and summer—"Lantphibex-62"—convinced Khrushchev that Washington would soon overrun the island.[120]

In May 1962 Khrushchev decided to defend Castro's government and to redress the Soviet-American strategic imbalance by deploying intermediate-range nuclear missiles on Cuban soil. "We had to think up some way of confronting America with more than words," Khrushchev later explained. "We had to establish a tangible and effective deterrence to American interference in the Caribbean. But what exactly? The logical answer was missiles." They were Khrushchev's magic bullet. "The main thing," he recounted, "was that the installation of our missiles in Cuba would, I thought, restrain the United States from precipitous military action against Castro's government . . . In addition to protecting Cuba, our missiles would have equalized what the West likes to call the 'balance of power.'" American threats to Castro's government jeopardized Moscow's credibility, but successful Cuban defense offered Khrushchev a startling strategic opportunity. The Soviet leader's haste to bolster his international stature drove him to the impulsive, and ultimately self-defeating, rocket deployments in Cuba.[121]

When Washington—thanks to U-2 aerial reconnaissance photographs—discovered the Soviet missile shipments on 15 October 1962, Khrushchev emphasized the "defensive" nature of the weapons. He believed that the utility of Moscow's nuclear deterrent required that he withstand American intimidation. U.S. strategic superiority led Khrushchev to take aggressive action in Cuba for the purpose of defending the exaggerated claims of Soviet nuclear strength. Once again, his rhetoric had outstripped his capabilities. After retreating from dangerous confrontations in Europe and Asia since 1958, Khrushchev took a big risk in 1962 for the purpose of bolstering Soviet power.

Moscow's nuclear maneuvers in Cuba foretold failure for Khrushchev. On 28 October 1962 the Kremlin retreated before American threats of military reprisal. In "the cause of peace" Khrushchev broadcast an urgent English text on Moscow radio. "The Soviet government," according to the conciliatory announcement, gave "a new order to dismantle the arms which [America] described as offensive." Instead of using the missiles in Cuba to buttress Soviet prestige, military personnel would now "crate and return" the weapons Khrushchev had invested with such great importance. Informed of the Kremlin's decision after the fact, Fidel Castro sent his discredited patron in Moscow an indignant but accurate appraisal of events. The Soviet Union had, in Castro's words, agreed to a "surprising, sudden, and practically unconditional" surrender.[122]

Khrushchev did get two things in return from the United States. The Kennedy administration publicly pledged not to invade Cuba. In secret the president also agreed to withdraw from Turkey a group of inferior American "Jupiter" missiles, which Washington had, in fact, considered dismantling for more than a year. In 1963 the United States quietly removed the Jupiters. More reliable and accurate "Polaris" submarine-launched nuclear rockets, first tested in 1960, replaced them.[123]

The withdrawal of Soviet missiles from Cuba loomed much larger than the American noninvasion pledge. Instead of bolstering the international prestige of the Soviet Union, Khrushchev discredited Moscow's commitment to its allies. He also failed to establish a new strategic beachhead for his nuclear forces near U.S. territory. If anything, the crisis contributed to perceptions in various communist states—especially China—that the Soviet Union would not use its nuclear power to pursue "national liberation," socialist development, and defense against capitalist incursions. When pushed by American force, the Kremlin retreated for its own self-protection.

Khrushchev admitted as much in his post-crisis correspondence with Kennedy. The Soviet leader wrote of untying the "knot" of war through new measures for Soviet-American trust, conciliation, and agreement. "I have been denouncing American imperialism," Khrushchev explained. "But on the other hand I consider it useful for us to continue to maintain the possibility of confidential exchange of opinion because a minimum of personal trust is necessary for leading statesmen of both countries."[124]

This was more than just good common sense. Following recurring difficulties around the two Germanys, China, and now Cuba, the Soviet leadership recognized that Khrushchev had failed in his energetic attempt to use nuclear weapons as a means of enhancing the Kremlin's power at home and abroad. Even if the Soviet Union managed to produce missiles "like sausages," these weapons offered little political leverage over adversaries and allies. Only active cooperation with hostile forces could convert the destructive military powers of the Soviet state to peaceful purpose.

▪ The Limits of Nuclear "Peace"

The Cuban missile crisis transformed international politics. It convinced the leaders of the United States and the Soviet Union that they must avoid war at almost any cost. Kennedy and Khrushchev resembled the doomed Kurtz character in Joseph Conrad's novella, *The Heart of Darkness*. Staring out at a foreboding landscape of nuclear dangers, they recoiled, like Kurtz, at the prospect of their imminent destruction: "the horror, the horror."[125]

The detailed records of White House deliberations during the Cuban missile crisis indicate that nuclear weapons became more of an albatross than an effective mechanism for pursuing "policy by other means." Despite all of Eisenhower and Kennedy's efforts to make their nuclear capabilities useful for state purposes, the events of October 1962 demonstrated that these military forces constrained the leaders who held them in greatest number. The giants of the international system possessed unprecedented power for destruction, but they were also incredibly vulnerable because their abundant nuclear arms restricted maneuver.[126]

The American president brought this realization to public attention in June 1963 when in a commencement address he argued that the superpowers must find new mechanisms for cooperation rather than conflict. Instead of threatening "massive retaliation" and pushing competitive new frontiers, Kennedy pointed to the shared dangers that nuclear weapons posed for the United States and the Soviet Union. "It is an ironic but accurate fact," he explained, "that the two strongest powers are the two in the most danger of devastation. All we have built, all we have worked for, would be destroyed in the first 24 hours." Instead of Cold War rhetoric about "bearing any burden" to defeat the enemy, Kennedy called upon leaders to "make the world safe for diversity." Highlighting the common military predicament, he emphasized that "our most basic link is that we all inhabit this small planet. We all breathe the same air. We all cherish our children's future. And we are all mortal."[127]

Agreements on a Limited Test Ban Treaty, a crisis "hotline" between Washington and Moscow, and a stable status quo around Berlin all followed from this post–Cuban missile crisis sentiment. Despite his past blustering about nuclear weapons, the Soviet leader appeared even more chastened than his American counterpart. For Khrushchev the Limited Test Ban Treaty constituted much more than a tactical measure. It marked what he called a "turning point in the history of contemporary international relations." "We are living at a time," Khrushchev wrote Kennedy, "when it is important to achieve progress together in international affairs. It is particularly important, I would say, that this be really tangible and actual progress creating a new situation—a situation of relaxation of tension, thus opening to us the prospect of solution to other pressing problems and questions."[128]

Khrushchev sought an explicit "pact of non-aggression" between East and West. He went so far as to call for a definitive "end of the Cold War." Instead of furthering the power and prestige of the Soviet Union, the specter of nuclear war forced the Kremlin to retreat from the most dangerous forms of military conflict with the capitalist states. Khrushchev and his successors focused their efforts on expanding Soviet power in areas that did *not* threaten direct confrontation with the United States. The Soviet Union continued to extend its influence abroad, but it was decidedly more cautious in its relations with Washington after the Cuban missile crisis. Stability and non-aggression replaced threats of war in Berlin and Cuba. Washington and Moscow recognized a common interest in avoiding nuclear conflict that superseded Cold War antagonisms, especially in Europe. For almost two decades neither state pushed for a change in the political status quo on the continent.[129]

Nuclear weapons proved supremely ill suited for alliances that expanded the military commitments and vulnerabilities of the superpowers for vague ideological purposes. Not surprisingly, as American and Soviet leaders recognized a common interest in avoiding war, the Kremlin continued its retreat from many of the close connections among communist states that began to fray in the late 1950s. After October 1962 the Soviet leadership gave clear priority to stable relations with the United States rather than preexisting commitments to Beijing and Havana.[130]

The decline in the prospects of full-scale war between the superpowers made direct Soviet-American confrontations far less frequent in the period after the Cuban missile crisis. Few would lament this consequence of the nuclear stalemate. The so-called nuclear "peace," however, came at great cost. Fearful of conflict, the leaders of the most powerful states curtailed their ambitions for international change. They accepted the political status quo they had criticized years earlier. Stability, not progress, became the watchword for diplomacy in the 1960s.

Nuclear weapons were a hindrance to, rather than a resource for, policy. The United States and the Soviet Union confronted excessive military constraints in a nuclear world. Politicians in France and China, following Adenauer's lead, exploited the superpower stalemate for their own purposes. Dissident groups in the United States, Europe, and Asia mobilized to criticize the growing gap between the ideological claims and the actual behavior of leaders such as Kennedy and Khrushchev. Emerging stability in U.S.-Soviet relations *destabilized* alliances and societies. Nuclear weapons contributed to international and domestic strains that spread throughout the 1960s.

2

POLITICAL CONSTRAINTS AND
PERSONAL CHARISMA

During the 1960s the dominant Cold War states grew at once more powerful and more constrained. This was the central paradox of the period. Nuclear weapons, mobilized economies, and enlarged administrative capabilities allowed governments to escalate the promises they made to their citizens—including "new frontiers" and "uninterrupted growth in the standard of living of the population." As new military technologies imposed frustrating international restrictions on policy, domestic political constraints also multiplied with the expanding webs of state bureaucracy. What sociologists call the "routinization" of authority produced strong pressures for consistency and compromise, rather than the rapid change initially sought by leaders such as Kennedy and Khrushchev. International alliances and domestic bureaucracies made daily politics a game of balance between various rational but disunited interests.[1]

Nationalist programs for wealth and power grew from more deep-seated and far-reaching hopes. They appealed to emotions that scholars have located in popular "imagination," "will," and, most of all, shared "memory." The political dependencies of the period curtailed widely held ambitions and contradicted the most compelling claims of "national purpose." By the mid-1960s leaders in the United States and the Soviet Union largely succumbed to these circumstances. In extolling the virtues of stability they sought to make a virtue of Cold War necessity.[2]

Other public figures, particularly in France and China, refused to accept these limitations on change. Charles de Gaulle and Mao Zedong, more than any other leaders at the time, struggled to create "charismatic" sources of authority that escaped the contradictions between Cold War stalemate and national purpose. Max Weber described charisma as the "magic" quality that allows an individual to transcend, at least in appearance, the normal restrictions on human endeavors. De Gaulle and Mao created "cultish" sources of domestic and international influence through shared scorn for "rational" be-

44

havior. Unlike Kennedy, Adenauer, and Khrushchev, they made a virtue of objecting to compromises that many perceived as necessary. Both men refocused politics on an inner, romantic vision of greatness that explicitly condemned the caution of other leaders at the time. They embraced risky, and sometimes foolhardy, policies to enhance their respective images of singular genius. De Gaulle and Mao rejected reform through existing political institutions, many of which they had themselves recently created. They advocated revolution against domestic bureaucracies and international alliances. By the middle of the decade they formed a curious personal connection in self-conscious struggle against Cold War constraints. De Gaulle and Mao used each other to build simple and alluring images that attracted huge public followings. In this sense, they were interdependent in their criticisms of the superpowers and their temporary acquisition of godlike prestige.[3]

After years of turmoil—instigated in large part by de Gaulle and Mao—the images of the two men shined brightly. This resplendence, however, came at the cost of widespread suffering and discontent. If anything, the Cold War constraints upon France and China tightened during the 1960s. Like their American and Soviet counterparts, de Gaulle and Mao faced consistent frustration as they searched for creative alternatives to existing policies that would reinforce their personal authority. Despite all their efforts, the uniquely charismatic leaders of France and China left a legacy characterized more by political and social chaos than by national achievement.

▪ The *Grandeur* of de Gaulle's France

Democratic politics often produce antidemocratic outcomes. French history since the late eighteenth century is a testament to this unsettling observation. Recurrent expressions of popular will have, time and again, brought the French state either into the grips of a dictator—Napoleon Bonaparte and Louis Napoleon—or into a period of violent anarchy—the post-1789 Reign of Terror and the Paris Commune of 1871. Memories of these experiences played an important role in the development of French politics after World War II.

Charles de Gaulle—the relatively unknown general who rallied France against the Nazi occupation of Western Europe from 1940 through 1944—was acutely conscious of the potentially antidemocratic consequences of French attachments to *liberté, égalité,* and *fraternité.* Unlike many of his military contemporaries in Europe, de Gaulle did not assume that legitimate authority derived from some particular "genius" of war or from a "science" of power isolated from popular will. He rejected assertions of any military or other "state within the state." For de Gaulle there could be only one unified France, with authority derived from a single source—direct popular will. Politics was too important to be left to either the generals or the politicians. De Gaulle perceived the power of the state as residing in the manifest consent of the French masses on all key issues.

During his years as leader of the post–World War II provisional government (1945–46) and, later, the Fifth French Republic (1958–1969), de Gaulle frequently used popular referenda to create sources of power *outside* the traditional institutions within the military, the National Assembly, and the bureaucracy. The general's standing as leader derived primarily from manifestations of broad popular acclamation—the voice of "le peuple." Confronted by opposition at home and abroad, de Gaulle silenced his critics with a stubborn appeal to the streets. "I have decided to proceed to a referendum, in order to verify the adhesion of the French to de Gaulle," the general characteristically intoned during one moment of political crisis.[4]

De Gaulle's consistent popularity among voters did not mask the twin specters of dictatorship and anarchy accompanying French democracy. As the leader of the provisional post–World War II government in Paris, the general sought to preserve his personal authority against partisan disputes about the state's political future. Despite various urgings, de Gaulle refused to join a political party or to base his power in a popularly elected assembly of representatives, as his counterparts in England, Italy, and later West Germany did. "As I saw it," de Gaulle recounted in his memoirs, "the state must have a head, that is, a leader whom the nation could see beyond its own fluctuations, a man in charge of essential matters and the guarantor of its fate." This executive, the general warned, must "not originate in parliament."[5]

The strong leader envisioned by de Gaulle would emerge from direct nationwide elections. The president would not simply represent but would actually affirm the unity and strength of the nation. Through policy, gesture, and ceremony the head of state would express the aspirations of the French public.

De Gaulle—the man who had guided France in her liberation from the ignominy of defeat in 1940—pledged to galvanize popular will in his person for a restoration of the nation's traditional greatness. France would maintain its popular revolutionary spirit, but the general would channel the will of the masses for collective purposes. Contemplating the prospect of communist and other local rebellions following the expulsion of the occupation regime, de Gaulle commented to his secretary that the rebels were not dangerous. "You don't have a revolution," de Gaulle explained, "without revolutionaries. And there's only one revolutionary in France and that's me!"[6]

As France's self-proclaimed revolutionary leader in 1945, de Gaulle "puri-fied" the state by unifying popular aspirations in his person. In October the general convinced two-thirds of French voters to limit the power of the newly elected Constituent Assembly, creating a separate executive office for the purpose of broad national policy, especially during periods of crisis. De Gaulle combined a deep faith in French popular will with a strong commit-ment to unified leadership. He extolled the virtues of building a democracy with important safeguards against disorder.[7]

The general believed that he alone could "preserve" France, amid her many contradictory impulses. The October 1945 vote revealed that although this view was tainted with a colossal ego and evident self-interest, many French citizens shared de Gaulle's amalgam of faith and fear in democracy. Years later, the general explained to his son that the government he sought to create after World War II followed neither Robespierre nor Napoleon—neither mass rule nor enlightened dictatorship. France needed a "popular monarch" who would preserve unity and national power while serving the interests of the people.[8]

De Gaulle's vision of a strong and unified France commanded popular ap-peal after World War II, but the pressures of reconstruction favored a state dominated by political parties—Socialists, Communists, Republicans, and Conservatives. Wary of too much power accruing in the hands of a single leader, the political elite within France and much of the American-led West-ern alliance pushed for the creation of a pluralist legislative system that would balance competing political perspectives, rather than allow one indi-vidual or party to assert overwhelming influence. As in Italy and West Ger-many, government by shifting party coalitions appeared to offer the best al-ternative to the experience of fascist dictatorship and communist revolution in Europe during earlier decades. This realization explains why more than half of the French public voted in late 1945 for left-leaning parties deter-mined to build a strong National Assembly. The majority of the electorate wanted de Gaulle to become president of the new state, but the French pub-lic also placed great faith in the legislative powers of a partisan parliament.[9]

Deliberations on the new French constitution quickly eroded most of the powers de Gaulle had hoped to invest in the head of government. The Con-stitutional Commission made the president explicitly dependent upon the National Assembly. Instead of direct popular election, only the members of the legislature would choose the national executive. In contrast to the domi-nant role de Gaulle had played in the governing Council of Ministers and the Committee on National Defense during the provisional period after liberation, the president no longer presided over these influential committees. Governing authority became more fragmented and less directly accountable. In judicial affairs the power of French courts also increased at the expense of the executive. The president, according to the constitution for the Fourth French Republic, could no longer overrule legal decisions through the use of a personal pardon.

By late 1945 de Gaulle found himself isolated within the emerging institutions of the French state. This was the paradox of the general's stubborn antipartisan posture. Without a network of close associates in the National Assembly, the courts, and other offices of government, de Gaulle could not shape the rules of power. His courage during the Nazi occupation continued to attract popular adulation, but within the ministries governing day-to-day organization of the economy, the army, and the judiciary de Gaulle's influence quickly slipped.

As Max Weber had predicted a half-century earlier, "legal domination" replaced the power of the single charismatic figure. By early 1946 the restrictions placed on the nonpartisan president by the institutions of daily governance forced de Gaulle, in the words of his biographer, to wear "a uniform that would have been too tight for a local mayor." Power diffused from the president to the National Assembly, the courts, and the various bureaucracies that controlled decisions about budget allocations, law, and the infrastructure of the reconstructed state. Frustrated by the restrictions on his power, de Gaulle resigned from the French presidency on 20 January 1946, explaining that "after terrible ordeals, France is no longer in a state of emergency." De Gaulle wished to separate himself from the emerging government of parties and bureaucrats. He also conveyed deep apprehension about the state's future. "As I retire," the general explained in carefully chosen words, "I would express my profoundly sincere wish that the government that will follow the one that I have had the honor to lead may succeed in the task that is still to be carried out."[10]

The central "task" for the French government remained, as before, to restore the state's greatness at home and abroad. De Gaulle believed that the divisions of authority in the Fourth Republic would bring only failure in this endeavor. Wishing to avoid association with an allegedly degenerate governing system, he withdrew to the political periphery. De Gaulle's biographer contends that this was only a "tactical" retreat—part of a larger plan for the general to return as a restored president, with unquestioned power, after the new government failed.[11]

De Gaulle's alleged plans for a heroic restoration seem prescient from the perspective of 1958, but recent scholarship has shown otherwise. While interlacing French bureaucracies after World War II detracted from the firm state unity that the general desired, they did assure national stability. As governing coalitions came and went—often within weeks of one another— highly educated engineers, economists, and planners remained firmly ensconced in the powerful ministries of foreign affairs, nuclear energy, finance, and education. Partisan divisions in the National Assembly allowed these civil servants to act with minimal intrusion from preoccupied political overseers. In critical policy areas the French planners formulated consistent and thoughtful initiatives, free of the political considerations that often required compromise and partial measures in other contexts. The bureaucrats used their expertise to serve both the financial interests of their particular ministries and the general international standing of the French state. One historian has termed this the "planning consensus" of Fourth Republic France that "restored" power to an unelected elite in an environment of continuing political discord.[12]

French nuclear policy provides one of the clearest examples of how planners made crucial decisions in place of politicians. In 1952 the National Assembly, convinced by members of the Commissariat à l'Energie Atomique (CEA) that nuclear energy would prove vital for the future electrical needs of industry, allocated 37.7 million francs for the construction of atomic reactors in France. Members of the National Assembly emphasized that French nuclear capabilities should serve only peaceful energy uses, not weapons proliferation in Europe and elsewhere. Despite this explicit prohibition on weapons capabilities, the CEA administrator general, Pierre Guillaumat, secretly oversaw the production of plutonium and other items that would allow France to build its own nuclear bombs. The CEA's only authorization for this activity was a vague encouragement received from Pierre Mendès-France at the end of his seven-and-a-half month tenure as president. Guillaumat could make France a virtual nuclear weapons state with little accountability because party wrangling within the National Assembly and uncertainty among rotating presidents prohibited the kind of consistent oversight required to control the CEA's activities. By the middle of the 1950s unelected administrators had secretly assembled much of the technology necessary for an independent nuclear capability. In 1958 de Gaulle merely confirmed a line of bureaucratic development already well in progress.[13]

During the late 1950s the CEA not only pursued a secret policy for French nuclear proliferation; it also aided other states—particularly Israel—in their endeavors to develop independent nuclear capabilities. In 1956, after the United States forced Britain, France, and Israel to withdraw from their recent occupation of the Suez Canal in Egypt, the CEA began work on a nuclear reactor for the Israeli government. French planners, operating without any public debate, built the Dimona facility from which Israel to this day assembles the critical ingredients for its nuclear arsenal. Shimon Peres—then an unelected aide to Prime Minister David Ben Gurion—arranged this deal with members of the French bureaucracy who were not authorized to make foreign policy decisions. The Dimona agreement between Israel and the Fourth Republic allowed France to project its still-undeclared nuclear power into the Middle East without political approval. In their reports to elected officials, members of the CEA emphasized the "peaceful" nature of the Dimona reactor despite its clear military purposes in design and planned Israeli application.[14]

French planners pulled off a similar feat of effective behind-the-scenes manipulation during the first years of Western Europe's postwar reconstruction. Despite the state's collapse in 1940 and subsequent occupation, by the end of the 1950s France had reestablished itself as a leader on the continent along with West Germany. Parisian economists and strategists authored a far-sighted agenda for cooperation with Bonn that included joint coal and steel production, trade tariffs, and even military collaboration. West Germany quickly became the industrial dynamo on the postwar continent, but French representatives—operating with little explicit political instruction at home—designed a Coal and Steel Community, followed by a Common Market, that gave the weaker economy west of the Rhine a dominant voice in Europe.[15]

De Gaulle often ridiculed the "European" bureaucrats in France who, he thought, sacrificed national interests to the mirage of a United States of Europe.[16] Despite this condemnation, the men who created the early Common Market did remarkable work to assure France an international position that far exceeded its relatively weak economic and military power. The bureaucrats, in many ways, accomplished what French politicians and generals could not. They used ideas and negotiating skills to compensate for material deficiencies. De Gaulle recognized this in his later continued adherence to the project of European cooperation and limited union.[17]

Between 1946 and 1958 France lacked the unifying public vision that the general desired. Nuclear developments and foreign policy in Europe, however, revealed that the bureaucratic Fourth Republic had provided the state with impressive stability and standing as a great power. The administrative postwar government that so rankled de Gaulle furnished many of the tools for the future exercise of French power.

By the late 1950s political debate in France no longer centered upon the capabilities of the state, as it had in the aftermath of the devastation wrought by Nazi occupation. Instead, a surprisingly strong French state struggled, within the context of a colonial war in Algeria and heightened Cold War tensions, to define a new national mission. This was the point at which the capabilities of the French bureaucracy proved insufficient.

A highly charged public debate about the future French role in North Africa prohibited skillful and flexible negotiations behind the scenes. Unelected ministers could not set the agenda for this issue so close to the hearts of the French people. Following the withdrawal of France's defeated forces from Indochina in 1954—and the decision to grant Tunisia and Morocco independence a year later—the nation's self-image as a great power became more firmly rooted in control of Algeria than ever before. Without this North African colony France would no longer have an empire or a claim to great-power status. The nationalist aspirations of French citizens and Algerian natives—both inspired in contradictory ways by the anticolonial struggles in Indochina, Tunisia, and Morocco—clashed violently. As armed conflict escalated throughout France and Algeria, the divided leadership in Paris found itself mired between a commitment to assert national interests and a desire to end the bloodletting. Concerns about France's future world status made Algeria an irresolvable issue without the kind of united political will that the Fourth Republic lacked.[18]

French leaders had to redefine their nation's interests if Paris was to withdraw its forces from North Africa. This required broad public persuasion, not behind-the-scenes administration. The government of the Fourth Republic had achieved a lot in other areas, but now its divisions and plodding qualities appeared most evidently deficient. Violence and recrimination around the question of Algeria's future required the "magic" of charismatic leadership for a resolution of disputes. This was the stage upon which de Gaulle initiated his second postwar revolution in French politics.

The years 1958–1969 witnessed unprecedented unity and purpose in French leadership circles. Firm government and emotional rhetoric about national greatness helped France accommodate its loss of empire in North Africa. In other international and domestic areas, however, the promises of de Gaulle's antibureaucratic politics produced far less than the general had hoped.[19]

The Algerian crisis brought de Gaulle back to power in May 1958. Evidence of a planned military coup against the civilian leaders in Paris forced the National Assembly to invest the general with powers to form a provisional "government of national safety." By the end of the year de Gaulle had overseen the creation of a new constitution, guaranteeing a strong executive. As the first president of the French Fifth Republic, de Gaulle ruled as the "popular monarch" he had hoped to become years before. In foreign and military affairs especially, the president forced the established bureaucracies to yield to his will.

France's recognition of Algerian independence in 1962 highlighted the dominance of de Gaulle in the new government. Despite opposition from members of the army, the political right, and the French settler community in Algeria, the president decided to cut his nation's losses in a colony it could no longer hold. Writing to the French army's chief of state in early 1959, de Gaulle explained that "it is possible a day will come when the integration of Algeria [with France] will be a possibility." "But," the president instructed his subordinate, "this day is not coming when we must kill a thousand combatants each month and, nevertheless, we find the insurrection active and intact before us for the last four years." Frustrated by calls for continued increases in French forces fighting in North Africa, de Gaulle exclaimed that "we have in Algeria 400,000 men, more than Napoleon had for conquering Europe." Algeria was an "abscess" that France had no choice but to remove. De Gaulle exploited a popular referendum for French disengagement from Algeria to outflank proponents—especially within the military—of continued armed intervention.[20]

Algeria was de Gaulle's triumph.[21] Relations with France's Cold War counterparts did not provide the president with similar successes. The structure of postwar Europe made the institutional sources of stability quite resilient against de Gaulle's attempts to heighten France's posture as a great power, beyond the more subtle maneuverings of the Fourth Republic. The alliances dominating Western and Eastern Europe—NATO and the Warsaw Pact—constrained the activities of a nation with resources far inferior to those of the United States and the Soviet Union.

De Gaulle understood the restraints of alliance politics as well as anyone. He lamented that "global affairs remain complicated, the fundamental reason always being the Russo-American rivalry." Despite his public words to the contrary, de Gaulle recognized that French security depended upon American military power. Paris simply lacked the resources to provide for its own defense. For this reason France needed NATO, and thus it had to tolerate some American influence on the European continent. When confronted with threats from the Soviet Union, de Gaulle consistently emphasized the importance of "cooperation" and "determination" among the Western allies.[22]

During the first five years after his return to power, de Gaulle attempted to reassert French *grandeur* within these obvious alliance constraints. As in Algeria, the president sought to capitalize on difficult circumstances. He hoped to elevate the international and domestic standing of his government by creating what he called a "permanent and organized concert" among the "three Western powers"—the United States, Great Britain, and France. Writing to President Eisenhower in September 1958, de Gaulle explained that the American-dominated organization of NATO "no longer addresses the necessary conditions for security which concern the free world." French and British interests in Asia and Africa, as well as priorities that differed from those of the United States in Europe, required more consultation and joint planning among Washington, London, and Paris. De Gaulle insisted that the Western alliance respect France as a great power despite its relatively weak military capabilities and disintegrating empire. Responding to a critic of his attempts to reform NATO a few years later, de Gaulle asked: "Yes or no must France be France? . . . You know how I chose."[23]

De Gaulle used public bombast rather than behind-the-scenes maneuvering to strengthen his nation's independence and prestige. Turning NATO into a forum for confirming France's equal standing with the United States and Great Britain was one important means to this end. Developing an inferior but publicly recognized French nuclear capability provided a second important symbol of the state's asserted great-power status.

While the bureaucrats of the Fourth Republic kept France's work on nuclear weapons secret, de Gaulle's government adopted Khrushchev-like tactics, exploiting the state's nascent nuclear capabilities for exaggerated public effect. Anxious to unveil France's bomb to the world, the president pushed for a test in the Sahara Desert "as soon as possible." Days before the detonation of the first French nuclear weapon (on 13 February 1960) de Gaulle went so far as to authorize significant public health dangers for the sake of an early explosion. "We must accept," the president wrote, "a notable margin of risk in this regard."[24]

"Our bomb will change the ideas of many," de Gaulle exulted. "It is a success, above all as proof of our capacity to undertake the most arduous and complicated techniques, and our resolution to follow our proper route without ceding to external pressures." De Gaulle asserted that France would maintain an independent "striking force" to deter Soviet aggression if America proved unwilling to risk its own security in defense of Western Europe. More significant, possession of a nuclear arsenal would corroborate the French president's claim that his state deserved equal standing among the three great Western powers.[25] One prominent American observer eloquently summarized de Gaulle's manipulation of nuclear imagery. For

France and other aspiring great powers, nuclear weapons became "the most potent status symbol since African colonies went out of fashion."[26]

In an effort to alter the image of France as a divided and decaying empire, de Gaulle used the nuclear tests in 1960 to emphasize that his state was "modern" and had "liberated" itself from the "chains" of inherited policies. Gaullist France would inject creative energy into stagnant domestic and international institutions. Above all, de Gaulle saw a need for emotional power, backed by displays of force, in a world that had become demoralized by the daily tensions of Cold War struggle.[27]

As he asserted French independence within the context of the Western alliance, de Gaulle attempted to build what he called a "real détente" between East and West. In this area he drew on the simultaneous efforts of West German chancellor Konrad Adenauer. Like his counterpart in Bonn, de Gaulle's vision of detente did not simply accept the status quo in Europe. It demanded nuclear disarmament among the superpowers and reconciliation between the divided halves of the continent. Instead of relying upon negotiations among numerous states (composing the United Nations Disarmament Commission), de Gaulle pushed for direct summitry between the great powers, with France at the center. Pragmatic leaders would iron out their differences head-to-head, without the dissension produced by the bureaucrats and "experts" de Gaulle derided as foreign policy "theologians."[28]

The general hoped that the May 1960 meeting of the great powers in Paris would allow France to broker an early step toward "real detente" in Europe. When the Soviet Union shot down an American U-2 reconnaissance aircraft in Russian air space a few weeks before the summit, the promising discussion among leaders became a forum for heightened acrimony rather than prudent compromise. De Gaulle regretted that the great powers had not yet learned to coexist to their mutual benefit.[29]

On this particular issue the general and British prime minister Harold Macmillan shared similar sentiments. Following the creation of the Fifth Republic the two leaders corresponded frequently. Both men believed that if they could overcome the accumulated superpower animosities and the inertia of the nuclear arms race, a long-term solution for stability in Europe would prove possible. During the Berlin crises in 1958–59 and 1961 de Gaulle and Macmillan opposed negotiations with the Soviets under duress. They did, however, push for West Germany's integration in an emerging European Economic Community that would help allay recurring fears of militaristic and "revanchist" behavior in the center of the continent.[30]

Despite their calls for stability and coexistence in the early 1960s, the differences in outlook between de Gaulle and Macmillan proved more significant than the initial similarities. The two leaders disagreed on how the European Economic Community should develop. The British prime minister had deep reservations about loosening London's ties to its Commonwealth of former colonies. This would be the necessary consequence of Britain's integration with the economies on the European continent. By July 1960, however, Macmillan realized that his nation's future political and economic standing required membership in "a loose confederal arrangement" among the European states. Excluded from the trading privileges of the Common Market, Britain could not hope to compete with the more dynamic German and French economies. For the purpose of building a more secure and anticommunist Western Europe, the United States also exerted strong pressure on Macmillan to join the emerging process of integration.[31]

Like Macmillan, de Gaulle was suspicious of any supranational structure that infringed on national sovereignty. The general wanted to strengthen French power through European integration. Instead of a larger Atlantic association dominated by the United States, de Gaulle sought to make an independent Europe, led by France, the core for reorganizing the Western bloc. "The Atlantic alliance must be founded on new bases," the general commented in 1960. "It is up to Europe to propose" a different framework for international partnership.[32]

De Gaulle's nationalist aims contradicted British attempts to use the Common Market as a limited avenue for halting imperial decline. Macmillan's Europe would remain part of a larger Commonwealth and Atlantic structure for foreign policy. In contrast, de Gaulle's Europe would bolster the independence, economic growth, and political influence of the continental states to the exclusion of foreign powers—the United States, the Soviet Union, and even Great Britain. De Gaulle sought to build a strong framework for France's cooperation with its neighbors—particularly West Germany—that would concentrate influence around Paris. By working closely with Bonn rather than London, de Gaulle felt he could direct West German power to favorable purposes while reinforcing the political "ascendance" of France.[33]

This was a strategy similar to that of the Fourth Republic planners. De Gaulle, however, relied upon public persuasion rather than private influence. Without popular mobilization the general feared that his state would remain divided internally and dominated externally. For long-term security and independence de Gaulle sought to create a distinct "personality" for Europe that matched the sense of greatness the Fifth Republic attempted to nurture in its citizens. The general even mused about a French-inspired popular referendum on Europe.[34]

In early 1963 the various elements in de Gaulle's vision of *grandeur* came together. On 14 January the general vetoed Britain's application to join the European Common Market. De Gaulle certainly harbored a prejudice against what he derisively called "Anglo-Saxon" influence in Europe, but he also had larger reasons for thumbing his nose at London. The December 1962 meeting between American and British leaders in the Bahamas—the "Nassau Summit"—had revealed that the "special relationship" between Washington and London would continue to threaten Paris' independence. In particular, the United States had agreed to provide Britain with national control over Polaris submarine-launched nuclear missiles. Anticipating similar French demands, President Kennedy considered limited "nuclear sharing" with de Gaulle as well. The American leader indicated, however, that he intended to curtail Paris' independent use of nuclear power. Washington had a double standard that clearly favored London over Paris. The two "Anglo-Saxon" states appeared intent on using their "special relationship" to constrain de Gaulle's activities.[35]

The general turned the evidence of "Anglo-Saxon" collusion to nationalist purpose. He argued that British membership in the Common Market would allow the "colossal Atlantic community" to expand its dominance on the European continent. A truly "European Europe" would require freedom from what de Gaulle later described as the attempts by Washington and London to "paralyze" independent cooperation among France, West Germany, Belgium, Luxemburg, the Netherlands, and Italy. De Gaulle's bold *"non"* to Britain established the French leader as the preeminent influence on the future shape of European integration. To the consternation of men like Jean Monnet, who sought a broader geographic conception of Europe, the general used his veto in the Common Market to increase France's international standing at the cost of Washington's and London's.[36]

Eight days after France's rejection of British membership in the Common Market, the general pulled a second rabbit from his hat. On 22 January 1963 de Gaulle concluded an agreement on Franco-German friendship with the West German chancellor. This remarkable treaty followed the agenda set by the French leader in his earlier meetings with Konrad Adenauer. From 1958 on de Gaulle had repeatedly told his West German counterpart that "there exists in Europe only one possible partner for France . . . and that is Germany." De Gaulle called upon the "new Germany"—represented by the Federal Republic—to work with France in building a cooperative, strong, and independent Europe. In the year before the conclusion of the Franco-German friendship agreement, the general explained to Adenauer that the future of the continent depended "essentially on our two countries and ourselves—you and me—animated in this regard with the same faith and the same hope." A close personal relationship between the two leaders would, he reasoned, deprive the more restrictive NATO institutions of power.[37]

Adenauer's signature on the treaty of friendship gave new impetus to French-led efforts to construct a "European Europe" in place of the American-led Atlantic community. Echoing the Gaullist tone, the West German chancellor commented that the "Franco-German entente which joins 100 million people will constitute, amidst the disorder of the contemporary world, an element of stability and confidence." According to the treaty, Paris and Bonn would organize frequent consultations among their respective leaders, foreign ministers, and military personnel. In addition, France and West Germany created interministerial commissions charged with expanding the areas of cooperation between the two states. Under the 1963 agreement defense officials in both countries would collaborate in training military officers, preparing for armed conflict, and producing new armaments. The treaty of friendship also aimed to increase youth exchanges between France and Germany.[38]

Noticeably absent from the Franco-German agreement were any references to consultation with NATO, and to the United States in particular. American diplomats with close ties to the West German government—especially former secretary of state Dean Acheson and former American high commissioner in Germany John J. McCloy—immediately recognized that de Gaulle's maneuvers jeopardized Washington's ability to control events in Europe. McCloy warned Adenauer that "the goals of European unity and Atlantic partnership toward which you have always directed your policies may be fatally disrupted" by de Gaulle. The French leader had apparently seduced the aging chancellor, undercutting in one fell swoop the stable alliance institutions that Americans and Europeans had labored to build, with great difficulty, in the years since World War II.[39]

McGeorge Bundy, President Kennedy's special assistant for national security affairs, described de Gaulle's charismatic appeal as the expression of a new, somewhat anti-American, nationalism in postwar Europe. "This [American] Government," Bundy explained, "was never in doubt of de Gaulle's desire to make France the first force in Europe." The French leader, however, startled Washington with his skillful use of rhetoric and symbols. He managed to manipulate Paris' defeats in Algeria and elsewhere for renewed nationalist purpose on the European continent. "Where we have been surprised," Bundy continued, "is in the degree of de Gaulle's success in achieving full political mastery over France . . . Few of us foresaw that de Gaulle would turn the acceptance of the loss of Algeria into a great victory, both national and international, and that by referendum and election he would break the influence of both the [mutinous army] and the traditional political parties. His emergence in full control of a strong, rich, prosperous, untroubled France was always possible but never really expected."[40]

De Gaulle's repudiation of the institutional limits on the power of the French state threw his opponents off balance. The general rejected compromise for the charismatic "magic" of personal will and national determination. De Gaulle promised to give France and much of Europe a new breath of independent power, free from the American and Soviet dominance that characterized the first decades of the Cold War. De Gaulle's vision was indeed inspiring to French citizens and to many frustrated counterparts, such as Konrad Adenauer. It also found a close parallel in mainland China. January 1963 marked the apex of de Gaulle's international and domestic *grandeur*. Events would quickly show that charisma without adequate institutional support provided the state with powers that proved more illusory than real.

By the end of January 1963 the general had exploited his charismatic appeal for maximum effect. After the conclusion of the Franco-German friendship treaty the dominant states in postwar Europe—the United States and the Soviet Union—reasserted their influence on the continent. They pressed France into a position of alliance subordination similar to its experience during the Fourth Republic. De Gaulle had shaken up the institutions of France, the emerging European community, and NATO, but he remained a creature of these inherited political structures. French military and economic weakness left the state dependent upon a strong and united Western alliance, despite the general's words to the contrary. De Gaulle's attempt to reshape European geopolitics through a partnership with West Germany that marginalized the United States was, in the words of one writer, profoundly "unrealistic."[41]

Frightened by the prospect of American disengagement from the European continent, members of Adenauer's government scrambled to attach a preamble to the Franco-German treaty that essentially nullified its effects. Bonn added a clause affirming West Germany's loyalty to NATO. This was a clear contradiction of de Gaulle's attempt to create an independent Franco-German power center in Europe. Adenauer's leadership was now also discredited. His party—the Christian Democratic Union (CDU)—forced the long-serving chancellor from office. In October 1963 the CDU replaced him with respected economics minister Ludwig Erhard. A strong critic of de

Gaulle's nationalist policies, Erhard favored an "Atlantic" vision of Europe's future over the general's calls for a "European Europe."[42]

More significantly, de Gaulle's public charisma inspired the very consequence the general feared most: Soviet-American negotiations on Europe's future without French participation. During periods of intense crisis, Washington had already displayed an inclination to make decisions absent allied deliberations. In the aftermath of the Cuban missile crisis, the Kennedy administration recognized that insufficient consultation raised apprehensions among America's European partners. U.S. attempts to design a "multilateral force" (MLF) that would allow Western Europe more say in its own defense—even as it preserved Washington's veto over nuclear decisions—sought to address these concerns. Since 1961 Undersecretary of State George Ball had worked with great ardor to create an effective MLF, but by the middle of 1963 this option appeared dead in the water. De Gaulle's strident calls for independent French nuclear power made deeper military cooperation between Washington and Paris inconceivable.[43]

Frustrated with its own friends in Europe, the Kennedy administration moved to negotiate the future of the continent with the Soviet Union in ever-greater isolation from Paris and Bonn. Discussions in Moscow during the summer of 1963 produced a Limited Nuclear Test Ban Treaty that hindered the ability of small powers to develop capabilities rivaling those of the superpowers. Prohibited from testing nuclear weapons above ground, nations like France would face greater difficulties in improving the quality of their independent forces. The opening of a "hot line" for direct communications between Moscow and Washington also increased the likelihood that during moments of tension the two superpowers would negotiate above the heads of the Europeans. Agreeing in the aftermath of the Cuban missile crisis that they could not tolerate uncertainty in critical strategic areas, Kennedy and Khrushchev came close to a tacit agreement on "non-aggression" in Europe that froze the political status quo between East and West. Stable bilateral consultations would, in this scheme, preserve the subordination of the European states to Washington and Moscow.[44]

Watching these Soviet-American deliberations from Paris, de Gaulle quickly recognized that the Cold War institutions managing the division of Europe—NATO and the Warsaw Pact—had proven more durable than his charismatic appeals for a "European Europe." The geopolitical status quo on the continent—and France's subordinate position—had become more fixed, not less. Through 1963 the superpowers tightened their hold over the ambitions of France's "popular monarch."

An indignant de Gaulle announced that France would not adhere to the Limited Test Ban Treaty or any other measures for a Soviet-American division of Europe. The general sent President Kennedy a sour letter, rejecting arrangements that left much of the continent under the Soviet "yoke." Paris would not endorse the actions of other states that infringed upon France's "right to possess its own arms." De Gaulle condemned the violations of state sovereignty inherent in Soviet-American negotiations.[45]

Adenauer and Erhard distanced themselves from Paris' angry pronouncements. West Germany abandoned the cooperative agreement it had signed with France in January 1963. Evidence of improved relations between Bonn and Washington—especially after Kennedy's visit to Berlin on 26 June 1963—led de Gaulle to limit the quantity of French territory available for joint German-American military exercises. The general acknowledged that despite his many efforts, he had failed to convert Bonn to his conception of a "European Europe."[46]

France could not supplant NATO and American influence in European affairs. De Gaulle had banged his head against this wall since the first days of his return to power. In late 1963 he largely abandoned his search for an alternative charismatic source of European leadership, resigning himself to accept the existing institutions of continental security. Instead of pressing for changes in alliance structures, de Gaulle simply limited France's commitments to NATO, the Common Market, and other European administrative bodies. The general had already removed the French naval fleet in the Mediterranean from NATO command in 1959, and in October 1963, pointing to the "essential divergence in strategic point of view between America and Europe," de Gaulle rejected proposals for integrated reforms in the military alliance.[47]

De Gaulle had said this many times before. By now he recognized that an independent European defense capability was more a pipe dream than a realistic option. France could refuse NATO directives—as it would on many occasions after 1963—but it could not change the basic policies of the Western alliance. During the first years of the Fifth Republic de Gaulle had condemned the "wishful thinking" of those who sought to maintain the last costly vestiges of the French empire in Algeria.[48] Now the general understood that national *grandeur* would not emerge from Paris' failed attempts to dominate the European continent. Late 1963 marked the most enduring shift in de Gaulle's charismatic search for French greatness. De Gaulle needed a new dramatic gesture to maintain his allure among an anxious public. At the moment when he was forced to abandon his program for reconstructing Europe in France's image, the general made an astonishing move to establish relations with another "great people" allegedly repressed by the international constraints of the Cold War: mainland China.

▪ Mao's "Great Leap" and Its Aftermath

After decades of struggle and civil war the Chinese Communist Party (CCP) took control of the mainland in October 1949. Beginning with a paltry roster of fifty-three members in 1921, the CCP accomplished a nearly impossible feat in less than three decades, bringing the vast population and territory of the Central Kingdom under its control following widespread violence, suffering, and revolutionary proselytism. On 1 October 1949 China's new leader, Mao Zedong, proclaimed that the ancient civilization had finally "stood up" to foreign imperialists and domestic warlords. This was an extraordinary moment of triumph for the CCP and the charismatic figure who had guided the party from obscurity to national predominance.

The years of upheaval since the collapse of the Qing dynasty in 1912 had destroyed many of the traditional impediments to China's "modernization." By the early 1950s, for example, the Communist regime had undertaken broad land reforms and given women many of the economic rights traditionally denied to their sex. In south central China the new government redistributed approximately 40 percent of the cultivated land from hereditary landlords to local peasants. By some estimates 60 percent of the population in the area benefited, receiving as much as two acres of farmland for each family of five.[49]

Assuring unity, prosperity, and security for China in a threatening world required much more than land reform and emancipation from traditional social practices. Having conquered the mainland, the CCP now had to organize society for effective economic development and projection of its power abroad. As it had during its years as a domestic insurgency, the CCP turned to the Soviet Union for aid and advice. Meeting in Moscow with Josef Stalin in December 1949 and January 1950, Mao explained that "China needs a period of three to five years of peace, which would be used to bring the economy back to pre-war levels and to stabilize the country in general." The CCP received a $300 million trade credit from the Soviet Union for purchases of industrial and military equipment. Whereas Moscow charged other "people's democracies" 2 percent interest on loans, Stalin made a point of requesting a rate of only one percent for the Soviet trade credits to Communist China.[50]

Despite his call for "three to five years of peace," Mao was prepared to use military force where possible for the unity and international standing of the new mainland government. During his 1949–50 discussions with Stalin, the CCP leader spoke about the "conquest of Formosa" (where the Guomindang leadership had fled in 1949) and a planned Chinese "attack on Tibet" (completed in October 1950). In 1950 Mao also supported, in conjunction with Stalin, North Korean leader Kim Il Sung's plans to attack South Korea. When American and other United Nations military forces came to the defense of the Seoul government, Beijing deployed its own "volunteer" army on the Korean peninsula. Chinese and American forces engaged in fierce but stalemated conflict for more than two and a half years before the negotiation of an armistice on 27 July 1953.[51]

Out of necessity, the CCP initially relied upon former Guomindang veterans, provincial residents, and untrained citizens to administer the institutions of the Chinese state. As the new government began a series of land reforms from Beijing, control of industry and agriculture remained in the hands of relatively autonomous local authorities. Mao and his closest advisers ruled the vast Chinese state in name, but they lacked the nationwide infrastructure to apply their power uniformly, especially in areas far from the capital.

The years 1952–1955 marked a period of what one scholar calls "organizational rationalization." CCP leaders worked to replace the "independent kingdoms" that continued to dominate society with a "professional" centralized bureaucracy. Following the Soviet model of governance, Mao charged government ministries with the task of formulating a national economic plan. This became the first Chinese Five-Year Plan, which allocated most agrarian and industrial resources to targeted peoples. Beijing established impersonal channels for regulating local behavior and reporting to the center. According to the New China News Agency, Communist modernization required the "strengthening of the concentrated and unified leadership of the central government."[52]

The First Five-Year Plan, and its accompanying centralization of economic and political power throughout China, created the foundation for what observers later called the "little leap forward." In early 1956 Mao proclaimed that "we want in a few decades and with great efforts to change the backward conditions of our nation's economy and its scientific culture, and speedily to attain advanced world levels." The CCP leader unveiled an ambitious Twelve-Year Agricultural Program. Through rapid and far-reaching farm collectivization Mao promised to raise grain harvests by more than 100 percent, and cotton production by more than 70 percent. This agrarian abundance, accompanied by a planned labor surplus, would provide the fuel for breakneck industrialization on the Soviet model.[53]

In March 1956 the government-controlled *People's Daily (Renmin ribao)* gave the "little leap" its official slogan: "The Party Center and Chairman Mao instructed us to undertake Socialist construction . . . faster, better, and more economically: this is the general direction." Combining ideological euphoria, faith in the Soviet model of development, and centralized administrative capabilities, Mao planned to use the "little leap" to catapult his regime ahead of its adversaries—especially the United States. The "organizational rationalization" that had created a more uniform and centralized bureaucracy in China during the mid-1950s allowed the CCP leader to pursue these inflated ambitions.[54]

By June 1956 the "little leap" had already proven a failure, especially in the countryside. Excessive investment by agricultural collectives contributed to mounting inefficiencies and bottlenecks in farm output. In industry an overemphasis on quantity and speed produced grave defects in quality, efficiency, and worker safety. In contrast to the euphoria of the March *People's Daily* editorial, the same newspaper published a more restrained report in June. It argued that the people must "oppose conservatism and also a disposition towards impetuosity." The later text criticized the CCP officials who, within the framework of the "little leap," had "attempted to do all things overnight."[55]

Deng Tuo, the editor of the *People's Daily*, wrote the June 1956 editorial. He sent it through the CCP Propaganda Department, which forwarded it to Mao for approval. The government published the editorial, but Mao, frustrated with the failure of his economic program, scrawled, "I won't read this" atop the *People's Daily* report. A year and a half later the chairman elaborated on this comment. "Why should I read something that abuses me?" he asked rhetorically.[56]

The failure of the "little leap" in 1956 left the CCP in a deep quandary, born of frustrating institutional constraints on ideological activism. Leaders in Beijing, including Mao, recognized that they could modernize the vast territory of China only with the help of a centralized and professional administrative apparatus. The governing bureaucracy created in the early 1950s implemented the overambitious plans formulated by the CCP elite, but it also tended to moderate and even reject party instructions when they failed to produce desired results—as in the "little leap." Mao wanted to initiate a series of "crash" programs, but the local administrative arms of the state wisely resisted these undertakings because of their harmful effects.[57]

By late 1956 the chairman and other influential members of the CCP found themselves torn between the practical requirements of governance and their desire for continued revolutionary activity. The extensive bureaucracy of the state provided instruments for economic and political policy that contradicted the goals of popular agricultural and industrial mobilization. Having completed his long war against the Guomindang regime on the mainland, Mao would spend the late 1950s and early 1960s struggling to balance the necessary organs of the state with a vision of exuberant mass activism that defied administrative regulation.

The Chinese leadership confronted a set of what Mao soon termed "contradictions among the people." These contradictions manifested themselves in conflicts between various groups of administrators, farmers, and industrial workers. What some called the "blooming and contending" of the period ultimately grew, however, from a deeper contradiction between the institutions of the centralized CCP government and Mao's devotion to an ideology that promised impossible accomplishments. After years of civil strife Chinese citizens found themselves torn, like the communist regime, between the practical necessities of daily survival and Mao's charismatic promises of a national "leap" into economic abundance.

February 1957 marked the first anniversary of Soviet leader Nikita Khrushchev's influential "secret speech" to the Twentieth Party Congress of the Soviet Union. Khrushchev's criticisms of Stalin's dogmatism and his "cult of personality" offered an encouraging opportunity for expanded freedom within the societies closely allied to the Kremlin. The "secret speech" also produced new risks of domestic disorder. Disturbances in Poland from June through October, followed by a revolutionary uprising in Hungary, illustrated the dangers inherent in Khrushchev's efforts to foster "de-Stalinization."[58]

Within China popular discontent also became evident. Chinese citizens— especially the educated residents of urban areas—were aware of the challenges to communist authority in Eastern Europe. Popular protests in Poland and Hungary inspired similar behavior in parts of the Central Kingdom. In Guangzhou, for example, workers organized thirteen separate strikes against government policy during late 1956. Students in Chengdu, Beijing, and other cities joined a proliferation of demonstrations. One group of middle school students had the temerity to protest that communism was "in no way superior" to other political systems.[59]

Beijing objected to Khrushchev's vituperative words about Stalin, but the CCP initially adopted the Soviet leader's criticism of bureaucratic rigidity and his encouragement of freer expression. The "Hundred Flowers" campaign, begun in early 1956, opened new space for discussion among intellectuals and educated citizens. Appealing for creative ideas that would contribute to China's development, Liu Shaoqi made the following remarks on behalf of Mao: "Our policy is to let 100 flowers bloom, to develop something new from the old . . . The remolding of culture requires strenuous efforts. You can't build Rome in one day."[60]

Mao encouraged popular activism against the stultifying tendencies of state bureaucracy. As the leader of the Chinese government, however, he could allow criticism to go only so far. The "contradictions among the people" were natural and healthy in some limited form, but they required forceful repression when they jeopardized the unity and strength of the state. For this reason, the CCP supported the bloody Soviet invasion of Hungary on 4 November 1956. Two months later Zhou Enlai, Mao's prime minister, traveled to Poland and Hungary, affirming that communist governments could not allow themselves to fall prey to domestic discord. The security of state institutions was more important than the urge for continuous revolution.[61]

Speaking to an enlarged session of China's Supreme State Conference in February 1957, Mao reflected at length on "the correct handling of [the] contradictions among the people." The Chinese leader observed that although the CCP was relatively secure in its control of the mainland, "there are still counterrevolutionaries." Mao affirmed the right of students and workers to "agitate to their heart's content," but he also explained that the state must remove "poisonous weeds" threatening the "fragrant flowers" of communist development.[62]

In his speech, Mao confessed to an attraction to anarchism in his early career as a revolutionary. He continued to harbor a strong disdain for the rigid and distorting effects of large government bureaucracy, but he admitted that the state's administrative institutions served a necessary purpose in purging dangerous domestic elements. Those who supported revolutionary principles at all cost "did not understand the complexity of the world"; they "did not understand arduous struggle." The state required a "democracy with leadership" rather than a "democracy of anarchism." Mao's government would encourage the creative expression of popular will, so long as it did not violate the basic tenets of the CCP's authority.[63]

For Mao "democracy with leadership" would resemble Karl Marx's "dictatorship of the proletariat." Central authorities would employ force, as required, to defend the basic sanctity of the revolution against threatening behavior at home and abroad. "What does dictatorship do?" Mao asked.

> What areas does dictatorship control? Dictatorship is used to handle [contradictions] between the enemy and us. To solve contradictions between

the enemy and us is a matter of forcing others to submit, but it is not a case of so-called total repression . . . Antagonistic classes—for example, the landlord class or imperialist elements—may not freely publish newspapers among us, nor may Taiwan. To prohibit the landlord class from publishing newspapers, to deprive them of freedom of speech and the right to vote all fall within the scope of dictatorship.[64]

The development of communist dictatorship justified not only the repression of dissidents, but also violence against domestic enemies. In his speech Mao admitted that the CCP had "unjustly killed" a large number of citizens during its first years in power. Mistaken acts of state-sponsored murder notwithstanding, the Chinese leader proclaimed that "basically there were no errors." Most of the 70,000 citizens executed by the Communist leadership "should have been killed," according to Mao; "if they had not been killed, the people would not have been able to raise their heads." "The people demanded the killing," Mao continued, "in order to liberate the productive forces. [Those killed] were fetters on the productive forces."[65]

"Contradictions among the people" were inevitable. Marxist analysis, after all, presumed a constant dialectical struggle between antagonistic elements. Mao sought to harness the tension produced by the contradictions in Chinese society for the purpose of making centralized state institutions more revolutionary. The dictatorship of the CCP would purge the state of dangerous enemies. It would also encourage people to agitate, work, and mobilize for common goals.

Mao wanted to create an active and energetic citizenry within a fixed agenda that stressed unity and modernization. The Chinese leader did not advocate a dogmatic application of ideological strictures. Instead, he attempted to use communist thought as an evolving guide for continued popular mobilization and organized social development. "Marxism," Mao explained, "still develops; Marxism is not [something] that is finished once studied. There is still the need to continue studying, [because] circumstances change. Dogmatism is not Marxism. Dogmatism is anti-Marxist. Opportunism, too, is anti-Marxist."[66]

In his attempt to merge an evolving interpretation of Marxism with a centralized state bureaucracy, Mao began to depart from what he perceived as the Soviet model of development. The Kremlin under Stalin and Khrushchev was, according to the Chinese leader, too rigid in its interpretation of communist ideology—"too leftist." Mao argued that the CCP could assure more reliable domestic stability than its Soviet counterpart. The turmoil in

Poland and Hungary indicated that Khrushchev's calls for de-Stalinization were self-defeating. Confronting difficult "contradictions," Mao planned to mix ideological flexibility and expanded central authority to "steel the Communist Party" against contrary international currents.[67]

The "contradictions" speech revealed the CCP's growing divergence from Moscow's leadership. The Soviet Union, however, remained an inspiration for the modernization of China. No goal was closer to Mao's heart than the development of his society as a powerful, prosperous, and respected great power. As de Gaulle spoke of the historic *grandeur* of France, Mao believed that the Central Kingdom had a right to dominate other states, especially in Asia. Soviet technological and military advances offered the most obvious route to China's acquisition of power.

Visiting Moscow in the month after the Soviet Union's triumphant Sputnik launch, Mao exulted in the evidence that a "relatively backward" empire—like Russia or China—could use communism to develop "into one of the world's most advanced countries." "We rejoice," the Chinese leader exclaimed in November 1957, "over the fact that the Soviet Union has taken the lead and launched a little moon of 500 kilograms." Only revolutionary principles and collective effort could transform "backwardness" into modern power so quickly. Mao urged his "Soviet comrades to launch even more sputniks in the future. When they build and launch one weighing 5,000 kilograms, then things will be even easier for us."[68]

Four days later Mao carried his post-Sputnik exuberance even further, laying the foundation for what would soon become China's disastrous effort to inaugurate a new "Great Leap" ahead of more prosperous Western economies through breakneck industrialization. Mao explained that "although today China is a major country politically and as far as the size of her population is concerned, economically she is still a small country. But our people are willing to exert themselves and work enthusiastically to turn China into a truly major country. Khrushchev has told us that the Soviet Union can overtake the United States in 15 years." "I can also tell you," Mao boldly proclaimed, "that in 15 years, we may have caught up with or overtaken Great Britain."[69]

The Great Leap upended rural society with a ferocity that far exceeded the efforts of 1955–56. Speaking in August 1958 to the Chinese Politburo, Mao proclaimed that agriculture required tighter control and more organized planting in state-run communes. "All levels should gradually strengthen their planning [system]," the chairman explained. "Production and distribution in [agrarian communes] should also gradually be brought under unified management. It won't do not to have tight planning and organization. Grain production should also be [well] planned . . . A socialist state is a tightly organized network."[70]

Mao spoke of "decentralizing" government control over provincial behavior in order to unleash the energy of the Chinese masses. At the same time, he also instructed that work in the countryside follow guidelines authored by the CCP leadership in Beijing. In this way, Mao delegated agricultural management to local authorities while enforcing strict production requirements through the centralized institutions of the state. "We must work hard, with all our might," the Chinese leader ordered. Through the "disciplined" planting and harvesting of the communes, the CCP expected to accrue rapid surpluses in annual grain and fruit inventories.[71]

During a visit to Hubei province Mao asserted that commune-directed activities would allow peasants to "eat more": "They can certainly eat five meals a day if they like." The chairman used these comments to justify the onerous work requirements mandated by the Great Leap. Consuming larger food rations than before, the residents of the countryside should be able to reach unprecedented harvest quotas. "Eating more" required citizens to produce more.[72]

Farm surpluses would fuel rapid industrialization. Mao's orders for unrealistic rural steel production reveal how he used his centralized powers to direct mass mobilization. "We must," Mao explained, "go all out for the next two years on [the production of] iron, steel, copper, aluminum, molybdenum, and other nonferrous metals."[73] China had produced 5.35 million tons of steel in 1957, and during the first months of 1958 the state showed impressive signs of exceeding that total. The CCP, however, endorsed a new annual steel production target of 10.7 million tons—a 100 percent increase over the prior year. This irrational "steel fever" was at the core of state policy during the Great Leap. Mao asserted that completion of the vastly increased steel targets "will be a victory." "We must," he concluded, "struggle with all our might. [We] must stress [this point] once a week; [since we] still have over a dozen weeks [left this year], it should be stressed over a dozen times."[74]

Under intense government pressure, families throughout the countryside sacrificed their kitchenware and other metal items for quixotic backyard steel production. Rural communes became sites for primitive furnaces forging metal from various collected scraps. Provincial party administrators turned peasants into farm and factory laborers working in frenzied conditions with little or no rest. This was a period of what Mao called "war communism": "Once an order is issued, everyone automatically goes to their work, idlers are few or none. Communism does not differentiate between superiors and subordinates."[75]

The Great Leap created a common struggle throughout China. It rejected what Mao called the "bureaucratism" dividing local officials from workers and peasants.[76] The Great Leap was, however, hardly an egalitarian grass-roots movement. Agrarian collectivization and backyard steel production followed orders emerging from the CCP leadership and, most especially, from Mao himself. Production targets superseded the authority of provincial officials and strongly affirmed the dominance of the central planners.[77]

Following from Mao's reflections on the "contradictions among the people," the Great Leap inspired the near-total mobilization of the population within a clearly delineated framework designed to further the unity, strength, and international standing of the Chinese state. The Great Leap was Mao's alternative to Khrushchev's campaign for de-Stalinization in the Soviet Union and Eastern Europe. Instead of the internal dissent that followed Khrushchev's "secret speech," Mao expected that his orders would allow a more modern Chinese state to overtake Western (and Soviet) economic predominance in a few years.

Mao's vision of surplus grain and what he called the "limitless forces" of industrial development quickly "tumbled into nightmare," according to one scholar.[78] From 1958 through 1961 the Great Leap created an exhausted, starving population of farmers and laborers. Chinese peasants franticly struggled to plant crops and produce steel in ill-suited areas of the countryside. On many communes peasants could not even gather the harvest because they had, following government orders, melted down their scythes for steel production. When harvesting tools were available, sufficient human labor often was not. Steel production elicited an enormous shift in the workforce away from agriculture. From 1957 to 1958 the supply of farm labor in China declined from 192 million to 151 million, and the number of industrial workers increased from 5.57 million to 35.5 million.[79]

China experienced rapid industrial growth, but at a cost that dwarfed any benefits. Heavy industry on the mainland increased output by 230 percent during the Great Leap. Chinese steel production, in particular, ballooned from 5.35 million tons in 1957 to a high of 18 million tons in 1960. The quality of output, however, suffered considerably. Steel forged from pots and pans in backyard furnaces lacked the strength and durability necessary for use in various building projects. After 1960 the CCP reduced quotas for steel production to 7 million annual tons in order to guarantee quality.[80]

Excessive investment in heavy industry contributed to plummeting production in other areas, especially grain harvests. Contrary to Mao's promises of "five meals a day," grain consumption per person across China declined approximately 25 percent from 1957 to 1960. In the province of Anhui, for instance, annual inventories dropped from 10.27 million tons in 1957 to 6.29 million tons in 1961. A mix of drought and flood conditions contributed to these devastating harvests, but the famine that resulted was largely the responsibility of the Chinese leadership.[81] By 1961 more than 30 million Chinese citizens had died from starvation and exhaustion. Most incriminating for the CCP, Mao received extensive evidence of suffering throughout the mainland during the period. Until early 1961 he refused to change course. Instead of admitting to mistaken judgment, the chairman used the centralized bureaucracy of the state to plow forward with an obviously disastrous set of policies. The combination of revolutionary hopes and state power that gave birth to the Great Leap Forward led China very far backward, on the corpses of a starving population.[82]

The Great Leap discredited Mao's revolutionary vision of China's rapidly surpassing Britain, the Soviet Union, and the United States. Following the long-overdue renunciation of this "crash" program in January 1961, CCP authorities remained firmly in place. Through an elaborate series of "emergency measures," the communist bureaucracy scrambled to import grain for distribution among China's starving population. Canada and Australia became the two primary sources of grain imports to the mainland, accounting for as much as 28 percent by 1963.[83]

Chinese domestic policy quickly changed course. During the Great Leap the government had forced laborers away from private plots in the countryside to communes and steel foundries. In 1961 the CCP ordered a massive "rustication." Workers returned to former farmlands where they mixed traditional agrarian ways with the continued existence of communes—now somewhat less restrictive in their supervision of the countryside. In Tianjin, for instance, the number of agrarian laborers had dropped from 193.1 million in 1957 to 154.9 million in 1958; during 1961 the farming population jumped again to 197.5 million. The post–Great Leap years lacked the ideological exuberance of the late 1950s, but the rapid movement of labor reflected the resilient power of CCP authorities in directing the behavior of the citizenry.[84]

Instead of addressing what Mao had called the "contradictions among the people" years before, from 1961 through 1963 the CCP bureaucracy focused upon restoring stability to the state. In discussions with the East German ambassador during this period, both Zhou Enlai and Liu Shaoqi emphasized that, after the havoc wrought by the Great Leap, China would have to abandon many of its revolutionary claims. According to Liu, Beijing required a method of "practice" that would modernize China in an incremental, safe, and undisturbed manner. The CCP bureaucracy needed a manageable policy, one that Liu hoped would prove "not too fast, but not too slow." Through "rustication" and increased foreign trade the authorities in Beijing sought a "prudent" tempo for development, rather than recurring "leaps" into a nonexistent communist utopia.[85]

A "prudent" policy tempo promised less suffering for the population on the mainland. It also presaged a retreat from the emotional and ideological claims that underpinned Mao's charismatic standing. Modest domestic development, managed by professional bureaucrats, would allow the "contradictions among the people" to fester and eventually eat away at the authority of the CCP. Prudence, in this sense, demobilized the popular mass energies behind Mao and his regime.

Mao remained a committed revolutionary in spite of the horrors his policies had wrought during the Great Leap. Like Charles de Gaulle in France, the Chinese leader blamed others for his frustrations. In particular, Mao condemned the institutions of government that he had created for sabotaging his policies. As Zhou Enlai, Liu Shaoqi, and other officials sought stability in 1963, Mao began another arduous search for revolutionary leverage in China. The new CCP "leap" would *not* address the "contradictions among the people" through a blending of communist ideology and state institutions. Instead Mao, like de Gaulle, turned to policies that explicitly rejected established authorities—other than himself—at home and abroad. The year 1963 marked the beginning of what we might call a "neo-Jacobin" period that brought Mao and de Gaulle together in a search for perpetual revolution.

▪ The French-Chinese Connection

Communist Chinese contacts with Western Europe and the United States increased during the late 1950s, despite the radicalism of the Great Leap and Beijing's threats against Taiwan. In August 1955 American and Chinese representatives opened a series of "ambassadorial talks" in Geneva. These meetings soon moved to Warsaw, where discussions focused upon tensions surrounding Taiwan, conflicts in Laos and Vietnam, and the fate of Americans held in Chinese prisons.[86] Beijing's contacts with French representatives also expanded during this period. Building upon discussions begun at the 1954 Geneva Conference on the future of Korea and Indochina, a number of prominent French politicians visited China in subsequent years—especially the former president of the Fourth Republic, Edgar Faure. From May 1961 through July 1962 French foreign minister Maurice Couve de Murville met periodically with his Chinese counterpart, Chen Yi, during another series of negotiations in Geneva—this time on the future of Laos.[87]

Personal contacts are a necessary foundation for effective diplomacy. The evidence of growing connections between China and the West made an improvement in relations more conceivable in the early 1960s than it had been since 1949. Prominent figures like Edgar Faure in France and Chester Bowles in the United States called for "normal" relations with Mao's government. None of these advocates condoned the domestic behavior of the communist regime. They hoped, in Bowles's words, "that some doors might be opened to reasonable negotiations" with China. Despite the tragedy of the Great Leap, the CCP appeared unlikely to collapse anytime soon. To ignore Beijing was to deny obvious "realities."[88]

China's leaders sent a series of signals indicating that they now sought improved relations with the West. In 1961 and 1962 American diplomats alerted their superiors that Beijing's representatives—particularly Wang Pingnan (the Chinese emissary to the ambassadorial talks in Warsaw)—appeared anxious to reconcile long-standing points of Sino-U.S. confrontation. The CCP intimated that it might consider concessions on the future of Taiwan in return for assistance in breaking out of the mainland's "international isolation." The deepening acrimony between Beijing and Moscow contributed to this positive Chinese turn to the West.[89] The CIA reported cautiously upon the new "signs of Chinese Communist friendliness." China specialist Franz Schurmann wrote from Hong Kong that the prospects for warmer Sino-American relations have "rarely been better than at the present moment."[90]

Many Western observers, including members of the U.S. government, reported that Chinese overtures served propaganda purposes more than any alleged change of heart. "These private approaches" from Beijing, one prominent State Department official wrote, "have for the Chinese Communists the advantage of portraying themselves as the aggrieved but reasonable party which desires an improvement in relations with the U.S." Peaceful propaganda was "particularly useful . . . at a time when the world has been impressed by [Beijing's] belligerent views."[91]

This analysis should not negate the importance of China's friendly signals to the West during the early 1960s. In the aftermath of the Great Leap the CCP entered a period of deep uncertainty. The regime needed new policies, and perhaps some new friends. Beijing's ambivalent feelers toward Washington set the stage for more explicit Chinese approaches to Paris.

De Gaulle harbored no illusions about what he called the "malevolent" actions of Mao's government at home and abroad.[92] The general remembered the role Communist China had played in supporting resistance to French imperial authority in Indochina and Algeria. From late 1953 through May 1954 Beijing had trained, equipped, and advised the Viet Minh soldiers who forced the French army to surrender at its encircled stronghold of Dien Bien Phu. The last half-decade of French rule in Algeria (1958–1963) coincided not only with the first years of de Gaulle's government but also with the CCP's moves to supply the rebel National Liberation Front with 150,000 guns and cannons for use against colonial forces occupying North Africa. In an ironic twist, Beijing's arms shipments to the Algerian resistance included 30,000 American-made weapons, captured by the Chinese government during the Korean War. Mao's government contributed to the final destruction of France's empire, including Algeria, the sacred territory from which de Gaulle had based his resistance to the Nazis during World War II.[93]

To French nationalists such as de Gaulle, Communist China seemed a natural enemy. The general recognized, however, that he could serve a "great interest" by fostering personal "contacts" with the leaders of the mainland. De Gaulle seized upon the ambiguous evidence of Chinese openness to send Edgar Faure on an extended visit to "a great people." By establishing more "normal" relations with Beijing, the French leader hoped to create new avenues for Paris' independent pursuit of *grandeur.* De Gaulle instructed Faure that France was not a "petitioner" paying tribute to the Chinese Son of Heaven, but instead a nation seeking to change the "current state of affairs" around the world. Ideological differences did not matter. France looked to relations with China as a lever for overcoming the restraints of both domestic and international politics in Europe.[94]

A dramatic opening with China would not only affirm the "reality" and "potential" of Mao's government. It would also symbolize the dynamism, creativity, and historic achievements of France. Paris would establish new connections with Beijing at the moment when Sino-Soviet relations became estranged and the United States remained isolated from the Asian colossus. De Gaulle exploited contacts with Beijing both to put his state on equal footing with "a great country like China" and to assert his independence from the superpowers.[95]

Faure secretly visited China on de Gaulle's behalf between 21 October and 2 November 1963. There he met with Foreign Minister Chen Yi, Premier Zhou Enlai, and Chairman Mao Zedong. Zhou, in particular, emphasized that China wanted to "reestablish" relations with France for the purpose of improving international conditions. In contrast to the other Western governments, Paris appeared poised for independent diplomatic activity that broke with Cold War divisions. Faure reported to de Gaulle that the CCP was serious about the prospect of wider economic, cultural, and political relations with France. Beijing and Paris had arrived, Mao explained, "at the time" for more independent and assertive behavior.[96]

After Faure's mission, neither government hesitated. The two longtime adversaries rapidly moved toward full diplomatic relations, including an exchange of ambassadors. During secret negotiations in December 1963, France agreed to jettison its official ties with Taiwan. Paris now recognized Mao's regime as the "only government that can speak in the name of China."[97] In response to protests from Chiang Kai-shek—the Taiwanese leader and former French ally—de Gaulle explained that "the situation formed and confirmed on the Chinese mainland does not reflect the expectations envisioned in the past. France will no longer ignore an established fact."[98]

De Gaulle, like most Western observers, had long understood that Chang Kai-shek's calls for the "liberation" of China from communist rule were at best impractical, at worst quixotic. At the same time, the "facts" of CCP control on the mainland did not appear unassailable to Western observers in the early 1960s. If anything, the trauma and dislocation of the Great Leap prompted serious ruminations about the possibility of communist collapse.[99] Accounts from foreign intelligence analysts predicted grave difficulties for the ruling regime on the mainland. The CIA, in particular, described both "a general erosion of cadre morale" and "mounting disorders and violence" in the post–Great Leap years.[100]

De Gaulle had access to similar accounts of political uncertainty in China, but he ignored these reports.[101] Instead, the last months of 1963 and the first weeks of 1964 marked a turning point in French-Chinese relations. On 27 January 1964 the two states dramatically announced that they would establish direct diplomatic relations. France and China affirmed what de Gaulle a few days later called the "evidence and reason" of mutual recognition. The general insisted that peace and stability around the world required closer relations between the two long-estranged governments.[102]

The leaders of both states invested the new French-Chinese relationship with unprecedented importance. Britain and other Western countries had established trading provisions with Communist China in the previous decade, but these commercial connections never included the political coordination that would soon characterize diplomacy between Paris and Beijing. Despite significant differences in professed ideology, de Gaulle and Mao saw themselves in similar circumstances. Each sought to escape from the restraints on a more independent, active, and charismatic set of political ambitions. A special relationship between Paris and Beijing promised novel opportunities for each government to achieve the "rank" it deserved at home and abroad.[103]

If a similar desire for political innovation brought the leaders of France and China together in 1964, a shared resentment of the superpowers dominated their early discussions. De Gaulle and Mao had already criticized American and Soviet hegemony on a number of occasions. The French-Chinese opening marked the final death of the capitalist and communist "monoliths" that had, with few notable exceptions, structured international politics since World War II.[104]

By the 1960s the world had become much more complex. After Khrushchev's "secret speech" and the Limited Test Ban Treaty, assumptions of "capitalist-communist conflict" made little sense. In contrast to the early Cold War years, the Soviet Union and the United States now appeared to act like a single international "monopoly," according to Zhou Enlai. Mao went so far as to argue that the Soviet Union had, since Stalin's death, undertaken a "restoration of capitalism," cooperating with American and British "imperialists" against China and other communist states.[105]

The French-Chinese opening became an important channel through which the two states, subordinated within Cold War alliances, worked for increased independence. From 1964 through 1966 French and Chinese leaders endeavored to counter the manifestations of Soviet-American "double hegemony" in Asia and Europe. Chinese foreign minister Chen Yi spoke for both Beijing and Paris when he explained that the United States and the Soviet Union "want domination of the world by two great despots." By cooperating with France, China would render continued superpower omnipotence "impossible."[106]

Both France and China developed independent nuclear weapons capabilities during the first half of the 1960s. The first French nuclear test, on 13 February 1960, grew from a series of vaguely authorized decisions within the Commissariat à l'Energie Atomique and de Gaulle's determination to possess an independent striking force. France's relatively small nuclear arsenal could never compete with the vast forces of the Soviet Union or the United States. Nuclear capabilities, however, allowed Paris to claim standing as a great power, possessing the most advanced military technology.

Like the French, Chinese leaders had embarked upon their own nuclear project years earlier. During the mid-1950s Mao began to doubt the assurances of protection from the Soviet Union. In 1959, fearful of Chinese belligerence, Nikita Khrushchev abruptly cut off Soviet support to what had been a joint program for nuclear development. In reaction, Mao vowed that China would produce its own nuclear bombs for military self-reliance. Independent Chinese nuclear power would show that the CCP could "catch up with advanced world levels." It would provide the same kind of *grandeur* that de Gaulle sought through French nuclear development.[107]

In a June 1963 letter to Khrushchev, Mao condemned his Soviet counterpart for "maintaining dominance over other socialist states" by substituting Moscow's nuclear umbrella for independent national capabilities. "You want to develop [nuclear weapons] alone and prohibit other brother states from building" their own bombs, the Chinese leader asserted. Khrushchev's nuclear policy forced other communist regimes to "obey you" while "you control [us] all." The chairman proclaimed that "the Chinese people will never accept the privileged position of one or two superpowers because of their monopoly of the nuclear weapons in today's world."[108]

The French and Chinese nuclear programs challenged the international dominance of the superpowers. After China tested its first fission bomb on 16 October 1964, Beijing announced that its new military capabilities would help the "Chinese people in their struggle to strengthen their national defense." Like France's independent striking force, Chinese nuclear power would resist the "monopoly" of the United States, the Soviet Union, and Great Britain (which possessed a small arsenal of its own). The Limited Test Ban Treaty concluded by these three states in July 1963 was, in Beijing's words, a "big fraud"—"an attempt to consolidate the nuclear monopoly . . . and tie the hands of all peace-loving countries." The Chinese government repeated Mao's famous description of nuclear bombs as "paper tigers": "This was our view in the past and this is still our view at present. China is developing nuclear weapons not because it believes in their omnipotence nor because it plans to use them. On the contrary, in developing nuclear weapons, China's aim is to break the nuclear monopoly of the nuclear powers and eliminate nuclear weapons."[109]

Neither Paris nor Beijing had any illusions about challenging American and Soviet military predominance. National nuclear forces provided a source of independent deterrence, discouraging threats to French and Chinese interests even as these states became less assured of protection from their powerful allies. More important, these nuclear programs served symbolic purposes. De Gaulle and Mao used their nuclear developments in the 1960s *against* their own allies, claiming status as great powers rather than strategic dependents.

This new assertion of nuclear power elicited deep anxieties in Washington and Moscow. Both superpowers worried particularly about China and how it might use its capabilities to undermine stability in Asia. The United States and the Soviet Union never intervened directly against China's nascent nuclear program, but proposals for joint action—including military force—received intermittent attention through the decade.[110]

The superpowers sought to isolate Paris and Beijing, discouraging other states from assisting these regimes in their political and military endeavors. Nuclear weapons, however, enhanced the international standing of France and China as "developed" nations worthy of respect and emulation. At home nuclear power symbolized strength and achievement—two associations at the core of charismatic claims to leadership. Deploying independent nuclear forces despite resistance from the "monopolists," de Gaulle and Mao showed that they could overcome great odds. Like mythic heroes, they used nuclear power to move mountains.

The French and Chinese nuclear projects progressed independently of each other, but diplomatic relations between the two states aided each program. In joint opposition to the Limited Test Ban Treaty, France and China reinforced their respective arguments about superpower "double hegemony." A reshuffling of Cold War alignments to accommodate shared interests between Paris and Beijing confirmed perceptions that communist-capitalist and East-West divisions no longer made sense. The dominant states now appeared to be driven by a common interest in protecting their privileges through nonproliferation efforts. The French-Chinese opening provided a channel for resisting superpower nuclear controls.

Economic exchanges also contributed to resistance against "double hegemony," furnishing independent sources for domestic development. From 1961 through 1965 total trade between France and China nearly doubled, from 257 million to 511 million francs. After the Great Leap the majority of French exports to the mainland consisted of wheat. By 1965 industrial products also filled many shipments to China. Industry throughout de Gaulle's state benefited from Chinese orders and a favorable balance of trade. Having overcome the Great Leap famine, Chinese society used industrial imports from France to reconstruct production facilities that had been destroyed by recent dislocations. In 1966 Paris and Beijing prepared for a series of joint

commercial expositions, followed by plans for collaborative naval construction, mining, and oil production. In the eyes of French and Chinese planners, bilateral trade served to "modernize" the two states while reducing de-
pendence on the superpowers.[111]

As American participation in the Vietnam War escalated, both Paris and
Beijing sought to expel the United States from Indochina. The French
Fourth Republic had played an important role in attracting American atten-
tion to this area in the first place, but by 1964 de Gaulle perceived U.S. activities as a threat to Paris' influence in Asia.[112] Deploring the widening scope of
American intervention, the French leader promised the Chinese ambassador
that he would pressure Washington to withdraw all forces from Indochina.
Despite continued Chinese aid to North Vietnamese and National Liberation
Front forces, de Gaulle agreed that the Chinese were not responsible for the
conflict. To assure peace, freedom, and development in Vietnam, the general
proclaimed, "it is necessary for the Americans to end their intervention and
withdraw."[113]

The French leader's criticism of American policy in Vietnam was part of a
larger dissent from the basic structure of the Western alliance. De Gaulle first
called for reforms in NATO's institutions during the late 1950s. Between
1959 and 1966 he progressively withdrew French forces from NATO exercises. By 1966 the general determined that independent French activity in
Asia and elsewhere required a complete break with the military component
of the alliance. This move had few immediate repercussions for France's security. The geography of the European continent ensured that NATO's defense of Belgium and Italy would necessarily protect France as well. Paris
also retained its representatives in the North Atlantic Council, NATO's main
political forum.

France's departure from the military leadership of NATO allowed the general to deploy his armed forces abroad without consulting the American-
appointed supreme allied commander. This move reinforced Paris' attempts
to assert its independence from the institutions dominated by the United
States. In de Gaulle's eyes, France now stood as an acknowledged great
power, not a subordinate to bipolar alliances.[114]

As the superpowers worried about their assertive allies, the governments
in Paris and Beijing rejoiced in the havoc they created with their defiant displays of national independence. During a May 1966 conversation French
foreign minister Maurice Couve de Murville and Chinese ambassador
Huang Chen highlighted their "common points" of resistance to Soviet-
American domination. "We are in close to the same position," the French-

man explained. Beijing's representative enthusiastically confirmed this sentiment. "We are very happy to establish," Huang announced, "that the present world is no longer the world of yesterday where two great powers, the United States and the Soviet Union, dictated their law, to which the other [states] had to submit."[115]

The French-Chinese connection transformed Cold War politics. Charles de Gaulle and Mao Zedong leveraged their new relationship to escape many of the limitations on their independent endeavors. As a consequence, the international system quickly grew less stable. De Gaulle and Mao embarked upon a period of self-consciously revolutionary behavior that unleashed long-repressed popular energies within France, China, and many other states.

Diplomatic relations between Paris and Beijing contributed to upheaval in both societies. The French student movement and the Chinese Cultural Revolution were very different in scope and origins. The politics of the French-Chinese connection, however, left a deep imprint on these divergent disruptions.

■ The French-Chinese Pursuit of Revolution

"The modern concept of revolution," Hannah Arendt observed in the mid-1960s, is "inextricably bound up with the notion that the course of history suddenly begins anew, that an entirely new story, a story never known or told before, is about to unfold." In addition to the "newness" implied by revolution, Arendt noted that revolutionary activity in the second half of the twentieth century drew on a "lost treasure" of accumulated memory and experience.[116] The cultural revolutions that convulsed the major states after 1966 manifested this search for a new beginning, coupled with the imagery of a past moment of popular, uncorrupted political engagement. In China and France leaders mixed their desire to build more independent modern states with the memory of mass engagement in past periods of revolution. Mao and de Gaulle portrayed themselves as twentieth-century Jacobins, freeing their societies from the oppressive institutions of bloated domestic administration and international alliance with the superpowers.

Frequent emotional references to what François Furet has called the "imagined" "popular will" of the French Revolution dominated diplomatic relations between Beijing and Paris after 1964. In a world in which alliances and bureaucracies constrained programs for radical change, the image of a pure and unadulterated popular will became an alluring alternative for leaders seeking to restore lost national greatness.[117] Both Mao and de Gaulle sought to recapture what they perceived as the "lost treasure" of revolutionary spirit.

Mao's unparalleled prestige within the CCP allowed him to ignite a new revolution as other leaders, including de Gaulle, could not. China's "Great Proletarian Cultural Revolution" sought to empower the alleged popular spirit of the nation's citizens against the corrupting administrative influences that Mao sought to destroy. During frequent discussions with their new French friends, Chinese leaders revealed that they hoped, in the second half of the 1960s, to transplant the mass enthusiasm of the French Revolutionary legacy to the mainland. Through a defiant international posture against the superpowers, as well as radical claims to charismatic authority, Mao endeavored to redirect Chinese Communism from its degenerate Soviet associations to the purer legacy of France in 1789.

This curious connection between French-Chinese diplomacy and domestic revolution became evident soon after the two states exchanged ambassadors. On the evening of 14 July 1964 (Bastille Day) Prime Minister Zhou Enlai, Foreign Minister Chen Yi, and approximately 160 other Chinese officials gathered in the garden of the recently opened French embassy in Beijing. To the great surprise of Paris' representatives, a Chinese band accompanied the visitors. The mainland musicians played a selection of French national songs—including the "Marseillaise"—before the night was out. Zhou, Chen, and the other Chinese guests displayed what Paris' ambassador described as "spontaneous" emotions upon hearing the songs that conjured images of the French Revolution, and early Communist Chinese tutelage in radical French circles.[118]

Zhou, Chen, and many other prominent members of the CCP (excluding Mao) first became active communists in the early 1920s, during a period of work-study in France.[119] Memories of revolutionary experiences and personal bonds forged early in life played an important role in Chinese Communist behavior throughout the second half of the twentieth century. Older members of the CCP showed unique respect for foreign figures with a somewhat similar pedigree. Zhou Enlai, Chen Yi, and even Mao believed that men like Soviet leader Josef Stalin, Vietnamese Communist party chief Ho Chi Minh, and Cambodian dictator Pol Pot commanded particular legitimacy because of their shared set of formative radical experiences.

Despite Stalin's limited and inconsistent support for the CCP, Mao continually took "advice" and requested "directions" from the old Bolshevik revolutionary.[120] The Chinese leader never used such deferential terms in his communications with Stalin's successors in the Kremlin and other communist states. Zhou Enlai's respect for Ho Chi Minh reflected an even more personal connection. "In 1922," Zhou explained, "I became acquainted with Chairman Ho [in Paris]. In 1925 Chairman Ho came to Guangzhou to support the Chinese revolution. This was a relationship of blood and flesh." As late as 1975 Mao showered Pol Pot with similar praise for implementing a revolutionary program in "one stroke" throughout Cambodia.[121]

The leaders of Gaullist France did not share anything resembling a revolutionary communist pedigree. They did, however, emerge from a political culture steeped in the rhetoric and images of an earlier French Revolution. De Gaulle's calls for national *grandeur* summoned the "popular will" of 1789. Chinese leaders found this French revolutionary tradition alluring, even in the mid-1960s.

On Bastille Day 1964 the aged Chinese leaders nostalgically reflected upon their past revolutionary esprit de corps, and its notable absence on the mainland after the devastating Great Leap Forward. Almost forgetting the communist criticism of "bourgeois" capitalist society, Chen Yi extolled the revolutionary legacy that united Paris and Beijing's representatives in sentiment and aspiration: "The French nation is a great nation of glorious revolutionary traditions . . . The Chinese people always had high esteem for the glorious revolutionary traditions of the French people." After offering extended criticism of American "intervention" in Asia, the Chinese foreign minister again stressed the revolutionary bond between his nation and France, toasting the historic "friendship" between the peoples of the mainland and the "French Republic."[122]

Chen Yi's emotional words constituted more than simple diplomatic courtesy. Following the Bastille Day celebrations in 1964, references to the French revolutionary tradition played a prominent role in Beijing's attempts to stir domestic energies for radical nationalist purpose. During the spring and summer of 1966—when Mao offered dramatic support for student criticisms of "rightist" administrators in Beijing and other cities—Chen Yi utilized his discussions with French representatives to emphasize the connections between the nascent Cultural Revolution and the French revolutionary model. Popular purges of self-serving bureaucrats throughout the mainland would, according to Chen, allow China to eliminate the last vestiges of feudalism and create a new atmosphere of freedom and popular will.[123]

In 1966 Mao reshuffled the Chinese leadership to expel alleged antisocialist bureaucrats and party officials—notably Liu Shaoqi and Deng Xiaoping. Mao endorsed what he later called the "havoc" of young Red Guard attacks on established authorities throughout society. The CCP announced that "the great proletarian Cultural Revolution now unfolding is a great revolution that touches people to their very souls and constitutes a new stage in the development of the socialist revolution in our country, a deeper and more extensive stage." Chinese leaders pointed to the Paris Commune of 1871 as a model for popular action against the repressive institutions of the state. Combining the thought of Lenin and Mao with the Marxist principles that motivated revolutionary activity in nineteenth-century France, the CCP explained that "in the course of the mass movement of the Cultural Revolution, the criticism of bourgeois and feudal ideology should be well combined with the dissemination of the proletarian world outlook of Marxism-Leninism, Mao Zedong's thought."[124]

During the late 1950s the Great Leap Forward had attempted to harness the central institutions of the state for rapid industrial development. The Cultural Revolution, in contrast, pursued modernization through anti-bureaucratic mass activism. "The aim of the Great Proletarian Cultural Revolution," the CCP announced, "is to revolutionize people's ideology and as a consequence to achieve greater, faster, better and more economical results in all fields of work. If the masses are fully aroused and proper arrangements are made, it is possible to carry on both the Cultural Revolution and production without one hampering the other, while guaranteeing high quality in all our work."[125] Goals set by central planners would not govern the new period of collective activity. Instead, the cryptic texts of "Mao Zedong Thought" became a "cultish" source for organization and action among Red Guards throughout China. Zhou Enlai explained in September 1966 that "whatever accords with Mao Zedong Thought is right, while that which does not accord with Mao Zedong Thought is wrong."[126]

Mao's vision for the Cultural Revolution derived from the model of French revolutionary militarization after 1789. Mao Zedong Thought would create an emboldened Chinese citizenry that would simultaneously destroy corrupting bureaucracies and strengthen the capabilities of the nation. An expanded and less hierarchical People's Liberation Army (PLA) would, in Mao's words, serve as a "big school" for the masses: "In this big school, the army should learn politics, military affairs, and culture, and engage in agricultural production . . . It can take part in mass work, factory work, and rural socialist education. After socialist education, there are always other kinds of mass work for it to do, to unite the army and people as one."[127]

Through the "big school" of the PLA Mao hoped to create a united mass citizenry, free of the divisions that hindered revolutionary action within existing state structures. "At the end of the eighteenth century in France," the Chinese leader explained to visiting French Sinophile André Malraux, "the people overthrew the royal family because a revolutionary people are the most strong. The weak [can] overthrow the strong." Mao expected that the Cultural Revolution would create similar strength among the relatively poor Chinese population.[128]

The CCP leader would become a "popular monarch" with a devoted and manipulated following that exceeded anything de Gaulle could hope for in France. Mao self-consciously modeled his rule on previous Chinese emperors and the French dictatorship of Napoleon Bonaparte. Mao would reign above the havoc of his society as a deity, not as a mere politician. He would soon command public adulation of an almost religious quality.

The Red Guards in the streets were Mao's *sans-culottes*. The students sent to the countryside and the PLA served as his revolutionary army. "[We] must train," Mao announced in August 1967, "a large number of revolutionary vanguards who have political vision, militant spirit, and readiness to make sacrifices."

> They are frank, honest, active, and upright. They seek no self-interest; they are completely dedicated to national and social emancipation. They fear no hardships; they are always firm and brave in the face of hardships. They are never boastful; they covet no limelight. They are unpretentious, realistic people. With a large number of people like this, the tasks of the Chinese revolution can be easily fulfilled.[129]

The Cultural Revolution required a radical vanguard, inspired by Mao, which would teach the people to banish the corrupt influences of bureaucracy and foreign intervention. Public upheaval would, to paraphrase Jean-Jacques Rousseau, force the citizens to be free. Chinese foreign minister Chen Yi composed a moving poem—"Ode to Jean-Jacques Rousseau"—in honor of the French writer's influence during the early days of the Cultural Revolution:

> So courageous in self-criticism,
> Your democratic ideas illuminated the future.
> One must prohibit whoever exploits others.
> Those who refuse to be tolerant must be hung.
> In your famous writings everywhere,
> You have spoken courageously in favor of the weak.
> I highly appreciated your confession.
> You always stood up against injustice.[130]

Communist China would carry Rousseau's ideas forward. Radical leadership from the top of society assured the ultimate "emancipation of the masses by the masses." China was the new spark that would ignite a modern "world revolution."[131]

Time and again Mao referred to the revolutionary history of France in the same context as the Cultural Revolution. This was the "lost treasure" the chairman hoped to uncover by unleashing widespread chaos. Searching for a foundation on which to build a new society that rejected both the Bolshevik and capitalist experiences, the Chinese leader returned to some of his early anarchist ideas and their historical connection with France. Mao seemed almost obsessed with the distant Jacobin and Napoleonic legacy.

Meeting with former French foreign minister Maurice Couve de Murville in 1970—after the first years of the Cultural Revolution—Mao praised the French Revolution as a model for national liberation. This was not merely polite conversation. The Chinese leader spoke at length about French history and asked many thoughtful questions about eighteenth- and nineteenth-century society. Mao lamented that although many foreign-authored biographies of Napoleon existed in Chinese translation, no mainland scholar had written an account of the French revolutionary dictator.[132]

Mao's detailed inquiries about Napoleon's life revealed an obvious connection in the Chinese leader's thoughts between Bonaparte's legacy and his own. Communism was always, at least in part, an imported ideology in China. The Cultural Revolution imported foreign images of popular mass action and charismatic imperial rule to the mainland.

Following his election to a new seven-year term as president in December 1965, Charles de Gaulle sought to initiate a period of popular activism in France. The general clearly did *not* desire the same level of chaos operating in China. He did, however, hope to inspire mass enthusiasm and charismatic reverence on a smaller scale.

"For the French people," the general wrote in late 1966, "the future must bring progress." This presumed "the free deployment of individual initiative." De Gaulle understood that the "great effort" he demanded from the nation required "decentralization" of authority from administrative bodies. French *grandeur* called for the creative participation of the masses behind the leadership of de Gaulle. Only the "popular monarch" could use the modern instruments of science and technology to "liberate" the citizenry, assuring that state power served the people and not vice versa.[133]

Living in what he called "fundamentally mediocre" times, de Gaulle attempted to inspire youth to active participation in the cause of national greatness. The veteran leader of France during times of war, resistance, and reconstruction sought a new cause to focus the will of the people. De Gaulle's calls for rapid modernization and national *grandeur* served this purpose. The general hoped that his second term as president would connect the revolution in French state power with the "great ambitions" of the young. De Gaulle sought youthful supporters who would criticize established government administrators and give the leadership a fresher, brighter image: "the Fifth Republic is our regime for us, the young."[134]

De Gaulle never went nearly as far as Mao in stirring revolution from above. The French leader harbored profound anxieties about unruly mass behavior. He read the history of the French Revolution, the 1848 upheavals, and the Paris Commune as warnings of mass excess rather than as manifestations of an enlightened popular will. In addition, the institutions of the French government—the National Assembly, the still-powerful bureaucracies, and the courts—prevented any single figure, even de Gaulle, from commanding uncontested public authority over the population. In contrast to China, revolutionary activity in France had to begin outside of government.

The Chinese Cultural Revolution was, in this sense, largely Mao's unique creation. Even without the French-Chinese opening of 1964, the upheavals on the mainland probably would have followed a similar path. As in the Great Leap Forward, the Chinese leader appeared intent on shaking up the stagnant elements in his society and on purging threatening figures from the CCP. The Cultural Revolution accomplished this purpose in a very chaotic but effective manner.

The unmistakable references to the French revolutionary tradition in the rhetoric of the Cultural Revolution reveal that this uniquely Chinese convulsion was not isolated from the currents of international politics. The French-Chinese opening of 1964 reflected a shared urge to separate personal leadership from a corrupting set of domestic and foreign attachments. Diplomatic connections between Beijing and Paris contributed to growing criticisms of established bureaucracies and dominant alliances. The French-Chinese opening boosted the charismatic claims of Mao and de Gaulle.

A "lost treasure" of mass enthusiasm and public will in the revolutionary tradition of France provided a common imagery for both societies after 1966. Mao and de Gaulle hoped to sweep away the detritus of accumulating government regulations, freeing the energy of their citizens for greater united accomplishment. The Chinese leader unabashedly followed this path through the Cultural Revolution he unleashed on the mainland. De Gaulle, in contrast, avoided such impetuous action only to find himself later the target of revolutionary upheaval against his own leadership.

Contrary to initial hopes, the course of international politics after 1966 created more restrictions for state leaders, not less. Striving for charismatic authority, Mao and de Gaulle inspired domestic energies that they could not control. In the late 1960s popular activism throughout China, France, and many other states operated against the desires for national unity and greatness that motivated the respective leaders. As early as July 1966 disorder in China hindered diplomatic and economic exchanges between Beijing and Paris. By 1967 Chinese and French leaders found themselves confronted with what Chen Yi called new "contradictions among the people."[135]

Despite the CCP's use of French Revolutionary imagery, on Bastille Day in 1967 neither Zhou Enlai nor Chen Yi attended festivities at the French embassy in China. Under siege by Red Guards in Beijing and more sparse protesters in Paris, French policymakers noted the new political "coldness" brought on by the consequences of the early French-Chinese opening. Popular mobilization in China had become self-defeating. The French government found itself condemned for insufficient radicalism on the mainland and at home.[136]

Charismatic national figures inspired widespread public activism, but in ways that often ran against their purposes. Charisma could not substitute for state administration. Instead of popular unity, the revolutions begun in 1966 created a descending spiral of chaos, division, and violence. Within a few years, French-Chinese politics would contribute to the "global disruption of 1968."

The charismatic allure of Mao Zedong and Charles de Gaulle masked growing political difficulties in China and France during the 1960s. These two leaders appeared strongest and most independent at the moment when their states confronted deep internal weaknesses and external dependencies. Mao and de Gaulle promised their citizens national greatness, but their policies could not overcome the resistance of domestic bureaucracies and the domination of the international superpowers.

The institutions of the Cold War inspired and restricted charismatic leaders at the same time. Mao and de Gaulle pursued "crash" programs for economic and nuclear development in hope of invigorating their societies with newfound strength. They also asserted national unity and independence by rejecting established structures of authority, especially in the international sphere. Despite their obvious bravado, these maneuvers produced little strength, unity, or independence. They elicited unrealistic popular expectations while encouraging more collusion among the most powerful countries—the United States and the Soviet Union—intent on securing their long-term hegemony.

The French-Chinese opening of 1964 revealed both the potential and the peril of charismatic leadership. Connections between the two states expanded when Mao and de Gaulle acted boldly, abandoning inherited ideological and alliance strictures. But violence and discontent overcame these two societies soon after the triumph of 1964. Mao and de Gaulle promised their citizens much more than they could achieve, even when they cooperated. In the second half of the decade the leaders of China and France struggled to meet the expectations they had nurtured and blamed others for their shortcomings.

If nuclear weapons created an inherent tension between the overwhelming muscularity of the superpowers and their practical inflexibility, charismatic leadership during the 1960s produced a similar paradox. The two men who commanded the most devoted popular followings could not channel their mass support to productive purpose. On the contrary, the crowds that cheered Mao and de Gaulle undermined the asserted *grandeur* of their respective states. Mass activism made charismatic authority possible, but it also undermined the intended uses of this "magic" leadership.

Edward Shils has called this the "perpetual strain" of charisma.[137] In the international history of the 1960s, this strain runs parallel to the "nuclear strain" that hindered innovative policymaking in the United States and the Soviet Union. China and France possessed more strategic flexibility than their larger allies. Their attempts to assert independence and greatness, however, exposed the limits on political leadership in Beijing and Paris.

The domestic disruptions that infected the great powers during the second half of the 1960s grew from the nuclear and charismatic strains of the time. Dissent became a global phenomenon before the French-Chinese opening. It spread with increased intensity thereafter.

THE LANGUAGE OF DISSENT

If politics is a form of controlled conflict, the balance of power shifted decisively to the young in the 1960s. The number of people between the ages of fifteen and twenty-nine increased dramatically from 1955 to 1975, reflecting the post–World War II baby boom that began in 1945 in Europe and America and in 1949 in China. Students now composed a large and restive segment of the population. Their condemnations of the alleged "false promises" and "hypocrisies" in contemporary society took aim at the Cold War stalemate. Leaders such as Kennedy, Khrushchev, de Gaulle, and Mao struggled with the obstacles that nuclear weapons, alliances, and bureaucracies posed to policy change. The growing mass of young citizens, however, demanded more radical politics.[1]

The youth culture of the early 1960s gestated in a relatively stable international environment in which young men—especially the most educated—were generally not involved in military conflict. More young women also entered college than ever before. This post–World War II generation of citizens enjoyed lives more secure and comfortable than their parents'. Security and comfort, however, did not preclude discontent and apprehension. The youth culture of the 1960s furthered domestic instability and upheaval.[2]

Extensive student interaction within the framework of crowded, usually urban, educational institutions provided the *infrastructure* for dissent within many societies. The words of prominent iconoclasts—writers as well as musicians and artists—supplied the *language* that allowed men and women to express their anger as they had not before. The American civil rights movement exemplifies how the language of dissent drew on an infrastructure of educated and energetic students. Throughout the United States, Europe, and Asia numerous protest movements emerged from a similar combination of dissident ideas and nascent youth organizations. In many cases student protesters mobilized around a powerful rhetoric of social criticism articulated by intellectual elites. Authors such as Michael Harrington, Aleksandr

Solzhenitsyn, Wu Han, and Herbert Marcuse contributed to the language that empowered youth around the world to organize and agitate in diverse ways.

The high tide of student and other domestic protests did not arrive until the end of the 1960s. The first half of the decade, however, set the stage for later social disruptions that in turn transformed Cold War politics. The language of dissent, formulated during the early years of university expansion, provided the critical tools for men and women to challenge state power.[3]

Demographics alone do not trigger social change. Education played a fundamental role in nurturing domestic unrest. During the late 1950s the leaders of the great powers expanded their citizens' access to school and college instruction. These educational reforms fit within a larger series of state modernizing programs aimed at building a technically sophisticated, skilled, and ideologically imbued population.

The United States and the Soviet Union provide the clearest examples of state-directed expansion in education. Fearing the challenges of ever more destructive military conflict, President Dwight Eisenhower and Premier Nikita Khrushchev created lucrative sources for the recruitment and training of national scientific elites. In America, the National Defense Education Act of 1958 offered student fellowships, enabling many working- and middle-class families their first opportunities to send their children to university.[4] In the Soviet Union, Khrushchev's push for scientific progress supported research facilities for the children of Russian peasants in Moscow, Leningrad, and new academic centers such as Akademgorodok. Between 1950 and 1965 the number of Soviet scientists rose from 162,500 to 665,000.[5]

Education reform was crucial for various attempts to formulate an activist foreign policy agenda. Looking to the future after the first Sputnik launch in October 1957, prominent observers emphasized the importance to state power of broad-based scientific sophistication. British scholar C. P. Snow famously called for an integration of the "two cultures"—literature and science—in education worldwide; only a more knowledgeable, well-rounded public could manage the increased "rate of change" and the "special danger" of a nuclear world.[6]

More than almost any other figure, James Conant worked to bridge the "two cultures" through international education reform. Conant had unique connections across universities and governments. He had served as the president of Harvard University, a scientific adviser to Presidents Roosevelt and Truman, and the U.S. ambassador to West Germany. In the late 1950s he argued that only a wider and more rigorous meritocracy of educated talent could cope with emerging foreign policy challenges. Commenting to President Eisenhower on his proposal for a "Commission on National Goals" in 1959, Conant explained that "today prophecies about the international scene are difficult to make even for a short period of years." "Having traveled around the country," he continued, he was "disturbed . . . by the present complacency and the confusion even among the leading citizens."[7]

Conant attempted to influence "public school people," encouraging reforms for improved student achievement in science and other fields. He worked during the early 1960s to make education more accessible and rigorous. In a study of urban and rural inequalities—*Slums and Suburbs*—Conant advocated different forms of instruction for young citizens of various talents. Policymakers could not expect that every child would attain the same high standards. The government should, according to Conant, create a calibrated system that maximized the learning and public contribution of each student. These proposals had a favorable reception in the U.S. Department of Defense, where officials worried about both civilian capabilities and educational achievement among military officers.[8]

National standardized testing, first pioneered by Conant for recruitment at Harvard in the 1930s, would now play an increasingly important role across the United States. These tests replaced a system of educational privilege with one of meritocracy, in which gifted students (according to exam results) found their way to the best educational institutions, and eventually to the most important positions in society. Other students, sorted by the "objective" tests, attained places in education and society appropriate to their talents. In this manner education reform sought to expand the training of all, creating a broad comparative advantage of abilities whereby each citizen performed for the public interest to the maximum of his or her capability.[9]

Conant did not confine his plans for an expanded meritocracy to the United States. He spoke of a "worldwide education revolution" that required more-coordinated government activities in the schools of each nation. Conant hoped to focus attention in Europe, as well as the United States, on developing "the potentialities of all youth to fit them for employment in a highly industrialized society." He believed that the future growth and stability of America's Cold War allies required significant changes in traditional modes of education.[10]

With a lucrative grant from the Ford Foundation, Conant carried his reform project to West Germany in 1963. The former ambassador knew the country well, and he recognized its symbolic importance for future developments around the world. Before leaving the United States with his wife,

Conant explained that "we are going to [West] Berlin because Mrs. Conant and I believe it to be of the utmost importance for the future of the free world that Berlin remain an outpost for freedom . . . Our hope is that Berlin will become a magnet drawing people from all over Europe who are interested in cultural and educational matters. I shall be assisting the Berlin authorities in building up a number of education enterprises which will have a certain degree of novelty and may be a point of direction for educators all over the world."[11]

Conant worked in Europe, as he had in America, to shake up the traditional institutions that confined education to a privileged elite and neglected important new subjects—especially in the sciences. Within German universities Conant attempted to break what he called the "frozen state" of instruction. Through public speeches, informal political pressures, and Ford Foundation grants he sought to increase the range of subjects studied and the number of both faculty and students. Conant endeavored, with mixed success, to revise German and other European education models in order to support "many teachers and educators for all kinds of students and undergraduates."[12]

The extraordinary expansion in the number and variety of institutions for higher education on the European continent—new universities, research laboratories, professional schools, and vocational colleges—reflected Conant's influence. Population pressures would have required the construction of additional educational facilities in any case; but the meritocratic model adopted by many of these institutions indicated that assumptions about schools in the service of the state carried great weight among leaders during the 1960s.

Conant's ideas appealed to combined worries about domestic complacency and international stagnation. His endeavors addressed the desire, shared by many politicians, to mobilize talent and forge creative policy alternatives. Because military resources and established state institutions appeared to constrain rather than to empower policy for ideological purposes, leaders turned to their growing young populations as a source for national achievement—what Kennedy called the "new frontier," and Khrushchev "communist construction."

This trend reached Communist China despite the country's relative poverty. One of the leading scholars on the subject describes the "pyramid" educational structure created by Mao's government to expand mass instruction at early ages and "guarantee quality" for the most talented students. During the early 1960s China implemented the rudiments of a state-sponsored meritocracy, increasing the resources for peasant literacy while building an educated elite at the top of the "pyramid." The expansion of higher educational opportunities in China, as in each of the other great powers, served clear political purposes.[13]

Demographic trends and education reforms converged to initiate a remarkable international expansion in higher education between 1955 and 1970 (see Figures 1–3 in the appendix). The enlargement of modern universities, colleges, and related postsecondary institutions followed the growth in both military resources and administrative functions controlled by states. By the 1960s higher education became a distinct sphere of government-sponsored activity, with its own clearly defined and regulated facilities.[14]

As an integral part of functioning society rather than an isolated elite privilege, institutions of higher education grew to accommodate both the expanding young population and the demands of political leaders. Although the precise structure and curriculum for higher education differed widely in each country, universities brought together a cross-section of the best-trained students, almost all of whom were literate and proficient in basic mathematics. In this context higher education groomed an aristocracy of talent and leadership, in contrast to earlier aristocracies of birth or manner.[15]

The statistics on the expansion of higher education in the 1960s are far from exact; differences in definition and disputes in reporting characterize all the historical data. The growth trends, however, are unmistakable. Just as the number of nuclear warheads and state bureaucracies increased across societies after 1955, so did the population of students in higher education. The expansion of universities, colleges, and other postsecondary schools occurred at a galloping rate in each of the great powers, with the notable exception of mainland China after the early 1960s (see Table 1 in the appendix).[16]

From 1955 through 1965 the number of students in higher education at least doubled in each of the great powers, with the sole exception of Great Britain, where university enrollments grew by 98 percent. This dramatic growth continued through 1970 everywhere but in China.

The experience of academic life—where intellectual study and separation from family are integral to student identity—became commonplace among a wide diversity of youths in the 1960s. Compulsory military service had often marked a distinct period in the maturation of young men, between childhood and full adulthood. The expansion in educational access created a freer, more intellectual transition for many citizens from diverse backgrounds, both male and female. Education reform, driven by demographics and state policy, provided the structural foundation for an international youth culture more integrated across gender and more politically aware than its predecessors.

Men and women attending university in the 1960s were not united by class, ethnicity, or national origin. Their commonality lay in their status as students. The influence of government within the expanding institutions of higher education exerted strong pressures on students for conformity with dominant ideologies. The experiences of McCarthyism in the United States, the Anti-Rightist Campaign against domestic critics in China, and the recurring purges in the Soviet Union, though very different in degree, attested to how coercive the forces of domestic order could become for students, intellectuals, and society as a whole.

The instruments of state "hegemony"—whereby the government uses education and other forms of indoctrination to reinforce its authority—operated effectively within the expanding institutions of higher education, but they also generated a series of powerful counterresponses ("counter-hegemonies"). The literacy, international awareness, and group interaction that served the purposes of educational indoctrination also empowered dissent against the aims of the state. Within universities students could produce their own literature (openly in the West, covertly in communist societies), distribute their materials to a large number of counterparts, organize their own social networks, and, most significant, turn their access to information against the claims of governing authorities.

In the early 1960s individuals in and around various universities used these sources of counterhegemony to transform students into dissidents. Agitators in the eyes of many, these individuals—often writing from outside the student community for young readers—played the role of Antonio Gramsci's "organic intellectuals."[17] Emerging from various age cohorts and backgrounds, a set of charismatic figures crafted a language of protest that inspired the growing body of students to resist the aims of state leaders.

The discontents that motivated dissent preceded this period. One writer notes that the "objective conditions" for protest were more acute in many societies before the 1960s.[18] Rebellion, however, required something more than a simple motive. Alexis de Tocqueville noted that "rising expectations" fuel protest during periods when social improvement stalls.[19] Scholars have also emphasized the importance of both organization and language in knitting various protests together for cohesive challenges to authority.[20] A number of influential intellectuals in the late 1950s and early 1960s filled this role. Drawing on the expanded university population, writers in each of the great powers provided the critical vocabulary that encouraged acts of dissent to proliferate.

The breakdown of the Cold War "domestic consensus" began in the early 1960s. Contrary to the conformist aims of state leaders, educational institutions nurtured a language of protest among students years before the Vietnam War and other international crises sparked broader criticisms of authority. Dissident voices communicated through journals, artwork, music, and television played a role somewhat similar to public criticisms shared in Parisian cafés before the French Revolution. They exposed the shortcomings of distinguished political figures and delegitimized what one historian calls the "royal touch" of government.[21]

An analysis of influential dissident texts sheds light on the proliferation of protest movements during the 1960s. Dissident writers contradicted the claims of established leaders and turned the energies of many citizens to alternative courses of action, including covert organization and extralegal protest. Operating under very different degrees of restriction, these dissidents voiced growing frustrations with the political status quo. They expressed hope for something other than a permanent Cold War. The expanded academic community in each of the great powers became a crucial forum for the transmission of these ideas, often in secret, and the organization of what many called "direct action." Protest movements such as the American civil rights movement had important nonacademic origins, but in the 1960s universities around the world became incubators for revolution.

Most modern revolutions have built on a series of influential texts and networks for social mobilization. The language of dissent in the 1960s produced a corpus of what one historian describes as the "forbidden bestsellers" that preceded prior upheavals. The extensive uprisings around 1968 grew from an international dissident culture, created in diverse ways by writers in each of the great powers. Authors such as Daniel Bell, John Kenneth Galbraith, Aleksandr Solzhenitsyn, Wu Han, and Herbert Marcuse were the Jean-Jacques Rousseaus of the twentieth century—inspirations for passionate reading, discussion, and public contention.[22]

▪ The Language of Dissent in the United States

In 1960 the American sociologist and longtime social-democrat Daniel Bell published one of those books that periodically capture almost everyone's attention. Bell's *End of Ideology* became the focus of countless debates in America and Europe. Prominent scholars and diverse students knew about the book's central contention that the old Cold War ideologies were, in Bell's judgment, "dead." "Ideology," he wrote, "which once was a road to action, has come to be a dead end."

> Few serious minds believe any longer that one can set down "blueprints" and through "social engineering" bring about a new utopia of social harmony. At the same time, the older "counter-beliefs" have lost their intellectual force as well. Few "classic liberals" insist that the State should play no role in the economy, and few serious conservatives, at least in England and on the Continent, believe that the Welfare State is "the road to serfdom" . . . In that sense, too, the ideological age has ended.[23]

Bell did not believe that conflict would cease to divide antagonistic interests at home and abroad. Despite his recurrent references to the "end" of ideology, he recognized that in the late 1950s the very *nature* of ideology had shifted decisively. The dominant language of social justice and legitimate authority no longer addressed the concerns voiced by articulate critics and a growing cohort of university students.

Bell's central insight was that superpower rivalry did not focus the energies of citizens as it had in prior years. He observed that "the old ideologies have lost their 'truth' and their power to persuade." In a world in which nuclear stalemate and administrative largess made stagnation within society palpable, there was little left to debate in the established language of politics. The promises of freedom offered by Marxist and liberal-capitalist ideologies appeared untenable when the largest states endeavored to restrain, rather than embolden, international pressures for change. Growing policy stagnation along a very moderate middle road between utopian visions made desired social reforms seem ever more distant. "The young intellectual," Bell explained, "is unhappy because the 'middle way' is for the middle-aged, not for him; it is without passion and is deadening."[24]

Many of the geopolitical disputes between the United States and the Soviet Union reached a stable "settlement" by the early 1960s. Bell recognized that domestic activists by no means considered their own aspirations settled. Politics among the great powers had become entrenched in a stagnant center that forced disgruntled voices to ever more critical extremes. This phenomenon proved most evident in the United States, but it surfaced in Western Europe, the Soviet Union, and China as well.[25]

Bell's analysis did not capture the full range of dissent within the great powers. His book did, however, predict that traditional centers of dominance could no longer hold. Government authorities—military and bureaucratic—clearly resisted the application of principle to dangerous problems. Cold War "peace" in the early 1960s ran against the moral rhetoric of "freedom" and "liberation" that had justified the post–World War II conflict in the first place. The failure to realize promised ideals opened a series of formerly taboo questions, especially among young thinkers. The language of dissent in the 1960s labeled existing leaders as illegitimate for failing to meet their own espoused standards of justice.

John Kenneth Galbraith, writing in 1958, had anticipated Daniel Bell's analysis. After 1960 Bell's critique added resonance to the Harvard economist's condemnation of America's hollow affluence. Galbraith's discussion in *The Affluent Society*—later extended by socialist writer Michael Harrington—provided the indispensable vocabulary for attacks on the underside of state achievements in the 1960s. In America and elsewhere the social failings of political policy received newfound attention thanks to Galbraith's evocative, if not fully satisfactory, polemic.

Galbraith recognized that although American affluence was incontestable during the Eisenhower years, its distribution belied claims to personal freedom. His best-selling book criticized American society for its obsession with wealth and its accompanying neglect of pervasive inequalities. Targeting the "social imbalance" between human needs and lucrative market priorities, Galbraith condemned the "paramount position of production" in America. "It is an index of the prestige of production in our national attitudes," he explained, "that it is identified with the sensible and practical. And no greater compliment can be paid to the forthright intelligence of any businessman than to say that he understands production."[26]

"Conventional wisdom" prioritized the production of material goods above what Galbraith saw as critical human investments in adequate health care, an improved living environment, and other public facilities. "Whether the problem be that of a burgeoning population and of space in which to live with peace and grace, or whether it be the depletion of the materials which nature has stocked in the earth's crust and which have been drawn upon more heavily in this century than in all previous time together, or whether it be that of occupying minds no longer committed to the stockpiling of consumer goods, the basic demand on America will be on its resources of ability, intelligence, and education." "The test," Galbraith proclaimed, "will be less the effectiveness of our material investment than the effectiveness of our investment in men."[27]

Despite its extraordinary wealth, America was in danger of failing this test. Inequalities among individuals and sectors of the economy were not the problem per se. Policy blindness to these inequalities was the central reason for Galbraith's urgency. The rhetoric of economic growth in America devoted little attention to a relatively small but significant cohort of impoverished citizens residing in rural lands like Appalachia and urban slums like Chicago's south side. Residents of these largely "invisible" regions suffered from inadequate education, poor nutrition, restricted economic opportunities, and a generally distempered social outlook. Galbraith did not deny that general economic growth had lifted many poor families, but he exposed the myth of universal mobility. "The most certain thing about modern poverty," Galbraith lamented, "is that it is not efficiently remedied by a general and tolerably well-distributed advance in income." Postwar America had produced great affluence, but many citizens remained stuck in poverty.[28]

Michael Harrington—a prominent Socialist Party activist—employed moving detail to reinforce the more literary claims of *The Affluent Society*. Extending an earlier article on "Our Fifty Million Poor" into a larger investigative exposé, Harrington reported in his landmark 1962 book, *The Other America*, on a wide range of experiences throughout the nation: unemployed coal miners, subsistence farmers, inner-city slum dwellers, segregated African Americans, mentally ill individuals, elderly citizens, and disadvantaged youth. Employing U.S. Bureau of Labor statistics that estimated an annual income of $3,500 for the subsistence of a family of four, Harrington computed that 50 million Americans—approximately one quarter of the population—lived in poverty.[29]

Harrington's argument proved more damning than a simple measure of relative suffering. He argued that contemporary poverty in America did not reflect the long-dreaded ravages of climate, war, and pestilence. In a world of sophisticated nuclear devices and far-reaching administrative institutions, flawed policy bore the burden of responsibility for continued suffering. Postwar programs for domestic economic growth and foreign competition benefited "those least who need help most." "These are the people who are immune to progress."[30]

Technological advances provided unprecedented farm and factory abundance for the nation. This abundance, however, came at the cost of isolating those least able to operate the new machines. "As the society [becomes] more technological, more skilled," Harrington explained, "those who learn to work the machines, who get the expanding education, move up. Those who miss out at the very start find themselves at a new disadvantage."[31]

Poverty, according to Harrington, had become much more than a cyclical condition, concentrated in "pockets" of the nation. The deprivations of the poor expanded into a pervasive "culture" that suffocated the creative aspirations underlying economic dynamism in America. Employing the image of a "vicious circle," Harrington described the dysfunctional families, communities, and morals that the poor propagated within the very fabric of abundance. "The United States contains," he exclaimed, "an underdeveloped nation, a culture of poverty."[32]

Harrington argued that this culture of poverty required comprehensive federal intervention. Otherwise, the depressed fatalism and dysfunctional influence of poverty would spread. Technology and administrative growth might, Harrington warned, "increase the ranks of the poor as well as intensify the disabilities of poverty." "There are," according to this somewhat apocalyptic vision, "millions of Americans who live just the other side of poverty."[33] *The Other America* focused exclusively on domestic areas, but many readers extended this analysis to the "developing world," especially in parts of Asia, Africa, and Latin America.

Harrington's strong words reflected a deep-seated apprehension that the structures supporting American affluence hindered whole segments of the population from enjoying the nation's wealth. President Eisenhower's calls for policy restraint and his admonitions about an emerging "military-industrial complex" only contributed, in Harrington's view, to the broad neglect of America's isolated poor. Stagnant politics produced surface successes. On deeper inspection, neglected social problems required urgent attention.

The criticisms of comfort articulated by Galbraith and Harrington were not new. The two authors popularized old arguments against conservative affluence at the moment when aggregate wealth appeared most evident. Galbraith and Harrington attracted wide audiences concerned about domestic problems—poverty in particular—unresolved despite America's international power in the 1960s.

"We can no longer afford the notion," Galbraith explained, "that foreign policy is a dance—an intricate minuet—which some people, peculiarly endowed with skill, experience, or a penchant for fast foot-work can do with unique proficiency." "I would hope," he continued, "that our foreign policy would soon become the subject of the same kind of social and political debate that focused the conflicting attitudes toward the New and Fair deals . . . The alternative, as I have noted, is agreement on an ungenerous and arid conservatism."[34] Domestic needs required a foreign policy that focused on social issues instead of restraint, stability, and the superficial signs of national affluence. Galbraith and Harrington did not elucidate a new policy blueprint, but they provided a powerful vocabulary for criticizing the short-comings of the status quo.

Criticisms of private materialism and political stagnation did not, contrary to the prejudices of some historians, arise only on the traditional left of the ideological spectrum. Eisenhower's restrained approach to foreign and domestic policy drew invective from self-proclaimed "new conservatives" such as William F. Buckley Jr. and Senator Barry Goldwater. Their condemnations of contemporary political leaders were as harsh as anything coming from the pens of Galbraith or Harrington. No longer could Eisenhower point to a conservative groundswell for politics aimed at preserving the status quo. The political right joined the left in calls for more policy activism.[35]

"Are we to fight the machine?" William F. Buckley asked. "Can conservatism assimilate it?" Buckley responded with rhetorical relish in *Up from Liberalism*, asserting that "the machine must be accepted, and conservatives must not live by programs that were written as though the machine did not exist, or could be made to go away." Conservatives would devise a new agenda—an alternative to nostalgia for a lost past or exuberance for a brave new world. Buckley demanded a "program that speaks to our time."[36]

In the pages of his weekly journal, the *National Review*, Buckley and his followers called for stronger defense of national ideals and increased community activism. They exposed the restraint of American policy at home and abroad for the materialism it claimed to abhor. The politics of Cold War competition became, for Buckley, an increasingly frustrating hindrance to a desired era of individual religious realization and creative experience. Instead of affirming enduring moral principles vested in the dignity of the individual and the omnipotence of God, Cold War moderation focused exclusively on methods and means without inherent value. Directing particular venom at theories of development and democratization closely connected with American foreign policy, Buckley exclaimed that "our preoccupation these days . . . is not so much with the *kind* of society democracy brings forth in a given political situation, as with democracy itself." Democracy, he continued, "has no program. It cannot say to its supporters: do thus, and ye shall arrive at the promised land."[37]

In an era without clear political ambitions, the constitutional procedures labored upon by Madison had become, in a word Buckley borrowed from contemporary college students, "dull." In place of procedure, restraint, and conformity, Buckley aimed to animate popular discussion with fire and brimstone. While Galbraith and Harrington carried themselves as socially conscious truth-tellers in a world of sham, the *National Review* crowd imagined itself as a populist intelligentsia, occupying the role of God-fearing preachers in a world too fearful to believe. Refusing to endorse either John F. Kennedy or Richard Nixon in the 1960 presidential election, Buckley explained that the new conservatives would gain "leverage on events" by dissenting from both established political parties.[38]

Buckley published *Up from Liberalism* as an explicit retort to *The Affluent Society*. The two texts, however, displayed striking similarities in tone and sentiment. Both writers hurled parallel invectives at the self-satisfied superficiality of American social thought during the Cold War. State power had created material abundance, but not the spiritual realization that made the Cold War, in the image of World War II, a righteous enterprise. The military and administrative strains of the early 1960s only presaged more stagnation in the domestic areas that demanded most concerted effort. Buckley and Galbraith were rabble-rousers. They drew upon neglected social energies in America to kick-start creative and probing thought. Young citizens attracted to the political right and left—heavily influenced by Buckley and Galbraith—set themselves against the dominant international trends toward political restraint.

Barry Goldwater, a U.S. senator from Arizona, emerged in the early 1960s to offer the spreading social criticism on the right a new political home. Goldwater failed to win election to the presidency, but he came to the forefront of American politics through a confluence of his own public maneuverings and the groundswell among critics of Republican policy. The energy Goldwater inspired among young conservatives at the *National Review,* on college campuses, and in selected areas of the country testified to the existence of a veritable, if limited, New Right movement born about the same time as the more famous "New Left."[39]

Goldwater's 1960 clarion call, *The Conscience of a Conservative,* set out an audacious agenda for criticism of American stagnation. The Arizona senator condemned the restraining impulses in contemporary politics. He spoke explicitly of "victory" in the Cold War through an unabashed emphasis upon America's superior capabilities. "Peace," Goldwater exclaimed, "*is* a proper goal for American policy—as long as it is understood that peace is not all we seek." "A tolerable peace . . . must *follow* victory over Communism. We have been fourteen years trying to bury that unpleasant fact. It cannot be buried and any foreign policy that ignores it will lead to our extinction as a nation."[40]

Goldwater sought to invigorate politics with moral principle. He focused his efforts on creating a more muscular, "offensive" American foreign policy, supported by reawakened patriotism at home. Calls for "victory" against communism provided an organizing mission that Goldwater found lacking in current Western leadership. "If our objective is victory over Communism," Goldwater explained, "we must achieve superiority in all of the weapons—military, as well as political and economic—that may be useful in reaching that goal. Such a program costs money, but so long as the money is spent wisely and efficiently, I would spend it. I am not in favor of 'economizing' on the nation's safety."[41]

According to Goldwater's vision, the United States would be in, but not of, the world. The American government would use overwhelming strength to protect its interests, and otherwise avoid entanglements that stifled creativity and hindered independent action. Goldwater wanted Washington to lead at home and abroad without becoming unnecessarily encumbered in complex arrangements with allies or adversaries. He argued that America's military muscle and its growing prosperity should serve as a beacon of freedom, not a restricting arm of administration. Freedom and prosperity would spread to more Americans, Goldwater promised, after victory over communist threats replaced the Cold War stalemate.

This rhetoric emboldened a wide range of dissident voices within universities and other communities. During the 1960s young men and women participated in chapters of Young Americans for Freedom (YAF) throughout the nation. YAF—founded at Buckley's Connecticut residence in September 1960—pledged itself to the vision of politics articulated most prominently by Goldwater. "In this time of moral and political crisis," the YAF "Statement of First Principles" explained, "it is the responsibility of the youth of America to affirm certain eternal truths . . . History shows periods of freedom are rare, and can exist only when free citizens concertedly defend their rights against all enemies." Echoing Goldwater, YAF proclaimed that "the forces of international Communism are, at present, the greatest single threat to [our] liberties . . . the United States should stress victory over, rather than co-existence with, this menace."[42] In later years Alabama governor George Wallace—campaigning for the presidency in 1968 and 1972— merged this New Right rhetoric with a broader racial backlash against civil rights reforms.[43] Ronald Reagan also drew on what one scholar calls "grassroots" conservatism, particularly in southern California, as he attacked the degenerate "big government" politics of mainstream Democrats and Republicans.[44]

Civil rights activists were the New Left counterparts to Goldwater, Wallace, and Reagan. Ministers, intellectuals, students, and grassroots organizers had built a powerful civil rights movement before the 1960s. Criticisms of Cold War stagnation augmented the number of young people—black and white —participating in protests against racial injustice. Civil rights leaders mobilized and revised the emerging language of dissent. Their rhetoric attacked the restraint of the U.S. government in its policies both at home and abroad.

Television in the 1960s gave racial discrimination new prominence in public perception. From the images of personal cruelty broadcast to an increasing number of households, many Americans became intensely aware of the contradiction between their nation's extolled freedoms and the realities of racial brutalization. This contradiction was particularly troublesome in the context of the Cold War, with the U.S. government trumpeting its worldwide defense of liberty against communism. Could the Cold War be a just war if it so clearly neglected justice at home?[45]

Many young Americans answered "no." In one of its first acts, Students for a Democratic Society (SDS) made race relations a litmus test for acceptable reform in the United States. This founding New Left organization prohibited membership to those who "would deny civil rights to any person because of race, color, creed, or national origin."[46] SDS gave the plight of segregated citizens central attention when it demanded alternatives to "stalemate" and empty rhetoric on race relations. Criticizing the restraint of both Eisenhower and Kennedy, SDS proclaimed: "Every time the president criticizes a recalcitrant Congress, we must ask that he no longer tolerate the Southern conservatives in the Democratic Party."

> Every time a liberal representative complains that "we can't expect every-thing at once" we must ask if we received much of anything from Congress in the last generation. Every time he refers to "circumstances beyond control" we must ask why he fraternizes with racist scoundrels. Every time he speaks of the "unpleasantness of personal and party fighting" we should insist that pleasantry with Dixiecrats [southern defenders of Jim Crow] is inexcusable when the dark peoples of the world call for American support.[47]

Young activists devised a set of protests that placed professed American values on public trial. They used university campuses, student publications, and television to highlight the pressing need for social change. The "sit-in

movement"—begun when four African-American students refused to relin-
quish their seats at a segregated Greensboro, North Carolina, lunch counter
on 1 February 1960—served as a striking testament to the unjust consequences of Cold War stagnation in America's reform agenda.

The Greensboro students initially expected arrest for their civil disobedience. The employees and customers at the targeted F. W. Woolworth lun-
cheonette, however, did very little when confronted by the sitters. Ignored
for almost an hour, the first sit-in ended without violence, police presence,
or even angry public exchanges. Instead, lunch service circulated around the
four quarantined stools until the store closed for the day. Franklin McCain,
one of the African Americans seated at the whites-only counter, later recalled his surprise: "Now it came to me all of a sudden. Maybe they can't do
anything to us. Maybe we can keep it up."[48]

This event became the organizing moment for the Students' Executive
Committee for Justice in Greensboro, soon expanded into the national Student Nonviolent Coordinating Committee (SNCC). Sit-ins with growing student participation quickly spread throughout the American South, engulfing cities in at least fourteen states by May 1960. Violent harassment,
police bullying, and public manifestations of race hatred followed the broadening student challenge to Jim Crow. More important, the sit-in movement
attracted widespread newspaper and television attention. In the month after
the first sit-in, reporters elevated race relations to a level of importance commensurate with the upcoming presidential election, the Soviet threat, and
Fidel Castro's Cuban revolution.[49]

Race relations in the United States took on an explicitly international
dimension during the 1960s. Broad dissemination of information made a
global "neighborhood" feasible at this time, even for downtrodden African
Americans in the Deep South. With great rhetorical force student activists
and civil rights leaders—particularly Martin Luther King Jr.—argued that a
global perspective on race relations revealed how far America lagged behind
other nations. Decolonization within the former European empires—especially the nonviolent Indian independence movement, led by Mohandas
Gandhi—inspired American social activism. King reveled in the emergence
of 1.3 billion free "colored peoples of the world." "They have broken loose
from the Egypt of colonialism and imperialism," he exclaimed, "and they are
now moving through the wilderness of adjustment toward the promised
land of cultural integration."[50]

In the early 1960s King expanded this vision to encompass a "new sense
of dignity on the part of the Negro," gained from "awareness that his struggle for freedom is part of a worldwide struggle." Visions of reform had clearly

turned away from the stagnant domestic policy debates. African Americans, according to King's broad international perspective, "watched developments in Asia and Africa with rapt attention." "Thirty years ago," he explained, "there were only three independent countries in the whole of Africa—Liberia, Ethiopia, and South Africa. By 1962, there may be as many as thirty independent nations in Africa. These rapid changes have naturally influenced the thinking of the American Negro. He knows that his struggle for human dignity is not an isolated event. It is a drama being played on the stage of the world with spectators and supporters from every continent."[51]

These rapid overseas transformations offered an alternative to the hidden suffering of the "Affluent Society" and the constrained politics of the Cold War. Liberation now appeared inevitable within the old colonial empires. Authentic freedom contradicted the established principles of legitimate authority. Civil rights agitation, in particular, became a primary channel for New Left direct action against the political status quo. The civil rights movement offered students—black and white—a new language for struggle and social change.

The Freedom Rides of 1961—organized by the two-decade-old Congress on Racial Equality (CORE)—were a defining experience for hundreds of men and women. James Farmer, CORE's national director, enlisted northern college students to ride public buses into the South during their vacation periods, challenging racially segregated facilities. Like the sit-ins of the previous year, these protests employed nonviolent civil disobedience, placing the onus for action upon southern law enforcement. In contrast to the lunch-counter confrontations, however, the freedom rides mobilized a large cross-section of students in defense of basic democratic rights. The Freedom Rides created a nationwide community of young, enthusiastic, and energetic social reformers.

Student defiance of segregation challenged liberal promises of gradual reform. Young activists believed that political pressures for stability and restraint had deferred the fulfillment of these promises for too long. The Freedom Rides demanded immediate change. Direct action was much more exciting than tedious, patient reforms. It gave young men and women a sense of mission. United in common action, they believed they could change society.

SDS sought to capture this "public spirit" and inspire more participation along similar lines. The first meetings of SDS predated 1961, but the Freedom Rides became the fundamental metaphor for the student movement. The Port Huron Statement—disseminated in June 1962 as SDS's "agenda for a generation"—explained that "when we were kids the United States was the wealthiest and strongest country in the world . . . Freedom and equality for each individual, government of, by, and for the people—these American values we found good, principles by which we could live as men. Many of us began maturing in complacency." But "our comfort was penetrated by events too troubling to dismiss. The permeating and victimizing fact of human degradation, symbolized by the Southern struggle against racial bigotry, compelled most of us from silence to activism." The SDS vision of social change embodied the ideals of "participatory democracy" in cooperation among black and white students to challenge the segregation of southern bus stations.[52]

SDS and other New Left organizations throughout America argued that social progress required the rejection of established authorities. Active participation in policy debates, grassroots mobilization, and public protest formed the youth agenda for the 1960s. This student message employed the language of writers such as Galbraith, Harrington, and even Buckley to challenge the restraint advocated by leaders struggling to strengthen existing institutions. The language of student protest attracted a broad following through its stark contrast with the seemingly stolid words of state authorities.

▪ The Return of Anti-Marxist History: The Soviet Union

If Galbraith and others used polemical words to expose the dark underside of affluence in the United States, Soviet author Aleksandr Solzhenitsyn deployed a literary evocation of his own experiences to puncture the "scientific" claims that legitimated communist authority in Russia and China. During World War II Solzhenitsyn had fought with valor against the invading Nazi armies. Josef Stalin's government forced Solzhenitsyn into a brutal labor camp (administered by a Russian agency known chiefly by its acronym, GULAG) and then into internal exile for his muted criticism of Soviet military leadership.[53] Entering mainstream Soviet society after an official amnesty in 1956, the former prisoner returned with fury to his literary ambitions. *One Day in the Life of Ivan Denisovich*, published in the Soviet Union with Premier Nikita Khrushchev's personal approval in 1962, became Solzhenitsyn's first, most moderate, but also most immediately influential condemnation of the communist political project.[54]

Khrushchev initially perceived publication of *Ivan Denisovich* as a means of separating his government from its predecessor. Solzhenitsyn's gripping account of gulag life, however, provided a compelling narrative that discredited both communist authority and its regime-saving reforms. The author occasionally singled out Stalin for criticism, but the sources of tyranny in *Ivan Denisovich* were decidedly impersonal. One man had not created the gulag. One misguided leader had not derailed a noble Bolshevik project. Communist pretensions to "scientific" authority had produced a vast machine of terror that negated personal freedom.

Solzhenitsyn focused on the regime's absolute control of personal time. It prevented any allocation of human effort for activities other than the work required by the state. For the individual, time "rolled by before you knew it," spent in unceasing efforts in the forced construction of communism. The promised liberation of classes and peoples had never arrived. Like the prisoners of the gulag, each Soviet citizen found, according to Solzhenitsyn, that his or her life "sentence stood still."[55]

Anticipated freedoms were a mirage. Despair replaced hope. Lying in his prison bunk during a moment of existential self-pity, Solzhenitsyn's protagonist—Ivan Denisovich Shukhov—reflected on the absurdity of life under communism:

> Shukhov stared at the ceiling and said nothing. He no longer knew whether he wanted to be free or not. To begin with, he'd wanted it very much, and counted up every evening how many days he still had to serve. Then he'd got fed up with it. And still later it had gradually dawned on him that people like himself were not allowed to go home but were packed off into exile. And there was no knowing where the living was easier—here or there. The one thing he might want to ask God for was to let him go home. But *they* wouldn't let him go home.

"Home" was the "peace," "bread," and "land" that Vladimir Lenin had promised during the heady days of the Bolshevik Revolution. The experience of the gulag revealed that, contrary to these promises, communist society ran on perpetual terror. "Relax for a minute," Shukhov lamented, "and somebody was at your throat."[56]

The forced labor, controlled time, and pervasive surveillance of the gulag were hardly exceptional. In the pages of *Ivan Denisovich* Solzhenitsyn presented the prison camp as a depressingly accurate reflection of how communist society as a whole operated. As in society at large, the commanders of the gulag allowed the inmates generous rights to petition for a "democratic" redress of grievances. Like claims to justice throughout the Soviet Union, the laws to protect the toiling masses proved hollow: "Four sealed boxes stood in front of the staff hut, and were emptied once a month by someone delegated for that purpose. Many prisoners dropped petitions into those boxes, then waited, counting days, expecting an answer in two months, one month . . . There would be no answer. Or else—'complaint rejected.'"[57]

Each person in a position of even minimal authority—the mailroom clerk, the cook, the guard, and the party commissar—manipulated the law for personal gain. There was no alternative. Contrary to the classless community promised by Marxist rhetoric, communist society heightened the necessity for each citizen to live off the opportunistic exploitation of another: "What the boss man doles out is all you will get. Only you won't get even that, what with cooks and their stooges and trusties. There's thieving on the site, there's thieving in the camp, and there was thieving before the food ever left the store . . . It's dog eat dog here."[58]

Solzhenitsyn's novella made the suffering of the gulag appear both inhuman and ordinary at the same time. The reader had to wonder how anyone survived the bitter deprivation of the Siberian prison camp. Looking around any city or collective farm, however, one could see the very same sources of individual suffering replicated many times over—even during the years of the Khrushchev "thaw." *Ivan Denisovich* made the gulag a metaphor for life in a society that continued to call upon its citizens for increased personal sacrifice while the prospects of communist utopia grew ever more dim.

In the aftermath of World War II, Stalin and his successors had used their victory over Nazi Germany as a renewed source of domestic unity against alleged capitalist enemies in the West.[59] Shukhov, like Solzhenitsyn, had fought heroically for his homeland. Instead of sharing in the Soviet mission after victory, however, Solzhenitsyn's protagonist joined countless other war heroes in state-enforced Siberian imprisonment. Shukhov—whose family name sounded eerily similar to that of the purged Soviet commander Georgy Zhukov—was just one more victim of the Kremlin's efforts to protect its monopoly on power. For war veterans, laborers on collective farms, and even the children of the party elite, state intrusions killed sincere hopes for building a more free and just future.

Soviet authority, during and after Stalin's reign, "barred" "the straight and narrow" desired by "ordinary people." Conniving for small handouts became the social norm. Even a distinguished navy captain who "had sailed all around Europe and across the Great Northern Sea Route," according to Solzhenitsyn, "bowed his head happily over less than a ladleful of gruel with no fat in it at all, just oats and water."[60] Insipid gruel, rather than a creative classless society, marked the future of the Soviet Union as revealed in Solzhenitsyn's public account of the gulag.

Solzhenitsyn's sharp words and his displays of personal courage throughout the 1960s attracted a large international following. Although he was only one of numerous dissidents, many of whom disagreed on important issues,

Solzhenitsyn was the single figure who caused the most immediate and lasting damage to the Kremlin's authority. *Ivan Denisovich* unleashed a flood of public complaints within the Soviet Union against the personal sufferings required in the name of building communism. Zhores Medvedev, a Soviet scientist and writer, recounts that the novella "breached" many barriers to a more "realistic" assessment of society. Even before its publication in November 1962, countless members of the university, literary, and scientific communities read the text in typescript. Despite later government renunciation and repression, Solzhenitsyn's unmasking of the inherent cruelty in Soviet communism was, in the words of one contemporary, "a literary miracle" that had "everybody" talking. Medvedev's own condemnation of the havoc wreaked on genetic studies by Marxist theory joined a large number of similar dissident works inspired by Solzhenitsyn's words.[61]

More than any other text, Solzhenitsyn's account of the gulag provided the vocabulary for a powerful culture of dissent within the Soviet Union. Reactions to the novella varied among citizens, but few could ignore its gripping portrayal of human suffering. "It has become clear," one reader of *Ivan Denisovich* explained in 1962, "that since the appearance of Solzhenitsyn's book we will never again be able to write as we have done till now."[62]

When Soviet authorities began to crack down again on dissident literature, around 1963, popular criticism went underground, augmenting the corpus of mimeographed and widely distributed *samizdat* ("self-published") texts.[63] Writing, distributing, and secretly discussing forbidden literature contributed to a vibrant subterranean culture beneath the enforced conformity of Soviet society. One former Moscow resident recounts how spontaneous nightly meetings of men and women—*kompanii* (singular: *kompaniya*)—sprouted up throughout the city during this period:

> . . . the *kompaniya* had sprung up as a social institution because it was needed. Our generation had a psychological, spiritual, perhaps even a physiological need to discover our country, our history, and ourselves. *Kompanii* evolved their own forms of literature, journalism, music, and humor. They performed the functions of publishing houses, speaker bureaus, salons, billboards, confession booths, concert halls, libraries, museums, counseling groups, sewing circles, knitting clubs, chambers of commerce, bars, clubs, restaurants, coffeehouses, dating bureaus, and seminars in literature, history, philosophy, linguistics, economics, genetics, physics, music, and art.[64]

Armed with the explosive analyses offered by Solzhenitsyn and others, the *kompanii* spread dissident ideas among a highly educated and predominantly young population. Friends and acquaintances from universities and other milieus would gather in someone's apartment—often with vodka as a lubricant—to talk, recite poetry, sing, and dance. The vernacular of these gatherings was not the official language of Soviet authority. Quite the contrary, the participants cultivated a "convict" slang that closely approximated the vocabulary of *Ivan Denisovich*. Referring to the Communist Party leadership, one *kompanii* song included the following lines:

> You've destroyed, you vermin, you have ravaged
> You have ravaged all my precious youth.

Another song line lamented:

> I sit in a cell, the very same cell my grandfather sat in.[65]

This was the language of Solzhenitsyn, *samizdat*, and the dissident culture of the Soviet Union in the 1960s. During *kompanii* meetings tape recorders and typewriters preserved and disseminated forbidden words. *Samizdat* became a true medium of alternative information, filling voids in "official" knowledge. *Kompanii* participants too young to remember World War II read and copied the unpublished memoirs of old revolutionaries, war veterans, and thousands of others who had suffered terribly under communist rule. Censored Soviet authors such as Boris Pasternak, Anna Akhmatova, and Aleksandr Solzhenitsyn reached a wide audience through the *kompanii* culture, as did foreign influences like Ernest Hemingway, Arthur Koestler, George Orwell, Elvis, and the Beatles.[66]

Young men and women in the expanding Soviet universities stood at the center of this dissident culture. In contrast to Khrushchev's enthusiastic rhetoric about the future accomplishments of communism, information distributed through the *kompanii* provided evidence that the promises of the state lacked historical credibility. If the past was filled with lies, why would the future prove any different?

Samizdat provided students with a vocabulary for expressing their disillusionment. In their poetry, music, and jokes men and women began to speak of contemporary society more as an absurd gulag than as a proclaimed workers' paradise. "What's the difference between socialism and capitalism?" one common joke began. "Under capitalism, man exploits man. Under socialism, it's the other way around."[67]

The disenchantment of Soviet youth in the 1960s was not unique to that generation. The entire history of communism, according to one writer, is a chronicle of ideals betrayed and illusion unmasked as tragedy.[68] Young Soviet citizens in the 1960s proved distinctive for their willingness to express this disillusionment. Earlier generations in the Soviet Union, lacking the infrastructure of expanded universities, mass literacy, and extensive urbanization, had had less opportunity to organize their discontents into coherent movements. Dissident ideas certainly existed in past Soviet society, but they remained much less articulate and much more diffuse.[69]

In addition to organizational difficulties, the long years of Stalinist rule had made dissent life-threatening. The pervasive use of terror by the government coerced citizens into silence. Having lived through revolution, famine, and war, earlier generations in the Soviet Union were generally willing to accept an unsatisfactory existence rather than face the far worse alternatives they had seen with their own eyes.

Men and women coming of age under Nikita Khrushchev and Leonid Brezhnev did not feel the same fears. Soviet citizens now possessed more information, personal security, and common organizational space. The Kremlin continued to deploy domestic terror against dissidents—including mandatory incarceration in "mental hospitals"—but not with the same cold-blooded determination as during the Stalin years.[70] Soviet leaders recognized that they needed a larger pool of educated, active, and creative citizens for their continued competition with the West. Stalinist terror had clearly become self-defeating for the regime. But contrary to the Kremlin's intentions, the readers of Solzhenitsyn and other *samizdat* authors exploited the controlled "thaw" of the 1960s to undermine the authority of the Soviet government.

Knowledge of past crimes against the population, combined with the virtual silence of older Soviet citizens, raised unsettling questions about guilt and complicity. Many of those who had survived Stalin's terror had done so at the cost of other innocent lives in what Solzhenitsyn called the "dog eat dog" world of communist society. In their attempts to make sense of this troubled past, young Soviet thinkers confronted an acute "problem of fathers and sons," described most poignantly a century earlier by the Russian novelist Ivan Turgenev.[71]

In Turgenev's *Fathers and Sons,* Nikolai Kirsanov, the son of a distinguished tsarist general and owner of a large country estate, encounters the unabashed hubris of Evgeny Bazarov, a university student, scientist, and self-proclaimed nihilist. As Kirsanov attempts to turn a profit from his estate by embracing gradual liberal reforms among the former serfs of the land, Bazarov accuses the estate owner of leading an "antiquated" life and of continued despotism. Science and rational analysis would, according to the young nihilist, replace inherited traditions of land ownership and chivalry with a more reasoned mode of existence in Russia. "Experiments," not "principles," guide the young student. "We act on the basis of what we recognize as useful," Bazarov explains on behalf of his fellow nihilists. "Nowadays the most useful thing of all is rejection . . . the ground must be cleared."[72]

Confronted by Bazarov's pointed criticisms, as well as by his own difficulties in balancing enlightened reform and order on the family estate, the older gentleman laments that his "song's been sung": "I seem to do all I can to keep up with the times," Kirsanov explains. "I've made arrangements for my peasants, established a farm, with the result that I'm called a 'Red' throughout the province; I read, study, and try to respond in general to the requirements of the day—but they say my song's been sung . . . I'm beginning to think perhaps it really has been sung."[73]

Kirsanov is the authorial voice of Turgenev, who suffered from what one scholar terms the recurring "liberal predicament" during a period of great ferment. Gradual, patient reform is always too radical for established conservatives and too plodding for young enthusiasts. Bazarov is, in the words of Isaiah Berlin, the "first Bolshevik," committed to rapid and even violent reform for the sake of "clearing the ground." Bazarov and his Soviet successors used force, violence, and the gulag to pursue what they perceived as a more "scientific," "rational" society, contrasted with the inherited traditions of tsarist Russia.[74]

The Soviet Union in the 1960s was the mirror image of Turgenev's Russia a century earlier. The Bazarovs had won, implementing "scientific" plans with little care for the human lives extinguished in pursuit of rational ends.[75] The single greatest horror in Solzhenitsyn's description of the gulag came from the realization that this terrible system of suffering operated with perfect rationality, maximizing the labor of each individual at the least possible cost to the state. The gulag was the supreme Bazarov-like "experiment" in "clearing the ground."

Citizens attending *kompanii* and reading *samizdat* rejected Bazarov, adopting a position closer to that of Kirsanov. The men in positions of authority throughout Soviet society supported a revolutionary edifice that, in the eyes of many students, imprisoned human beings in a terribly destructive experiment. The actions of the Bolshevik Bazarovs had destroyed the noble motives behind the revolution. Through their private gatherings, illicit writings, and muted public actions Soviet dissidents sought to restore the human values violated in the headlong pursuit of communism. "If Turgenev were living at this hour," Isaiah Berlin wrote, "the young radicals whom he would wish to describe, and perhaps to please, are those who wish to rescue men from the reign of those very 'sophisters, economists, and calculators' . . . who ignore or despise what men are and what they live by." Speaking of young dissidents in the Soviet Union and other societies during the 1960s, Berlin observed that "they want to build a society in which men treat one another as human beings with unique claims to self-expression, however undisciplined and wild, not as producing or consuming units in a centralized, worldwide, self-propelling social mechanism . . . Better anarchy than prison."[76]

Soviet students did not protest quite as openly as Bazarov, but they expressed their criticisms with growing vehemence in the years around the publication of Solzhenitsyn's *Ivan Denisovich*. In 1963 an attentive reading of the official Soviet press revealed that youth resistance to Communist Party authorities had become quite prevalent, eliciting unprecedented government hand-wringing. Radio Liberty—a radio broadcast and research organization formed in Western Europe to circumvent Kremlin censorship— reported that "skepticism, because it is so widespread among Soviet intellectuals, in particular the young people, is the subject of much attention in the Soviet press. And surprisingly the basic cause is frequently suggested in the press—the disparity between communist theory and Soviet reality."[77]

Soviet newspapers admitted that the Communist Party found it increasingly difficult to recruit citizens for military duties, farm labor, and basic public services. The Communist Youth League—the Komsomol—reported that students avoided mandatory activities and, when present, displayed a marked lack of interest. The informal *kompanii* had clearly supplanted the state-controlled Komsomol. When provided with full doses from the Soviet canon of heroic socialist films and books, students openly voiced their preference for the realism of Solzhenitsyn and *samizdat*. "I want to read about real youth, not about an invented one," one citizen boldly proclaimed. Another student inveighed that "one must portray not 'cut outs' but living people in books."[78]

Youth preferences in film, poetry, and art increasingly departed from the standards sanctioned by the state. The complexity of "real life" in communist society became the focus of student cinematic productions. Young poets began to identify themselves with Western "beatniks" and the "lost generation" of American authors in the decades between the world wars. The paintings of young artists replaced the heroic icons of hearty Soviet workers with abstract displays of shape and color that challenged superficial claims to popular communist contentment. The disoriented visions of the "nonconformist" artists drew the viewer to deeper, more complex, and often somber reflections on Soviet society.[79]

Soviet leaders made a point of condemning the degenerate, "licentious" behavior of young artists. Nikita Khrushchev exclaimed that when he viewed the canvases of abstract painters he could not tell "whether they have been painted by a man's hand or splashed over an ass's tail." During a visit to a Moscow exhibition in December 1962, the general secretary labeled the "nonconformist" art perverse. Berating one painter, Khrushchev asked: "You know what your art is?" In one of his most graphic diatribes, the Soviet leader answered his own question: "You go into one of those outdoor bathrooms, you climb down through that hole, and from there, from the bottom, you look up at what's above you when somebody sits on the toilet. You look up and see that part of the body. That's what your art is. And that's where your place is . . . you sit in a shithole."[80]

The abstract artists transformed this crude condemnation into a badge of honor. They ridiculed detractors for their superficiality and stupidity. During *kompanii* discussions, participants recounted Khrushchev's meeting with the artists in the following form:

> *Khrushchev:* What's this turd-on-canvas supposed to symbolize?
> *Guide:* That, Nikita Sergeyevich, is *Dawn on the Volga.*
> *Khrushchev:* And what's this finger-painting?
> *Guide:* This, Nikita Sergeyevich, is *A Symphony of Light.*
> *Khrushchev:* What's this fat ass with ears?
> *Guide:* This, Nikita Sergeyevich, is a mirror.[81]

Komsomolskaya Pravda, the official Soviet journal most directly concerned with youth issues, became obsessed with the troubling "psychology of contemporary young people." Men and women frequently wrote to the newspaper, explaining that they felt bored, unchallenged, and depressed. Soviet society was relatively stable in the 1960s, but it offered, according to a letter from students in Novosibirsk, little space for interesting and creative work. One eighteen-year-old adopted the language of existential angst. He wrote that "I've lost faith in the future, faith in life." A public survey conducted by Soviet authorities in 1964 revealed that more than four out of every five students refused to heed the leadership's call for the cultivation of "virgin lands."[82]

Komsomolskaya Pravda reported with dismay on the proliferation of *kompanii* that distracted students from their patriotic work. Young men and women joined "degenerate" groups such as the self-proclaimed "World Association of Troglodytes" rather than the distinguished Komsomol. Mocking the manipulated self-righteousness of state-controlled clubs, the Troglodytes declared that they were fed up with communist society. The group explained that it would seek the "gradual transformation of man into monkey."[83]

The irreverent humor of Soviet youth in the 1960s reflected the typical rebellion exhibited by young men and women nearly everywhere. Disillusionment and even existential angst are youth phenomena that cross time and space. The public discussion of these voices in the Soviet press, however, revealed that leaders recognized a much deeper problem. *Kompanii* meetings and *samizdat* publications included a cacophony of frivolous and diffuse subjects, but they almost universally rejected the state's communist claims. Discussion of the future classless society and competition with capitalist imperialists received minimal attention. These guideposts for behavior in Soviet society failed to focus the attention of the young.

Solzhenitsyn's *Ivan Denisovich*, in particular, illustrated how communist claims furthered human suffering. Visualizing society as a gulag rather than as a classless community, young men and women refused to take the sanctimony of their elders seriously. Few openly revolted against the system, but many avoided their patriotic duties whenever possible. Passive resistance and social stagnation became palpable within Soviet society as the dissident culture infected many of the central institutions of authority.

▪ The Return of Anti-Marxist History: China

Chinese society offered far fewer opportunities than its Soviet counterpart for the communication of dissident voices. The Chinese system of education expanded rapidly during the late 1950s, but the educated young remained a distinct minority in what was still a predominantly peasant society. The failure of Mao Zedong's economic policies did, however, elicit words of public reproach that would prove particularly important in the lead up to the Cultural Revolution.

In 1961 Wu Han—a distinguished historian, deputy mayor of Beijing, and acquaintance of Mao—produced a play that served, in some ways, as the Chinese equivalent of Solzhenitsyn's *Ivan Denisovich*. In the late 1920s Wu had become a scholar of the Ming period (1368–1644). Then a student at Shanghai's China College, he followed Liang Qichao's influential call for a "New History" that would provide twentieth-century China with a usable past as it transformed itself into a "modern" nation.[84] Confronted by recurring Japanese attacks on Chinese sovereignty and pervasive political corruption on the mainland, in 1932 Wu wrote a scathing criticism of the Guomindang regime: "Everywhere in the present national situation, the leaders of the party and nation sell the nation, the government sells the nation, the high border officials sell the nation . . . If you open the history of any country or any dynasty you cannot find this sort of shameless, depraved, crazy government and it is also difficult to find this sort of innocent, naive, benumbed people."[85]

Wu's first encounter with Mao occurred in late 1948—the last months of the civil war on the mainland. During a series of meetings the two men discussed Wu's biography of the founding Ming emperor, Zhu Yuanzhang. Both the Chinese Communist leader and Wu were interested in the Ming concept of the "good emperor" and its relevance for the contemporary world. The historian became convinced that Mao would bring the best attributes of Ming leadership to a disunited mainland in need of strong, virtuous direction. Before the end of 1948 Wu wrote to Mao pledging that he would devote his scholarly energies to the service of the Communist Party.[86]

A decade later Wu began to regret this decision. The tragedy of the Great Leap led him to search for political virtue in areas removed from the apparent corruption of the Communist Party. His 1961 play, *Hai Jui's Dismissal*, utilized Ming history to locate important values in ordinary individuals rather than in the leaders of society. Hai Jui—the stubborn, well-educated, but modest official who dared to reproach the emperor—became Wu's hero rather than Zhu Yuanzhang, the founding Ming Son of Heaven. Condemning the corrupt officials who serve the interests of the local elite, Wu gave Hai Jui the following words near the end of the play:

> You pay lip service to the principle
> that the people are the roots of the state.
> But officials still oppress the masses
> while pretending to be virtuous men.[87]

Wu set his play in Hua Ting county (Songjiang prefecture) in the years 1569 and 1570.[88] The family of the distinguished scholar and former imperial minister Hsü Chieh dominates the area. In the words of one peasant, they "simply will not allow the people to go on living." Through control of virtually all local land and law the Hsü family oppresses hard-working citizens, even stealing their daughters for concubinage. When peasants appeal to government officials, corrupt ministers punish the wronged, not the influential Hsü family.[89]

After his appointment as the new governor of the prefecture Hai Jui attempts to "restore the fabric" of local justice and to "destroy the tyrants." Instead of residing in a grand house designated for someone of his distinguished stature, Hai Jui makes a point of wearing ordinary clothes and living close to the people. "I shall dwell," he proclaims, "in the countryside as the universal hope of the peasants here." When he learns that "the gentry and the evil officials are feeding on the fat of the people," Hai takes decisive action *without* consulting the emperor or his other representatives. He orders that all the peasants' private landholdings be restored to them. The corrupt members of the local elite receive immediate death sentences. "The law will be as firm and solid as a mountain," Hai proclaims, "showing no mercy." The return of private landholdings and the execution of local tyrants lead the peasants to sing with joy:

> These days we shall look up to Heaven above,
> We shall plow and sow diligently,
> restoring orchards and gardens.
> While we have land, what worry have we for clothes and food?
> A promising future lies before our eyes.[90]

Resisting intense pressure from the local elites, Hai Jui carries out the death sentences he has ordered for transgressors of the law. He does not, however, succeed in restoring the land to the peasants before his forced removal from office. Utilizing their great wealth and their influence with the imperial court, the Hsü family manages to replace Hai with a more ordinary, corrupt minister. The departure of the single upstanding official brings the play to a sad close.

> Heaven is cold, the earth is freezing,
> and the wind whistles mournfully.
> The thoughts of all the people
> go with this official as he leaves.[91]

The Chinese emperor does not appear in Wu Han's play. The text, however, presents the ways in which figures of distinguished standing corrupt central authority. The self-serving Hsü family, for example, maintains a virtually unassailable position in the prefecture because of its scholarly achievements and its personal service to the emperor. Hai Jui has attained scholarly and imperial standing of his own, but, in contrast to Hsü Chieh, he is hardly a favorite of the emperor. Having already served a prison sentence for his criticism of the previous Chinese ruler, Hai's social standing derives primarily from his reputation as an "honest, good official."[92] Simple acts of virtue, not accumulated learning, drive Hai:

> Poor students for twenty years,
> studying diligently as they learn
> to write their essays,

talking of Confucius and Mencius,
discussing the *Book of Songs* and *Book of History,*
these people end up losing their direction
all because of you [Hsü Chieh].[93]

Wu Han's play attacks the virtuous claims of the "good emperor." Despite
the sovereign's intentions, central authority in the vast Chinese landscape
represses ordinary citizens. The millions of Chinese peasants unable to communicate with the emperor are forced to suffer from the arbitrary, senseless,
and inhuman application of state power in what amounts to an immense
gulag without fences.

Imperial principle—Confucian and Communist—produces local oppression. The world of the peasants in Wu Han's play departs markedly from the
virtuous civilization the historian had earlier associated with the founding
Ming emperor and the promises of Mao's leadership. Crushed by the corruption of government officials, Chinese society becomes unable to "distinguish
right from wrong."[94]

Hai Jui attempts to enforce justice against the corruption of central authority. He invokes a natural law that transcends the dictates of the emperor.
Hai explains that he must at times disobey the Son of Heaven out of loyalty
"to my sovereign" and love of "my country." Justice and virtue override political orders. Hai Jui is heroic because he not only recognizes this truth but
also lives by it. He risks life and social position in defense of the peasants
against the authority of the emperor. In this way Wu Han's play glorifies "local knowledge" rather than the encompassing vision of a central leader or
party.[95]

If Wu Han's admiration for the Ming emperor Zhu Yuanzhang brought
him close to Mao and the Communist Party in 1948, by the early 1960s the
historian had found new heroes. Many readers immediately recognized Hai
Jui as a historical metaphor for the disgraced Chinese minister of defense,
Peng Dehuai, who had strongly criticized Mao's Great Leap Forward in
1959. "I belong," Wu Han explained in the preface to his play, "in the ranks
of those who dare." "Dare to think, dare to speak, and dare to do has been
the new style since the Great Leap Forward."[96]

Wu Han's account of Hai Jui echoed a long-standing Chinese tradition of
voicing political criticism through historical analogy. Even so, in its not-so-
subtle condemnation of the Communist Party's claims to enlightened authority, the play was quite daring. Wu's depiction of the inherent corruption
of imperial administration made the connection with the tragedy of the
Great Leap almost unavoidable so long as "good emperors" attempted to ex-

ert their power over the vast Chinese countryside. The local and personal virtues glorified by Wu provided an alternative vocabulary for power and authority. In this sense, *Hai Jui's Dismissal* was a very "usable history," primarily for dissent against the existing regime.

Wu Han was hardly alone in his allegorical criticism of the Chinese regime's excesses. Other prominent communists, including Deng Tuo (the former editor of the state-run *People's Daily*) and Liao Mosha (the head of Beijing's United Front Work Department), published essays attacking the corruption of misguided central government. These two writers collaborated with Wu Han on a series of columns—"Notes from a Three-Family Village"—expanding on many of the themes found in *Hai Jui's Dismissal*.[97]

Drawing on the history of China in the ancient Qin-Han period, Deng Tuo published an essay that drew a distinction between what he called the benevolent "Kingly Way" and the degenerate "Tyrannical Way." "That which is called the Kingly Way," Deng explained, "can be interpreted as the honest ideological workstyle of a mass line based on practical reality. And that which is called the Tyrannical Way can be interpreted as the blustering ideological workstyle of willful acts based on subjective and arbitrary decisions."[98] Readers of this essay—printed in a February 1962 issue of *Beijing Evening News (Beijing wanbao)*, with a circulation of 300,000—could clearly recognize the references to "blustering ideological workstyle" and "arbitrary decisions" as attacks on the leaders responsible for the Great Leap.[99]

From 1961 through 1964 Chinese society benefited from a hesitant "thaw" in the restrictions on public criticism. Wu Han, Deng Tuo, and Liao Mosha attracted a broad readership among the increasingly literate population. During this period Vice Premier Chen Yi encouraged dissident voices for the purpose of inspiring creative and productive activities across the mainland. Chen drew upon the language of Wu Han when he warned that without a new openness to debate (including explicit criticism of the Great Leap) "our country's science and culture will lag behind forever."[100]

Recognizing the appeal of the emerging dissident vocabulary, Mao attempted to ally himself with the public critics rather than the government officials whom he blamed for the failures of the Great Leap. In 1962 and 1963 the Chinese leader praised the message in *Hai Jui's Dismissal*. At a dinner attended by Ma Lianliang, the actor who played Hai Jui, Mao exclaimed that "the play is good, and Hai Jui was a good man!" As a show of his appreciation for the work of the playwright, Mao inscribed a copy of the fourth volume from his *Selected Works* for Wu Han. The chairman encouraged Wu to continue his research and writing on Ming history.[101]

Within a couple of years, however, Mao turned on Wu Han and his fellow critics. In November 1965 Yao Wenyuan—a Shanghai journalist who became a prominent government polemicist during the Cultural Revolution—published the first in a series of articles condemning the dissident writers as traitors "who have taken the capitalist road to seize leadership." He accused them of "preparing public opinion for a capitalist restoration." Yao singled out Wu Han for advocating a "reactionary" program that glorified gradualism and local initiative instead of communist principles.[102]

Yao Wenyuan's attacks sparked the first public protests against party cadres and intellectuals that convulsed much of China after 1965. With cryptic but determined action, Mao encouraged Yao and the Red Guards to condemn the writers the chairman had praised a few years earlier. Mao maneuvered behind the scenes to use public attacks as instruments for purging challengers to his leadership, especially Liu Shaoqi, the party official credited with helping China overcome the disastrous consequences of the Great Leap.[103]

The "Great Proletarian Cultural Revolution" began in China with the official denunciation of Wu Han. Ironically, the language adopted by the Red Guards to condemn Wu and other figures had originated with the men now under attack. In urban areas such as Shanghai and Guangzhou student groups from universities, high schools, and lower schools divided into factions. All, however, voiced criticism of allegedly corrupt, degenerate party administrators.[104] Public calls for undiluted personal virtue and a return to the simple lifestyle of the native peasant echoed the themes of Wu Han's play. A *People's Daily* editorial in December 1966 urged the "masses" to "elect Cultural Revolution groups." "Members of these organizations," the *People's Daily* continued, "must not be appointed by superiors, nor is behind-the-scenes manipulation to be allowed."[105]

Like Hai Jui, the "simple" and "righteous" students showed no mercy in eradicating the individuals responsible for everyday political compromises. Dressed in simple military attire, students made the Cultural Revolution into a popular "campaign" for a community of uncorrupted virtue, free of privilege and patronage. One Red Guard, reflecting on his experiences years later, remembered the exhilaration of the young rebels as they chopped the governing elite down to size:

> At that time I had this fantasy. I thought that those big shots should somehow only be up there in the same way as the heads of these mass organizations were. That meant that when the masses were dissatisfied with them, they could remove them from office. Officials normally kept their posts for the rest of their lives. If the masses had the power to remove them then they

wouldn't dare do so many of the things which were against the interests of the masses . . . Ah, I realized what it meant for a country to have democracy. That was it![106]

Hopes for democracy through mass revolt tragically failed to reach fruition. Mao manipulated the language of the Red Guards to fashion himself as a twentieth-century Hai Jui. Like the revered Ming official, Mao used a simple and eclectic collection of aphoristic "truths" to guide action against the corrupt influences of his own government.[107] Addressing a crowd of Red Guards in July 1966, the chairman confirmed that "sitting in offices listening to reports is no good." Socialist revolution must "rely on the masses, trust the masses, struggle to the end . . . If you want to carry the revolution through to the end, you must discipline yourself, reform yourself in order to keep up with it. Otherwise you can only keep out of it."[108]

As the inspiration for the Red Guards, the chairman did not base his claim to leadership on his position as the head of the government or the Communist Party. Mao presented himself as an honest, simple, and modest thinker committed to restoring justice in a corrupt state. Despite his unparalleled role in the construction of the existing political institutions, Mao placed himself above government or party as Hai Jui had done in his criticism of the distinguished families and the emperor himself. This was also a tactic that Charles de Gaulle used to great effect in France. The chairman described state bureaucrats as "vampires," whom those with a "revolutionary spirit" should replace.[109]

Mao lambasted members of the Communist Party who "feared" for the consequences of mass revolution: "You People! If you don't make revolution, the revolution will be directed against you."[110] Wu Han had issued a similar warning a few years earlier. In his play Hai Jui explains that the repressed anger of the peasants "bubbles and boils; their resentment will be hard to overcome."[111]

The Maoist "cult" that developed among protesting students during the second half of the 1960s grew from the dissident language formulated by writers like Wu Han to criticize the chairman in the aftermath of the Great Leap. Mao manipulated the Cultural Revolution for his own purposes, but he did this by tapping into a preexisting ferment among intellectuals, students, and millions of others touched by the failures of past communist policies.[112] The attacks on Wu Han, Deng Tuo, and Liao Mosha in late 1965 served as what I will call "discursive kidnappings" for the Chinese leader. Mao eliminated the most important independent writers, capturing the dissident language they had authored for his own purposes. Mao turned Hai

Jui's criticisms of the centralized state against his potential rivals in the Communist Party, insuring his own personal rule over Chinese society.[113]

The language of dissent in both China and the Soviet Union developed as a criticism of the personal suffering induced by the state's exercise of centralized power. In the Soviet case, Solzhenitsyn contributed to a growing community of writers and artists who became increasingly alienated from the state during the 1960s. In China, Wu Han provided one of several public criticisms of corrupt political power that helped inspire the antistatist rhetoric of the Red Guards.

Mao proved far more slippery than his counterparts in Moscow. While Nikita Khrushchev and Leonid Brezhnev endeavored to repress dissident voices initially unleashed for the Kremlin's purposes, the Chinese leader managed to place himself at the head of the young radicals. Mao crafted an image of himself as a dissident who happened to run a state corrupted by others. Unlike Khrushchev and Brezhnev, Mao did not draw back from the chaos that internal contention created for the Communist Party. To the surprise of many foreign observers—especially those in the Soviet Union—he encouraged attacks against the basic institutions of authority on the mainland. Only the chairman escaped public rebuke. In the cauldron of the Cultural Revolution he alone remained unassailable. This was pure dictatorship, not party rule.

Mao manipulated domestic ferment to reinforce his personal authority. Standing above the chaos he acquired the divine image that Max Weber originally associated with the concept of charisma. Mao would soon find, to his immense frustration, that his "supernatural" power allowed him to sponsor widespread destruction but left little room for necessary construction. In the late 1960s disorder and discontent on the mainland undermined the chairman's aim of strengthening China.

■ Internationalizing the Language of Dissent

The dissident writers of the 1960s created an emotional language critical of established political authorities. Herbert Marcuse went one step further. He argued that the organization of contemporary society—West and East—was inherently inhumane.

Born in 1898 to a Jewish family residing in Berlin, Marcuse associated with a group of philosophers who sought—especially after their forced exile from Nazi Germany in 1933—to formulate a "critical theory" of society.

Unsatisfied with analyses of fascism and authoritarianism that focused on personality and political maneuverings, the self-proclaimed "critical theorists" devoted themselves to investigating the deeper sources of oppression within modern civilization. In 1951, when some of the critical theorists returned to their prewar institutional base in Frankfurt, Max Horkheimer, a prominent member of the group, proclaimed that critical theory must "transcend existing society." "Without this intention," Horkheimer explained, "questions will neither be put in the correct way, nor will sociological thinking arise at all . . . A certain critical attitude to what exists is, so to speak, part of the job of the social theorist."[114]

Marcuse never returned permanently to Frankfurt, and he eventually broke with Horkheimer and other former associates. A professor in the Department of Political Science at Brandeis University after 1954, Marcuse applied critical theory to what he called "similarities in the development of capitalism and communism." He devoted his energies to studies of the contemporary world that transcended apparent national differences in ideology, culture, and political organization. Marcuse sought to uncover what he perceived as the global restrictions on human freedom.[115]

In a widely read examination of Soviet Marxism, published in 1958, he argued that communist and capitalist societies shared a similar "spirit" of individual repression under the label of "technical progress." "The Soviet state," Marcuse explained, "seems to foster the disciplining, self-propelling, competitive-productive elements of this spirit in a streamlined and politically controlled form." Capitalist states proved less overt in their discipline, according to the author, but they effectively repressed human freedom by organizing life around constant labor, rather than natural sexual instinct (Eros).[116]

Communism and capitalism, according to this analysis, produced the same human chains. Marcuse argued that although other thinkers had observed this phenomenon, they had failed to offer a viable alternative for society in the twentieth century. In his writing and activism Marcuse set out to blend theory and practice, reaching across national boundaries in America, Europe, and parts of Asia to build resistance against established political institutions. Critical theory, in this context, provided a vocabulary for diverse protests. It made Marcuse into an internationally renowned celebrity, especially among young readers.

One-Dimensional Man, published in 1964, catapulted its author to stardom. Marcuse's language managed to simplify many complex and diverse developments. In contrast to his earlier writings and those of other critical theorists, Marcuse designed his text to be easily readable. Citizens in different parts of the world could readily understand the book's message because it used recognizable concepts, rather than the pedantic philosophical language usually employed in works of this sort.

The author laced *One-Dimensional Man* with references to the American, European, and even Soviet dissident voices of the early 1960s. In addition to John Kenneth Galbraith's exposition on the "affluent society" and Daniel Bell's ruminations on the "end of ideology," Marcuse merged radical sociologist C. Wright Mills's concept of the "power elite," French existentialism, and criticism of the "new class" of communist bureaucrats with ideas rooted in the tradition of critical theory.[117] The language of dissent employed by Marcuse, more than the classical texts of Western philosophy, circulated widely among young readers during the period. One journalist reported in the second half of the 1960s that the students he surveyed had never read Max Weber, John Dewey, or John Stuart Mill; very few had read Lenin, Trotsky, or Marx. Almost all, however, had read some of C. Wright Mills, French existentialist Albert Camus, and, most popular of all, Herbert Marcuse. Connecting his analysis to an already emergent dissident framework of discussion, Marcuse produced a grand synthesis, focusing diverse thoughts among readers.[118]

One-Dimensional Man proclaimed that the most powerful states—those pursuing industrial "progress" in one form or another—exploited pressures for production, administration, and national defense to create new instruments of domination. The "rational" arguments made by leaders for preserving existing institutions of governance turned technology and science against the human hope for liberation from danger. "The industrial society," Marcuse wrote, "is organized for the ever-more-effective domination of man and nature, for the ever-more-effective utilization of its resources." Each life had become a "means" for manipulation by state policy rather than a respected "end" in itself. Echoing the words of his early academic mentor, Martin Heidegger, Marcuse lamented the "instrumentalization of things." In a world of nuclear weapons, sophisticated machines, and vast institutions for human administration, technical progress "turns into a fetter of liberation; the instrumentalization of man."[119]

Aggregate wealth and stability in industrial societies had, according to Marcuse, come at the cost of personal freedom in family and community. The state was everywhere, "containing" rather than enabling new experiments in individual living. The expanding arms of government administration had "invaded the inner space of privacy and practically eliminated the possibility of that isolation in which the individual, thrown back on himself alone, can think and question and find. This sort of privacy—the sole condition that, on the basis of satisfied vital needs, can give meaning to freedom and independence of thought—has long since become the most expensive commodity available to the very rich (who don't use it)."[120]

Marcuse argued that society—West and East—had become dangerously homogeneous. Drawing on the imagery of Thomas Hobbes's *Leviathan*, he wrote that the imperatives of economic production and national defense allowed governing authorities to exclude alternative modes of behavior from everyday language. Continuous diversion of human energy from personal reflection acquired the label of "progress." Proliferating military dangers were defined as sources of "peace." Lacking the space for personal privacy and the capabilities for self-reliance, "People depend for their living on bosses and politicians and jobs and neighbors who make them speak and mean as they do . . . In speaking their own language, people also speak the language of their masters, benefactors, advertisers."[121]

This was not a new phenomenon. Marcuse contended that the growth of state power had made the restrictions on free speech more onerous than ever before, even in democratic societies. Competitive international pressures interacted with the new mechanisms of mass communication—in particular television advertising—to silence alternative visions of social order. What Marcuse called the consistent "mystification" of industrial production and state administration enforced "frozen relationships among men." Instead of functioning as independent thinkers, the educated population in each state became "one huge captive audience."[122]

Citizens could, at least in Western Europe and the United States, debate the relative merits of communist and capitalist organization. Marcuse argued, however, that even the most democratic societies lacked the basic vocabulary to imagine alternatives in place of this bipolar Cold War framework. The communist-capitalist debate framed political discussions, restricting thought to the shared assumptions of both systems: consistent mobilization of society's resources and continuous expansion of state authority.[123]

Marcuse perceived the repressive tendencies of contemporary society as particularly resistant to change. In a competitive international system with growing domestic needs, old and new industrial societies could not turn back the clock. Daily survival seemed to demand ever more adherence to the assumptions of "progress" that protected basic social order and economic sustenance. In terms reminiscent of Michael Harrington's *Other America*, the critical theorist argued that citizens in the United States, Europe, and Asia confronted a truly "vicious circle" of limited horizons.[124]

Marcuse's diagnosis of contemporary repression broke new ground in its ability to connect circumstances across very different societies. The analysis, however, proved somewhat shallow in its prescriptions for popular liberation. Marcuse's early writings had emphasized the importance of creating alternative social settings for human love and sexual instinct. In *One-Dimensional Man* he also advocated "pacification" rather than further industrialization. Seeking to turn social energies away from weapons production, material accumulation, and the expansion of state authority, Marcuse envisioned a world in which technology would support human leisure, not competitive toil.[125]

A culturally rich population would replace the one-dimensional men of the twentieth century when society truly fostered the "free development of human needs and faculties." In Marcuse's utopia, technology would find use in abolishing poverty, not in extending the risks of destruction. "Socially necessary labor would be diverted to the construction of an aesthetic rather than repressive environment, to parks and gardens rather than highways and parking lots, to the creation of areas of withdrawal."[126]

True freedom required a "Great Refusal"—"protest against that which is." Marcuse called upon his readers to reject all accommodation to the continued demands of technological "progress." Instead of building more machines, he advocated that citizens return to the neglected world of art—in particular, literature—where "higher culture" could rejuvenate the "autonomous personality," the "humanism," and the "tragic and romantic love" lost in contemporary civilization. Using Thomas Mann, Johann Wolfgang von Goethe, Gustave Flaubert, and Honoré de Balzac as his models, Marcuse explained that profound works of literature created an alternative reality that, in language and image, challenged existing assumptions about society. Art allowed for a reconstruction of reality and a reassertion of individuality. In his later writings, Marcuse referred to pensive literature, music, and painting as touchstones for the "radical imagination" which individuals must force a shallow society to "remember."[127]

This appeal to art as a salvation for the human spirit attracted young readers while it contradicted the very sentiment that had brought more men and women into universities during the 1960s. James Conant and others had expanded educational institutions in order to bridge the "two cultures" of art and science. They had hoped to build a more technically productive mass citizenry. Marcuse demanded just the opposite. The corruption of literature by "technological thinking" harmfully narrowed the range of human experience, according to Marcuse. Independent artistic evaluations of society provided the necessary material for probing the human soul. With the merger of science and art, Marcuse predicted that the pressures for "useful" products would narrow the personality of the individual. Society needed more artists who refused to follow state demands. Otherwise, human relations would descend to a "common denominator" in which "commodities" replaced thought and creativity.[128]

In the years after the publication of *One-Dimensional Man*, the author became more specific about who would lead the Great Refusal he advocated. In addition to artists and writers, Marcuse associated himself with antiwar protesters in America and Europe. Student rebels appeared to constitute an educational shock force that would reestablish humanistic concerns in a depraved world civilization.[129] Looking also to those who suffered from what he called "historical backwardness," Marcuse glorified revolutionaries in Vietnam, the Congo, and other areas who could perhaps succeed in "turning the wheel of progress to another direction." Authentic rebellion—like the most profound works of art—would demonstrate an alternative reality for the citizens of capitalist and communist societies. "Technical and scientific overdevelopment," Marcuse wrote in 1966, "stands refuted when the radar-equipped bombers, the chemicals, and the 'special forces' of the affluent society are let loose on the poorest of the earth, on their shacks, hospitals, and rice fields. The 'accidents' reveal the substance: they tear the technological veil behind which the real powers are hiding."[130]

Marcuse grouped civil rights activists in the United States with third world revolutionaries. He argued that these "rebels" could inspire the active, sometimes violent Great Refusal necessary within the dominant states. "The spread of guerrilla warfare at the height of the technological century" was "a symbolic event: the energy of the human body rebels against intolerable repression and throws itself against the engines of repression."[131]

Marcuse's diagnosis of "one-dimensional man" and his advocacy of the Great Refusal made the German émigré philosopher the "celebrated mentor" of protesters throughout America and Europe. He often differed with the strategies of his readers, but Marcuse provided a framework for dissidents to envision their behavior in international terms. Influenced by *One-Dimensional Man*, many men and women believed they were part of a shared struggle to reclaim human culture from the clutches of political destruction.[132]

Accumulating ever more dissident voices in his writings, Marcuse formulated a common language for a global Great Refusal, especially among the young. In West Germany one of the most influential student leaders of the decade, Rudi Dutschke, adopted Marcuse's analysis in his criticism of the allegedly repressive "formed society" that managed Cold War politics. Dutschke drew on Marcuse to justify "external pressures" on established institutions of authority.[133]

Among American students Marcuse also became a revered figure. One former activist recalls that *One-Dimensional Man* revealed "the magnitude of what we were up against" and "our helplessness": "Impossible and necessary: that is how we felt about our task."[134]

Marcuse's language, like rock-and-roll music, became an incredibly popular antidote to the political rhetoric that alienated many young citizens. Marcuse and rock bands—especially the Beatles—were synthesizers on a grand scale.[135] They brought a series of diverse dissident sounds together, producing a startling effect on an audience already poised for something new. The German-Jewish philosopher quickly became a most unlikely celebrity, drawing crowds that strangely resembled excited music fans. "On Friday evening a few years ago," one contemporary recalled, "I was standing in the midst of a noisy, happy crowd of students in an auditorium at Brandeis [University], waiting for a concert to begin, when word suddenly came up the line: Marcuse's here!"

> At once there was a hush, and people divided themselves up to clear a path. A tall, erect, vividly forceful man passed down the aisle, smiling here and there to friends, radiant yet curiously aloof, rather like an aristocrat who was a popular hero as well . . . The students held their breaths and gazed at him with awe. After he had got to his seat, they relaxed again, flux and chaos returned, but only for a moment, till everyone could find his place; it was as if Marcuse's very presence had given a structure to events.[136]

Marcuse knew very little about China, and even less about Vietnam, Cuba, and other parts of the third world. After the publication of *One-Dimensional Man*, however, he began to search for the Great Refusal in these unfamiliar areas. Marcuse's writing highlighted how resilient both capitalist and communist societies had become in resisting internal reform. Anxious to offer his readers a hopeful message, Marcuse's eyes wandered eastward, where violence in the less industrialized societies seemed to offer the most impressive spark for fundamental change in the international system.

"In Vietnam, in Cuba, in China," he wrote, "a revolution is being defended and driven forward which struggles to eschew the bureaucratic administration of socialism. The guerrilla forces in Latin America seem to be animated by that same subversive impulse: liberation." Marcuse recognized that resistance to American and Soviet influence by allegedly "weaker" populations could inspire something akin to a global revolt. Events in 1968 offered preliminary evidence for this nascent Great Refusal across diverse societies. Marcuse described what he perceived as the "genuine solidarity" among "young radicals" who drew their "elemental, instinctual, creative force" from guerrilla fighters in the third world and the Chinese Cultural Revolution.[137]

The murderous consequences of American military activity in Vietnam demonstrated the bankruptcy of the most advanced industrial society, according to Marcuse. The Cultural Revolution in China, however, promised "liberation" from the assumptions about technological "progress" that drew the author's most trenchant condemnations. Observing how Mao Zedong encouraged students to "reeducate" the bureaucrats who administered the state, Marcuse praised the evident "break in the unity of the communist orbit." Mao—like Che Guevara and Fidel Castro in Cuba—appeared to reject the "collaborationist" Soviet-American "community of interests" that placed the people of the world under the control of nuclear weapons, complex machines, and bloated state governments.[138]

Marcuse understood that the arbitrary violence of the Cultural Revolution did not constitute his envisioned utopia. The upheavals in China nonetheless offered a "concrete alternative" to the status quo, the possibility of a "new society." Marcuse saw in the Cultural Revolution an effort, led by Mao, "to construct socialism by developing and creating a genuine solidarity between the leadership and the liberated victims of exploitation." Instead of a dominant bureaucracy, government would now have an assertive "popular base."[139]

Anxious to break out of the political structures that held "one-dimensional man," Marcuse and many of his followers in America and Europe became enthralled with the illusory image of Chairman Mao. In the late 1960s the Chinese leader seemed to represent the opposite of everything that supported advanced industrial society. Mao's calls for near anarchy blatantly contradicted the demands for international stability and patient reform voiced by other leaders. Mao's revolution appeared as the closest thing to a genuine remaking of society along the lines of youthful instinct.

Marcuse and his followers rarely spoke of what the Chinese Cultural Revolution had accomplished because they knew too little. They recognized the disorder, the dislocation, and the violence, but they also admired the promise of a "new society." Desperate for hope and ignorant of detail, activists in the West found in Mao an icon for the more instinctual and individualistic society they desired—even though the Chinese reality thoroughly departed from this aspiration. "The new radicalism," Marcuse wrote, "militates against the centralized bureaucratic communist as well as against the semi-democratic liberal organization."

> There is a strong element of spontaneity, even anarchism, in this rebellion . . . [and] sensitivity against domination: the feeling, the awareness, that the joy of freedom and the need to be free must precede liberation. Therefore the aversion against preestablished leaders, apparatchiks of all sorts, politicians no matter how leftist. The initiative shifts to small groups, widely diffused, with a high degree of autonomy, mobility, flexibility.[140]

During the late 1960s dissident voices throughout the United States, Europe, and Asia came together in various "small groups" to create widespread havoc. Marcuse, internationally recognized by this time, provided a common anthem for what the CIA called the "world-wide phenomenon" of "restless youth." An expanded cohort of students in nearly every society adopted a "truly radical concept of industrial society." "Revolutionary heroes"—in particular Mao Zedong—offered an inspiration for action as men and women put dissident language into practice on countless city streets.[141]

The domestic unrest of the 1960s grew from different social conditions in every state. An examination of local particularities does not, however, explain how a "world-wide phenomenon" of "restless youth" took shape through the decade. The growth in the youthful population and the expansion of educational institutions during the early 1960s provided the *infrastructure* for dissent in each of the great powers. Exposed to new ideas in crowded settings where they could interact and organize informally, students in universities, high schools, and even lower schools were an easy cohort to mobilize in protest. If young men and women had been more scattered, less numerous, less literate, and less free of military discipline one can easily imagine a decade without such widespread upheaval.

Demographic and institutional expansion throughout the 1960s ran against the tightening international stalemate. Many educated men and women wanted to play an active and immediate role in policy change, along the lines promised by the Cold War rhetoric of "new frontiers," "communist construction," national *"grandeur,"* and "great leaps." When leaders who had learned the difficulty of implementing these simplistic ideas prudently restrained citizen expectations, popular enthusiasm turned to anger, cynicism, and violent resentment.

The *language* of dissent emerged in this environment. A diverse group of polemicists offered biting criticisms of political elites for failing to fulfill domestic promises and accomplish national goals. Dissidents across countries had very different grievances, but they articulated a similar disillusion with Cold War rhetoric that ignored the changed diplomatic and social conditions of the 1960s. Michael Harrington, Aleksandr Solzhenitsyn, Wu Han, and Herbert Marcuse did not create the unrest of the 1960s. They provided dissatisfied citizens with a new vocabulary for articulating and acting out their anguish.

Recognizing these conditions, Kennedy, Khrushchev, de Gaulle, and Mao attempted to exploit dissident language. Heretics served a useful purpose in the early 1960s—shaking up conservative institutions, purging threatening members of the "old guard," and inspiring new creativity. This explains, at least in part, why critics were initially allowed to publish in censored societies such as the Soviet Union and China.

By the middle of the decade, however, the dissident language became too heretical for government leaders to tolerate. As critics proliferated they encountered growing opposition from the political center in each state. Mao Zedong is the notable exception to this trend. While he persecuted dissident figures like Wu Han, the chairman used the Cultural Revolution to "kidnap" social ferment in China and to increase his personal authority at the expense of the Communist Party.

Mao's posture as a rebel in command of a state made the chaos on the mainland profoundly perplexing to participants and observers alike. Historians (including this one) still have trouble making sense of the Cultural Revolution. Placing the disruptive impulses of the 1960s in a larger international context does not equate events in China with those elsewhere. Instead, a broad perspective reveals that each of the great powers experienced the gestation of influential dissident forces early in the decade. Domestic unrest had an international dimension that preceded the Cultural Revolution as well as the Vietnam War and the global disruption of 1968.

John F. Kennedy speaking at the University of Wisconsin–Madison, 1960.
(University of Wisconsin–Madison Archives)

Nikita Khrushchev and Fidel Castro at the United Nations, 1960.
(Hank Walker/TimePix)

Charles de Gaulle waving to a crowd, 1960. *(Jon Brenneis/TimePix)*

Willy Brandt standing in front of the Brandenburg Gate and the no-man's land separating East and West Berlin. The sign behind Brandt reads: "Attention! You are now leaving West Berlin." *(Robert Lackenbach/TimePix)*

Mario Savio addressing a student rally in Berkeley, 1965. *(Bill Ray/TimePix)*

Lyndon Johnson and Walt Rostow consult on the grounds of the White House, 1967. *(LBJ Library Photo by Yoichi Okamoto)*

A student bookstore displaying the common idealization of Che Guevara and other "guerrilla" revolutionaries during the 1960s.
(University of Wisconsin–Madison Archives)

Students at the University of Wisconsin confront riot police.
(University of Wisconsin–Madison Archives)

Chinese Red Guards waving their "little red books." *(Co Rentmeester/TimePix)*

Above:
President Johnson and his staff watch television reports of Martin Luther King Jr.'s assassination, April 1968. *(LBJ Library Photo by Mike Geissinger)*

Above right:
Workers and students marching in Paris, May 1968.
(Henri Cartier-Bresson/Magnum Photos)

Below right:
Citizens of Prague confront invading Warsaw Pact troops, August 1968.
(Josef Koudelka/Magnum Photos)

Richard Nixon and Mao Zedong shake hands, February 1972.
(Richard Nixon Library and Birthplace)

Richard Nixon and his wife, Pat, share a laugh with Zhou Enlai, February
1972. *(Richard Nixon Library and Birthplace)*

Richard Nixon and Leonid Brezhnev share a toast at the Moscow Summit, May
1972. *(Richard Nixon Library and Birthplace)*

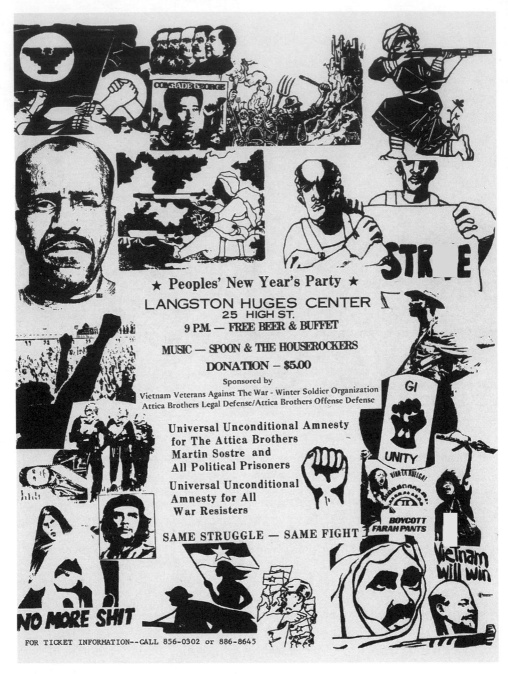

A poster employing the "urban guerrilla" imagery of the 1960s to encourage attendance at a "Peoples' New Year's Party." *(Wisconsin Historical Society)*

4

THE ILLIBERAL CONSEQUENCES
OF LIBERAL EMPIRE

Liberal democracies rarely fight wars with one another. The respect for individual freedoms, the "norms" of peaceful conflict resolution, and the divided domestic powers that characterize liberal democracy predispose these states to seek compromise, rather than armed conflict, with similar counterparts. Liberal democracies are not pacifist, but they are biased to peaceful change by broad consensus.[1]

Despite their tendency to avoid war with one another, liberal democratic nations frequently seek conflict with illiberal adversaries. This is the dark side of the "liberal peace"—what one scholar calls "liberal imprudence." In the eyes of democratic statesmen, "fellow liberals benefit from a presumption of amity; nonliberals suffer from a presumption of enmity." Two liberal democratic leaders can identify with one another, at least in terms of basic political values. Relations between democrats and dictators are more often filled with misunderstanding and distrust.[2]

In the so-called third world the sources of "liberal peace" have often encouraged "liberal imperialism." Assumptions about good governance and economic development have mixed with racism to produce policies that neglect local particularities. Attempting to remake the "underdeveloped" areas of the world in their own image, liberal democrats have elicited animosities that resemble the criticisms of less well-intentioned imperialists. Nationalists, in particular, have condemned the meddling of self-proclaimed do-gooders from abroad. Liberal empires are distinctive in their attempts to foster *mutually beneficial* economic and political development, but they are similar to illiberal alternatives in the resistance they inspire.[3]

All empires confront resistance at some point. The difference between the American liberal empire and its predecessors is the *degree* to which Americans really thought they were improving the rest of the world. Elements of this "civilizing mission" infused earlier empires, but not to the same extent as in the United States. Liberal faith in individual rights and market relations was at the core of America's expansion overseas. Even critics who have pointed to the self-interest and hypocrisy of U.S. imperial activity have also noted the powerful influence of liberal ideology.[4]

Throughout the twentieth century America consistently allied itself with liberal democratic states, especially in Europe. The nation also engaged in a series of armed conflicts against the preeminent illiberal countries—late Wilhelmine Germany, Nazi Germany, Fascist Italy, Imperial Japan, and, of course, the Communist Soviet Union. The strongest exponents of America's confrontation with these enemies were, not coincidentally, the most eloquent liberal spokesmen. Woodrow Wilson, Franklin Roosevelt, and John Kennedy championed the cause of individual liberty and external intervention in the very same breath. They represented what one scholar calls the "crusading" strain in American thought. Peace-loving liberals advocated far-reaching uses of military force to make the world "safe for democracy."[5]

The United States found few liberal democrats in Latin America, Africa, and Asia after World War II. Decades of colonial exploitation, widespread poverty, and broad social dislocation denied the basic conditions for stable democratic development in these areas. Apprehensive about the attractiveness of communism and other illiberal ideologies, the United States attempted to balance support for local anticommunists with encouragement for liberal reforms. Washington pursued a series of "reformist interventions." Centralizing power in the hands of a few local figures, U.S. policymakers hoped that their chosen allies could ensure stability and economic growth in former colonial territories. "Democratization" would follow, in the long run.[6]

Washington's attempts to liberalize illiberal areas produced decidedly mixed results. The world surely would have become a less democratic place if the United States had not intervened directly in Western Europe, Japan, and other areas during the twentieth century. The horrors of American participation in the Vietnam War, however, tend to overshadow the accomplishments of liberal nation-building elsewhere.

During the three decades after World War II, the United States, the Soviet Union, and the People's Republic of China escalated their military, economic, and political commitments in Southeast Asia. These states did not act to defend clearly defined national interests. Instead, they asserted their ideological leadership in what appeared to be an open space—a "new frontier," in the words of John F. Kennedy. The nations emerging from European colonial domination in Southeast Asia offered, according to American secretary of state Dean Acheson, a "blank sheet of paper, a white page on which the future [is] to be written."[7]

Leaders in Washington, Moscow, and Beijing wanted to show that they had the best ideas to fill in the open spaces. All three states criticized the legacy of imperialism in the third world, and each pledged to stand up for the rights of formerly exploited peoples. The United States advocated "self-determination." The Soviet Union employed Marxist terminology, proclaiming its commitment to "national liberation" from the chains of international capitalism. The People's Republic of China called for an Asian "intermediate zone" that would assure independence against intruders from the West.

Neither Washington, nor Moscow, nor Beijing had any particular interest in Vietnam. Leaders in each state were drawn to the area by the potential it offered for foreign initiative, especially during a period of international stalemate. Reconstructing a former colonial territory as a "modern" society— liberal-capitalist or communist—was a goal of policymakers looking for a place where they could safely implement it. Vietnam served this role because of its apparent isolation from the most dangerous areas of superpower confrontation. Contrary to the ambitions of many leaders, however, intervention in Vietnam only furthered international stalemate and the dangers of superpower confrontation.

A decade after the French retreated from the Indochinese peninsula in 1954, Charles de Gaulle recognized that Washington, Moscow, and Beijing all wished to cut their mounting losses in the region. When the French leader encouraged his counterparts to withdraw, he learned that each was afraid to vacate the area before the others. Instead, the great powers continued to follow a costly path of increased support for local belligerents, fearful that any change of policy would delegitimize their larger ideological claims. In this sense, the war in Vietnam followed the same dynamic as the nuclear arms race. The superpowers spent more for less in return. In their attempts to break out of a stalemated Cold War world, the most powerful states extended their stalemate to Southeast Asia.[8]

Discontent with the international status quo led the United States to pursue its liberal vision in a most inhospitable setting. The nation's commitments in Vietnam grew in deliberate response to the military, administrative, and alliance constraints of the period. By the middle of the 1960s events in Indochina clouded perceptions of the U.S. government at home and around the world. Domestic critics who had demanded a more principled foreign policy condemned the American government for becoming embroiled in a military quagmire. Among allies, Washington's calls for assistance in Vietnam inspired resistance to America's international leadership.

The foremost advocate of liberal democracy had apparently become, in the words of some of its own citizens and allies, the worst "imperialist."[9]

The difficulties for the Soviet Union and China took a different form. American military activity in Vietnam confirmed Leninist assumptions about "capitalist imperialism." The opportunity for "anticapitalist" resistance in Southeast Asia, however, increased the distrust between Moscow and Beijing. Each feared that the other would use its assistance to North Vietnam for the purpose of establishing dominant influence in the region. Never during the 1960s did the two communist states collaborate as closely as they had during the Korean War a decade earlier. Assistance to North Vietnamese forces exacerbated the growing rivalry between Moscow and Beijing. Ho Chi Minh encouraged competition between the Soviet Union and China by demanding that each patron exceed the other's pledges of support. Competitive bidding of this sort made Vietnam a proxy war for domination of the communist world. Leaders in Moscow and Beijing intervened in the region to bolster their respectability as revolutionaries, but their rivalry further imperiled their credentials.[10]

Vietnam became a self-defeating venture for all foreign participants. It was a trap for the most powerful states, especially the United States. A total of 58,193 Americans died in Vietnam (this number pales in comparison to the millions of Vietnamese who died from war). Well-intentioned American efforts to foster "development" and "democracy" in Vietnam triggered upheaval within the most developed democratic state. The nation's failures left a deep scar on its psyche, shattering much of the optimism that underlay its liberal vision. America's liberal pursuits in a tiny part of the globe undermined democracy and liberalism around the world.[11]

▪ The Origins of American Intervention in Vietnam

World War II united many divergent groups in Asia against the menace of Japanese militarism. Ho Chi Minh, who had petitioned for Vietnamese independence from French rule as early as 1919, collaborated after 1942 with allied resistance to the Japanese. Ho was a communist, but he understood that he could appropriate the rhetoric of "self-determination" and "democracy" for the purpose of combating Japan and creating an independent Vietnamese state.[12]

Despite their criticisms of colonialism, many Americans shared the racism and imperial condescension evident in London and Paris. Ho Chi Minh's communism contributed to the American government's apprehensions about Vietnamese "immaturity." It also convinced a number of influential policymakers that France should retain temporary control of the region. In 1947 Secretary of State George Marshall explained that Washington must "not lose sight [of the] fact that Ho Chi Minh has direct Communist connections . . . it should be obvious that we are not interested in seeing colonial empire administrations supplanted by [the] philosophy and political organizations emanating from and controlled by [the] Kremlin."[13]

The Korean War pushed the United States to transform its largely informal influence in Asia into more direct intervention. When North Korean soldiers—assisted by the Soviet Union and Communist China—invaded South Korea on 25 June 1950, Ho's forces launched an attack on French positions in Indochina. Fearful of communist advances, the Truman administration expanded its assistance to the French, increasing aid by the following year from $10 million to $107 million. Washington's mission in Indochina retained its official noncombatant status, but the United States now offered high-level advice and military training to French and anticommunist Vietnamese soldiers. The Truman administration's commitments after the Korean War engaged American credibility and prestige with the fate of Indochina as never before. The threat of Soviet and Chinese-supported incursions in Southeast Asia was very real in the early 1950s. The alleged danger of "losing" the region to communism, however, reflected Washington's fears more than actual conditions.[14]

Perceptions of Vietnam as a test of firmness became self-fulfilling. Each time a president increased America's commitment in Vietnam as proof of the nation's anticommunist resolve, enemy advances challenged Washington's claims. This tragic dynamic of self-fulfilling dangers drove American intervention in the Vietnamese civil war during the 1950s and 1960s. A more sophisticated understanding of economics and geopolitics—like that offered by many contemporary critics—would not have created quite the same quagmire for Truman's successors.[15]

President Dwight Eisenhower redoubled American efforts to contain communism, bankrolling as much as 80 percent of French costs in Vietnam. Despite U.S. aid, French forces never gained the initiative over Ho Chi Minh's independence movement. The village of Dien Bien Phu became the site of a prolonged siege that marked France's last stand in Indochina, and the beginning of America's direct military commitment in Paris' place. During May 1954 Ho's army at Dien Bien Phu defeated the heart of the French military, leveling a knockout blow against European colonial power.[16]

At this very moment the great powers met, by prior arrangement, for deliberations on the future of Asia. The Geneva Conference began on 26 April 1954, cochaired by Great Britain and the Soviet Union. France and China also attended, along with delegates from Cambodia, Laos, Ho Chi Minh's Democratic Republic of Vietnam, and the American-supported State of Vietnam. The United States participated in the conference, but only as an "interested party." The Eisenhower administration wanted to avoid any implied recognition of the Chinese or Vietnamese communists present for the discussions.

Following his stunning victory against the French at Dien Bien Phu, Ho Chi Minh was poised to take full control of Vietnam. This had been Mao Zedong's promise months earlier. At Geneva, however, all the great powers sought to preserve stability in Indochina and the region as a whole. China joined the Soviet Union, the United States, France, and Britain in endorsing a division of Vietnam at the Seventeenth Parallel. Ho's government would control the North, and the regime of Emperor Bao Dai would rule in the South. The Final Declaration of the Geneva Conference prohibited "the introduction into Vietnam of foreign troops and military personnel as well as . . . all kinds of arms and munitions." All-Vietnam elections would occur in July 1956, according to the terms agreed upon by the great powers.[17]

China, the Soviet Union, and the United States pressured their respective allies in Vietnam to accept the terms of settlement, but not the prohibitions on external military aid. China provided Ho with food, labor, technical aid, and a grant of 800 million yuan ($200 million) in 1955. The Soviet Union gave Ho's regime 400 million rubles ($100 million) in the same year, along with various agreements on technical assistance, trading privileges, and personnel exchanges.[18]

Eisenhower similarly worked to fortify the government in the South. At his urging, Bao Dai appointed Ngo Dinh Diem as prime minister. A devout Catholic with ties to many prominent Americans—including Montana senator Mike Mansfield and the Kennedy family—Diem quickly became the Vietnamese equivalent of Syngman Rhee and Chiang Kai-shek. Authoritarian anticommunists, these men received extensive military support from the Eisenhower administration as stalwarts against communist aggression in Asia. They built centralized states and nascent market economies, but they failed to carry out many of the democratic measures that Washington urged—especially land reform.[19]

America's military commitment to South Vietnam gave Diem enormous leverage over his patrons. On a number of occasions Eisenhower considered dumping Diem, but, as in South Korea and Taiwan, no more reliable anticommunist appeared on the scene. In October 1955 Diem used a rigged ref-

erendum to depose Bao Dai and declare himself "chief of state." In 1956
Diem refused to hold the all-Vietnam elections promised under the Final
Declaration in Geneva. By the end of the decade Diem's family ruled almost
exclusively over the people of South Vietnam, executing opponents at will.

Eisenhower remained committed to Diem for the sake of containing communism. The president sought to accomplish this end with direct military
assistance but minimal loss of American lives. Washington's aid to the region
grew throughout the 1950s, including military equipment, army training,
and operational advice. In early 1961, however, fewer than 700 American
soldiers actually served in Vietnam. This was a policy of containment with
few immediate risks for the United States.[20]

▪ Kennedy's Liberal Vision in Vietnam

John F. Kennedy broadened Eisenhower's cautious commitment to Southeast Asia into a self-imposed ideological test. Vietnam offered what one historian calls an "insidious temptation."[21] In this peripheral area, safe from direct nuclear conflict with the Soviet Union, the White House could display
its capacity for innovation. Here the United States would not simply accept
the status quo as it did in Europe and Cuba.

Vietnam promised to redeem the new frontier vision. It would provide an
injection of energy in a part of the world where the future battles of the Cold
War focused on the "hearts and minds" of former colonial subjects. Success
in Vietnam offered the Kennedy administration a rare chance to demonstrate its idealistic credentials to critics of Realpolitik. The American public
was ambivalent then, as during later years, regarding the merits of economic
and military intervention in South Vietnam. A widespread desire for political and social change, however, influenced deliberations in the White
House.[22]

Vietnam became an ideological testing ground not because of its intrinsic
qualities, but because it appeared—like the "space race"—available for Kennedy's purposes. If not in Indochina, the United States probably would have
fought a Vietnam War somewhere else at the time. In retrospect, members
of the Kennedy administration wished they had indeed pursued their new
frontier in another place.[23]

Kennedy's attitude toward Southeast Asia reflected, in part, the emergence
of the National Liberation Front for South Vietnam (NLF), often called the
Viet Cong. Founded on 19 December 1960, the NLF was an umbrella organi-

zation for insurgent groups opposed to Diem's government and American influence. It exploited nationalist sentiment to "rally all patriotic classes and sections of the people."[24]

The NLF received support from North Vietnam, China, and, to a smaller extent, the Soviet Union. At the same time, the rebel group carefully constructed an image of moderation. The "Ten Point Manifesto," issued by the NLF at the end of 1960, did not mention the word "communist" once. Instead, it called for the creation of a "national democratic coalition administration." The NLF pledged "to overthrow the disguised colonial regime of the U.S. imperialists and the dictatorial Ngo Dinh Diem." It would replace them with a government devoted to "land reform" for impoverished peasants, "equality between men and women," and "a foreign policy of peace and neutrality." In order to appear independent, the NLF did not demand immediate reunification between North and South Vietnam. Recognizing widespread fear of Ho Chi Minh's regime, it promised only "to work toward the peaceful reunification of the Fatherland."[25]

Despite this moderate rhetoric, the NLF was a communist organization intent on spreading the influence of Hanoi (and, indirectly, Beijing and Moscow). American observers often exaggerated the extent of external subversion in South Vietnam, but foreign communist parties certainly aided the rebellion against Diem. Neither the NLF nor its Southern opponents operated as an indigenous, grassroots force. By the early 1960s the United States, China, and the Soviet Union were deeply involved in a Vietnamese civil war.[26]

After a visit to Vietnam in early 1961, Assistant Secretary of Defense Edward Lansdale predicted "a fateful year." "The Communist Viet Cong," he explained, "hope to win back Vietnam south of the Seventeenth Parallel . . . Vietnam can be kept free, but it will require a changed U.S. attitude, plenty of hard work and patience, and a new spirit by the Vietnamese." President Kennedy authorized action along these lines. During his first week in the White House, he sent an additional $41 million aid package to Diem's government, funding a 20,000-soldier increase in the South Vietnamese army. The new administration also proposed to train and equip a South Vietnamese "Civil Guard."[27]

The president called for a more direct challenge to Ho Chi Minh's regime, including military attacks on North Vietnamese territory. Employing the same "guerrilla" tactics used by the enemy, the United States would now sponsor its own "guerrilla forces." Under "Operational Plan 34A" the American military dropped agents behind North Vietnamese lines, developed an internal resistance movement, and undertook a series of airborne and seaborne "destruction raids" above the Seventeenth Parallel. Covert operations were one element of what grew into a multifaceted "counterinsurgency" doctrine.[28]

Lansdale's ideas about counterinsurgency provided an early channel for the energy and drive of the Kennedy administration. Lansdale soon lost influence in the White House because of his eccentric personality, but a group of social scientists took up where he had left off. Trained in economics, systems management, and international relations, these academics now serving as government officials sought to integrate their desire for rapid change within a disciplined policy model. Counterinsurgency doctrine offered a framework for defeating communist enemies while sponsoring "modernization" and "development" overseas.[29]

Walt Rostow, an economist with long-standing connections to the foreign policy community, became the most influential architect of American counterinsurgency activities. He brought a coherent framework of analysis to affairs in Vietnam, emphasizing that economic development in the region—as in Western Europe after World War II—would provide the best insurance for anticommunist governance. Drawing from his widely read book, *The Stages of Economic Growth*, Rostow argued that Vietnam had reached the critical period of "take-off," when outside assistance and enforced order could guarantee a transition to rapid industrial growth. Increased American aid, through Diem's government, promised to promote the "definitive social, political, and cultural victory of those who would modernize the economy over those who would either cling to the traditional society or seek other goals."[30]

The analysis in *The Stages of Economic Growth* lacked any empirical basis in Vietnam. Kennedy's search for new initiatives, however, gave the model remarkable influence in the formulation of counterinsurgency doctrine. According to Rostow, the American-sponsored "take-off" in Southeast Asia would stabilize a "mature" capitalist society with heavy industry, large-scale agriculture, and organized labor. Social and economic achievement would be open to "modification," but not the radical shifts that could disrupt established patterns of healthy economic growth. The "mature" development that the United States hoped to sponsor in Vietnam was invested in building an affluent and muscular anticommunist state.[31]

Rostow's language quickly seeped into policy deliberations, replacing Eisenhower's emphasis on military containment with appeals to the "hearts and minds" of peasants in Southeast Asia. In May 1961 the president's interdepartmental task force on Vietnam proposed "A Program of Action to Prevent Communist Domination" in the area. Applying Rostow's model for extensive foreign assistance during the critical "take-off" transition, the task force argued that "the most effective means of establishing Vietnamese confidence in the political and economic future of their country would be for the United States to commit itself to a long range economic development program." The region would become a second Western Europe, with its own Marshall Plan. "Under peaceful circumstances," the task force asserted, Vietnam "would unquestionably be one of the most rapidly developing countries in the area." Diem's government required "a minimum of $50 million of U.S. development grant assistance." The money would go to industrial investments, infrastructural improvements, public administration, education, health services, and mechanized agriculture.[32]

NLF infiltration required the United States to provide more than just foreign aid for successful "take-off." South Vietnam needed increased security to thwart communist subversion of the development process. This is where counterinsurgency doctrine merged Rostow's economic model with the use of armed force. In January 1962 Kennedy created a "special group for counterinsurgency" to coordinate aid programs and military activities. Kennedy did not commit ground forces to combat at this time, but the United States deployed military resources as a "prophylaxis" for social and economic stability in Vietnam. This included a series of aerial "defoliant operations" that sprayed herbicides designed to expose and starve out NLF bases. Systematic deforestation and crop destruction in Southeast Asia began with the Kennedy administration and its hasty exploitation of destructive technology to assure "development."[33]

Adapting its economic model to the insecurities of the Vietnamese countryside, Washington set out to create a series of "strategic villages" (more commonly called "strategic hamlets") in place of traditional rural settlements. Roger Hilsman, then director of the State Department's Bureau of Intelligence and Research, produced a general outline for this program: "The struggle for South Vietnam, in sum, is essentially a battle for control of the villages." Calling for more than communist containment alone, Hilsman argued that "the struggle cannot be won merely by attempting to seal off South Vietnam from the North. It must be won by cutting the Viet Cong off from their local sources of strength."[34]

Hilsman formulated a three-part "strategic concept" for South Vietnam. First, American-supported forces had to deny "the Viet Cong's access to the villages and the people." Seeking to build the cohesion of the South Vietnamese state from the bottom up, Hilsman advised that the United States should tie the villages into a strengthened "network of government administration and control." Second, the United States had to assist the South Vietnamese government in smothering the terrorist activities of the NLF: "Physical security, coupled with controls on the movement of people and supplies, will protect the villagers from being intimidated into selling the Viet Cong rice and from being persuaded or intimidated into joining the Viet Cong." Third, "Counterguerrilla forces must adopt the tactics of the guerrilla himself." The United States should deploy "special forces" (including the "Green Berets," created by the Kennedy administration) to isolate the rural population from the NLF. "Mobility, surprise, and small unit operations are basic," Hilsman wrote. Anticommunist forces in the countryside "should be highly mobile, never sleeping twice in the same place, and patrolling and ambushing at will."[35]

The "strategic hamlets" at the core of Hilsman's program embodied the three-part "strategic concept." They operated as self-contained residential units protected by military force. In this sense, they were more like prisons than popular bases for economic growth and democratic development. Destroying loosely connected rural settlements, the United States created a feudal landscape that approximated the walled cities of medieval Europe. "Each strategic village," Hilsman explained, "will be protected by a ditch and a fence of barbed wire . . . It will include one or more observation towers, guard posts, and a defense post for central storage of arms . . . The area immediately around the village will be cleared for fields of fire and the area approaching the clearing, including the ditch, will be strewn with booby-traps (spikes, pits, explosives, etc.) and other personnel obstacles."[36]

Villagers in South Vietnam found themselves uprooted from their land, denied mobility, and virtually imprisoned in their homes. Under these circumstances, NLF calls for "liberation" naturally grew more attractive. In March 1962, when the strategic hamlets program began, only 70 of the first 205 Vietnamese families agreed to voluntary resettlement. South Vietnamese and American personnel used force to move the remaining 135 families. From the 205 families settled in the first strategic hamlet, only 120 adult males reported for village service. The remaining local male population fled to join the communist rebels, not because of any ideological predisposition, but because the NLF offered freedom from oppressive government controls.[37]

In 1962 and 1963 Vietnamese resistance to American counterinsurgency activities mounted. Kennedy, however, remained firmly committed to the interrelated programs that included strategic hamlets, defoliant spraying, and covert attacks on the North. Instead of rethinking his assumptions about economic development, the president continued to increase military and financial outlays to South Vietnam. In January 1961 America had fewer than 700 military personnel "in country," with limited resources. By late 1963 more than 16,000 troops from the U.S. Army, Navy, Air Force, and Marine Corps—as well as various intelligence agencies—flew helicopters, resettled villages, and penetrated NLF lines.[38]

The Kennedy administration saw no alternative to protect its vision of a prosperous, stable, anticommunist state in Southeast Asia. "Nation-building" in Vietnam became a symbol of America's redoubled energy, ingenuity, and determination. Washington's intervention in the region promised to make the new frontier a reality at limited cost. The United States would not "take over" in Southeast Asia, but would instead provide the necessary assistance to foster economic and political "take-off." In the early 1960s this became a process of destroying villages in order to save them.[39]

Thousands of South Vietnamese citizens condemned the brutality of American-sponsored "nation-building." In June 1963 a Buddhist monk, Thich Quang Duc, burned himself in public as a protest against Diem's repression of religious dissidents. Duc's self-immolation shocked viewers around the world. It displayed the depth of popular indignation toward the Saigon regime. Diem did not respond with a series of needed reforms, as Americans hoped. Instead, he increased the use of police force—including persecutions, arrests, and even public shootings. Under these circumstances, popular support for the communist insurgency grew throughout South Vietnam. American officials reported that urban professionals, intellectuals, and students "blamed" the United States for the corruption and repression under Diem.[40]

This observation frustrated the Kennedy administration. Why hadn't America's counterinsurgency programs produced favorable results? One could blame either the programs or their implementers. Almost unanimously, the president and his closest advisers condemned the latter. American attempts to foster development in South Vietnam could not possibly be flawed. After all, the assumptions about modernization and economic growth that underpinned the administration's policies had "scientific" support. They reflected the accumulated wisdom of extensive American thought and experience.[41]

The United States focused exclusively on Diem's failings. Kennedy hoped to reform his ally and to improve political conditions in Vietnam. If that failed, the administration would support a change in the Saigon government. Continued assistance to a corrupt regime threatened American goals at home and abroad. "We cannot stay in the middle much longer," Secretary of Defense Robert McNamara reported in October 1963. The time for decisive moves had come.[42]

Despite American pressures, Diem resisted domestic reforms. Henry Cabot Lodge, the U.S. ambassador to Saigon, conveyed the South Vietnamese leader's stubbornness to Washington. He reported that at a formal dinner Diem "attacked American activities in Vietnam." Instead of appealing to domestic and international public opinion, Diem wanted to expand the repression of his opponents. He demanded increased American aid, but he imposed strict limits on Washington's influence. Attempts to persuade the South Vietnamese leader otherwise became, in Lodge's words, "frustrating and long-drawn-out." Isolated and increasingly paranoid, Diem often responded to American requests with "a blank stare" or the exclamation "I will not give in!"[43]

Lodge judged that a military coup against Diem would salvage American hopes in Southeast Asia. Policymakers in Washington, however, expressed reservations. Diem was a frustrating ally but also a known commodity. A sudden change of regime raised a host of uncertainties. More important, policymakers worried about the consequences of a failed coup. NSC adviser McGeorge Bundy explained to Lodge that the United States did not want a foiled military takeover "laid at our door." That would turn international opinion against Washington. It might also push Diem to more rash and erratic behavior.[44]

Despite these apprehensions, in late October 1963 members of the Kennedy administration debated a change in South Vietnamese leadership. Robert Kennedy argued that "to support a coup would be putting the future of Vietnam and in fact all of Southeast Asia in the hands of one man not known to us before." Along with Chairman of the Joint Chiefs of Staff Maxwell Taylor and Director of Central Intelligence John McCone, he opposed any coup at this time. Secretary of State Dean Rusk and Undersecretary Averell Harriman supported a change of leadership. "If the Diem government continued," Rusk predicted, "the war effort would go down hill."[45]

President Kennedy appeared to side with Rusk and Harriman on the merits of a coup, but he doubted that the South Vietnamese generals could pull it off. Instead of instructing his ambassador to reject any proposals for a military takeover in Saigon, Kennedy discouraged a coup *only* if it appeared doomed to failure. In the case of probable success for the plotters, his position remained uncertain but not opposed: "The President said the burden of proof should be on the coup promoters to show that they can overthrow the Diem government and not create a situation in which there would be a draw . . . The President reiterated his suggestion that Lodge should tell the Generals that they must prove they can pull off a successful coup or, in our opinion, it would be a mistake to proceed."[46]

Lodge and the coup plotters in Saigon interpreted this message as a green light. On 1 November 1963 they moved against Diem's government. A desperate Diem telephoned the American ambassador to request assistance. Prepared for this moment, Lodge resolved to deny the deposed leader any immediate help. Disingenuously, the ambassador stated: "I do not feel well enough informed to be able to tell you [the attitude of the United States]. I have heard the shooting, but am not acquainted with all the facts. Also it is 4:30 A.M. in Washington and [the] U.S. Government cannot possibly have a view." Diem responded with disbelief: "You must have some general ideas. After all, I am a chief of state. I have tried to do my duty. I want to do now what duty and good sense require."[47]

At this point Lodge encouraged Diem to resign instead of fight. "I am worried about your physical safety," the ambassador cynically explained. Contradicting his claims of ignorance about the coup, Lodge revealed that "those in charge of the current activity offer you and your brother safe conduct out of the country if you resign. Have you heard this?" Diem recognized that he was doomed.[48]

By the next morning, the South Vietnamese army had deposed Diem and established a new government under the leadership of General Duong Van Minh ("Big Minh"). Various elements of the military voiced their support for the coup, and the civilian population in urban areas showed no serious signs of protest against the change in regime. The leader of the American Military Assistance Command in Vietnam, General Paul Harkins, sent a message to Washington advising that the United States must back the new government to assure unified action against communist forces. He warned of a "greater danger" if South Vietnam were "left without clear political and military leadership, for the Viet Cong will certainly move to exploit the resultant vacuum."[49]

The White House learned on the same morning that the coup plotters had murdered Diem and his brother Nhu. Kennedy's former advisers have reported on his visible "shock and dismay" at the news. The president, according to these accounts, never intended to condone such brutality. Events in Vietnam had begun to spiral out of control. Kennedy allegedly recognized that he had to act with a newfound caution.[50]

These accounts illustrate the Kennedy administration's penchant for self-delusion. The president did not worry about the moral and political implications of a coup. The documentary record reveals only a hesitation to endorse a military takeover that might fail to achieve its goals. Kennedy and his closest advisers approved the removal of Diem, so long as it occurred with speed and efficiency. Ambassador Lodge maneuvered to this end with the full knowledge of the White House.

Recovered from his alleged "shock," Kennedy wrote Lodge to praise him for "pulling together and directing the whole American operation in South Vietnam in recent months." The coup was "a Vietnamese effort," the president explained; "our own actions made it clear that we wanted improvements, and when these were not forthcoming from the Diem Government, we necessarily faced and accepted the possibility that our position might encourage a change of government." Having contributed directly to the military takeover, Kennedy admitted that "we thus have a responsibility to help this new government to be effective in every way that we can."[51]

The coup against Diem was a natural consequence of the new frontier and American counterinsurgency programs in Vietnam. It grew from a patchwork of Kennedy initiatives that connected reform ideals at home and abroad. The administration channeled its search for economic development and democratic change into a series of activities that included village relocation, crop defoliation, covert attacks, and a change in indigenous leadership.

This commitment to action instead of restraint on the periphery redeemed the new frontier spirit, but it also created a host of difficulties. Following Diem's death, South Vietnam suffered a series of coups that only deepened domestic turmoil in the region. The November coup contributed to a prolonged civil war within South Vietnam, continuing through the next decade.

After Kennedy's tragic assassination on 22 November 1963, the new American president, Lyndon Johnson, faced escalating Indochinese commitments. Kennedy's legacy connected the promises of political reform with counterinsurgency activities in an increasingly unstable region. The assassination of the president occurred as America had begun a steep descent toward more direct participation in South Vietnam's civil war. Despite his confidence that Kennedy would have altered U.S. policy if he had not died prematurely, Robert McNamara recounts how, after receiving news of the assassination, "we were in such shock that we simply did not know what to do. So, as best we could, we resumed our deliberations."[52] The trajectory of America's Vietnam policy did not change.

The pressures for a new frontier amidst deepening international stalemate made "victory" in Vietnam necessary for America's liberal self-image. Lyndon Johnson found himself in a position similar to that of Harry Truman. Promises of achievement against illiberal adversaries made violent action almost unavoidable. Truman dropped two atomic bombs on Japan to conclude Franklin Roosevelt's war against fascism. Johnson deployed more than 500,000 American soldiers in Vietnam to finish Kennedy's crusade for international liberal development. The dead presidents might have recoiled from the actions of their successors, but they created strong political and ideological biases for the escalating violence their defenders later condemned.

▪ Johnson's Liberal Vision in Vietnam

If Franklin Roosevelt provided the lodestar for liberalism in postwar America, no president had more liberal instincts than Lyndon Johnson. He did not need to read about poverty from Michael Harrington or listen to Martin Luther King Jr.'s sermons on the evils of racial discrimination to understand the urge for social reform in the 1960s. More than any other twentieth-century president, Johnson combined his overwhelming personal ambition with a profound commitment to help those less fortunate—those with a background similar to his own. The American activities Johnson inherited in Vietnam became a vital test for the New Deal legacy in the Cold War.[53]

Born on a farm in the Texas hill country, Johnson was a self-made man. He financed his own education at Southwest Texas State Teachers College and later taught elementary school to the children of poor farmers and Mexican laborers. Johnson began his political career in 1935 as the state director of the newly formed National Youth Administration (NYA), one of the New Deal agencies created to address the widespread suffering in America during the Great Depression. Relying on school aid programs, roadside construction projects, and behind-the-scenes efforts to aid African-American youths, Johnson's activities at the NYA illustrated how government could develop pragmatic programs for the down and out.[54]

This was the bright New Deal vision that Johnson carried with him as he left the NYA in 1937 for a long career in the U.S. House of Representatives and later the Senate. He worked tirelessly in Washington to transform federal offices into agents for development, aid, and public service. Faith in a broad welfare state occupied the center of Johnson's politics. He was never a compelling orator, a revolutionary thinker, or a grand strategist. He was, instead, a master manipulator who sought to make government do whatever necessary to improve the lives of his constituents. Civil rights activists who interacted with Johnson throughout his career attest to his remarkable compassion for the unfortunate. He left abstract debates about ideology, morality, and ethics to better-educated men with more privileged backgrounds.[55]

In attitude and experience Johnson was out of place in the Kennedy

White House, where the highly educated and privileged controlled the reins of power. As vice president he attended many high-level meetings, but historians have uncovered few instances when the Texan significantly influenced important administration policies. Johnson served primarily as the president's goodwill ambassador abroad, especially for countries in the third world. His eleven overseas trips in less than three years included Senegal, India, Pakistan, Taiwan, Thailand, the Philippines, Laos, and South Vietnam. Dispensing with diplomatic etiquette and reverting to his down-home Texas style, the vice president mingled with foreign crowds, shaking hands, hugging babies, and distributing pens and lighters inscribed with his initials.[56]

This was, according to one biographer, Johnson's way of displaying his deep belief in "American democratic habits."[57] He frequently remarked that the men and women he met in foreign crowds were just like his brethren in Texas. "The ordinary people need decent houses," Johnson reported. "They need schools. They need better conditions of health. They need the productive industries, the thriving agriculture and safe and adequate transportation and communications which will make all these things possible. They need an understanding government which is close to them and in which they feel a stake."[58]

Johnson saw foreign policy, like everything else, in New Deal terms: How could American activity overseas contribute to the spread of the welfare state, which guaranteed personal security, material comfort, and, ultimately, world peace? Communists were enemies not so much because of their ideology or strategic threat. They posed grave dangers when they distorted the New Deal welfare state with excessive militarism and policies that denied domestic development. Johnson equated communists with those "who would confiscate the farms of Texas and place Texas farmers under the lash of the commissar's whip."[59]

Johnson believed that the United States had to sponsor an international New Deal, bringing quality education, decent employment, and a functioning economy to those most in need. This was both domestic and foreign policy. It focused on the disadvantaged whom Johnson had seen firsthand at home and abroad. Despite extensive travels, his vision carried a condescending assumption of American superiority, coupled with a profound ignorance of foreign cultures. Johnson understood poverty in international terms, but he knew little about non-American peoples beyond their material deprivations.

The vice president brought this worldview to South Vietnam in May 1961. During the long flight from Washington to Saigon, Arthur Goldschmidt—an old New Dealer who had become an economic specialist at the United Nations—briefed Johnson on a series of ambitious public works proposals. Goldschmidt described how a network of dams built at the mouth of the Mekong River could transform the social and economic landscape. A project of this sort would allow for industrial development and regional cooperation in Southeast Asia, modeled on the granddaddy of all New Deal public works, the Tennessee Valley Authority (TVA). Goldschmidt convinced Johnson that a similar Mekong River Delta project could guarantee Vietnam economic development instead of poverty and recurring conflict.[60]

In his report to Kennedy, the vice president called for increased American economic and military assistance to South Vietnam. He wrote that the "will" to undertake necessary human "improvements" existed in the region. "The effort to achieve them," however, was "frustrated and disrupted by the agents of terrorism as well as by the ever-present shadow of the massive communist armed forces in North Viet Nam." American grants and weapons would play a vital role, ensuring the necessary "mutual security" for development in the South. Without increased assistance, Johnson predicted that "the great efforts and sacrifices, the vast amounts of aid which have poured into this country in the interests of peace and security may go down the drain." Such a setback would damage the energetic image of the new frontier and contradict the hopeful promise of an international New Deal. Johnson's determination to fulfill "FDR's mission" only grew during his years on the sidelines of the Kennedy administration.[61]

When he emerged from his predecessor's shadow with a decisive electoral victory in November 1964, President Johnson returned with renewed gusto to his hopes for expanding the New Deal at home and abroad. On 15 March 1965 he gave his most memorable speech to a joint session of Congress. Following the violent confrontation between civil rights marchers and Alabama state troopers on 7 March, Johnson called on the nation to "make good the promise of America." Linking his proposed Voting Rights Act for African Americans with his earlier pledges to wage a "war on poverty" and construct a "great society," Johnson explained that he did not want to build "empires." Instead, he announced, "I want to be the president who educated young children to the wonders of their world."

> I want to be the president who helped to feed the hungry and to prepare them to be taxpayers instead of taxeaters. I want to be the president who helped the poor to find their own way and who protected the right of every citizen to vote in every election. I want to be the president who helped to

end hatred among his fellow men and who promoted love among the people of all races and all regions and all parties. I want to be the president who helped to end war among the brothers of this earth.[62]

Less than a month later, Johnson applied this same New Deal rhetoric to Vietnam and his plans for a Mekong River development project. Speaking at Johns Hopkins University on 7 April 1965, the president admitted that Vietnam "is far away from this quiet campus. We have no territory there, nor do we seek any. The war is dirty and brutal and difficult. And some 400 young men, born into an America that is bursting with opportunity and promise, have ended their lives on Viet-Nam's steaming soil." From this somber observation Johnson went on to mouth the mantras of communist containment. The speech presented these familiar words with little emotion or rhetorical flourish.[63]

Johnson's presentation became more lively and heartfelt as he turned to what he called "our objective in Vietnam." The president announced that the United States would use its abundant resources to provide the region with peace and prosperity. Like poor Texans, he explained, the people of Vietnam "want what their neighbors also desire: food for their hunger, health for their bodies, a chance to learn, progress for their country; and an end to the bondage of material misery."[64]

The road to a better life in Southeast Asia, as elsewhere, would come only with struggle and sacrifice, according to Johnson. Military force served a vital purpose, protecting freedom and enterprise from communist saboteurs bent on disrupting the stages of human progress. Arms, however, provided only the foundation for what the president envisioned as the long-term "work of peace." He called upon the "countries of Southeast Asia," including North Vietnam, "to associate themselves in a greatly expanded cooperative effort for development." Drawing upon the precedent of the Marshall Plan in Europe, the president pledged a $1 billion investment in the region. "The task is nothing less than to enrich the hopes and the existence of more than a hundred million people."[65]

With these ringing words Johnson had only just begun to bask in his long-held vision of an international New Deal. "I also intend," he continued, "to expand and speed up a program to make available our farm surpluses and assist in feeding and clothing the needy in Asia. We should not allow people to go hungry and wear rags while our own warehouses overflow with an abundance of wheat and corn, rice and cotton."[66]

Self-consciously adopting Martin Luther King Jr.'s exhortation to "dream" about a better world, Johnson revealed how Vietnam fit within his plans for the future. He echoed the calls for renewed idealism advocated by New Left and New Right activists. "Our generation has a dream," the president announced. "It is a very old dream. But we have the power and now we have the opportunity to make that dream come true . . . For all existence most men have lived in poverty, threatened by hunger. But we dream of a world where all are fed and charged with hope. And we will help to make it so." Johnson argued that armed forces were necessary but also symbols of "failure": "They are witness to human folly." Government, he stated, should foster development among the poor, not war.[67]

The president closed with a call for action lifted from the words of university students in America and other nations at the time: "This generation of the world must choose: destroy or build, kill or aid, hate or understand. We can do all these things on a scale never dreamed of before . . . we will choose life . . . we will prevail over the enemies within man, and over the natural enemies of all mankind."[68]

None of Johnson's predecessors could have given this speech. It lacked the strategic wisdom of Eisenhower and the muscular eloquence of Kennedy. Instead, it possessed a depth of personal introspection rarely manifested in great-power politics. Johnson's words grew from his sincere urge to accomplish big things, expanding the New Deal agenda set out by Franklin Roosevelt.

This ambition had little to do with Vietnam, but as in the case of Kennedy's new frontier, the divided Southeast Asian nation provided an almost unavoidable testing ground. Johnson inherited a commitment to the region that dated from World War II. Current policies clearly had not worked. Withdrawal from the area had its strong proponents, but such a retreat would call the entire idea of an international New Deal into question. If America's overwhelming capabilities failed to improve the lives of Vietnamese citizens, how could the United States expect to succeed in other parts of the world? In this sense, Johnson did not fear extreme militarists who wanted to eliminate the prudent limits on American force in Southeast Asia.[69] He worried, as Roosevelt did, about those critics who sought to curtail the brightest promises offered by a compassionate government acting on behalf of the downtrodden.[70]

Liberal ideas did not make American intervention in the Vietnam War inevitable. Kennedy and Johnson had many opportunities to change course. The widespread desire for new initiatives that emphasized American capabilities and ideals—rather than the conservative restraints that characterized Eisenhower's policies—drove leaders in the 1960s to increase their commitments in Southeast Asia. The realists who rejected idealism and the racists who saw little value in helping "Orientals" were the earliest and most consistent opponents of U.S. activities in Vietnam. Liberals were much more divided, driven to use American power for good purpose overseas and horrified at the consequences.

Johnson had to win in Vietnam. Withdrawal without victory would smother the promise of an expanded New Deal in the 1960s. It would be the equivalent of closing down the Tennessee Valley Authority. Johnson remembered how a few setbacks in 1937 had allowed Congress to curtail Roosevelt's program prematurely, bringing an early end to needed reforms. The Texas New Dealer would not accept similar constraints during his tenure in the White House.[71]

▪ Lyndon Johnson's War

Johnson suffered from excessive ambition but not from naiveté. He knew that he faced trouble in Vietnam from his first days as president. A Mekong River development project would surely help the region, but convincing Ho Chi Minh to accept this vision would prove no easy matter. In South Vietnam, Johnson recognized that he could not rely on the parade of corrupt strongmen who had succeeded Diem. At home and among allies, observers were profoundly uneasy about the growing costs—human and financial—that accompanied the application of ideals in a faraway land. America's commitment in Vietnam threatened to undermine the rest of the president's reform agenda.

In late May 1964 Johnson called one of his trusted friends, Senator Richard Russell of Georgia. Dispensing with pleasantries, he opened an agonizing twenty-eight-minute conversation: "I've got lots of trouble. What do you think about this Vietnam thing, I'd like to hear you talk a little bit." Russell replied without hesitation. "It's the damn worse mess I ever saw. I don't see how we're ever gonna get out without fightin' a major war with the Chinese and all of 'em, down there in those rice paddies and jungles."[72]

"Our position is deteriorating," Russell continued, "and it look like the more we try to do for them, the less they willin' to do for themselves. There's no sense of responsibility there on the part of any of their leaders." Russell was an old New Dealer, but he also harbored a deep disdain for what he called the Asian "complex" that "glorified the individual" rather than the interests of the nation. Convinced that American assistance could not reform South Vietnam, he expressed a sincere desire to "get out."[73]

Russell was one of several figures—including Montana senator Mike Mansfield and Undersecretary of State George Ball—who shared Johnson's

New Deal aspirations but also recognized the forbidding environment in Southeast Asia. Russell, however, understood that although withdrawal from Vietnam might make the most sense in military and economic terms, America's ideological commitment to the area prohibited immediate disengagement. He disagreed when Johnson mused that Americans "would impeach a president that run out," but he also confirmed that "anything you do is wrong. It's one of these things where heads I win, tails you lose."[74]

Johnson listened intently and agreed with most of Russell's comments. Already, in May 1964, the president recognized that Vietnam was not the proper showcase for his plans to extend Roosevelt's New Deal. These were the wrong downtrodden people to help at this moment. In his conversation with Russell, Johnson never offered a strategic justification for containment in Vietnam. He did not mention markets, natural resources, the infamous "Munich analogy," or the "domino theory."

Johnson recognized that great powers cannot compartmentalize their commitments. After World War I the United States had betrayed its pledge to "make the world safe for democracy" when it declined to join collective security arrangements in Europe. During the Truman presidency, Washington had failed to deter communist aggression in Korea when it extended the range of containment while stubbornly returning the Treasury to a prewar budget. Johnson devoted his energies to avoiding similar setbacks. He had to escape the obvious contradiction that would emerge if he preached activism but practiced withdrawal. The president believed that he could not disengage from America's most conspicuous overseas development case and still stick to his domestic reform program. If he gave up abroad, people would expect him to do the same at home.

Americans did not want a war "10,000 miles away from home," Johnson told McGeorge Bundy. They also would not support the ambitions of a president who suffered defeat in an area of long-standing commitment. "It just worries the hell out of me," Johnson confessed. "I don't see what we can ever hope to get out of this . . . and I don't think that we can get out." "That's exactly the dilemma," Bundy meekly replied. Grasping for some kind of solution, Russell pleaded that "there's undoubtedly some middle ground somewhere."[75]

Filled with doubts, the president told Adlai Stevenson, one of the leading liberal Democrats throughout the 1950s and the U.S. ambassador to the United Nations from 1961 to 1965, "I shudder at getting too deeply involved there [in Vietnam], and everybody thinks that's the only alternative." "Well," Stevenson replied, "I've been shuddering on this thing for three years, and I am afraid we're in a position now where you don't have any alternative, and it's a hell of an alternative. It really gives me the shakes."[76]

Following the advice of Adlai Stevenson, Robert Kennedy, Robert McNamara, and McGeorge Bundy, the president undertook a cautious escalation of America's commitment in Vietnam. He enlarged aid programs designed to win "hearts and minds," and he expanded the use of American military force to counter NLF and North Vietnamese incursions in the South. Johnson also implemented the covert action program devised during the Kennedy years to undermine Hanoi's government.[77]

Johnson planned for a "limited war" that, according to McNamara, would allow for the proportional application of American capabilities in a manner that proved "the least costly in terms of men's lives and in terms of the nation's security." "The military tools and concepts of the [South Vietnam]/ U.S. effort are generally sound and adequate," he advised. "Substantially more can be done in the effective employment of military forces and in the economic and civic action areas." The secretary of defense called for "graduated overt military pressure" that "would include air attacks against military and possible industrial targets" in North Vietnam but avoid full-scale American participation in the war. "We intend," McGeorge Bundy concurred, "that Communism shall not take over Southeast Asia, but we do not intend or desire the destruction of the Hanoi regime. If terror and subversion end, [a] major improvement in relations is possible. It is only if they do not end that trouble is coming."[78]

Trouble, as Johnson had feared, came very quickly. A safe "middle ground" allowing for New Deal programs in South Vietnam and limited military deployments simply did not exist. In search of compromises that would allow for something other than war or surrender, the president continually asked: "Who are the best people we have . . . to talk to about this thing?" Who "might be fresh . . . might have some new approach?"[79]

No one could devise a "magic bullet" solution that would make over South Vietnam in the image of Texas, as Johnson desired. McNamara reported that the NLF controlled about 40 percent of the territory in South Vietnam and that "large groups of the population are now showing signs of apathy and indifference." The government in Saigon risked further weakening in the future as a result of corruption, disorganization, popular resistance, and increased communist subversion.[80]

One historian has observed that during 1964 policymakers in Washington cultivated a contempt for the South Vietnamese because of their failure to "develop" and "mature" as expected. The United States accordingly deepened its direct intervention. In addition to combating the communist-supported NLF and North Vietnamese forces, Washington worked with growing disregard, and frequent disdain, for the very people it ostensibly wanted to help. Paradoxically, the president's sincere commitment to New Deal principles made America behave as a classically imperialist state in Vietnam. The pursuit of ideals brought dehumanizing and frankly self-serving consequences.[81]

If the domestic weakness of the South Vietnamese state created a crisis that pulled the United States deeper into the vortex of a civil war, surrounding circumstances contributed to this dynamic. William Bundy—McGeorge's elder brother and Johnson's assistant secretary of state for Far Eastern affairs—recounts that with each passing month the news from East Asia as a whole grew worse. Communist China had recovered from the Great Leap famine. As it prepared for its first independent nuclear test in October 1964, Beijing became noticeably more assertive in its support for communist groups in Indonesia, Cambodia, and North Vietnam. A small guerrilla insurgency also emerged in northeastern Thailand, apparently aided by China. Washington watched nervously in June 1964 as leaders from Hanoi visited Beijing, receiving pledges of increased military assistance. The darkening picture in Asia elicited widespread American fears that the entire area would soon collapse.[82]

South Vietnam was no longer merely a domino that could push over other states in the region; it had become a crucial finger in the precarious dike containing Chinese advances in Asia. Johnson planned to build new dams along the Mekong River in the future, but for now he had to focus on rapid military action for the sake of regional stability.

The president and his closest advisers believed that a failure to employ additional force in South Vietnam would leave Washington with little territory for future development programs in Asia. The alternatives became starkly polarized. The White House perceived a choice between acting decisively in Indochina or letting the area fall into communist hands. During the election campaign of 1964 Johnson was careful to show that although he rejected risky measures, he would act with resolve against proliferating threats.[83]

On the morning of 2 August 1964 three North Vietnamese patrol boats attacked an American destroyer—the *Maddox*—conducting surveillance in the Gulf of Tonkin. Hanoi claimed this area as part of its restricted "national" waters. Turning out to sea, the American ship lured the smaller enemy boats into international waters, at least sixteen miles from the shore. The *Maddox* called in support from a nearby American aircraft carrier, and the North Vietnamese boats fled back to their base.[84]

When news reached Washington the president immediately called for caution, fearing a hasty descent to full-scale war, including the risk of direct Chinese intervention. Instead of tit-for-tat retaliation, he prepared for a deliberate increase in American pressure against North Vietnam. Johnson hoped to provide the sagging Southern regime with a morale boost.[85]

A number of historians have alleged that after the attack Johnson provoked a second incident, one that would justify planned American bombing raids over North Vietnam. On 3 August four South Vietnamese patrol boats, supported by American destroyers, initiated a series of raids on Hanoi's coastal facilities. Stepping up covert activities of this sort during a period of increased tension, the U.S. government appeared to expect (and perhaps desire) a North Vietnamese response.[86]

If Johnson sought an excuse for bombing North Vietnam, the fact that he initially withheld any military action other than these relatively limited and preplanned covert raids seems curious. A confirmed attack on an American vessel in international waters justified some sort of retaliation. Despite growing pressures, the president refused to authorize a larger war after 2 August. This fits the pattern *not* of alleged provocation from Washington, but of uncertainty and groping attempts to find a safe "middle ground" between passive acceptance of communist aggression and full-scale war.

American forces should defend themselves, Johnson told Senator George Smathers, but the White House must act with caution before authorizing broad retaliation. Conscious that small steps and misperceptions could unintentionally lead to a conflagration, the president explained that "you can't give them order to chase the hell out and destroy a boat that they don't even know if they've seen." This comment was an ominous, if unintentional, prediction of the next few days of heightened tensions in the Gulf of Tonkin.[87]

During the night of 4 August the *Maddox* and a second American destroyer—the *Turner Joy*—mistook a number of unidentified radar sightings for North Vietnamese aggression. Virtually all the historical evidence—airplane sightings, communication intercepts, and interviews—indicates that the tense U.S. sailors overreacted to a false alarm, a surprisingly common occurrence when watching for an attack by radar under anxious circumstances. Crisis conditions in the Gulf of Tonkin had—despite Johnson's caution—produced false perceptions of escalating hostilities.[88]

Word of the reported North Vietnamese attack reached Washington at around dawn. A show of U.S. strength now appeared necessary both to punish the enemy and to avoid charges of weakness. Within hours, the story of the alleged engagement at sea leaked to the press. Johnson had to do something, he told congressional leaders, as reporters prepared to publish stories announcing that "some of our boys are floating around in the water." The president feared that his opponents—including Republican presidential candidate Barry Goldwater—would accuse him of "appeasing" aggressors if he did not react with obvious force.[89]

The analogy to the Cuban missile crisis dominated White House discussions. Like Kennedy almost two years earlier, Johnson had to take new military risks to prevent further losses of American forces in the region. Despite his clear misgivings about U.S. policy in Vietnam, Richard Russell explained that without a military response "it is possible we would be giving up the right to sail through the Gulf [of Tonkin.] If we did that, psychologically our prestige possibly would be seriously affected in Hanoi and other places. They might come to the wrong conclusion about what we are willing to do, which would be much more serious."[90]

Pressed by events to protect America's threatened position in Vietnam, Johnson authorized retaliatory strikes against North Vietnamese petroleum tanks, aircraft, naval vessels, and other military installations. This was the first direct U.S. attack north of the Seventeenth Parallel. The air strikes caused minimal damage, but they clearly raised the stakes of the conflict. Hanoi had anti-aircraft guns ready to fire on U.S. planes. The North Vietnamese government was determined to inflict heavy casualties on the American forces now overtly engaged in combat.[91]

Johnson's retaliation after the second alleged Gulf of Tonkin incident received widespread support. Even the president's opponents approved his expansion of the Vietnam War. Goldwater told Johnson, "I think it's a proper course of action. I think you've taken the right steps."[92] On 7 August the House of Representatives and the Senate overwhelmingly passed the Gulf of Tonkin Resolution, authorizing the president to "respond instantly" to "any unprovoked attack against the armed forces of the United States." If requested by a Southeast Asian nation, Johnson could also undertake "all measures including the use of armed force" to repel "aggression or subversion." Every congressman and all but two senators voted for this military blank check in Vietnam.[93]

Johnson remained cautious after the air strikes. Covert naval raids against North Vietnam continued, but American ships did not travel as close to the coast as they had before. When another report of North Vietnamese attacks on U.S. destroyers reached Washington on 18–19 September, the president refused to retaliate despite Secretary of State Dean Rusk's urgings.[94]

The Gulf of Tonkin incidents marked an important escalation in the Vietnam War, but Johnson continued to avoid additional use of force wherever possible.[95]

Caution gave way to combat in 1965. On 7 February NLF forces used trails across the Laotian and Cambodian borders to attack South Vietnamese and American forces in Pleiku, 240 miles north of Saigon. Visiting South Vietnam at the time, McGeorge Bundy reported to Johnson that the situation "is deteriorating, and without new U.S. action defeat appears inevitable . . . There is still time to turn it around," Bundy warned, "but not much."[96]

The president had to do something dramatic to reinforce American commitments and hopes in South Vietnam. Bundy called for "sustained reprisals against North Vietnam"—"a policy in which air and naval action against the North is justified by and related to the whole Viet Cong campaign of violence and terror in the South." By gradually increasing the number of air strikes against targets in North Vietnam, the United States could raise morale in Saigon while discouraging enemy attacks. Washington would set "a higher price for the future upon all adventures in guerrilla warfare." A systematic bombing program, rather than tit-for-tat operations, promised to give the White House new initiative.[97]

On 7 February, before Johnson had the opportunity to discuss Bundy's proposal with his advisers, he authorized retaliatory air strikes against North Vietnam. American planes bombed military barracks and storage depots across the Seventeenth Parallel, despite the presence of Soviet premier Aleksei Kosygin in North Vietnam at the time. Accumulating American frustrations since the Gulf of Tonkin incidents stiffened the president's determination to launch these new air strikes. The United States would not wait while Kosygin appeared to give the North Vietnamese "substantial help." On 11 February Johnson ordered a second air strike, followed two days later by his formal approval of "Rolling Thunder," the program for systematic attacks proposed by Bundy. The United States would now send bombers across the Seventeenth Parallel "about once or twice a week," directed at "two or three targets" chosen by the White House.[98]

The initiation of "Rolling Thunder" was, in Bundy's words, the "watershed" for the rest of Johnson's presidency. The policy of "sustained reprisals" never boosted Southern morale, and it never discouraged enemy attacks. Johnson had now associated himself, and his vision for an international New Deal, with an air war against North Vietnam. To cease military activity in the region without success would surely discredit American reform efforts in Southeast Asia and elsewhere. Retreat would, according to the president, trigger broader "defeat."[99]

Johnson felt compelled to escalate his commitment to war with each month. The more force the president used, the more he lost and had to redeem with future successes. On 2 March 1965 alone, North Vietnamese anti-aircraft guns destroyed six U.S. planes. American personnel rescued five of the six downed pilots on this occasion, but the losses of life and machinery had already begun to mount. After the commencement of "Rolling Thunder" Johnson had to prove that accumulating casualties—American and Vietnamese—had not come in vain.[100]

McGeorge Bundy advised the president to consider placing a "substantial allied ground force" in South Vietnam. The U.S. air attacks showed no signs of curtailing enemy advances or the chronic instability of the Saigon regime. American ground forces would help maintain order, guard air and embassy facilities, and lead counterinsurgency missions. On the border between the two states, U.S. troops could also interdict North Vietnamese supply lines. Without the deployment of more American soldiers, the air strikes offered little chance of building a viable South Vietnamese state. "Guerrilla wars," Robert McNamara agreed, "could not be won from the air."[101]

Johnson had worked himself into a corner. To avoid a humiliating defeat, especially after the commencement of "Rolling Thunder," the president had to open an American-led ground war in Vietnam. On 1 April 1965 he secretly authorized the deployment of two battalions in active combat. Convinced less than a week later that this small U.S. contingent was not enough, the president made preparations to send another two armed divisions.[102]

As he engaged the United States in its first extended ground war since Korea, Johnson redoubled his public commitment to an international New Deal. On 7 April he gave his speech proposing a Mekong River development project. Bundy explained that U.S. leadership in a "regional Southeast Asia development operation" would serve the same purposes as the Marshall Plan in Western Europe after World War II. American aid would improve the lives of poor citizens and insulate the area against communist infiltration. Increased military activity in Southeast Asia protected short-term stability, but long-run peace in the region required economic growth. American air strikes and combat troops served as forward forces, preparing the ground for rural electrification and other ambitious projects. Military commitments and promises of New Deal–style programs were part and parcel of the same Vietnam policy for Lyndon Johnson.[103]

The tragic pattern was now set. From early 1965 through the end of 1967 Johnson consistently increased the number of American soldiers fighting in South Vietnam. He continued to promise that he would rebuild the region in the image of rural Texas during the 1930s. Every combat death made success in this hopeless endeavor more necessary to sustain the president's reform vision. In late March 1965 the United States had 28,000 "noncombat" soldiers in Vietnam. By early 1966, 184,000 Americans were fighting in difficult terrain against forces supported by North Vietnam, China, and the Soviet Union. In January 1968 the number of U.S. troops in Vietnam reached its peak of 535,000.[104]

As American involvement in Vietnam peaked, Johnson struggled to reconcile excessive commitments at home and abroad. In a December 1965 meeting with his closest advisers, the president acknowledged that the rising cost of the war was diverting resources from his domestic "great society" initiatives. Without a quick victory or a settlement on favorable terms in Southeast Asia, Johnson predicted, "We're going to suffer political losses." Torn by his devotions to communist containment and social reform, he lashed out at the "damn fool liberals who are crying about poverty." Johnson pointed out that he had "doubled" funding for welfare and education in one year. That obviously wasn't enough. Both the great society and the Vietnam War demanded a growing share of depleting government resources. "We need money for all these programs," the president explained. "How do we divide up this money?" he asked with evident frustration.[105]

Johnson never found a satisfactory answer to this question. His refusal to make any sacrifices in his social agenda or his anticommunist resolve prevented him from succeeding in either effort. Attempts to provide more "guns and butter" brought America's long post-1945 economic expansion to an abrupt end. Washington's profligate spending triggered an international financial crisis that undermined political authority in the United States and Western Europe.[106]

During 1966 the American public began to turn against the president for his failures in trying to do too much at home and especially abroad. Special Assistant Bill Moyers alerted Johnson that the "administration is being criticized from both ends." These voices represented, in Moyers words, the "first signs of American impatience with [a] long war."[107]

A majority of U.S. citizens never supported an immediate withdrawal from Vietnam. In 1966 and 1967, however, evidence of public dissatisfaction with the military stalemate grew considerably. Despite McNamara's assurances that American forces "will win the war and end the fighting," Johnson recognized increasing resistance to his leadership. The president admitted that he was "frightened" by the implications of public trends for his foreign and domestic programs.[108]

During the summer of 1967 riots inflamed Detroit, Newark, and other major cities. These urban disturbances reflected long-simmering racial and economic tensions, but they were surely exacerbated by public frustrations with the Vietnam War. Johnson despaired that the administration was now susceptible to "the charge that we cannot kill enough people in Vietnam, so we go out and shoot civilians in Detroit." Domestic violence discredited the promises of the great society. Instead of fortifying a broad consensus for reform, America's overseas activities had derailed the president's policies at home. "The main front of the war," Johnson told his advisers, "is here in the United States."[109]

The president continued to promise that he could win the war in Vietnam and implement his domestic agenda, but even he had serious doubts. With the spread of urban violence at home, Johnson felt he now had to push hard for a quick victory or an honorable peace settlement in Southeast Asia. Salvaging his reform program and winning reelection depended on results overseas. In late 1967 the president told his senior advisers that "our people will not hold out four more years." He made arrangements to expedite the latest deployment of U.S. troops to Vietnam. America would now have a colossal force of 535,000 men fighting on the ground.[110]

William Westmoreland, the commander of American forces in Vietnam, proclaimed that he had "never been more encouraged" by the prospects in Southeast Asia. Ellsworth Bunker, Washington's ambassador to Saigon, sent a long telegram to Secretary of State Rusk, praising the American and South Vietnamese soldiers who displayed "great valor" in combating enemy forces. These "small heroes" were "fighting communism" and protecting the "entire free world position."[111]

Assessments of this kind told the president what he was desperate to hear. International and domestic difficulties had grown so intractable that wishful thinking replaced careful analysis. Overcome by the resistance they confronted on a variety of fronts, members of the government had become dangerously isolated from both public opinion and battlefield conditions. Events days after Bunker's long telegram triggered months of political crisis that would end only after Johnson's successor, Richard Nixon, assumed the presidency. Failing in his ambitions to do so much for so many, in 1968 Lyndon Johnson lost control over both his foreign and domestic agendas.

One of the most decisive U.S. military victories in Vietnam marked the final destruction of Johnson's reform vision. In the early hours of 30 January 1968—the beginning of celebrations for Tet, the lunar New Year—North Vietnamese and NLF forces launched a coordinated assault on more than 100 cities and towns in South Vietnam. The attackers, engaged in what became known as the Tet Offensive, sought to force a collapse of the Saigon government. For a few hours they appeared on the brink of success. After the smoke cleared, however, a survey of the landscape revealed that enemy forces had suffered a punishing defeat. They lost as many as 40,000 lives in battle, compared with less than one-tenth that number for the American and South Vietnamese armies.

During the months after Tet, U.S. soldiers fought with a new ferocity in Vietnam. Under Westmoreland and his successor, General Creighton Abrams, American troops took the initiative. In late February 1968 U.S. marines and South Vietnamese soldiers recaptured the old imperial capital of Hué from the enemy forces who had overrun it three weeks earlier. American leaders exposed the torture and brutality inflicted on the local population, more than 2,000 of whom the communist-supported fighters had killed in cold blood.[112]

The ferocious fighting of 1968 put the NLF and its North Vietnamese supporters on their heels, retreating time and again. Enraged American soldiers began to act with the same battle fanaticism that had given the NLF an edge in earlier years. This new fierceness in battle, however, also led many U.S. soldiers to commit atrocities strikingly similar to those of the enemy.[113]

The My Lai Massacre demonstrated how low some American forces had sunk in their determination to win the war. On the morning of 16 March 1968 a group of U.S. troops entered the South Vietnamese village of My Lai. This settlement had long served as a base for NLF forces. By the time the American soldiers arrived, members of the NLF had retreated from the area. Only old men, women, and children remained in the village. Frustrated by the unwillingness of these frightened residents to cooperate in locating enemy fighters, American soldiers proceeded, in a few short hours, to murder more than 200 civilians. Many of the villagers died when U.S. troops herded them into a ditch, firing upon the population en masse.[114]

The American public did not immediately learn of the My Lai Massacre, because the military command covered it up until late 1969. In the weeks after Tet, families watching the nightly news across the United States did see just how violent the war in Vietnam had become. On 2 February 1968, 20 million television viewers and many more newspaper readers saw the gruesome image of a summary execution on the streets of Saigon. In front of American cameras, South Vietnamese national police chief Nguyen Ngoc Loan fired a bullet, at point blank range, into the head of an unnamed enemy suspect.

Weeks later Walter Cronkite, the widely watched anchor of the *CBS Evening News,* described South Vietnam as "a burned and blasted and weary land." The future, according to Cronkite, promised more violence, not less. Contrary to the claims of the president, American forces did not appear poised for any kind of meaningful accomplishment in Vietnam. "To say that we are closer to victory today," Cronkite explained, "is to believe, in the face of the evidence, the optimists who have been wrong in the past. To say that we are on the edge of defeat is to yield to unreasonable pessimism. To say that we are mired in stalemate seems the only realistic, yet unsatisfactory conclusion." Cronkite's verdict and the accompanying images of the war reached far beyond the United States, fueling anger and disillusion on a global scale.[115]

Johnson's efforts had only reinforced the international stalemate that he and Kennedy had worked so hard to transcend. The ferocious fighting in Vietnam made talk of a Mekong River development project, or any other New Deal efforts, completely unconvincing. After Tet, the war in Vietnam became a contest to limit losses and balance risks on the model of the Korean conflict in the early 1950s. "Winning," if that were even possible, now meant sacrificing the very purposes behind America's commitments during the Kennedy and Johnson years.

In 1968 the "language of dissent" that had already emerged in North America, Europe, and Asia focused upon the Vietnam War. Large student protests against U.S. activities convulsed almost every major urban center across the world. The Vietnam War did not create the initial sources of dissent, especially among the young; but the evidence of American brutalities without recognizable purpose catalyzed public anger.[116]

The Vietnam War was a high-stakes venture. Success in fostering Southeast Asian economic development might have alleviated popular anguish about stagnation in the West. Both Kennedy and Johnson understood this. Their determination to display a new activism at home and abroad contributed to escalating American intervention in Vietnam. When Washington's efforts produced devastation instead of development, public anger turned against the U.S. government. By the middle of 1968 Lyndon Johnson was a prisoner in the White House, besieged by early liberal supporters turned radical critics.[117]

America's "time of troubles" served Soviet and Chinese purposes, in principle. Public criticism in the West, however, inspired similar urges in Eastern Europe and the Soviet Union that hindered the political control of the Kremlin. An emboldened leadership in Hanoi also challenged its communist patrons, triggering greater rivalry between the already estranged Soviet and Chinese governments. The Vietnam War became a nightmare for Lyndon Johnson in 1968, but it hardly left Leonid Brezhnev and Mao Zedong with occasion for calm repose.

The Vietnam War has long overshadowed the history of the 1960s. America's failure to reconstruct Indochina in the model of a liberal democratic state is central to understanding the decline of the Cold War consensus that ordered great-power politics after 1945. The atrocities perpetrated in the name of "development" and "progress" discredited the authorities who had advocated these aims. No longer would skeptical men and women so readily accept patriotic calls to "pay any price" for inherited ideals.

American behavior in Vietnam was not the sole cause of this crucial change in attitude. The legacy of French colonialism and the aggressive actions of other states—in particular North Vietnam, China, and the Soviet Union—led the United States to make unwanted commitments in a place few could identify. Liberal ambitions drove two presidents to transform Vietnam into a showcase for recharging American ideals. Kennedy and Johnson dreaded war in Vietnam, but calls for policy activism and evidence of communist expansion made withdrawal almost unthinkable. Instead of accepting Cold War stalemate, U.S. leaders increased their commitments in Southeast Asia, hoping to find a breakthrough.

The Vietnam War contributed to the global disruption of 1968. In this fateful year each of the great powers confronted profound (and often violent) conflict at home and among allies. The actions taken by leaders to forestall growing dissent in the early 1960s had the contradictory effect of multiplying difficulties by the decade's end.

5

THE GLOBAL DISRUPTION
OF 1968

The entire world shook in 1968. Across cultures, people of all generations recognized the significance of the moment. A global wave of urban protests produced a crisis of authority in nearly every society. Many of the demonstrators who took to the streets in 1968 were young citizens, angered by what they perceived as a stagnant political status quo. Domestic revolution threatened to undermine the international balance of power—what one scholar calls a "long peace"—that had ensured stability among the great powers after World War II.[1]

The revolutions of 1968 did not begin with a vanguard party or a workers' uprising. The upheavals grew from less glamorous political and social difficulties. Nuclear stalemate between the great powers, unresolved alliance disputes, and the increasingly impersonal nature of domestic institutions alienated citizens from their governments. The growing university population in each of the largest states had the resources to translate discontent into active protest. The brutality of the Vietnam War catalyzed public anger, contradicting the promises of "development" and "progress" espoused by national leaders.

These circumstances gave rise to a global disruption.[2] A very wide chasm—one that still exists today—opened up between the aims of established elites and of social activists in every major society. Cold War divisions between communist and capitalist, East and West, and "developed" and "developing" lost much of their meaning. "National security" had always included international and domestic components, but after 1968 the latter gained importance over the former in many states. The urban crowds of protesters created serious anxieties for the most powerful political figures. By the end of 1968 the politics on the streets had changed the politics of government, but not as any of the protesters had hoped.

* * *

Many scholars have examined the historical patterns of revolutionary up-heaval. Most of their work has focused on why promising movements for radical change fail, frequently producing dictatorship in one repressive form or another. Why popular protests spread across diverse societies has received surprisingly little attention. The events of 1968 require a transnational analysis of social change.[3]

During the 1960s one factor was preeminent in igniting the flames of revolution. Leaders promised their citizens more "progress" than ever before—through education, material consumption, and individual equality. Even in China, Mao had pledged that through the Great Leap the impoverished state would soon surpass Great Britain. The government in Beijing consistently repressed freedoms on the mainland, but it did so in the name of a higher communist cause that many, including the chairman, believed would bring a better future for all citizens.

A number of societies—particularly in North America and Western Europe—were remarkably successful in creating affluence during the second half of the twentieth century. They failed, however, to meet the rising popular expectations that they inspired. The rhetoric of both capitalism and communism became harmfully exaggerated in the context of Cold War competition. A perception of "false promises" among young and ambitious citizens pervaded the language of dissent and contributed directly to protest activities in nearly every state.[4]

In this context of festering discontent, relatively innocuous incidents, especially on university campuses, sparked broad demonstrations. When local and national authorities overreacted with excessive police force—as they did in many cases—protest activities grew more radical, and often violent. Resistance to perceived police brutalities provided angry men and women with an apparent link between their local grievances and what they came to perceive as a larger "culture" of government repression.

Attempts by authorities to limit popular demands and prohibit public unrest only contributed to more of the same. From a small number of relatively isolated places, violence spread throughout many of the largest states. Governments deployed sufficient police power to anger large crowds, but they did not use enough force to smother future demonstrations.

Organizational ties between protesters across different societies were a minimal factor in these developments. Domestic conflicts grew from local conditions that, though unique in each case, produced a similar dynamic of rising expectations and attempted repressions. Men and women on diverse city streets perceived themselves as participants in a shared "movement" against the police, the military, and the established political institutions.

These were the common "others" that bonded dissidents together in struggle. Beyond daily street battles, however, protesters within and across societies did not have anything resembling an international program for political and social change. As protests escalated, the demonstrators in various societies became more united in their attacks on the existing order, but also more divided on what should come next.

Protesters never had to reach a consensus on the future. Despite the violence on the streets, governments managed to maintain their control over domestic society, with the notable exception of China during the height of the Cultural Revolution (1966–1969). In the United States and Western Europe, domestic order required virtual military occupation of entire cities. In Eastern Europe, the Soviet Union, and China, governments used even greater force, including foreign invasion, mass arrests, and forced migrations. Leaders repressed revolution, but they also contributed to a cycle of violence that deepened the chasm between public expectations and official authority.

The global disruption of 1968 grew from the declining ability of leaders to manufacture consent at home. Events during the year made this problem far more intractable. Political elites displayed their determination to retain power through the use of force, but they did so at the cost of their domestic legitimacy. No longer could political figures attempt to lead largely by persuasion. Order and unity now relied more heavily on police activities.[5]

▪ Berkeley: "A State of Perpetual War"

Before the 1960s few Californians foresaw the domestic cataclysm on the other side of the state's golden horizon. Perched on a tract of former cattle-grazing land on the eastern side of the San Francisco Bay, the city of Berkeley and its public university grew from a backwater into one of the preeminent Cold War institutions after 1945. Scientists at the school—particularly Robert Oppenheimer and Ernest Lawrence—were pioneers in American research on atomic energy (and bombs). As a state-run institution, blessed with large federal research grants, the University of California at Berkeley was a sprawling empire with a convoluted structure of authority that included various regents, a president, and countless decentralized departments, institutes, and allied organizations.[6]

Student enrollments at Berkeley expanded in line with its counterparts around the world. By 1968 the university's student population totaled 28,132, compared with only 7,748 in 1944 and 21,909 in 1946, when an unusually large number of war veterans returned to school. Formerly a conservative white suburb of San Francisco, Berkeley developed into a diverse city in parallel with the growth of the university. By 1960 more than 100,000 people of widely varying incomes resided within the town limits, more than a quarter of whom were black, Asian, or Hispanic. Military, political, and social trends after World War II made Berkeley into a large and cosmopolitan community.[7]

Berkeley's startling Cold War expansion produced profound vulnerabilities. The resources and intelligence packed into this small slice of northern California coalesced into a powderkeg of energy and ambition. Dissident impulses, born of the international and domestic difficulties in the late 1950s, spread with ease among the thousands of men and women gathering each day at the university and the various bars and cafés around town. Berkeley was a republic of letters where independent newspapers, poetry, music, art, and theater proliferated, transmitting dissident thoughts to a large community. University and government officials attempted to control the public discourse, but the diverse setting around the campus made this an impossible task. By the 1960s the city of Berkeley was large enough to nurture a cosmopolitan exchange of ideas, but it remained small enough to protect a space for youthful experimentation relatively free from the commercial pressures that naturally dominate an urban metropolis.

From 1964 through 1968 this university community spearheaded the development of a national protest movement in America. The ideas of the New Left provided students with an initial language of dissent during the early years of the decade. Protest activities in Berkeley converted words into action. Confrontations on and around campus—beginning with the Free Speech Movement in late 1964—sparked a series of disruptions that reached a crescendo within a few years.

The disruptions began when the university attempted to enforce a long-standing ban against political activities on campus. For many years activists had set up tables to publicize their causes on the edge of the university grounds. These facilities violated school regulations, but administrators generally ignored them. In September 1964, however, worries about growing student dissent—and the ferment around the civil rights movement in particular—led officials at Berkeley to change course. They prohibited groups such as the Congress on Racial Equality (CORE) from organizing on campus.

The Free Speech Movement rallied students, faculty, and local residents against the university restrictions. Representatives from CORE and other groups moved their tables in front of Sproul Hall, the main administration building. The university responded by calling in local law enforcement officers and suspending eight students. On 1 October 1964 hundreds of young men and women staged a sit-in to prevent the police from arresting CORE activist Jacob Weinberg. After a tentative compromise between the students and the university broke down, members of the Free Speech Movement organized a long series of rallies on campus, culminating in an occupation of Sproul Hall on 2 December.[8]

Police promptly arrested the students who occupied the building, but their sit-in became a source of inspiration for many observers. Like their counterparts in the civil rights movement, the students channeled various energies into a form of "direct action" that highlighted the unjust use of authority by established institutions. Sitting peacefully, the students appeared morally pure. Using force to remove sitters, the police looked brutal and menacing.

Mario Savio, one of the leaders of the Free Speech Movement, recognized that this was the beginning of a crusade that would not end soon. Speaking to a large group before the sit-in at Sproul Hall, he merged New Left language with a call for immediate action. "There is a time," Savio exclaimed, "when the operation of the machine becomes so odious, makes you so sick at heart, that you can't take part; you can't even passively take part, and you've got to put your bodies upon the gears and upon the wheels, upon the levers, upon all the apparatus and you've got to make it stop."[9]

Less than a week after the Sproul Hall sit-in, the faculty voted to lift most of the bans on political activity. Many professors and administrators sympathized with the students, but they also feared that dissent could quickly get out of hand. Berkeley's pedagogical and research responsibilities required the maintenance of order on campus. External entities, including the federal and state governments, pressured the university to avoid embarrassing scenes. By adopting less stringent restrictions on student speech, the faculty hoped to appease the large mass of restless youth in the area. Berkeley gave political activists more freedom in the hope that they wouldn't actually use it.[10]

This tactic might have worked if it hadn't been for the Vietnam War. America's military commitment in Southeast Asia, and the accompanying fear of the draft among Berkeley's young population, inspired larger student protests. In the spring of 1965 Jerry Rubin and Stephen Smale—a former sociology student at Berkeley and a young professor of mathematics—founded the Vietnam Day Committee. This group directed the protest energies inspired by the Free Speech Movement against Lyndon Johnson's policies in Southeast Asia. Following the first antiwar teach-in at the University of Michigan in March 1965, Rubin and Smale organized a number of public discussions at Berkeley.[11]

Students, faculty, and other activists traveled to the nation's capital in

April to participate in the first antiwar march. Twenty thousand young men and women from schools across the country formed a picket line around the White House. They then staged a rally at the Washington Monument. The Free Speech Movement had now gone to Washington on a national scale.[12]

Back in Berkeley, Rubin and Smale rallied more students against American intervention in Southeast Asia. On 21–22 May men and women from the community gathered for more than thirty hours on a softball field to debate the war. Celebrity antiwar activists such as journalist I. F. Stone, writer Norman Mailer, socialist Norman Thomas, and pediatrician Benjamin Spock lectured on the evils of U.S. military activities. Performers such as the musician Phil Ochs and the San Francisco Mime Troupe entertained the crowd. This Vietnam Day Committee rally became the model for similar gatherings in Berkeley that grew in size and frequency as American military activity escalated in Southeast Asia.[13]

The Vietnam War provoked a continual series of student demonstrations that included strikes, marches, sit-ins, teach-ins, and building takeovers. A majority of Berkeley residents never participated in these activities. What had been a very small cohort of protesters at the time of the Free Speech Movement, however, grew into a formidable insurrectionary mass. Roger Heyns, the newly appointed chancellor of the university in the fall of 1965, commented that the atmosphere in Berkeley had grown "sick." Radical critics of American policy and dogmatic conservatives polarized the city, creating what one historian calls "a state of perpetual war."[14]

The *Berkeley Barb*, founded as an antiwar weekly in August 1965 by a local activist, reflected the trend toward radicalism inspired by the Vietnam War. The raggy newspaper proclaimed that the "quality of the American war in Vietnam [has] rubbed off on Berkeley. The Vietnam War is beyond brutality. It is obscenity." U.S. military activities in Southeast Asia made it clear, the *Barb* announced, that citizens must "nettle that amorphous but thickhided establishment that so often nettles us."[15]

From 1965 through 1969 the *Barb* advocated and reported on protest activities. Its circulation rose from 1,200 to 90,000, exceeding the circulation of all other local newspapers. Surely every *Barb* reader did not take to the streets. Yet the astonishing growth of this radical paper—founded without any significant financial support or even a permanent staff—revealed how the climate of opinion in Berkeley became progressively insurrectionary during the second half of the 1960s.[16]

The *Barb* was a unifying source of information for diverse groups. Calling its expanding cohort of readers the "dissenting element of American society," the newspaper explained that each daily act of protest, no matter how small, demonstrated a benign refusal "to cooperate with the power structure which makes and enforces the rules." This was a "new style of confrontation" that promised to reverberate throughout the Bay Area and the rest of the nation.[17] We are fighting a "revolution," the *Barb* announced; "nothing short of basic change will restore peace . . . Will the establishment recognize this at home—or are they after subjugation through extermination as in Vietnam?"[18]

In late 1967 the antiwar forces in Berkeley mobilized 10,000 demonstrators to block draft induction centers in Oakland and other areas nearby. Confronted by 2,000 law enforcement officers on 20 October, the protests turned violent, engulfing twenty city blocks in brawling instigated by both angry demonstrators and unprepared police. "Dissent is through!" the *Barb* angrily announced in its account of the violence. Police brutality required active, and sometimes forceful, retaliation: "Resistance is here!"[19]

Berkeley's protesters had become national leaders, setting a tone for demonstrations throughout the country. On 21 October more than 50,000 people from around the country traveled to Washington for another antiwar rally, this one modeled on the first Vietnam Day Committee gathering in Berkeley. The young men and women who assembled at the Lincoln Memorial marched across the Potomac River to the Pentagon, where they hoped to occupy the center of American war planning.

Prepared for this event, Secretary of Defense Robert McNamara coordinated military maneuvers from the roof of the Pentagon. He deployed army and marshal service soldiers to remove the demonstrators attempting to block the building. The protesters were hardly innocent in their intentions, but the scenes around the Pentagon made the government forces appear brutal and callous. Soldiers brandished rifles against unarmed civilians, employed strong-arm tactics to arrest demonstrators, and herded men and women into buses for imprisonment. In addition to 647 arrests, 47 antiwar protesters suffered injuries requiring hospitalization.[20]

In the aftermath of the Oakland and Washington demonstrations, the *Barb* proclaimed that "the Berkeley style wins on both coasts." Antiwar protests in the Bay Area and other parts of the country continued through the last weeks of 1967 and the early days of the new year. According to reports, attendance at Berkeley rallies against the Vietnam War increased threefold.[21]

The *Barb* described the "normal" protest routine that continued into 1968: "Berkeley SDS [Students for a Democratic Society] Anti-Draft Union car pools arrive at the [Oakland] Induction Center every Monday through Friday at 6:30 A.M. Individuals picket the building and talk to inductees, pre-induction physicals, and enlisters." The *Barb* reported that "various people who had been down to the center related instances of inductees walking out of the center in response to conversations and leaflets." Students harassed the administration of the university with frequent "mill-ins" in Sproul Hall. Protesters organized various public condemnations of the U.S. government.[22]

The student population in Berkeley was hopeful and frustrated at the same time. Largely peaceful protests, beginning with the Free Speech Movement, had drawn widespread support for demands to expand civil rights and end the Vietnam War. The revolution, however, still seemed far away. The U.S. government continued its participation in the Vietnam War, with no end in sight. Washington's preoccupation with Southeast Asia drew resources away from the antipoverty and antidiscrimination programs that President Johnson had extolled when he succeeded his slain predecessor. During the early days of 1968 radicals in Berkeley and other cities could point to few accomplishments despite the increasing momentum of protest activities.

The language of warfare in Vietnam displaced the promise of peaceful domestic reform. The youth and civil rights movements of the 1960s had initially emerged, at least in part, from an extended pacifist tradition in American thought.[23] After the Oakland and Washington events, however, protest activities veered toward more violent language and tactics. The year 1968 marked the point when demonstrators became militarized in parallel with the militarization of American foreign policy in Southeast Asia. The *Barb* reported that calls to "kill a white cop" received loudest applause at student gatherings. Arguments for nonviolent change garnered far less enthusiastic support.[24]

The image of Argentine-born revolutionary Ernesto "Che" Guevara—wearing soiled battle fatigues and a tattered beret—became ubiquitous in the Bay Area. His death in October 1967 at the hands of Bolivian military forces only added to his cult stature. Che's murder was the first in a series of political assassinations that fed a new idealization of the "guerrilla" fighter, especially among young men.[25]

Todd Gitlin, the former president of Students for a Democratic Society, who moved to Berkeley at this time, reported seeing the following spray-painted message on the streets of the East Bay: "Che is alive—he is working in Oakland." In his determined fight for local freedom against the established sources of state power and concentrated capital, Che became an iconic "hero" for student protesters. He served, especially after his death, as a model for continued struggle. Writing to his colleagues in Berkeley, Gitlin called for more "ordinary heroes" who would fight for their ideals like the Argentine martyr.[26]

Che's image proliferated on Berkeley's sidewalks, but the streets of the city remained eerily quiet during the weeks around the Tet Offensive. This was the calm before the storm. Rumors about an anti–Vietnam War "convocation," local strikes, and race riots circulated throughout town. One professor wrote to the president of the university, warning of widespread "treason." California governor Ronald Reagan condemned the entire atmosphere in Berkeley as "obscene."[27]

No group struck government officials as more "obscene" than the Black Panther Party. Formed in 1966 by two Berkeley area residents, Bobby Seale and Huey Newton, the Panthers glorified the use of violence.[28] They promised self-help and armed defense for African Americans who suffered from poverty, discrimination, and disproportionate Vietnam draft duties.[29] By 1968 the Panthers had more than 2,000 followers, many of whom carried weapons in public, wore black berets reminiscent of Che Guevara, and distributed copies of Chairman Mao's book of quotations around the Berkeley campus. The Panthers taunted the area police, calling them "pigs." At one event, members of the group encouraged local children to chant: "We want a pork chop, off the pig!"[30]

A "guerrilla" mystique dominated Berkeley's protest rhetoric in 1968. The sit-ins of the Free Speech Movement gave way to mob action against government installations. The threatening image of Black Power replaced the inclusive, multiracial examples of the freedom marches earlier in the decade. Violence, not pacifism, now fused the frustrated aspirations of the civil rights and youth movements. Talk around town focused on "arming" the right people for revolution.[31]

Stokely Carmichael, a prominent figure in the influential Student Nonviolent Coordinating Committee (SNCC), commented that "it's time to end this non-violence bullshit."[32] Even groups with "non-violence" in their title, like SNCC, turned to guerrilla warfare in 1968. The war in Vietnam, fought to carry American developmental ideas abroad, had now come home in ways that threatened to spiral out of control.[33]

▪ West Berlin: "Today Vietnam, Tomorrow Us"

If Berkeley developed as a microcosm of the Cold War, West Berlin was at the center of the Cold War. The city served as a crucial battleground between the United States and the Soviet Union. Located deep within East German territory, its residents experienced recurring threats of forced isolation and armed conflict. During the Soviet-enforced Berlin blockade of 1948–49, the Korean War of 1950–1953, the Berlin Crises of 1958–1961, and the Cuban missile crisis of 1962 Western policymakers feared an imminent communist takeover of the city. Recently declassified war plans reveal that the Soviet Union and its East European satellites did indeed contemplate the use of force to cut off West Berlin, in addition to attacks deeper into Western Europe.[34]

The Free University, founded largely on student initiative in November 1948, became an integral part of the Western alliance's "magnet" strategy in West Berlin, and Central Europe in general. Contrary to the rigid administration of East Berlin's Humboldt University, the Free University encouraged experimental courses and creative pedagogy. Students in the Western institution had an extensive voice in admissions and curricular decisions. West Germany, the United States, and institutions such as the Ford Foundation funded this unique school because they recognized its attraction for men and women in the East. Between 1949 and 1961 more than one-third of the student population at the Free University's West Berlin campus came from East Germany. East-West contacts in this setting allowed Western authorities a unique opportunity to exert informal influence upon some of the best and brightest emerging from the communist milieu.[35]

During its first decade the Free University managed to balance Cold War pressures with a liberal environment for education and social interaction. The construction of the Berlin Wall in August 1961 undermined this enterprise. East German students could no longer travel by streetcar to the Western university. State-sponsored anticommunist propaganda became more dominant. The West German government began to discourage, and even repress, potentially dissident experimental ideas.[36]

The Wall transformed West Berlin from a battleground into a showcase. Chancellor Konrad Adenauer and his successors used the city to display the best of their society. They hoped to impress those in the East who peered into this now closed-off capitalist island in a sea of communist authority.[37]

Ironically, the Free University developed in this context as the "Berkeley of West Germany." It symbolized the remarkable political and economic accomplishments of the Federal Republic while cultivating radical dissent. Students in West Berlin revolted against the division of the city, the government in Bonn, and the Cold War in general. By the late 1960s "most active groups among the student body," according to West German philosopher Jürgen Habermas, "desire[d] the immediate overthrow of social structures." Radical students became "the backbone of an extra-parliamentary opposition that [sought] new forms of organization in clubs and informal centers, and a social basis wider than the university."[38]

German youth dissent grew particularly disruptive in late 1966. Students blamed the U.S. government for prolonging the division of Germany and supporting a "Grand Coalition" of the dominant West German parties—the Christian Democratic Union (CDU) and the Social Democratic Party (SPD)—which constrained political debate. In December groups of young men and women demonstrated throughout West Berlin, including the crowded shopping area known as the Kurfürstendamm. One student leaflet pledged to restore "democracy, a socialist alternative, [and] a new left party" in West Germany. The protesters proclaimed their opposition to the "bankruptcy of the established parties."[39]

Altercations between students and law enforcement officers in West Berlin, including alleged incidents of police brutality, escalated through the end of 1966 and into the early months of 1967. In January West Berlin authorities entered the offices of the Socialist German Student Union, one of the leading West German youth groups. They searched through the organization's materials, confiscated membership files, and accused the group of conducting illegal activities against the government. This heavy-handed police behavior had the effect of strengthening public support for the student protesters. In addition, it contributed to a more confrontational climate, especially in West Berlin. The social tension in this old Prussian city now approximated the polarized atmosphere of Berkeley.[40]

West German authorities worried not only about the mounting protests of the New Left. They also confronted a resurgent nationalist right. In 1967 and 1968 the National Democratic Party of Germany (NPD) won between 7 and 9.8 percent of the vote in local elections. Friedrich Thielen and Adolf von Thadden, the leaders of the NPD, called for a strong, independent, and reunited Germany, free of the "alien" interests that allegedly corrupted the states on both sides of the Berlin Wall. "Our nation," the NPD Manifesto proclaimed, "is being merged into two antagonistic systems . . . Territorially alien powers are assuming the guardianship of the peoples of Europe and jointly maintaining the division of Germany and of Europe for their own political aims."[41]

Like the students on the left, the NPD attacked what it called the "unrestrained materialism" that harmed the people's spiritual and moral health. The party's 28,000 members condemned the "Grand Coalition" for repressing traditional German family and community norms. Instead of increased federal aid to universities, the NPD argued that the "youth want and need decent, clean standards to look up to." The NPD demanded a strong central government that would eliminate "public immorality."[42]

In retrospect, the challenge from the nationalist right appears quite tame. The NPD never crossed the 5 percent threshold in national elections required for seating in the West German Bundestag. During the late 1960s, however, worries about the party animated radical students and government officials. Protesters at the Free University renounced the alleged return of "fascists" to German politics. Policymakers feared that continued student radicalism would inspire more counterdemonstrations on the right. Excessive repression of left-leaning protesters could also legitimize the militant rhetoric of the NPD. Student demonstrations at the Free University posed a very difficult dilemma for a society scarred by memories of both the Weimar period of social disorder and the Nazi years of excessive state power.[43]

Washington's attempts to secure West German financial and moral support for the war in Vietnam added another layer to the Federal Republic's troubles. Repeatedly, President Johnson argued that anticommunist commitments in Southeast Asia were vital to NATO's international credibility. Allowing communist advances in Vietnam would encourage enemy incursions in Europe as well.[44]

Student protesters in West Berlin turned this argument on its head. They contended that America's support for South Vietnamese dictators discredited the democratic claims of the anticommunist states. The war in Southeast Asia was not an isolated, distant event for the men and women attending the Free University. They felt the presence of military forces—Warsaw Pact and NATO—all around them. They feared that the indiscriminate and brutal violence exhibited by the allegedly most advanced societies in Vietnam would reverberate in their contested territory. The dogmatic reaction of local police and university officials to the protests of late 1966 only heightened these student anxieties. "Today Vietnam, Tomorrow Us," the protesters predicted.[45]

The "America House" in West Berlin—established to build cultural contacts between the United States and West Germany—became a favored target for demonstrations and physical attacks in 1967. Early in the year members of the Socialist German Student Union defaced the building, throwing makeshift water balloons filled with red paint at its glass and concrete exterior. They accused the United States of propagating imperialism through its cultural, economic, and military programs overseas. Protesters argued that Washington acted as an "occupying" power in West Germany, stifling creative, sometimes socialist-inspired, reforms. The America House in West Berlin found itself under student siege for much of the next decade.[46]

Vice President Hubert Humphrey visited the city on 6 April 1967, seeking to reinvigorate German-American friendship after the first attacks on the U.S. cultural center. Humphrey hoped to arouse the same public displays of goodwill that had greeted President Kennedy's "Ich bin ein Berliner" speech in 1963. Kennedy had also spoken to an enthusiastic Free University audience about the "unity of the West" and future work for the "peaceful reunification of Germany."[47]

Humphrey's appearance in West Berlin succeeded only in extinguishing the lingering legacy of Kennedy's earlier trip. Before his arrival, rumors spread of an assassination attempt organized by some of the West German students who had attacked the America House. On the eve of the vice president's visit the police in West Berlin arrested eleven young people and tightened security. Kennedy had traveled in a topless car, mingled with crowds, and delivered his famous oration from an open platform. Humphrey, in contrast, gave a short, nondescript speech to the Berlin House of Representatives, avoiding any uncontrolled contact with citizens on the street.[48]

During Humphrey's short time in West Berlin more than 2,000 students demonstrated against American policies. The vice president was so dismayed by his treatment that he lashed out against his critics. In a meeting soon after his return to Washington, Humphrey uncharacteristically interjected that the "Europeans have rejected the world after the loss of their colonies. They resent U.S. power . . . The Europeans are selfish. We should challenge them to participate in the world outside their borders. We must keep pounding at them on this problem."[49]

Humphrey correctly identified rising anti-American sentiment in West Berlin. Protesters had seized the initiative in the streets; they were now the ones pressuring state officials. Student demonstrations continued after the vice president's visit, including a sit-in of more than 300 men and women at the meeting of the Free University's Academic Senate. For the first time in its history, the rector of the school had to call police on to the campus. Fears of disorder and excessive reaction rose yet again as university officials struggled to punish disruptive individuals while avoiding additional provocation.[50]

In June another foreign visitor, Shah Mohammed Reza Pahlavi, undermined these efforts to preserve social peace. The Iranian dictator and his glamorous wife traveled around West Germany in an attempt to foster closer economic and cultural ties between the two societies. Leaders in both states saw themselves as emerging "middle" powers, poised to challenge Soviet and American global dominance, as well as growing Chinese power in Asia. During an extended discussion, the shah and West German chancellor Kurt

Georg Kiesinger highlighted new opportunities for collaboration in weapons development and industrial production. West Germany would provide technical know-how and some capital; the Iranians would supply their own capital, labor, and, of course, oil. Working together the two states hoped to escape the constraints of the bipolar international system.[51]

For residents of West Berlin, however, it appeared that deeper relations with the shah would only perpetuate Cold War injustices. At the Free University a number of Iranian émigrés publicized the brutalities of the government in Tehran. The shah's security forces beat, tortured, and often murdered critics at home. No one could question the authority of the absolute ruler. The shah and his close associates flaunted ostentatious riches while the majority of the country's citizens were mired in poverty.[52]

The Iranian leader was an anticommunist and a modernizer who maintained friendly relations with the Western powers in an important strategic area, but he was hardly a democrat. In the rush to build deeper economic and cultural ties with the shah, the Federal Republic, like the United States and other Western nations, neglected the Iranian leader's grave domestic shortcomings.[53] "We Germans," one student leaflet proclaimed, "have, with the help of the other great powers, supported a dictator. We cannot legitimize such a dictator with assistance and heartfelt reception . . . Through our demonstration, we want to direct your attention to the true conditions in Iran."[54]

The domestic brutalities perpetrated in Iran, with Western aid, were not isolated occurrences. Students in West Berlin recognized that communist containment, economic development, and concerns for international stability frequently led democratic leaders to underwrite domestic violence. In Southeast Asia and Latin America this trend was so common by the 1960s as almost to escape notice. In Europe—especially West Germany—the widespread acceptance of the polarized status quo reflected a choice for security over self-determination. "Iran is for us," the protesting students explained, "just one example of the difficult problems in the developing countries today." The "realities" of international politics appeared to smother real democracy. By demonstrating against the Iranian shah, the American vice president, and other allies, members of the Free University hoped to inspire greater concern for "basic democratic rights." Although they did not completely overlook the violence of "leftist" regimes, especially those in the Soviet bloc, protesters focused on the brutalities of "right-wing" anticommunists.[55]

The shah arrived in West Berlin on 2 June 1967. Throughout the day protesting students trailed his entourage, shouting "Freedom for Iranians" and

"Shah, Shah, Charlatan." In the evening, as the foreign guests traveled to the opera house for a performance of Mozart's *Magic Flute*, more than 800 men and women attempted to block the streets. An army of police officers and the shah's personal bodyguards reacted to the aggressive crowd with brutal force. After the delayed dignitaries finally reached their destination, Iranian personnel used large sticks and other projectiles to beat the protesters. According to some reports, the local police acted similarly.[56]

Amidst the disorder on the Berlin streets, a plainclothes police officer fired two shots. Benno Ohnesorg, a twenty-six-year-old Free University student, fell to the ground and died soon thereafter. By almost all accounts Ohnesorg was only a peripheral participant in the demonstrations. No one provided evidence that he directly provoked the West Berlin police in any way. According to the bishop of his church, Ohnesorg was "not a fanatic" but a good citizen, active in the student religious community.[57]

Ohnesorg's murder threw the city into chaos. The anguish displayed by students and other sympathetic citizens after the incident rivaled the emotions unleashed by the construction of the Berlin Wall almost six years earlier. The mayor of West Berlin, Heinrich Albertz, gave an address on television the next day, pleading for "security and order." He accused an extreme minority of "terrorizing" the population.[58]

This student minority grew in size and unruliness during the following days. On June 3 more than 4,000 men and women gathered to condemn the entire West Berlin city government for Ohnesorg's death. The angry protesters demanded the resignation of the mayor, the police chief, and other officials. They also called for legal action against the West German media magnate, Axel Springer, for encouraging police violence during the demonstrations.[59]

Mayor Albertz soon resigned. The Springer press came under increasing attack throughout the Federal Republic. The city of West Berlin never regained the "security and order" that government and university officials demanded. A frustrated Chancellor Kiesinger lamented that the youth of his nation had fallen victim to an "international sickness" that had infected all the major states. The West German government struggled to repress proliferating student demonstrations without provoking more radicalism or an NPD-advocated reaction.[60]

In the second half of 1967 one fiery student emerged as the chief agitator for protest activity in West Berlin. Rudolf "Rudi" Dutschke came from the province of Brandenburg in East Germany. The communist government had barred him from higher education when he refused to participate in mandatory military service during the late 1950s. As a consequence, Dutschke attended the Free University, the only institution from which he was not excluded. After the construction of the Berlin Wall he fled to the western half of the city, continuing his studies in sociology, philosophy, and political science.

Unlike most other students in Western Europe and the United States, Dutschke had personal experience with the domestic cruelties of the Soviet bloc. In West Berlin, however, he found many of the promised freedoms unfulfilled. Dutschke took particular aim at the "manipulation" of power that allowed dominant political and economic groups to make policy without popular consent. He blamed government "bureaucracy" for prolonging Cold War divisions in Europe, supporting dictators around the world, employing violence in Southeast Asia, and neglecting inequalities between rich and poor. The established political institutions in West Germany "blocked" necessary reforms. "We must always make more people conscious and politically mobilized," Dutschke announced. Active students would harass established elites, creating the foundation for what he called an "antiauthoritarian camp."[61]

Dutschke's rhetoric combined the example of protests in Berkeley with the writings of Herbert Marcuse and Mao Zedong. "We must use direct action," he explained. Halting the machinery of everyday politics, individual citizens would gain a "critical awareness" of the injustices around them. Dutschke admitted that he had no "concrete utopia" to offer, but he believed that the "great refusal" advocated by Marcuse would eventually lead to a society that better approximated the "Garden of Eden." West Berlin would have almost daily Berkeley-like demonstrations with the added sophistication of rhetoric inspired by the German "critical theorists."[62]

Sit-ins, demonstrations, and organized student heckling prohibited regular instruction at the Free University throughout late 1967 and early 1968. Dutschke's followers did much more than voice radical rhetoric. At times student activity became explicitly violent. Men and women began to identify themselves as members of an "academic proletariat" that, in Marxist terms, required the use of force against its oppressors. During protest marches students hurled tomatoes, rocks, and even bricks at the police. Dutschke was careful never to advocate student violence, but when pressed he refused to condemn it.[63]

Free University students saw themselves as players in a global revolution. In his diary Dutschke wrote with relish about the emergence of an international movement against both American and Soviet domination. He overlooked the domestic abuses of Mao Zedong, Che Guevara, and Fidel Castro because these figures publicly challenged the Cold War status quo. They were vanguards for radical change in image, if not in reality. Following Mao's inspiration in particular, Dutschke called on students around the world to lead a "long march" through the institutions of society, overturning established centers of power from within and without. "The third front is set up," Dutschke wrote in his diary. Like guerrilla fighters in Bolivia and South Vietnam, men and women in West Germany would wage a militant struggle to smash the existing order.[64]

The Vietnam War provided both an inspiration and an opportunity for the student protesters in West Berlin. Dutschke and others saw the fierce fighting around the Tet Offensive as confirmation of the destruction that followed from Western attempts to foster foreign "development." In South Vietnam, American bombs and guns protected an unpopular, corrupt government that looked more like the shah's dictatorship than a democratic state. America and its West European allies had become "imperialists." Vietnamese villagers and German students would struggle as a united "third front" to "revolutionize the masses."[65]

American setbacks in Vietnam opened the possibility for successful resistance from the periphery and from within. "Comrades, Antiauthoritarians, People!" Dutschke exclaimed, "We have an historic opening . . . Real solidarity with the Vietnamese revolution comes from the actual weakening and upheaval in the centers of imperialism." Students, natives, and guerrilla fighters had all become proletarians under the domination of repressive "fascists." The time for a global "emancipatory struggle and national self-determination" had arrived. After Tet the tide of history appeared to move in favor of the weak and downtrodden.[66]

In February 1968 students at the Free University organized an international Vietnam Congress, using the war to bring together 10,000 protesters and intellectuals from all across Western Europe. Reform through existing institutions had become "hopeless," Dutschke remarked in his diary. "We must do something else." "We will make the Vietnam Congress," he wrote, "into an international manifestation of solidarity with the bombed and struggling people." Accordingly, at the congress Dutschke called for "revolutionary struggle" against the domination of the great powers in Asia, Latin America, and other parts of the world.[67]

Demonstrations throughout West Berlin and the rest of West Germany grew more confrontational in succeeding weeks. Students besieged government buildings, foreign embassies, and the offices of university administrators. Instead of sitting in, men and women now staged "go-ins" that included physical harassment and deliberate property damage. Almost all institutions of authority came under attack, including communist-supported organizations that appeared hesitant to join the student radicals.[68]

On the afternoon of 11 April 1968 Josef Bachmann, an unemployed worker, shot Rudi Dutschke three times at close range. Dutschke miraculously survived, but he never fully recovered before his death in 1979. Students immediately blamed the government and the press for encouraging the attack. That night more than 5,000 men and women marched to the center of West Berlin, angrily condemning the entire "system." The next day another 5,000 students protested in front of the city hall. Demonstrations with even larger numbers continued, reaching a crescendo in May. When the West German Bundestag passed the long-debated "emergency laws" for public order, protesters demanded popular "agitation" to undermine the existing regime. By this time, the youth revolt had become a self-conscious "guerrilla" struggle.[69]

The men and women who took to the streets did not achieve the radical changes they desired. They did, however, reorient West German society. Before 1968 West Berlin was a Cold War frontier, an outpost of communist containment. The East Germans and the Soviets constituted the greatest threat to the city. After 1968 the most pressing danger to West Berlin and the Federal Republic came from within. Moscow did not want war but expanded trade and economic assistance from the West. University students who received more financial aid from the state than other citizens were now the main enemies of order. They continuously attacked the government through words, demonstrations, and, in some cases, acts of terror. During the next decade, extreme "extraparliamentary opposition" would remain a source of violence and uncertainty for the West German leadership.[70]

▪ Washington, D.C.: "You Better Get Out of Here"

In early 1968 Dr. Martin Luther King Jr. remained the most recognized civil rights leader in America, but the national movement he had so effectively led since the beginning of the decade showed signs of coming apart. Groups such as the Black Panthers and SNCC challenged the nonviolent tactics of King and his followers. A white backlash against the civil rights movement gained momentum throughout both the South and the North, spearheaded by Alabama governor George Wallace. Most significant, King's efforts to address poverty and the injustice of the Vietnam War failed to attract the sympathetic following that his calls for racial equality elicited. The violent segregation of the South was a far easier enemy to defeat than the less visible suffering of rural families, inner-city residents, and drafted soldiers.[71]

King's approach to all these problems involved broad public mobilization. He relied upon an eloquent appeal to democratic values and Christian faith to inspire listeners. He used peaceful displays of personal courage—marches, boycotts, sit-ins, and strikes—to attract sympathy from onlookers. King was, in the words of one historian, the "epitome of the liberal spirit"—a leader committed to reforming a political system that failed to fulfill its promises. He appealed to inherited American ideals for the purpose of correcting American behavior.[72]

King remained consistent throughout the 1960s, but the world around him changed dramatically. By 1968 he had become a "liberal spirit" swimming against a strong illiberal tide. The polarization of American society in the wake of the Vietnam War left little room for consensus building. Berkeley and other cities grew deeply divided between radicals and conservative opponents. Groups at both ends of the political spectrum resorted to frequent violence out of frustration and fear.

In August 1965 the decade's first major urban riot by poor African Americans began in Watts, a formerly peaceful enclave of southern Los Angeles. During the next two summers similar upheavals occurred in Chicago, Newark, Detroit, and more than forty other cities. These disruptions arose from diverse sources, but they all reflected a turn to violent protest rather than peaceful reform. Citizens and law enforcement personnel resorted to vicious assaults on one another. In 1968 nearly every observer, including King, expected more of the same.[73]

Violence consumed the civil rights movement and its great leader within two months of the Tet Offensive. In late March 1968 King led a demonstration through downtown Memphis, Tennessee, on behalf of striking African-American sanitation workers. Young participants disregarded nonviolent urgings, breaking store windows and looting area businesses. As the peaceful march turned into a riot between rowdy youth and nervous police, King had to flee the scene for his own self-protection.

The civil rights movement's tried and true tactics for peaceful change no longer focused the energies of protesters. "We live in a sick nation," King observed after the disastrous Memphis march. "Maybe we just have to admit that the day of violence is here, and maybe we have to just give up and let violence take its course." King prepared to deliver a sermon to his congregation, at Ebeneezer Baptist Church in Atlanta, titled "Why America May Go to Hell."[74]

Before this scheduled lecture, King visited Memphis again on 3 April 1968 to plan another march, one that he hoped would remain peaceful. In the swirl of violence during this period, King's closest advisers observed that he had become preoccupied with death. He continued to refuse bodyguards, and he revealed a prevailing sense of doom. "We've got some difficult days ahead," King announced to one crowd. Describing the "promised land" of equality that awaited his followers, he admitted that "I may not get there with you."[75]

King's fatalism was well justified. On the evening of 4 April 1968 James Earl Ray shot the civil rights leader on the balcony of his Memphis motel. All evidence indicates that Ray acted alone, but he was hardly the only individual after King's life.[76] If not Ray, someone else would probably have attempted to assassinate King within months. He had already received countless death threats.

America had become a violent place. Instead of inspiring broad support among diverse groups, moderate advocates of peaceful reform became primary targets for attack. King understood this. He expected that he would be only one of many people to die as frustrated citizens turned from the logic of reason to the "voice of violence."[77]

The public reaction to King's assassination differed considerably from the national agony that had followed John F. Kennedy's murder less than five years earlier. In late November 1963 the nation was paralyzed with shock. Life seemed to slow down as the president's casket lumbered down Pennsylvania Avenue in Washington, D.C. Many Americans went on a spending spree, fearful that if this tragedy could occur to the most privileged of men, it could happen to anyone. Why save for a future that might never come?[78]

King's death had a different effect, occurring in a different America. Life now sped up. The future was not uncertain anymore; it was fatally doomed, as the slain civil rights leader had feared. A depressed American public did not pause in anguish over King's death, nor did it enter upon a binge of hedonistic living. Many youth—especially African-American men residing in poor inner-city areas—raged against all signs of established authority. Rioters took part in what historians have called a "carnival" of violence that released pent-up anger and temporarily turned the structure of power in society upside down.[79]

The upheavals beginning on the night of 4 April 1968 were not strategic undertakings, promising any durable accomplishment. Black Americans suffered the vast majority of all property damage and human injury during the riots. The violent reaction to King's assassination reflected a widespread desire to lash out against the circumstances of poverty and discrimination that the African-American community seemed unable to overcome. "If we must die," Stokely Carmichael exclaimed, "we better die fighting back."[80]

Riots occurred in more than 120 cities following King's murder. The most devastating of disturbances took place in Washington, D.C., beginning only hours after James Earl Ray fired his fatal shot in Memphis. When news first reached the large African-American community in the nation's capital, local figures forced city businesses to close out of respect for their slain leader. By 10:30 P.M. parading groups of African Americans began to smash windows and loot displayed merchandise. More than 500 individuals marched into other, largely white neighborhoods. Some carried what they could—televisions, radios, clothing—from ransacked stores that they could not, under normal circumstances, afford to enter. Others stood in the middle of the street, throwing rocks and bottles at passing vehicles. After midnight, growing mobs began to light fires across town. When firefighters attempted to put out the blazes, they came under attack as well.

During the early hours of 5 April, the city where King had spoken of his "dream" for peaceful racial integration five years earlier became a war zone. Angry African Americans controlled many of the streets in the nation's capital. They heavily outnumbered the local police officers hastily dispatched to maintain order. When Mayor Walter E. Washington attempted to survey the scene by car, he could only watch as the looting and burning continued around him. Instead of escorting the local leader through the damage, fearful police officers advised the mayor that "you better get out of here." Despite their use of tear gas, nightsticks, and other implements, law enforcement personnel could not control or contain the rioting.[81]

The mayor was not the only government official in danger. President Johnson, scheduled to address a fundraising dinner at the Washington Hilton Hotel, had to cancel his appearance for reasons of personal safety. Instead, Vice President Humphrey attended the affair. Substituting for the president in an environment filled with street violence, Humphrey must have felt a sense of déjà vu from his ill-fated trip to West Berlin almost exactly one year earlier. As the riots spread through Washington, D.C., police officers had to surround the Hilton in large numbers to ensure the security of the vice president and other guests.[82]

Public looting spread to within ten blocks of the White House. Congressmen, cabinet officials, and other high-ranking figures became prisoners in their homes and offices. The rapid escalation of violence made the leaders of the "free world" fearful of walking or driving on their own streets. The U.S. government had contained adversaries abroad with relative success, but it was now physically imperiled by enemies within. Each additional sidewalk lost to the raging mobs represented another fallen domino, another further encroachment on the nation's security by its own citizens.[83]

On 6 April more than 11,000 troops from the U.S. Army entered Washington, D.C. They placed the nation's capital under military "occupation," with virtual martial law. Two to four soldiers patrolled each city block in the riot-torn areas. Personnel stationed at checkpoints on area highways stopped and searched all vehicles entering the city. Mounted machine guns appeared on the steps of the Capitol. A 6:00 P.M. to 6:00 A.M. curfew required all residents to remain indoors during the hours of darkness. Citizens and soldiers alike compared the circumstances in Washington, D.C., to "pacification" of villagers in Vietnam.[84]

By the next morning the city had returned to an eerie quiet. Army troops remained in Washington through the following weekend, gradually lifting the curfew and other restrictions on citizen activity. Twelve civilians died during the riots, a relatively small number compared with the toll from similar disorders in other cities. This number should not, however, disguise the extreme violence of the events. During a four-day period local police fired more than 8,000 canisters of tear gas at unruly crowds, and 1,190 people suffered injuries at the hands of rioters or those attempting to enforce order. Law enforcement personnel arrested more than 7,600 people. Property damage and government expenses during the riots exceeded $27 million.[85]

"Our nation is moving toward two societies," the National Advisory Commission on Civil Disorders had warned before April 1968, "one black, one white—separate and unequal."[86] The upheavals that followed Martin Luther King Jr.'s assassination confirmed this pessimistic observation, but they also pointed to a more discouraging phenomenon. America was divided not only by race but also by age. The rioting mobs on the streets of Washington and other cities were disproportionately composed of young men. Unlike their elder counterparts who had participated in the peaceful demonstrations of the civil rights movement, these urban youths saw little hope in gradual reform. They thought of themselves as "guerrilla" fighters, not spiritual healers.

The African-American crowds that ransacked the nation's capital shared more in language and behavior with their white counterparts at Berkeley and the Free University than with the earlier civil rights marchers. Although the material conditions of the inner city differed markedly from the privileged circumstances of elite colleges, youth from different races harbored a common disaffection with the established channels of social reform. Martin Luther King Jr.'s death appeared to provide incontrovertible evidence that nonviolent change could not work. Revolutions required armed struggle. A growing cohort of young Americans—black and white—believed that they could redress inequalities and end the war in Vietnam only through increased violence. Members of the Black Power movement and student radicals forged loose alliances during the tumultuous months of 1968.[87]

Political leaders, including President Johnson, recognized this radical inclination among many young Americans. One could no longer dismiss them as an extremist fringe. With violence building in cities and universities, something clearly had to be done. Middle-aged leaders unaccustomed to dealing with angry young men and women were confounded and, frankly, scared.[88]

▪ Paris: "There's a Battle Raging"

French President Charles de Gaulle was not someone easily scared. Comparing the 1960s with the harrowing days of World War II, the former leader of the French Resistance lamented that he now lived in "mediocre" times. De Gaulle expressed frustration with the difficulties of governing a large nation during a period that "is certainly not dramatic." Charismatic leadership required a consensus on big threats. Public fear, in this sense, could prove very useful. De Gaulle—like John F. Kennedy years earlier—longed for a major challenge that would allow him to demonstrate his courage and galvanize popular support.[89]

Soon after de Gaulle deplored his "mediocre" times, an overriding public threat emerged in France. The president now had a clear "enemy," but it was one he proved poorly equipped to confront. De Gaulle had fought foreign adversaries, communists, and domestic militarists throughout his career. He had never, however, dealt with broad generational conflict. A public divided by age rather than party affiliation showed frustrating indifference toward the president's appeals to a common French language, culture, and historic *grandeur*. Young French citizens in the late 1960s had no recollection of World War II and the Resistance—the formative experiences for de Gaulle and his counterparts. Instead of national strength and unity against foreign challengers, university students looked to a "glorious revolutionary tradition" that harkened back to public protests and radicalism before the formation of the Fifth Republic.[90]

The Gaullist vision of national *grandeur* created what many citizens called "cultural alienation." They contended that contemporary political decisions reflected the interests of national security but not the social concerns of the population. Hierarchies of authority limited freedom in the workplace, the university, and the local community. Students condemned what they called the contemporary "blockage" against "self-determination." Instead of de Gaulle's "popular monarchy," they wanted a less hierarchical and more contentious democracy. The current government, one student pamphlet explained, "is for the people but is no longer operated by the people."[91]

As violent upheaval swept the streets of Berkeley, West Berlin, Washington, D.C., and other cities in early 1968, Paris initially remained quiet.

Nanterre, a new university on the outskirts of the French capital, became a center for student protests, but these activities received little public attention. Opened in 1964 to serve the burgeoning population of students, Nanterre was a "wasteland campus" without any cafés, movie theaters, or even a library. The 15,000 men and women at this university quickly grew dissatisfied with their insufficient facilities. In April 1967 a group of male students, led by Daniel Cohn-Bendit, used a sit-in at one of the all-female dormitories to voice their discontent with the social limits of university life. Without cafés and other locales where they could informally meet women, men rebelled against the prohibitions upon entrance into female campus residences. Police forces quickly dispersed the Nanterre demonstrators with little fanfare. Protests of this sort did not seem serious.

These apparently innocuous events were the early winds of a gathering storm. Daniel Cohn-Bendit, a sociology student whose Jewish parents had fled Germany for France during the Nazi years, gained notoriety among his colleagues for his intrepid challenges to authority. In addition to condemning restrictions on student freedom, Cohn-Bendit attacked the so-called Fouchet Plan, designed to make higher education in France more disciplined and preprofessional. He also criticized the use of police power on university campuses and alleged French complicity in the Vietnam War. On the latter issue, students advocated more active protests, and even assaults, against American facilities in France.[92]

During March 1968 young men and women organized a series of anti-American demonstrations throughout Paris. At one event, protesters threw rocks at an American Express travel office, shattering its windows. The police arrested six Nanterre students who had participated in the violence. Simultaneously a rumor circulated that the university rector had compiled a "black list" of troublemakers—including Cohn-Bendit—for punishment and even extradition. Cohn-Bendit held German, not French, citizenship. He was therefore subject to possible deportation.[93]

Nanterre students reacted to the arrests and the talk of a "black list" with their largest demonstration to date. On 22 March more than 150 men and women, heavily influenced by recent protests in Berkeley and West Berlin, occupied the main administration building on campus—the first such student takeover in France. The protesters demanded that the university and the government stop trying to "run society like an army." Broadening their agenda beyond the controversies surrounding university facilities and the Vietnam War, they called for a "vast debate" on the nature of capitalism, imperialism, and the "workers' and students' struggle in the East and the West." In order to prevent a planned student teach-in on 29 March, the rector of Nanterre closed the school from 28 March through 1 April. This move only increased the ire of the protesters, whose numbers grew in reaction to the hard line of the university administration.[94]

More than 1,000 students assembled on 2 April to condemn the university's restrictive policies. They formed the "22 March Movement," designed to expose what they perceived as the systemic injustices of capitalism and imperialism. The students employed Marxist rhetoric in their criticism of class repression in France, but they deliberately distanced themselves from communists, whose primary allegiance remained with the party, not the men and women taking to the streets. The 22 March Movement marked the beginning of a broad-based anti-Soviet left among student radicals in France.[95]

By late April similar protest activities took shape in Paris around one of the nation's most distinguished universities, the Sorbonne. When a committee there summoned eight students participating in the 22 March Movement for possible discipline, demonstrations in the Latin quarter began in earnest. Suddenly French newspaper readers discovered the existence of a youth rebellion in their midst, similar to more publicized movements in Berkeley and West Berlin. Journalists began to write about a student "insurrection."[96]

As in West Berlin, large public demonstrations in Paris drew both radical students and right-wing organizations. Like their counterparts at the Free University, leftist groups at the Sorbonne announced that "exceptional domestic and international conditions" opened a unique opportunity for "revolution." According to one student leaflet, the "defeat of American imperialism in Vietnam" and the "radical crisis in the United States" gave formerly powerless people an opportunity to change the politics of the Cold War. The mobilization of allegedly "proletarianized" students and workers would promote an international "democratization of power" across Europe, North America, and Asia.[97]

Right-wing groups condemned this revolutionary rhetoric for applying alien ideas to the unique circumstances of French society. Members of an organization known as Occident called for an emphasis upon nationalism. Proclaiming themselves "neither Gaullist, nor communist," they wanted a reformed "New France" that would assert itself more forcefully abroad. They also pledged to rebuild France's bloated domestic institutions, allowing for more freedom, creativity, and civic spirit. Like the NPD in West Germany, Occident accepted the radical diagnosis of contemporary social stagnation. The organization sought to build a more vibrant state with new leaders who could inspire the young. Occident promised even more *grandeur* than de Gaulle.[98]

On 3 May 1968 the rector of the Sorbonne hastily called the Parisian police to remove student demonstrators—leftist and rightist—blocking buildings at the university. Never in recent memory had the police entered the grounds of the Sorbonne. The crowds of protesters appeared threatening, but they remained relatively small, at least until law enforcement personnel arrived. The police allowed female demonstrators to leave the area peacefully. They herded male students into black vans for arrest.

News of alleged police brutality brought many people to the area. As the vans with the detained men drove away, onlookers attempted to block the vehicles. Students "ripped up the iron gratings from around the trees on the pavement to block the vans, threw everything they could lay their hands on at them, [and] burnt newspapers to prevent the motorcycle police from getting through." "It was a great battle," one young woman remembered, "a festival! I felt happy. The violence was restoring to the student movement what it had lost since the end of the Algerian War." These sentiments reflected the intoxicating experience of crowd protest for many participants. Similar feelings would draw more students to the street in the next few weeks.[99]

Extended urban violence, reminiscent of the unrest experienced in Paris during the late 1950s, constituted the worst nightmare for local leaders. In response to the obstruction of their vehicles, the police used brute force against the students, hoping to smother any future thoughts of rebellion. They attacked the crowd with truncheons and exploded large doses of tear gas to disperse people from the streets. By the end of the day, the police had arrested 590 men and women. Eighty officers suffered injuries, in addition to several hundred students and other civilians.[100]

These violent altercations provoked an immediate escalation of protests at the Sorbonne and other schools around Paris. Daniel Cohn-Bendit, who traveled from Nanterre to join the demonstrations in the Latin Quarter, later commented that 3 May was the "day that really mobilized student opinion; the first great ripple of a swelling tide."[101] High school pupils soon joined protests throughout the city. Imitating the Paris Commune of 1871, young men and women began to construct street barricades on the night of 10–11 May. These makeshift fortifications provided students with temporary freedom from police authority in the areas around various schools. The barricade builders moved cars, assembled building debris, and gathered whatever they could find to block off city streets. Various student factions united behind the Sorbonne's "Action Committee," pledging to deploy "all the forces" available to "abolish dictatorial power" in France.[102]

The barricades symbolized the group autonomy that many young men and women desired. Transforming their immediate surroundings, the students hoped they would become the vanguard for a "new society." "We oppose," one Sorbonne group exclaimed, "the hierarchical military and Napoleonic organization of the state." Students would experiment with new forms of living in order to make their education, and the nation as a whole, respond "to the real needs of society."[103] In this context, the Sorbonne Action Committee argued that violence might prove necessary. Like the heroes of Victor Hugo's *Les Misérables*, men and women resorted to barricades and guerrilla fighting because "the entire world does violence to us." Revolution against police brutality required more than peaceful protest.[104]

Student communities behind the barricades really did approximate Hugo's story. Young men and women used their newfound freedom to read radical literature and engage in "free love." As Marius and Cosette found one another behind the barricades in *Les Misérables*, many students developed romantic attachments amidst the protests, spending hours together on the streets and living in close proximity.

Protest behind the barricades was serious, but it was also great fun. Demonstrations against authority provided much more romance, excitement, and esprit de corps than the daily drudgery at school or university. Lilly Métreaux recalled her exhilaration during these heady days. Before May 1968 "I had begun to acquire a real culture, Marxism, to understand what was at stake in Vietnam, to take on responsibilities although I was still very young . . . one morning, my young brother comes running home, out of breath, with his little satchel, saying: 'Come quick, there's a demonstration!' So instead of going to school I followed him and we found ourselves on the Boulevard Saint-Michel in the middle of this huge demonstration."[105]

The whirl of the crowd whipped its participants into an orgy of love and violence. "There was a sort of magic island coming out of nowhere, and it was us, the young ones, who were pulling it out," Métreaux explained. "My brother's best friend, Nicholas, and I fell in love, became lovers . . . I helped them bring out their school on strike, going from classroom to classroom. All the kids ran into the streets."[106]

De Gaulle's government would not accept the anarchy and "free love" of the students' "magic island." The police must "clean up the streets," Minister of the Interior Christian Fouchet exclaimed. "That's all." "Power does not retreat," the president declared, as he had during previous periods of unrest.[107]

Charismatic authority depended upon the image of omnipotence that de

Gaulle had cultivated so assiduously throughout his career. The man who had refused compromise with the likes of Hitler and Stalin—and, to a lesser degree, Kennedy and Johnson—could not afford to retreat when confronted by a few thousand unarmed youth. Compromise in these circumstances would diminish de Gaulle's asserted *grandeur*.

During the early hours of 11 May 1968 riot police stormed the student barricades. Journalists on the scene provided close coverage of this event. Over the radio, an announcer who usually described soccer competitions offered colorful play-by-play for the bloody street match: "Now the [riot police] are charging, they're storming the barricade—oh, my God! There's a battle raging. The students are counter-attacking, you can hear the noise— the [riot police] are retreating . . . Now they're re-grouping, getting ready to charge again. The inhabitants are throwing things from their windows at the [riot police]—oh! The police are retaliating, shooting grenades into the windows of apartments."[108]

By 6:00 A.M. on 11 May law enforcement personnel had won their match with the demonstrators, but at great cost. More than 376 people had suffered injuries, a third of whom were members of the riot police. Government authorities had arrested almost 500 men and women. Street fighting had caused serious damage to more than one hundred cars and countless storefronts.[109]

Pictures of riot police attacking unarmed students appeared on the front pages of newspapers in France and much of the rest of the world. Paris was again the epicenter of a worldwide revolution. Men and women at the Sorbonne spoke of participating in upheavals "everywhere in Europe." The use of brute force to destroy the barricades pushed the students off the streets, but it also killed the "Old Regime." University and city life would never recapture its pre-May 1968 form. Mutual suspicion between students and administrators—and the general fear of future rioting—would mar any attempted return to "normalcy" in France, or in the rest of Europe for that matter.[110]

Adopting the language of the Chinese Cultural Revolution, one student publication explained that the "reign of the Mandarins is finished." Through their use of force, established elites had admitted that they could not command popular legitimacy among the young. De Gaulle's regime would remain in power, but now only with the assistance of frequent violence.[111]

Self-doubt began to creep in on the aging French president. When Parisian students called a nationwide strike and were joined by factory workers across France, de Gaulle despaired that "in five days, ten years of struggle against the rottenness in the state have been lost." For the first time in his life de Gaulle suffered from insomnia, unable to reconcile his faith in the French "spirit" with the growing manifestations of popular protest against his leadership.[112]

By 24 May striking students, workers, and various sympathizers had brought the city of Paris to a virtual standstill. Fearful of street violence, businesspeople and other citizens avoided any confrontation with the protesters or the police. French television ceased to report on the Paris upheavals because the state broadcasting company could not find enough working personnel. Truck drivers did not make many of their deliveries to the city, creating acute food and fuel shortages. Gasoline rationing prevented most citizens from driving. Government authority in Paris became, in the words of the metropolitan police chief, "a theater of shadows."[113]

De Gaulle ordered Prime Minister Georges Pompidou to negotiate with laborers but not with students.[114] Despondent, tired, and confused, the French president made a curious journey with his wife to the West German town of Baden-Baden. De Gaulle's advisers could not discern whether the president wanted to flee for his personal safety or to organize a military campaign against the revolutionaries who had shut down the government. Pompidou feared that de Gaulle would never return.[115]

When de Gaulle arrived in Baden-Baden he went to see General Jacques Massu, the commander of French forces stationed in West Germany. No one was more surprised by the president's unannounced arrival than Massu. He received a call at 2:40 P.M. indicating that de Gaulle had entered his military base. The surprised general allegedly exclaimed: "Look, I'm naked in bed and I am having my siesta. Give me five minutes to get ready." The French president had never before made an unannounced visit to foreign territory. Massu was accustomed to quiet, languid days on duty.[116]

Agitated and nervous in contrast to his slumbering subordinate, de Gaulle announced that "it's all over." Lamenting the "total paralysis of the country," he explained that "I'm not in charge of anything any more. I'm withdrawing . . . since I feel that I and my family are threatened in France, I've come to seek refuge with you . . . People don't want me anymore."[117]

Massu urged the president not to resign, "for the country's sake, for your own sake . . . Everything that has been done over the past ten years cannot disappear in ten days. You will open the floodgates and accelerate the chaos that it is your duty to control. You must fight till the end," Massu advised, "on the terrain that you have chosen . . . If you leave power, it must only be after consulting the people."[118]

His spirits lifted by this strange meeting in Baden-Baden, de Gaulle returned to Paris on 30 May. Confident of support from Massu and other military officers, the president dissolved the National Assembly. He called for new elections as a referendum on the student protests and his leadership. In a radio address to the nation, de Gaulle warned that the street demonstrations threatened to bring a "dictatorship" of "totalitarian communism." Playing upon public frustrations with continued disorder throughout Paris and much of the rest of the country, he argued that only a reaffirmation of his authority could assure "progress, independence, and peace."[119]

As de Gaulle stood firm against the student protesters, Pompidou worked to buy off the striking workers. He offered them a general wage increase of 10 percent, accompanied by a 35 percent rise in the minimum pay for agricultural and industrial work. Pompidou also promised a shorter work week, a 5 percent increase in medical expenses reimbursed by the state, expanded union rights, and, most startlingly, 50 percent back pay for days on strike. The unions in France initially rejected this generous offer, hoping to get even more from a desperate government. During the early weeks of June, however, the continuing costs of striking and the increasing use of government force led most workers to accept what Pompidou proposed.[120]

On 30 June voters overwhelmingly backed de Gaulle's supporters, electing them to 360 of 485 seats in the National Assembly. Once again the president had made an effective call upon "le peuple." He exploited the uncertainty and frustration born of the disorders in Paris and other cities. In a reprise of 1958, citizens backed de Gaulle as a bulwark against revolutionary upheaval on the streets.[121]

Fifth Republic France remained intact, but it was badly shaken. Demonstrations continued across the country during the second half of 1968. If anything, the June elections proved that society was in fact "blocked," as protesters claimed. De Gaulle made the vote a referendum on order or chaos, "popular monarchy" or radicalism. Many citizens wanted to escape these polarities. As late as November 1968 students continued to agitate on the streets and in print for a "third force." Protesters gave increasing attention to the "Great Refusal" preached by Herbert Marcuse and the grassroots mobilization advocated by Mao Zedong's "Great Proletarian Cultural Revolution." More factions and internal antagonisms dominated French society in late 1968 than at any time since de Gaulle's return to power a decade earlier.[122]

No consensus emerged in France on what would constitute an effective and desirable "third force." The president had played upon this uncertainty in June 1968, but he could not continue to do so for very long. The demonstrators did not accomplish their revolution, but they did undermine de Gaulle's leadership. His initial hesitancy and confusion revealed the limits of his charisma. De Gaulle no longer commanded the allegiance of the crowd. His vision of French *grandeur* did not have the same appeal, especially among the young, as in prior years. The great man now appeared very small.[123]

When de Gaulle submitted his plans for government reorganization to a popular referendum in April 1969, 53 percent of voters rejected the initiative. Humiliated and exhausted, he immediately resigned. This time he did not bother to consult with General Massu or any other members of the military.

De Gaulle had never regained the self-confidence that he lost in May 1968. He recognized that he could no longer lead the nation, that he no longer embodied "le peuple." The demonstrations in Paris and other cities made it clear that he could only expect more "difficulties." De Gaulle admitted that the 1968 rebellion had diminished "the figure that History has made of me." The students had worn the old man out.[124]

▪ Prague: "We Want Light!"

Prague in the late 1960s was the Paris of Eastern Europe. The city's long history as a magnet for artists, intellectuals, and interlopers made it a natural home for dissident thinkers. Under the watchful eyes of communist authorities, writers and students in the capital of Czechoslovakia continued to push the limits of accepted opinion. The Soviet-supported government had outlawed capitalism, but it could not eliminate the traditions of Bohemian iconoclasm.

During the years after the Hungarian revolt of 1956, the Czechoslovak leadership worked to smother the potential for a similar uprising in Prague. While the Soviet Union and other East European countries pursued de-Stalinization, Czechoslovak leader Antonín Novotný condemned most manifestations of "revisionism." Ironically, the clash between the strong-arm tactics of the state and a remarkably resilient dissident tradition produced the very revolutionary explosion that Novotný feared.[125]

In 1967 Czechoslovakia's most distinguished writers—Milan Kundera, Pavel Kohout, Ludvík Vaculík, and Václav Havel—condemned the tightening restrictions of communist censorship. Speaking at the Fourth Czechoslovak Writers' Congress, Havel publicly defied government authorities, pledging his "respect" for Soviet dissident Aleksandr Solzhenitsyn's "true ethical stance" against the communist system. Vaculík went even further. He argued that under a repressive leadership Czechoslovak society had "lost so much moral and material strength." Despite the spread of education and industry, he observed, "We have not contributed any original thoughts or good ideas to humanity."[126]

The Czechoslovak Communist Party expelled the writers for their defiant words, making them official outcasts. This action, however, failed to repress what had become a mounting social crisis by the last quarter of 1967. Czechoslovakia suffered from all the signs of youth apathy and discontent evident in the Soviet Union at the time.[127]

Like its counterpart in Moscow, Novotný's government found it increasingly difficult to motivate citizens for patriotic duty in the military and the Communist Party. Warsaw Pact representatives observed a threatening decline in the operational effectiveness of the Czechoslovak armed forces as recruits challenged regimental discipline. The student population grew during the 1960s, but the number of men and women affiliated with the state-sponsored Czechoslovak Union of Youth declined by 33 percent, from 1.5 million in 1963 to barely 1 million in 1966. Students accounted for less than 0.5 percent of the Communist Party membership in 1966. Czechoslovakia was a state with aging leaders and a large cohort of young, disaffected citizens. Even state authorities spoke of a "youth problem."[128]

Czechoslovakia had become a dark and drab society, a "closed-minded," medieval world, according to Milan Kundera.[129] Young citizens longed to enliven the city of Prague with bright and energetic ideas, many inspired by dissident figures in both the East and the West. Students distributed typed copies of Vaculík's scandalous speech at the writers' congress, they read Solzhenitsyn and other Soviet dissidents, they listened to rock and roll, and they followed the agitations for a "third way" in West Berlin, Paris, and the other cities of Europe. Forbidden thoughts reached the educated young in Prague through self-published (samizdat) journals, American-sponsored Radio Free Europe broadcasts, and occasional foreign visitors.[130]

Young women in Czechoslovakia, for example, managed to obtain feminist literature from abroad. Betty Friedan's book The Feminine Mystique was particularly popular.[131] Even though Friedan focused upon the difficulties of the white, upper-middle-class American "housewife," her words resonated among disillusioned women in Prague. In late 1967 Friedan visited the city, meeting with the members of the new Czechoslovak Union of Women. "I found developments there very fascinating," Friedan wrote; "they certainly increased my insight into the depth and importance of the unfinished revolution . . . all of us are fighting to complete." This was one manifestation of a broader cultural and intellectual connection developing among angry, often young, citizens on both sides of the Iron Curtain.[132]

Novotný's heavy-handed repression of popular writers converted anger to rebellion. Frustrated with the restrictions on their freedom, 1,500 students, mostly from the Czech Technical College, took to the streets of Prague on 31 October 1967. The most recent in a series of electrical power outages at a local dormitory sparked the protests. Carrying candles, student demonstrators chanted: "We want light!"—a plea for both electrical power and an openness to new ideas.[133]

Novotný deployed special Public Security Police to disperse the protesters. Law enforcement personnel initially relied upon tear gas. When the demonstrators organized a mass meeting, the police attacked the unarmed men and women. Thirteen students suffered injuries, as did three of the uniformed officers.[134]

The overreaction of the police provoked more protest from students and sympathetic intellectuals in Prague. On 8 November a group of students from Charles University held a five-hour meeting, independent of Communist Party supervision. They adopted a resolution demanding punishment of the police officers responsible for attacking the students. More significant, the students condemned the official state media for distorted news coverage and called for more open and accurate reporting. Like the famous figures who had spoken out at the writers' congress in June, students wanted a freer press. According to one analysis, the protesters in Prague contributed to a "broad oppositional front" with other rebellious intellectuals.[135]

Alarmed by the boldness of student criticisms, the Czechoslovak government expressed regret about the violence on 31 October. Authorities in the Ministry of the Interior pledged to improve conditions for student life, especially with regard to electrical power in the dormitories. Novotný's regime, however, refused to admit any errors in "restoring public order." The state would not tolerate protests that challenged the one-party dictatorship.[136]

Through November and early December tensions in Prague continued to rise. Discontent among students, intellectuals, and other citizens bubbled to the surface throughout the city. The streets remained orderly, but young people became overtly critical of Novotný and his fellow party bosses. Students threatened future demonstrations if the government refused to initiate new reforms. They formed a coordinating committee for this purpose, against official prohibitions. In alliance with dissident writers, students demanded the right to publish their own journal, free of Communist Party censorship.[137]

Novotný's government faced an upsurge in domestic resistance that threatened imminent disorder. With each day, the demands of students and intellectuals seemed to grow. Foreign observers began to worry that Czechoslovak society would either descend into chaos or suffer from a round of violent neo-Stalinist repression. American Ambassador Jacob Beam reported that the population of Prague was visibly "unsatisfied"; unable to inspire or even enforce citizen loyalty, the Communist Party had entered a period of "internal confusion."[138]

Confusion quickly gave way to strife among leaders. Alexander Dubček, the first secretary of the Slovak Communist Party (subsumed within the larger Czechoslovak apparatus), criticized Novotný for following a method of governance that was too "conservative." Novotný's unwillingness to pursue necessary reforms contributed, Dubček argued, to threatening conditions among "concrete people." Confronted with student unrest, intellectual dissent, and many other domestic difficulties, the time appeared right for a new "long-term party program" that would strengthen communism, rather than brute repression.[139]

Dubček's criticisms resonated with other party leaders. A group of respected officials—Mária Sedláková, František Kriegel, and Josef Špacek—joined Dubček in demanding more energetic leadership and drastic policy change. Students and intellectuals had not overturned the ruling party, but they had made the political status quo appear untenable. The Czechoslovak leadership had to undertake new measures, either along a more conservative Novotný path or perhaps in a more "liberal" direction.[140]

Alarmed by the divisions within the Czechoslovak Communist Party, Soviet leader Leonid Brezhnev made an emergency visit to Prague on 8 December. He spent forty-eight hours in the city, meeting with different members of the regime. Brezhnev later reported that during his stay he had had only three hours free from discussion for "personal hygiene and food." Although this was surely an exaggeration—particularly for a self-indulgent man like Brezhnev—the description of marathon deliberations captures the urgency of the moment.[141]

Brezhnev was initially disposed against any change of leadership in Czechoslovakia. He came away from his visit, however, with the impression that "Comrade Novotný hasn't the slightest idea about the true state of affairs." His dictatorial control over government activities had inspired dangerous resentments among well-meaning communists. Groups seeking to resist state authority were taking advantage of the leader's failed policies and the divisions among his associates. Brezhnev found Dubček's call for a new Communist Party program more promising than Novotný's continued adherence to a dogmatic hard line. He lamented that the longtime Czechoslovak leader "does not know what collective leadership is" or "how to handle people."[142]

Brezhnev did not explicitly endorse any side in the dispute among the

Czechoslovak communists. He emphasized that Czechoslovakia required a strong and unified government to deter external challengers. "Unity," Brezhnev explained "is a supreme principle that begins at the nucleus of the [Communist] Party." This call for unity favored the arguments of men like Dubček who promised new ideas, rather than more of the same dead-end policies. The Soviet leader's failure to back Novotný against his challengers sealed his fate. Novotný could no longer rely on Moscow to ensure his legitimacy and, more important, his access to military force. Soon after Brezhnev's departure, Novotný resigned.[143]

Alexander Dubček became the new leader of the Czechoslovak Communist Party on 5 January 1968. His mandate from the Central Committee reflected concerns about domestic discontent. In order to revitalize the public standing of the government, the party called for "far greater encouragement of an open exchange of views" within society. Dubček announced that the government would direct "all of our endeavors . . . toward a true invigoration and unification of all constructive and progressive forces in the republic . . . This is the necessary prerequisite for a new inception of socialism." The future strength of the Czechoslovak Communist Party required the cultivation of what Dubček called "democratic forms" originating "from below"— among workers, scientists, intellectuals, and students.[144]

The new Czechoslovak leader believed in the sanctity of the Communist Party. He also understood the importance of following Soviet tutelage in Eastern Europe. For these reasons, he emphasized the "leading role" of the communists and the virtues of "centralism": "We want to rally all the citizens of our republic to implement the progressive objectives of socialist development and strengthen confidence in the party."[145]

Dubček hoped to build a new political consensus somewhere between the dogmatism of Novotný and the raucous behavior of the Prague students. As he preserved the anticapitalist shibboleths of the Communist Party, Dubček promoted "voluntary discipline" that would strengthen the Czechoslovak state. "Today more than ever," he explained, "the important thing is not to reduce our policy to a struggle 'against' but, more importantly, to wage a struggle 'for' . . . We cannot preserve past values simply by defending them all the time." Dubček called for all factions in society to explore "new problems boldly in the face . . . We shall tackle these in a new and creative manner, in a manner dictated by our present reality."[146]

Singling out students for attention, Dubček argued that Communist Party reforms required "far greater participation" from the nation's youth. Young men and women in Prague were better educated than their forebears.

They could infuse Czechoslovak society with the creative energies needed to overcome what Dubček perceived as a contemporary malaise. Calls for open discussions served as a direct appeal to the young. Co-opting them in a project to strengthen the state rather than suppressing their dissident thoughts, Dubček expected that he could coax the unruly students into becoming loyal communists. Reforms would channel rebellious energies for constructive purpose.[147]

The "Action Program," published in April 1968, followed along these general lines. It affirmed the "leading role of the Communist Party," the continuing struggle against capitalist "imperialism," and the fundamental importance of Prague's alliance with Moscow. At the same time, the Action Program called for domestic pluralism. "The [Communist] Party does not want to and will not take the place of social organizations . . . The role of the Party is to find a way of satisfying the various interests without jeopardizing the interests of society as a whole." In this context, Dubček went so far as to advocate "freedom of speech" and expanded rights of personal choice in profession and "lifestyle." The Communist Party would lead by persuasion, not by coercive force.[148]

Czechoslovakia's East European allies, especially in Poland and East Germany, quickly grew skeptical of Dubček's reforms. They worried, in the words of Polish leader Władysław Gomułka, that Czechoslovakia risked following a "path to counterrevolution." Free speech would allow "imperialists" to gain support among students and workers. "Why not draw conclusions from what happened in Hungary [in 1956]?" Gomułka asked. "That all began in a similar way."[149]

Leonid Brezhnev had the same apprehensions, but he also recognized the promise of Dubček's reforms. If the Czechoslovak leader could revitalize his society, he would inspire improvements in morale and unity throughout the Soviet bloc. Brezhnev understood the necessity of pursuing a more dynamic "route" to "socialist democracy." Although the Soviet leader did not want to encourage the now-repudiated excesses of Khrushchev's de-Stalinization, he realized that one could not return to the days of dictatorial terror. Novotný had tried to rule like Stalin, and he had produced a stagnant, discontented, and divided society.

Brezhnev warily endorsed the Czechoslovak Action Program. He wrote a personal letter to Dubček explaining that "I understand very well that your work is aimed at overcoming certain difficulties, the most important of which is that amidst the healthy trends, revisionist and hostile forces are seeking to divert Czechoslovakia from the socialist path." "You can always count on our full support," the Soviet leader pledged, "in the struggle to bolster the cause of socialism, the cohesion of the socialist countries, and the unity of the world communist movement."[150]

Brezhnev warned about the "great dangers" that accompanied "crash" reforms. Referring indirectly to Khrushchev's failures, he advised against the urge to seek "immediate solutions to all the problems that have accumulated." The older Brezhnev adopted a paternalistic tone with his younger Czechoslovak counterpart: "I can tell you quite frankly that life and experience show that overly hasty corrections of past mistakes and imperfections, and the desire to solve everything at once, can make for new and even greater mistakes and consequences. That's why I want to point out the danger that the current emphasis on immediately solving a broad array of complicated questions, which can evoke disagreements, could possibly undermine the very important process of consolidation that you've started."[151]

Brezhnev desired a gradual opening in Czechoslovakia. Dubček, however, saw a need for rapid reform. Both men sought to strengthen the authority of the Communist Party, but they disagreed fundamentally on tactics. Dubček's methods allowed new freedoms for protesting students and intellectuals, exposing his regime to domestic criticism. Brezhnev feared the consequences of freer dissent among Czechoslovak citizens. The Soviet leader's gradualism was rooted in a desire to maintain stability above all. Ironically, Dubček's radicalism—like that of the Prague students—was much more orthodox in its socialist theory.

"The Prague Spring," as unleashed by the forty-six year-old Czechoslovak first secretary, aimed to build a more utopian society based on shared needs. In place of large bureaucracies and coercive police forces, government would run on a pledge to make everyone's life better. Encouraging innovative ideas, public criticisms, and independent groupings, the Communist Party would serve as an umbrella organization bringing together the concerns of all citizens. A truly classless society would emerge as everyone cooperated on equal footing. This was a vision of democratic socialism, inspired by a long tradition of nineteenth-century European thought. Dubček hoped to build a workers' and intellectuals' state without the exploitative characteristics of either capitalism or Soviet-bloc communism.[152]

Brezhnev's worries about this program were well founded. By the middle of 1968 the promise of the Prague Spring had encouraged many students and intellectuals to challenge the "leading role" of the Communist Party. In June Ludvík Vaculík published a bold manifesto, "Two Thousand Words," that extended his criticism of the Communist Party voiced a year earlier at the Czechoslovak Writers' Congress. Referring to the years immediately after World War II, Vaculík recalled that "most of the nation"—including him-self—had "welcomed the socialist program with high hopes." The promise of independence from foreign domination and equality among citizens came upon "evil days" because power "fell into the hands of the wrong people." The Communist Party captured "all the offices" in government, filling them with "power-hungry individuals," "cowards," and "people with bad con-science."[153]

Despite Dubček's reforms and the high-minded Action Program, Vaculík observed that the "retrograde" communists who had corrupted postwar Czechoslovakia "still wield the instruments of power, especially at the dis-trict and community level." Within the Soviet bloc as a whole, repressive "self-willed" figures continued to oppose reform and threaten interven-tion; "the struggle between opposing forces has merely become less open." Vaculík argued that "the fight" among reformers and hard-liners "continued over the content and formulation of laws and over the scope of practical measures." "Superior forces" in the Communist parties of Eastern Europe remained antagonistic to the hopes of the Prague Spring.[154]

Instead of relying upon the wisdom of the Czechoslovak Communist Party to manage society, Vaculík contended that citizens must "someday elect statesmen with sufficient courage, honor, and political acumen." This objective required the forced resignation of many communists and an elimi-nation of the party's monopoly on power. Vaculík advocated "public criti-cism, resolutions, demonstrations, demonstrative work brigades, collections to buy gifts for [communists] on their retirement, strikes, and picketing at [Communist Party] front doors." Through informal "civil committees and commissions," the author called for grassroots agitation to select new lead-ers. Vaculík's vision would replace Communist Party dominance with a di-rect, pluralist democracy.[155]

Like his fellow dissidents in Berkeley, West Berlin, and Paris, Vaculík rec-ognized that a crucial moment for change had arrived in 1968. Support for "democratization" had risen rapidly among students, intellectuals, workers, and even members of the ruling elite in Czechoslovakia. At the same time, the forces of "intervention" had also gathered, fearful of the dangers to es-tablished authority in the Soviet bloc. At this crossroads, Vaculík pleaded for citizens to pursue the opening for broader reform at once. Instead of trem-bling before the tightening fist of Warsaw Pact reaction, he called for cour-age, determination, and immediate action. "This spring a great opportunity was given to us once again, as it was after the end of [World War II] . . . Again we have the chance to take into our own hands our common cause."[156]

More than seventy prominent Czechoslovak intellectuals, scientists, and athletes signed Vaculík's manifesto. The text appeared in four widely read journals—*Práce, Mladá fronta, Zemědělské noviny,* and *Literární listy.* The last publication alone had a circulation of 300,000. Almost immediately an outpouring of letters from inspired citizens arrived at newspaper, radio, and television offices throughout the country. Pressured by their followers to support Vaculík's eloquent clarion call, the Czechoslovak media advocated broader political pluralism.[157]

In a television address, Dubček offered a mild response to Vaculík's challenge. He emphasized the importance of national unity and continued Communist Party leadership. In another speech he contended that "strikes and demonstrations" would not help the cause of reform. The Czechoslovak leader admitted that many problems required further domestic self-criticism, but he warned against a lapse into the extreme of either Novotný-like reaction or radical exuberance. As in January, Dubček spent the early summer of 1968 searching for a middle ground that would revitalize Czechoslovak society by building popular support for existing Communist Party institutions.[158]

Brezhnev's earlier worries about the course of the Prague Spring now turned to panic. In July 1968 he sent an urgent letter to Dubček warning against the "destruction of the leading role of the Communist Party." Singling out Vaculík for attack, Brezhnev argued that the "whole content of the 'Two Thousand Words' platform is directed against the Communist Party of Czechoslovakia and is intended to weaken the position of socialism in Czechoslovakia." The letter expressed dismay at the "indiscriminate belittlement of party cadres."[159]

Brezhnev spared no insult for those who dared to advocate political pluralism in place of the Communist Party's monopoly on power. Dissidents "are bringing together under one political roof everyone who can serve their anti-socialist aims, ranging from the muddle-headed and those who are disoriented by the complicated political situation to open class enemies of the socialist system, from right-wing social democrats to former Hitlerites." These groups allegedly used "various 'clubs' and other organizations for their subversive aims."[160]

The Soviet government called on Dubček to take more vigorous action against "anti-socialist" forces before they brought "death" to the Communist Party. Abandoning the earlier hope that Dubček could inspire "unity in general" throughout Czechoslovakia, the Kremlin prohibited compromises that jeopardized established Eastern-bloc authority. Brezhnev's letter demanded that the Czechoslovak regime "rally all communists" and "normalize" the domestic situation. A crackdown on critics and a strengthening of "healthy forces in the party" would ensure necessary order.[161]

Meeting with the leaders of Poland, East Germany, Hungary, and Bulgaria, Brezhnev voiced even more strident criticisms of the Prague Spring. In a long, rambling speech he exclaimed that "Czechoslovakia is at a dangerous phase on the path leading out of the socialist camp." As happened during the years of Khrushchev's leadership in the Soviet Union, limited reforms "snowballed" out of control. Brezhnev feared that Czechoslovakia "was only a small step" away from "open repudiation of Marxism and of socialism in general."[162]

Soviet fears of spreading disorder—in Czechoslovakia and throughout the Eastern bloc—led to direct military intervention. Brezhnev really did not want to send Soviet tanks into Prague. He hoped that through both persuasion and threat he could convince Dubček to take a harder line with domestic opponents. The Soviet Union and its other East European allies called upon authorities in Prague to mobilize "all means of defense," reassert "control over the mass media," and close "the ranks of the Party" against dissident elements. These actions would protect the interests of the communist states without the cost of armed intervention against a "fraternal" nation.[163]

Brezhnev pleaded with Dubček to crack down on critics of the Communist Party. The Czechoslovak leader had, however, lost control of events. On 13 August Brezhnev telephoned Prague to press for an immediate internal restoration of order. Exhausted and distraught, Dubček explained that "it is impossible" to squash popular support for reform "in as short a time as you are suggesting."[164]

The exuberance of the Prague Spring had infected all institutions of authority in Czechoslovak society. Dubček risked triggering a massive wave of protests if he attempted to call in military or police forces, as Novotný had tried in late 1967. "This is a complex process," the Czechoslovak leader told Brezhnev. It "has encompassed the whole party, the whole country, the whole nation." Confronted with Soviet demands for immediate action, Dubček responded that he did not have the capacity to make society over with a few simple moves: "I can't just resolve these matters myself. It's not so simple, Comrade Brezhnev, to resolve such matters." Even if he wished to resort to force, Dubček could not count on the loyalty of the Czechoslovak army.[165]

The Soviet leader would not accept Dubček's calls for patience while citizens attacked Communist Party authority. On the night of 20–21 August 1968, 165,000 soldiers and 4,600 tanks entered Czechoslovak territory from across the Polish, Hungarian, and East German borders. This marked the beginning of "Operation Danube"—a Warsaw Pact plan to smother the Prague Spring and restore power to a reliable set of conservative leaders. The Soviet Union authored the plan, and it supplied the majority of the men and equipment.[166]

Hours after the invasion, Kirill Mazurov—one of Brezhnev's representatives in Prague—reported that despite the successful military operation, events had gone "haywire." "Thuggish elements have been throwing explosives and grenades at tanks, trying to provoke our soldiers. Crude anti-Soviet broadcasts are being transmitted on radio and television from various stations throughout the day." The hard-liners who Brezhnev hoped would create a more disciplined regime had "gone to pieces." In "shock" at the depth of public resistance to Warsaw Pact forces, conservatives in the Czechoslovak Communist Party failed to show what Mazurov called the necessary "initiative and firmness of purpose." "Our friends," he reported, "have made no real progress in forming a new government."[167]

The Warsaw Pact invasion transformed the Prague Spring from a broad search for domestic reform into a popular resistance movement against foreign occupiers. Tad Szulc, the *New York Times* bureau chief in the Czechoslovak capital at the time, witnessed countless manifestations of public rage. Men and women reacted with particular violence against Soviet soldiers. According to Szulc they "spat at the tanks and troopers, hurled garbage and insults, and, in many instances that first morning, tried and succeeded in setting the armored vehicles afire." Some students threw burning, gasoline-covered rags into the tanks that occupied the streets. Others painted swastika signs on foreign military vehicles. Prague descended into "guerrilla warfare." Szulc remembered watching "young people, many of them long-haired boys and girls in slacks, [fight] the tanks with their bare hands, setting them on fire with flaming torches and hitting at them with branches fallen from the trees."[168]

At the behest of defiant underground Czechoslovak radio broadcasts, citizens combined "guerrilla warfare" with passive resistance in the weeks after the invasion. Residents of Prague and other cities removed street signs and painted over house numbers. Unfamiliar with their surroundings, foreign soldiers found it difficult to conduct their activities without address markers. Workers initiated a series of general strikes, paralyzing necessary services throughout the country. Czechoslovak citizens denied foreign soldiers food and water. Communist Party officials who courageously defied Soviet authority issued a proclamation that captured the widespread sense of public resistance. "Do not aid the foreign troops," the reformers advised. "Pay no attention to them, ignore them!"[169]

Public condemnation of the Soviet invasion came from many communist countries. Rumania's leader, Nicolae Ceauşescu, feared that Moscow might invade his state on the pretext of domestic "counterrevolutionary" developments. He argued that the Kremlin had no right to violate the sovereignty of its allies. "The problem of choosing the ways of socialist construction," Ceauşescu explained, "is a problem of each party, each state, and of every people . . . it is necessary to put an end once and for all to interference in the affairs of other states and other parties."[170]

The Yugoslav government contended that the Soviet invasion of Czechoslovakia was the equivalent of America's war in Vietnam. "The peoples of our country," the Communist Party of Yugoslavia announced, "once again raise their voice in protest, as they have been doing in the matters of American aggression in Vietnam . . . Viewed historically, the action against Czechoslovakia is all the more grave and far-reaching in its harmful effect on progress, peace, and freedom for having been undertaken by socialist countries ostensibly to protect socialism." "The progress of socialism is being opposed," the Yugoslav government proclaimed, by "the forces of stagnation and conservatism" in the United States and the Soviet Union. These two regimes had become the sources of "bloc divisions," "imperialism," "hegemony," and "war."[171]

The Yugoslav condemnation of Kremlin activities echoed the critical words that had come out of Beijing since the early 1960s. Moscow's hesitancy to support North Vietnam in its war against "American imperialism" had fueled Chinese allegations that Brezhnev opposed real socialist revolution. Beijing argued that the Soviet Union, like the United States, had become a "hegemon" pursuing domination rather than progressive change. In Vietnam, Eastern Europe, and the rest of the world, China contended that it was now the true guiding light of revolution. "Armed with Mao Zedong's thought," the Chinese government would "resolutely support the struggle of the people the world over against U.S. imperialism and Soviet modern revisionism."[172]

These criticisms of Soviet "hegemonic revisionism" and comparisons to American behavior in Vietnam resonated in Czechoslovakia, Poland, and even the Soviet Union. On 25 August 1968 eight demonstrators unfurled a collection of homemade banners in Moscow's Red Square, condemning Soviet aggression. They demanded "hands off the [Czechoslovak Socialist Republic]" and "freedom for Dubček." Another banner proclaimed "shame on the occupiers." The protesters included a student from the Moscow Institute of Historical Archives, the mother of a young girl, and the grandson of former Soviet foreign minister Maxim Litvinov.[173]

When authorities placed the demonstrators on trial, ninety-five Soviet intellectuals circulated a letter condemning the prosecution. Similar criticisms of the government's repressive behavior circulated by *samizdat* and word of mouth. Government reports observed "negative processes" among students, intellectuals, and workers throughout the Soviet Union. One KGB informer reported that university attendees sympathized with the aims of the Prague Spring and condemned the Warsaw Pact invasion: "The very word 'opposition' is something students find appealing." Reported acts of student dissent and "hooliganism" within the Soviet Union increased during the next few months.[174]

Brezhnev protected the "leading role" of the Communist Party in Czechoslovakia, but only at great cost. In response to domestic resistance throughout the Soviet bloc, he returned Dubček—after his initial incarceration—to power in Prague. Protests against the party's authority in Czechoslovakia continued until April 1969, when the Kremlin replaced Dubček with a more Novotný-like leader, Gustav Husak. Husak used concerted force to repress domestic critics.[175]

In Eastern Europe, the Soviet Union, and Asia, Brezhnev's government never recovered the authority it had possessed before 1968. Open protests occurred less often in the early 1970s, but public disillusion became more palpable in every communist state.[176] China, engaged in a self-proclaimed Cultural Revolution against superpower domination, emerged as a more credible model than the Soviet Union for radical change. While Mao's followers waved a "little red book" pledging power to the masses, the Soviet leader could only offer the so-called Brezhnev Doctrine, a commitment to the use of force in defense of the status quo. In the eyes of many men and women, the heirs to the Russian Revolution had aged into a conservative Old Regime.[177]

▪ Wuhan: "The People's Commune of China"

Mao's China appeared to offer a "new direction" for revolution in a world dominated by conservative leaders. This image was, however, more myth than reality. By the middle of 1967 China had entered a period of virtual civil war.[178]

Rival Red Guard factions of students and workers fought one another with escalating violence in almost every major urban area. From April through June 1967, according to one estimate, more than 100 clashes occurred in the industrial city of Wuhan alone. Of the 2.5 million people residing in this entrepôt of central China, 70,000 took part in street altercations. In less than three months, 158 people died from violence, and 1,060 suffered serious injuries. In Shanghai, Guangzhou, and Xinjiang factional disputes produced similar brutality.[179]

During 1965 and 1966 Mao had roused public passions for the purposes of purging his opponents in the Communist Party and connecting his leadership with a growing cohort of restive youth. By 1967, however, this manufactured mass upheaval endangered the very foundations of Mao's authority. The street violence of the Red Guards undermined the functioning of Chinese society. The Great Leader could not lead in anything more than name when the basic institutions of government control suffered continued attack.[180]

"Mao Zedong thought" became detached from the purposes of its author. Each Red Guard faction pledged its loyalty to the chairman's guiding light, but precise interpretations were a source of intense dispute. "Ultra-left" groups such as the "Hunan Provincial Proletarian Revolutionary Great Alliance Committee" and the "May 16 Corps" sought not only to purge "counterrevolutionary" elements in the state bureaucracy, but to create their "own political party" that would destroy all established ruling organizations, including Mao's CCP.[181]

"Problems cannot be solved by merely dismissing a few officials," members of the Hunan group announced in an essay titled "Whither China?" Inspired by Mao, student radicals wanted to launch a revolution that would "negate the past 17 years" and "smash" the authority of old communists on the mainland. Criticizing the Great Leader's timidity, the "ultra-lefts" observed that "all of the basic social changes which must be carried out by the first Great Cultural Revolution, such as the overthrow of the new bureaucratic bourgeoisie, changes in the armed forces, and the establishing of communes, have not been carried out." Radical Red Guards wanted to transform the People's Republic of China into the "People's Commune of China." Revolutionary upheaval would become a "permanent" way of life, and society would function without any institutionalized leadership.[182]

The People's Liberation Army—China's military—reacted to the growing domestic disorder by taking matters into its own hands. Soldiers arrested hundreds of Red Guard activists. Military commanders created their own "revolutionary committees" to organize basic services and repress radical elements. The army also prevented the Cultural Revolution from spreading to frontier regions.[183]

In Wuhan members of the military openly revolted against Mao's authority. On 13 July 1967 an entourage including Mao and Zhou Enlai came to the city, hoping to arrange an agreement between army and radical groups fighting one another in the streets. When Wang Li—a former mayor of Wuhan, and now the chairman's chief negotiator—showed some favor toward the "rebel" demands, local military officers launched a violent coup.[184]

On 20 July soldiers kidnapped Wang and his associate Xie Fuzhi. They attacked other members of the Beijing entourage and bludgeoned protesting Red Guards with the butts of their rifles. A Japanese journalist reported that soldiers "tied Wang up . . . before he was given a good beating. After that, Wang was taken to the headquarters of the military region command and paraded before demonstrators. For more than ten hours, Wang was insulted and savagely beaten up."[185]

Mao secretly left Wuhan for Shanghai the next day. Fearful for his security against rioting members of the military, the chairman fled the situation. He sent naval gunboats and a unit of airborne paratroopers to Wuhan to restore order. On 25 July the Chinese government organized a mass rally in Beijing's Tiananmen Square to condemn the "Wuhan reactionaries" and welcome Wang Li's recent release. Two days later the mutiny crumbled, and Beijing purged the military leaders in the region.[186]

The Wuhan mutiny marked what one writer calls "a decisive turning-point in the development of the Cultural Revolution."[187] The army's heavy-handed actions inspired radical denunciations of the military for "separating itself from the masses." For the first time, Red Guards seized weapons from army depots and barracks across the country. The rebels now became armed "guerrilla" fighters.[188]

Startled by this new wave of "ultraleft" disorder, army units reacted with more force of their own. Local commanders exerted direct control over their immediate jurisdictions. As in Wuhan, soldiers battled local rebels. The Chinese military frequently acted against protesters without Beijing's explicit approval. Everyone claimed to follow "Mao Zedong thought," but no one was beholden to the chairman's immediate orders any longer.[189]

Mao really had only one choice in late 1967: to back the military against the most rebellious Red Guard groups. In earlier months the chairman had begun to advocate a "three-way alliance" among the revolutionary masses, the army, and the Communist Party. He frequently warned of the dangers arising from "extreme anarchism."[190] After the Wuhan mutiny these exhortations showed favoritism to the Chinese military. Mao recognized the army's vital role in protecting domestic order and, most important, his personal authority. On 1 January 1968 the *People's Daily, Liberation Army Daily,* and *Red Flag (Hongqi)*—all government-controlled newspapers—asserted that "the army is the fundamental pillar of the Cultural Revolution." They emphasized the importance of reinforcing, rather than destroying, established leadership in China.[191]

These statements marked the beginning of a government campaign to repress radical students who had gone too far in their challenges to authority. A *People's Daily* editorial written by Mao announced that the nation must "resolutely overcome lack of discipline, or even, in many places, anarchy." In later months the chairman called upon students to remain in their urban and village schools and in general to follow the orders of PLA officers.[192]

Mao demoted the Red Guards from the vanguard of the Cultural Revolution to a secondary place, behind the more orderly soldiers in the military. Loyal worker organizations—those that rejected wage bargaining ("economism") as practiced by Western trade unions—also attained a new prominence in the chairman's calls for a return to factory and agricultural production. An August 1968 directive from Mao stipulated that "our country has 700 million people and the working class is the leading class." He demanded "working-class leadership" and "cooperation with [People's] Liberation Army fighters." Workers, like soldiers, had the "practical experience" that radical students lacked. Mao had confidence that they would use revolutionary ideals for productive, not destructive, purposes.[193]

In the second half of 1968 bodies of men and women began to wash up on the beaches of Hong Kong. Many were bound with rope, hand and foot, in a method called the "great binding of five flowers." The use of this technique revealed the handiwork of organized military reprisals against radical protesters, rather than acts of random violence. The Chinese army not only repressed Red Guards; it now also summarily executed threatening elements throughout society. Mao probably learned of these brutalities from Western reports if not from his own mainland sources. The chairman made no apparent effort to curtail this military violence.[194]

Men and women who escaped the harshest acts of the army often found themselves "sent down" to the countryside for "reeducation." According to one scholar, the Chinese government forced more than 1.7 million urban youths to live and work in rural areas during 1968. The number of mandatory resettlements increased to approximately 2.7 million in 1969. By 1975 almost 12 million city-educated men and women had become rural toilers, many against their will. Resettlement in the countryside became a central element of the Cultural Revolution. Mao removed Red Guards from cities, where they caused trouble, and dispersed them in villages, where the challenge of producing for daily sustenance reduced the opportunities for making revolution against the Communist Party. Resettled youths from Shanghai, for example, worked in the countryside to build canals, dig ditches, and tend the crops on collective farms. Instead of agitating for new policies, former radicals became intensive laborers, contributing to the Communist Party's rural development projects.[195]

The chairman spoke of peasants, workers, and soldiers in the countryside "reeducating" students and intellectuals, in direct contrast to the ideological proselytism he had advocated in earlier years. Mao turned to the peasants as a conservative force that could temper violent student anarchism. The "practical experience" of village residents would make sophisticated revolutionaries more humble and obedient. "It is absolutely necessary," the *People's Daily* explained in late 1968, "for educated young people to go to the countryside." "They must be re-educated by workers, peasants, and soldiers under the guidance of the correct line [so that] their old thinking may be reformed thoroughly."[196]

Despite his criticisms of Soviet and American "hegemony," Mao also acted in hegemonic ways. He employed antiauthoritarian rhetoric to launch the Cultural Revolution, but when public protests imperiled his authority he crushed advocates of radical change. Mao eventually relied upon the firepower and discipline of the military to maintain public obedience.[197]

The "correct line" enforced by Mao had nothing to do with "Mao Zedong thought." Ideas of revolution had become sources of dispute among Red Guard factions. The "correct line" represented a return to the same "democratic centralism" Lenin and Stalin had used to purge critics within the Soviet Union during earlier decades. Leonid Brezhnev employed similar rhetoric to repress fellow communists in Czechoslovakia. Mao did not invade a neighboring state in 1968, but he followed the Soviet example in deploying military force against idealistic communists who threatened to undermine his political dominance. The chairman used "reeducation" to close off creative thought and internal reform, as the Soviet leader had with his Brezhnev Doctrine.

Protesters in Paris, West Berlin, and Berkeley continued to identify Mao with the promise of a "third way"—a revolution against both American capitalism and Soviet communism. Students associated him with Che Guevara and the image of "guerrilla" warfare. In reality, Mao was a ruler (with some aspects of an emperor's power) and not a revolutionary in the late 1960s. He sought to maintain and expand his power at virtually all costs.

Most contemporary observers failed to notice Chinese criticisms of Che for abandoning the discipline of the Cuban Communist Party.[198] Similarly, Beijing was very circumspect in its support for student radicals overseas.

Urban disorders in Europe and the United States served China's interests by undermining rival governments, but Mao remained suspicious of the demonstrators because they acted independently. Even the self-proclaimed student "Maoists" did not appear sufficiently loyal to the chairman; in his eyes, they were still "bourgeois." Like Soviet, American, and West European leaders, Mao favored order and discipline against the ubiquitous manifestations of popular protest in 1968.[199]

▪ The Social Crisis of the Nation-State

As the 1960s came to a violent close the leaders of the largest states still controlled most of the guns, finances, and communications media. The protesters on the streets remained relatively weak. The weak, however, now had momentum. The strong were on the defensive. Political power had lost its social component—its ability to command domestic obedience *without* force, in short its legitimacy.

Leaders in 1968 had to work much harder than in previous years to fight off challenges from their own citizens. University sit-ins, urban riots, and acts of assassination became almost normal occurrences. Public mobilization behind government programs was now increasingly rare. If the 1950s ended with widespread despair about conformist "organization men" who wore "gray flannel suits," the 1960s closed with the commonly sung lyrics to the Beatles' "Revolution" and John Lennon's solo "Power to the People."[200]

A burst of violent energy convulsed every major society. Local grievances initially triggered protest activities, but dissatisfaction with Cold War politics broadened the range of public criticism beyond provincial concerns. Although street demonstrators in various countries drew inspiration from what they perceived as an international protest movement, they acted with little coordination or common understanding. Protesters operated in parallel, reflecting the similar—though certainly not identical—discontents and constraints that transcended national boundaries.

The combined effect of these activities was a truly "global disruption" that challenged the basic authority of the modern nation-state. A large cohort of radicals in each society sought to overturn the fundamental political structures that they perceived as corrupt and irredeemable. In the context of increasing domestic violence, gradual piecemeal reform no longer seemed feasible. This sentiment made the Chinese Cultural Revolution powerfully attractive as a mythic movement to dissolve inherited institutions.

Leaders in the United States, West Germany, France, the Soviet Union, and China managed to keep their states running, but they never recovered the allegiance of many citizens. The legitimacy and prestige that had made the nation-state the accepted form of political organization for at least three centuries now confronted an unprecedented number of detractors. Leaders could no longer count on persuading the population at home to support their programs. Most often, they could expect the opposite from skeptical citizens. Leaders now had to formulate policy *against* their constituents.

Great-power politics after 1968 operated under a self-conscious siege mentality that drove Charles de Gaulle, Lyndon Johnson, and others from office. The strongest states struggled to maintain their domestic cohesion. Men such as Leonid Brezhnev and Mao Zedong no longer commanded the public respect they demanded. To preserve their personal authority and the general strength of their states, policymakers had to find new sources of power away from home. This endeavor became the foundation for what contemporaries called the politics of "detente."

6

THE DIPLOMACY AND DOMESTIC POLITICS OF DETENTE

The distinction between foreign and domestic politics is artificial. During the 1960s nuclear stalemate, alliance disputes, and the Vietnam War were issues of domestic, as well as foreign, policy. Excessive institutional growth, intellectual criticism, and public protest had international, in addition to obvious internal, repercussions. Social and cultural influences created tectonic shifts across frontiers, even in the largely "closed" lands of the Soviet Union and China. As the sources of international stalemate tightened and the evidence of transnational social unrest mounted, leaders in all the major states became aware of their precarious hold on power. Cold War antagonists now unexpectedly recognized their interdependence. Not only could they virtually annihilate one another; they also shared difficulties in maintaining basic order within their boundaries.

Policymakers cooperated to protect their authority against a wide range of internal challengers. Detente was, in this sense, a direct reaction to the "global disruption" of 1968. From 1969 through 1972 leaders in each of the major states attempted to reconstruct order from the international "top" down to the domestic "bottom." They used agreement with foreign adversaries to contain increasingly virulent internal pressures. They used promises of international peace to deflect attention from domestic difficulties and to free their resources for repressive measures. Cooperation among the great powers reinforced established authorities.

Despite the chaos on the streets, the years after 1968 witnessed *no* significant institutional change in any of the major states. The politics of this period were profoundly conservative. At its core, detente was a mechanism for domestic fortification.

Like the protesters around them, leaders during the late 1960s questioned many of the inherited assumptions about hostility between capitalist and communist states. New domestic challengers made old international adversaries seem more benign. After two decades of Cold War rivalry, policymakers felt that they understood their foreign enemies and could rely on their consistency and pragmatism. They were known quantities.

One could not say the same of the protesters. They appeared uncompromising, unpredictable, and unorganized. For leaders accustomed to the cautious world of diplomacy, dealing with radical critics posed a series of difficulties for which they were poorly prepared. State sovereignty made questions of national leadership relatively clear. The spontaneity of dissident activity, in contrast, offered few broadly representative figures with whom one could negotiate. Fragmented domestic authority made effective compromise and consensus-building virtually impossible.

State elites cooperated with their counterparts who faced similar domestic difficulties. They worked to sustain the existing structures of domestic and international authority—now stripped of much of their ideological baggage—in the interest of stability. Jettisoning long-standing policies—such as "nonrecognition" between the two Germanys and between the United States and China—the great powers now affirmed one another's legitimacy as sovereign states.

Nuclear arsenals and other military facilities, constructed because governments had refused to coexist peacefully, remained in place. In many instances—especially with regard to strategic striking forces—Cold War capabilities continued to grow despite the new amity between leaders. Attitudes among elites changed, but state institutions stagnated. As a result, the Cold War did not end in the 1960s, as some suggest it should have. Its basic structures—military and political—guaranteed a predictable status quo that leaders held to in the face of an uncertain future. Detente emphasized continuity over change, and stability over reform. Detente "normalized" the Cold War instead of replacing it with something better.

Politicians were profoundly insecure and fearful that the forces of history had aligned against them. Secrecy has always played an important role in the relations among governments, but leaders now became obsessive about shielding their activities from their citizens, their domestic bureaucracies, and even their chosen advisers. The people at home were the greatest perceived threat to prudent policy.[1]

Idealistic protesters grew disillusioned with the impediments to reform. By the late 1960s they recognized that far-reaching change would not come from a quick burst of activity. The radicals had many effective instigators, but few figures capable of constructing a real alternative to contemporary politics. Students could shut down universities and other institutions, but they could not operate them on their own. Protesters lacked the resources, unity, and clarity of purpose necessary to build a viable replacement for the existing political order. Criticism and protest alone produced widespread frustration.

Now more cynical than idealistic, dissidents learned to live under what they perceived as illegitimate—or at least deeply flawed—governments. Many turned away from their former political activism to a self-imposed isolation from what they saw as the corrupt world of state power. Social criticism found expression in what one observer called "new types of community," formed among educated men and women who left the city streets for life in self-governing communes and artistic colonies. In communist societies, citizens often totally withdrew from official activities, creating their own isolated groups. The majority of former protesters did not choose these alternative communities. Instead, they adjusted themselves to existing circumstances by either confining their dissident instincts to thought or changing their ideas to make a virtue of political necessity.[2]

All these responses furthered social fragmentation. Several scholars have pointed to a dramatic decline in connections among citizens—"social capital"—beginning in the late 1960s. Educated men and women now devoted far less time to public activism than before. Groups within society became smaller and more isolated from one another. Social relations grew noticeably more uncivil.[3]

The trends toward "countercultural" and "antipolitical" behavior that many writers have identified were the unintended consequences of detente. Leaders isolated policymaking from public accountability. They used secrecy, manipulation, and lies to accomplish this end. Protesters furthered this process of public alienation by refusing to engage in the hard work of daily compromise required for effective reform. Too many radicals rejected institutional change altogether because their revolution had failed. Isolated elite politics and widespread disengagement in the 1970s replaced the mass politics and public protests of the 1960s. This was detente's social legacy.[4]

If one defines national power in broad terms—including economic productivity, technological innovation, cultural attractiveness, and military capabilities—the United States was *always* predominant after 1945. By the late 1960s, however, the Soviet Union possessed a formidable quantity of nuclear weapons, enough to destroy the United States swiftly and completely. China had also become a nuclear power, capable of inflicting horrific damage throughout Asia. France and Great Britain possessed modest nuclear arsenals of their own.

Under these circumstances, with war among the great powers guarantee-

ing almost complete annihilation, cooperation made sense. Large-scale conflict had become too costly. The dominant states avoided dangerous provo-
cations—such as the Cuban missile crisis—and worked together for their
common survival. The *balance of power*, in this context, created a stable international equilibrium. This is the traditional interpretation of the origins of
detente.[5]

Balance-of-power explanations focus too narrowly on nuclear weapons.
Leaders in the late 1960s worried more about domestic unrest than about
nuclear war. They formulated foreign policy as a barrier against escalating
internal turmoil. Great-power cooperation reduced the public tensions fueled by ideological conflict. Cold War antagonists now criticized each other
less often, reduced their support for subversives, and more readily ignored
their adversaries' acts of repression. Detente had a powerful domestic component that exceeded a mere agreement to avoid nuclear armageddon.

Responding to both domestic and international pressures in the late
1960s, leaders pursued what I call a *balance of order*. This involved a desperate attempt to preserve authority under siege. It emphasized stability over
change, repression over reform. It was less about accepting nuclear parity
than about manipulating political institutions to isolate and contain a variety of nontraditional challengers. Detente brought together an international
array of threatened figures who coordinated their forces to counterbalance
the sources of disorder within their societies.

The "peace" created by detente entrenched the social and political status
quo. Cooperation among the great powers became a substitute for both domestic and international reform. It served as a balance against what policymakers saw as unreasonable public expectations. Diplomatic arrangements
made war less likely, but they also froze most of the initial sources of antago-
nism in place. These circumstances could never provide a foundation for
long-term harmony among states and peoples. The profound shortcomings
of detente were evident in its immediate origins.[6]

▪ The West German Origins of Detente

In July 1963 West Berlin mayor Willy Brandt and his close aide Egon Bahr
attended a conference of notables in a little-known location outside Munich,
the Tutzing Christian Academy, conscious that Cold War politics had reached
a dead end. Like Chancellor Konrad Adenauer, they found American policy
regarding the future of the two Germanys unsatisfactory. In addition to
the nuclear dangers that worried the long-serving leader of the Federal Republic, Brandt and Bahr recognized emerging domestic pressures for policy
change.

Brandt praised the chancellor's recent overtures to the Soviet Union. He called not only for more of the same, but also for creative measures aimed at improving living conditions in Central Europe. "There is no hope for us," Brandt warned, "if there is no change." Germans must "break through the frozen front between East and West." Progress required peaceful diplomacy coupled with a "dynamic transformation."[7]

Brandt argued for a closer integration of domestic and foreign policy. Openness to East Germany, especially through economic relations and human contacts, would undercut the enforced division in Central Europe. This assessment followed from what Brandt called the trends toward a "deconcentration of power" away from the traditional centers that had managed affairs on the continent since World War II. As he affirmed the importance of Bonn's partnership with Washington and the West European capitals, Brandt argued that improved relations with the East must stand and fall on the actions of German citizens, mobilized for the cause of peace and freedom. Grassroots overtures had now become the "real test for German foreign policy." Bonn had a "duty" to sponsor richer and more diverse connections across the Berlin Wall.[8]

Egon Bahr elaborated on Brandt's general pronouncements. He emphasized the importance of "recognizing the other side's interests." "The [East German] zone must be transformed," Bahr explained, "with the consent of the Soviets." Cold War adversaries had to respect one another's fundamental security concerns. Mutual recognition between states would allow nongovernmental groups to create new connections, improve living conditions. and, ultimately, eliminate national divisions. Bahr advocated an increase in "interzonal trade" between East and West. Not only would West German products improve the lives of consumers in the Soviet bloc; they would also create sources of dialogue and common interest. Trade would break down many of the barriers that the Federal Republic's stubborn policy of isolating the East—the so-called Hallstein Doctrine—appeared to reinforce. Economic exchange could operate with Soviet approval to build bonds between people in separated states.[9]

If military conflict had stalemated in an era of nuclear weapons, human interactions through trade promised a more flexible avenue for policy influence. As the strongest and most dynamic economy in Europe, the Federal Republic could offer Soviet-bloc leaders and their citizens many attractive consumer products in return for greater access to their societies. Instead of simply reinforcing the status quo through strategic cooperation, trade would allow West Germans to work with their Eastern counterparts for liberal, anticommunist purposes. According to this vision, Bonn would induce the Kremlin and its satellites to dig their own grave.

West German politicians began to use the term *Ostpolitik* for this proposed departure from previous Cold War policies. Instead of trying to force change through strength, Bahr argued that West Germany should encourage "change through rapprochement." Social and economic engagement would replace enforced division and mutual deterrence. Bonn had to encourage some risky contacts and concessions to the Soviet Union. Bahr and Brandt believed that there was no alternative in the pursuit of German reunification.[10]

The West Berlin mayor and his assistant pursued this vision with remarkable consistency during the 1960s. In the months before the Tutzing Conference, Brandt and Bahr initiated a series of secret contacts with Soviet diplomats, aimed at creating opportunities for citizens to travel across the Berlin Wall. After meeting in early 1963 with Victor Belezki, a representative from Moscow's embassy to East Berlin, Bahr reported to the mayor that the Soviets appeared to want a "modus vivendi" that would prevent future crises. They accepted tentative proposals for more trade and human interaction between East and West.[11]

In December 1963 the East German government, responding to pressures from Moscow, issued the first travel passes since the construction of the Berlin Wall, allowing West German citizens to visit their relatives in the East. Bahr called this a "very interesting example" of the accomplishments possible from informal diplomatic contacts and increased activism within the Federal Republic. He hoped it marked the first step on a "long road" to "friendship" between states and peoples divided by the Cold War.[12]

Bahr employed the German equivalent for the term *detente—Entspannung*—in a June 1964 speech delivered at the University of Hamburg. "The only hope for solving the German question," he explained, "is to push forth the development of detente." There were "no guarantees" that the Soviets and East Germans will allow more travel passes and other East-West contacts in the future, he warned, "but there is a chance, and we do not have any other alternatives."[13]

Ludwig Erhard, Konrad Adenauer's successor as chancellor, generally opposed any rapprochement with the East. Pressures from Brandt, Bahr, and other West German citizens, however, led him to make some guarded overtures, especially in the area of trade. Erhard admitted in late 1964 that Bonn must make it evident that "German reunification in peace and freedom also serves Soviet interests." Without more East-West contacts, the Federal Republic could not conduct what Foreign Minister Gerhard Schröder called an "active, daily, direct pursuit of reunification."[14]

Erhard concluded bilateral trade protocols with Poland, Rumania, Hungary, and Bulgaria. Bonn did not maintain embassies in the other East European states, but West Germany now established economic missions throughout the region as points of contact between ministers, businesspeople, and even some ordinary citizens. In order to provide the Soviet-bloc states with the hard currency they needed to purchase West German products, Erhard's government began to offer generous credits labeled "development aid." Trade and aid, the foreign ministry explained, helped the cause of freedom and self-determination without jeopardizing security or stability.[15]

By 1966 economic and person-to-person contacts with the East dominated Erhard's foreign policy. Washington had become distracted with the war in Vietnam, and President Johnson—despite his advocacy of "building bridges" between Eastern and Western Europe—appeared uninterested in European affairs.[16] France and other Western states opened their own trade links with the East, jeopardizing West Germany's ability to control the future development of Ostpolitik. Members of the Foreign Ministry began to fear that de Gaulle might build such strong connections with the communist states that East-West reconciliation would bypass Bonn. In this nightmarish scenario, German hopes for reunification would get lost once again in the maneuvers of other states. Erhard had to pursue more aggressive overtures to the East, as Brandt and Bahr continued to advise.[17]

In March 1966 West Germany issued a "Peace Note," addressed to the Soviet Union and its East European allies. Rejecting Cold War divisions in Central Europe, the document proclaimed that

> the German people . . . consider it their greatest national task to remove the partition of Germany under which they have suffered for many years . . . The German people would be prepared to make sacrifices for the sake of their unification . . . The German people desire to live on good terms with all, including their East European neighbors. Hence the Federal Government has been trying in various ways to improve relations with the states and peoples of Eastern Europe.[18]

Erhard's commitment to "make sacrifices" for reunification marked the triumph of Brandt and Bahr's vision. The West German Foreign Ministry admitted that while the Cold War had reached a stalemate in Central Europe, the citizens on both sides of the Berlin Wall had grown visibly "restless," living with the painful division of their nation. Domestic pressures for broader East-West connections—beyond the diplomacy of the Adenauer years and the trade of Erhard's tenure—had "sharpened" the need for a more active and perhaps riskier Ostpolitik. The Peace Note indicated an important turn in West German foreign policy to embrace Bahr's call for "change through reconciliation."[19]

In December a new West German "Grand Coalition" government formed between the two dominant parties, the Christian Democratic Union (CDU) and the Social Democratic Party (SPD). It made improved relations with the Federal Republic's Eastern neighbors one of its most prominent aims. The "Declaration of the Grand Coalition" explained that the German people "want reconciliation with Poland whose sorrowful history we have not forgotten and whose desire ultimately to live in a territory with secure boundaries we now . . . understand better than in former times." "The German people also wish," the declaration continued, "to come to an understanding with Czechoslovakia."[20]

As foreign minister for the Grand Coalition, Brandt worked to create better state-to-state relations between the Federal Republic and its Eastern neighbors. He also sponsored expanded economic and person-to-person contacts for the sake of transcending the "sterility" of great-power politics. Central Europe, he proclaimed, must become a "European zone of detente," characterized by nuclear disarmament in the region, freer movement of citizens, and a "normalization" of borders—even those between the two German states.[21]

Brandt and Bahr believed that a true detente required greater independence from external powers and inherited policy assumptions. Given the opportunity, the citizens of the two Germanys would surely create living conditions far better than those enforced by Cold War rivalries. In the long run, reunification required much deeper coordination between leaders and publics. "Foreign policy," Bahr explained, "begins with domestic policy."[22]

Brandt felt that he could provide this connection, but the politics of the Grand Coalition constrained his options.[23] The CDU remained deeply suspicious of the states in the East. Both Brandt and Bahr criticized the conservative inclinations of their coalition partners. When they took over as the leaders of West Germany in October 1969, however, they also abandoned much of their optimism about the reconciliation of citizens in the East and West. After the domestic upheavals of 1968 even the earliest and most progressive advocates of detente pursued conservative policies.

As early as 1966, Egon Bahr had warned of a crisis within the Federal Republic. "Twenty-one years after the end of the war," he wrote Willy Brandt, "there exists a new generation." Bahr worried about rising "extremism on the right" and "extremism on the left." Ostpolitik offered the opportunity for creating a new political middle between right and left, but it also risked unleashing unrealistic public expectations. Domestic contention could jeopardize the stability required for any durable overtures to the East.[24]

This was exactly the difficulty that Brandt and Bahr confronted at the end of the decade. Their concept of Ostpolitik called for broader public connections between citizens in the East and West. Domestic radicalism in the Federal Republic and other European states, however, made leaders fear that young people, when given opportunities for more freedom and movement, would create new sources of disorder and conflict. The student protests throughout West Germany indicated that if not properly managed, "change through reconciliation" between societies could spark increased violence.[25]

Speaking to a group of fellow politicians in September 1968, two weeks after the Warsaw Pact invasion of Czechoslovakia, Brandt made this very point. "Young people in many of our countries," he lamented, "do not understand why we, the older ones, cannot cope with the problems of [our] age." Counseling against extensive public criticism of Soviet intervention in Prague or America's war in Vietnam, Brandt argued that leaders had to control "dangerous tensions" through pragmatism and "reason"—two qualities frequently absent from the naive behavior of protesters. Policymakers needed to temper popular urges for well-intentioned but reckless political change.[26]

In contrast to protesters in West Germany, Brandt refrained from any significant condemnation of the foreign policies pursued by Moscow and Washington during the late 1960s. He feared that criticism of the superpowers would create new barriers to East-West reconciliation. West Germany pursued a more independent foreign policy than ever before, but Brandt remained acutely aware that the functioning of Ostpolitik was dependent on the consent of the more powerful governments—the Soviet Union and the United States—that continued to dominate the European continent.[27]

This was an accurate strategic assessment, but it alienated many of Ostpolitik's supporters in the Federal Republic. Brandt's caution appeared to perpetuate the great-power politics of the Cold War. Once again, it seemed that the people of Central Europe had to sacrifice their interests for the sake of international stability. Once again, leaders accepted repression in Europe, instead of promoting resistance and change.

West German youths who traveled to the Soviet bloc as participants in a series of cultural-exchange programs supported by Brandt, became his most vocal critics. They observed the repressive conditions in the East, but they also imbibed the condemnations of political leaders circulating among protesters in the West. During one meeting between students from the two

Germanys in East Berlin, speakers from both sides called for more attention to "our freedom," allegedly smothered by domestic institutions, East and West. Disparaging all German leaders, they demanded that power devolve from national figures to student groups. Other meetings of Eastern and Western students inspired discussions about the alleged absence of moral values in politics on both sides of the Berlin Wall.[28]

By 1969 Ostpolitik had produced some important convergences between East and West, as Brandt hoped, but in a form he found most threatening. Radicalized by protest movements in their respective states, students now formed East-West networks of criticism against established authority. Citizens traveling from the Federal Republic to the East curiously neglected the issue of reunification for discussions about what many called a common "system" of repression throughout Europe. Peace and national unity would come, one group of Eastern and Western students proclaimed, when "existing communists and capitalists can meet one another on the socialist road." Another group explicitly condemned the great powers for prolonging the Cold War. They called for grassroots, all-German answers to political and social problems that state leaders, including Brandt, appeared unable to solve.[29]

Accompanied by the spread of radicalism throughout Europe, Ostpolitik contributed to growing domestic upheaval within the two Germanys. Events followed the earlier pattern of educational expansion and proliferating dissent. East-West connections supported by Brandt and Bahr for the purpose of improving internal conditions had the opposite effect. With more knowledge and human contact, Germans on both sides of the Berlin Wall grew more restive, disorderly, and violent. Increased interaction between the two German states did not foster reconciliation and reunification, as Brandt and Bahr had hoped. Instead, Ostpolitik contributed to a set of new domestic dangers for the future of the Federal Republic.

The members of the CDU who had only reluctantly embraced Ostpolitik in the 1960s took advantage of Soviet aggression in Czechoslovakia and domestic unrest in the Federal Republic to criticize Brandt's policies. Rainer Barzel and Franz-Josef Strauss (the latter from the CDU's sister party, the Christian Social Union) claimed that concessions to Moscow would legitimize Soviet tyranny in the East and prevent German reunification. They accused Brandt of undermining the stability of the Federal Republic by advocating an overly optimistic foreign policy. The chancellor did too little for Ostpolitik in the eyes of social activists, but he was reviled by the CDU for doing too much.[30]

Embattled on both the political left and right at home, Brandt and Bahr shifted gears. Late 1969 marks the point when they turned their overtures to the East against their own citizens. As chancellor, Brandt made Ostpolitik more elitist, centralized, and secret, emphasizing political control and speed at the expense of public deliberation and debate. Through Bahr, Brandt personalized his foreign policy to prevent interference from both established bureaucracies and allegedly irresponsible domestic groups. One historian has compared Bahr to a "greyhound" who moved so quickly in 1969 and 1970 that he left his detractors—young radicals and CDU conservatives—"spluttering with shock and indignation."[31]

As Brandt's "state secretary"—the rough equivalent of the American national security adviser—Bahr opened an unprecedented channel between Bonn and Moscow. Secret meetings with Soviet representatives created what Bahr describes in his memoirs as a "relaxed atmosphere" among the small group of participants. Other members of the West German government—including Foreign Minister Walter Scheel—knew little about what transpired during these discussions. The public remained almost entirely ignorant of their occurrence.[32]

Brandt and Bahr acted with secrecy and haste to contain their internal opposition. Lingering public debate about their policies would allow criticism to coalesce on both the right and the left. Instead of following the deliberative approach common to West German foreign policy, Brandt and Bahr rushed to create a *fait accompli* that assured a series of openings between East and West, but also established limits on how citizens could use Ostpolitik. While diplomatic, economic, and cultural contacts would increase across the Berlin Wall, the two German states would remain firmly intact, further empowered to control activities within their respective borders.

Bahr explained to President Nixon's national security adviser, Henry Kissinger, that the chancellor sought to "normalize" political authority in Central Europe. West Germans would interact more with their Eastern neighbors, but not in the free and uninhibited way that Brandt and Bahr had contemplated years earlier. The leaders of the Federal Republic no longer sought reunification, except perhaps over the very long term. In the context of growing domestic upheaval, they wanted to use Ostpolitik to improve living conditions throughout the region while reinforcing existing sources of state authority. Any new challenges to political leadership threatened to unleash dangerous forces within the societies on either side of the Berlin Wall.[33]

In 1970 Bahr extolled the virtues of coupling agreements for increased human movement with reinforced state boundaries. He argued that this maneuver would increase the political flexibility available for embattled leaders. West German families receiving frequent travel passes to visit relatives in the East would react favorably. Businesspeople and social activists would also appreciate a softening in European divisions. At the same time, the strengthening of existing frontiers promised that the region would remain stable and orderly. Ostpolitik, in this form, promoted social and cultural change, but only on the political and strategic margins.[34]

This was a more conservative vision of East-West relations than Brandt and Bahr had voiced at Tutzing seven years earlier. Political stability, not progressive change or what Brandt had called "deconcentration," emerged from the Bonn-Moscow channel. Cold War divisions in Central Europe became less rigid while they also grew more permanent. Instead of eliciting new openings for popular initiative, Ostpolitik confined the activities of citizens within a very limited framework.

Bahr called this "respecting realities," but his secret negotiations with Moscow revealed that many of the inherited East-West animosities had in fact dissipated.[35] Although domestic unrest in Berlin and other cities had replaced recurring superpower crises as the greatest immediate threat, the leaders of the Federal Republic used the old reality of Cold War division to control the new reality of internal weakness. In the early 1970s Brandt, Bahr, and their Soviet counterparts preferred managed great-power conflict to the risks of fundamental political and social change.

East German leader Walter Ulbricht attempted to exploit the opening of relations with the Federal Republic to increase his regime's autonomy from Moscow. The Soviet Union, however, acted quickly to limit his room for maneuver. During the first half of 1970 Leonid Brezhnev cautioned Ulbricht to "pause for reflection" before embracing the alluring offers of trade that accompanied Bonn's attempts to open East German society to Western influences. The Soviet leader wanted to make sure that he, not Ulbricht, controlled events in Central Europe.[36]

Moscow rejected Ulbricht's argument that the Soviet bloc should encourage East-West dependency for the purpose of financing communism. This vision promised more unrest within the Eastern, as well as the Western, half of Europe. Brezhnev and a number of prominent East German Communist Party officials pressured Ulbricht to use contacts with Bonn for the purpose of stabilizing existing Cold War divisions, rather than risking new efforts at domestic development. The Moscow Treaty, signed in August 1970 by the leaders of West Germany and the Soviet Union, enforced Brezhnev's control over the East European responses to Brandt and Bahr. It preceded Ulbricht's forced "resignation" in May 1971, and his replacement by Erich Honecker, a more deferential Kremlin ally.[37]

The text of the Moscow Treaty made the conservative inclination of Ostpolitik obvious. Article 1 pledged the signatories to a "normalization of the situation in Europe" and "peaceful relations among all European states," without any mention of German reunification. Article 3 stipulated that "peace can only be maintained in Europe if nobody disturbs the present frontiers." Acknowledging the permanence of East-West political divisions, Brandt and Bahr promised to "respect without restriction the territorial integrity of all states in Europe," including "the frontier between the Federal Republic of Germany and the German Democratic Republic."[38]

At the signing ceremony for the treaty, West German foreign minister Walter Scheel handed his Soviet colleagues a letter stipulating that the document "does not conflict with the political objective of the Federal Republic of Germany to work for a state of peace in Europe in which the German nation will recover its unity in free self-determination."[39] Scheel's note, never formally acknowledged by the Soviets or appended to the treaty, indicated what was missing from Bonn's relations with the East. The language of the treaty associated "peace" with the acceptance of current divisions. Signing the agreement, Brandt legitimized Soviet domination in Eastern Europe and the existence of a separate East German state. In return he received promises of future stability in the area. Leaders from Bonn and Moscow promised to accept and strengthen the "actual situation" in Central Europe, no matter how morally reprehensible.[40]

Nowhere did the treaty, or even Scheel's letter, provide any of the measures for improved living conditions, increased human interaction, and East-West integration promised by Brandt and Bahr throughout the 1960s. Family visits and trade across Central Europe continued to increase, but the respective societies also became more separate than ever before. Restrictions on personal freedom and the discussion of dissident ideas tightened in the Soviet bloc just as Brandt and Bahr rushed to justify territorial boundaries. The West German leaders gave the Soviets the political legitimacy in Eastern Europe that they had long desired without any accompanying advances for the cause of reunification. The August 1970 treaty ensured that East-West relations would remain, in Bahr's words, under "full control," and not subject to dangerous public emotions.[41]

In the next four years Brandt's government concluded major treaties with Poland, East Germany, and Czechoslovakia. Each document emphasized the "inviolability of frontiers" and the "normalization" of diplomatic relations. None of the treaties mentioned reunification or any other measures designed to promote self-determination for citizens living under tyrannical rule in Eastern Europe. Increased trade between East and West received attention in these treaties, but only within a framework of assured political stability.[42]

Ostpolitik had now come full circle. The Berlin crises of 1958–1961 had pushed Konrad Adenauer to seek new diplomatic measures for overcoming East-West division. Through the 1960s Willy Brandt and Egon Bahr had expanded on Adenauer's vision to include many additional proposals for person-to-person cooperation and eventual German reunification. They had spoken with eloquence about the promises of "change through reconciliation." By the early 1970s, however, domestic instability throughout Europe turned Ostpolitik into a mechanism for reinforcing, not transcending, the political structures of the Cold War.

In September 1971 the four powers that controlled Berlin after World War II—the United States, the Soviet Union, France, and Great Britain—gave up on reunifying this city or the larger German nation. They pledged "mutual respect" for the division of Berlin, and restraint against "unilateral changes." The leaders of the two German states signed an agreement indicating that the Berlin settlement was a "contribution to detente in Europe."[43]

Ostpolitik was, according to one scholar, a "motor" for detente.[44] Brandt and Bahr displayed remarkable energy, but they really did not travel very far. Their activities after 1969 froze the international system in place. They answered public calls for an end to the Cold War with efforts to make the Cold War seem more "normal." Over time, Brandt and Bahr hoped that people would associate normality with legitimacy, and even with justice. Despite their progressive inclinations, domestic circumstances led these two men to pursue a form of detente that opposed change. By the early 1970s they had pioneered a new international conservatism, quickly emulated by the leaders of the other major states.

▪ Detente with Chinese Characteristics

Despite the violence unleashed by the Cultural Revolution, China's Foreign Ministry managed to follow the development of Ostpolitik very closely during the late 1960s. Publicly, Beijing opposed any agreement between the Federal Republic and its communist neighbors to the East. Mao Zedong's government argued that the forced division of the German nation, like the separation of Taiwan from the mainland, could find resolution only in the formation of a unified socialist country. The policies pursued by Brandt and

Bahr legitimized two German states, setting a dangerous precedent for Beijing's relations with Taiwan.[45]

In the context of rising Sino-Soviet tensions, Mao's government also worried that the stability promised by Ostpolitik would allow Soviet leaders to transfer more of their military forces to their disputed eastern border. The Kremlin might form temporary alliances with West European nations—and even the United States—against China. All of these were serious possibilities that leaders in both Moscow and Beijing contemplated after 1968.[46]

The Chinese Foreign Ministry spoke out against Ostpolitik, but it also made a series of overtures to Bonn that preceded similar openings to the United States by a number of years. In early 1967 Beijing conveyed a message to Paris, requesting assistance in establishing new connections with West Germany. The Chinese did not desire "only economic contacts." They sought "political" relations as well.[47]

Paris passed Beijing's message to Bonn.[48] In May a high-ranking official in West Germany's Foreign Ministry, Klaus Schütz, met with one of Beijing's informal envoys, Fei Yiming. Fei described China's reasons for pursuing better relations with the Federal Republic. First, he explained, the Sino-Soviet rift had become "unbridgeable." Moscow did not assist communist development, but exploited Chinese resources for its own selfish purposes. Beijing needed new friends, like West Germany, to counteract Soviet hostility.[49]

Second, relations between China and East Germany had also turned sour in recent years. Fearful of new communist heresies, Moscow had pressured its allies to condemn Mao's government. The economic and cultural contacts that had briefly flowered between Eastern Europe and China during the early 1960s declined in the context of the Sino-Soviet rift. Fei observed that Beijing and Bonn now had similar enemies in East Germany and the Soviet Union.[50]

Third, and most important of all, China's envoy revealed that the mainland had a strong desire for West German imports. Fei intimated that the domestic dislocation caused by the Cultural Revolution had made leaders in Beijing desperate for industrial goods manufactured abroad. The Federal Republic could serve as the ideal partner. West Germany had become the dominant industrial producer in Europe, and, as Schütz explained to Fei, it was anxious to open new export markets. Politicians in Bonn did not share Washington's inhibitions about trading with Communist China.[51]

Schütz provided West German leaders with an optimistic report of his meeting. He explained that Beijing and Bonn shared an interest in "constant contact." Both the Federal Republic and China could exploit bilateral connections to balance Soviet behavior, as Adenauer had predicted years earlier. Expanded trade also served domestic needs, especially in the chaotic circumstances of the Cultural Revolution and the slumping conditions of the recent European economic cycle.[52]

By the end of 1967, only seven months after the Schütz-Fei meeting, West Germany's exports to China had grown by 60 percent. During the next two years informal contacts between the People's Republic and the Federal Republic continued to expand. As trade increased, representatives from both states began to speak more favorably about each other in public. China continued to oppose Ostpolitik, but it confined its criticisms almost exclusively to the Soviets.[53]

Egon Bahr interpreted Beijing's overtures as an indication that opportunities would soon open for broader agreements between the Western and Asian states. He noted that the dangers of the Sino-Soviet split and the stalemated war in Vietnam motivated China to seek cooperative arrangements with capitalist states. Trade links to more productive economies—West Germany, Japan, and even the United States—offered Beijing great promise for needed domestic development.[54]

Discussions between Beijing and Bonn convinced the leading proponent of Ostpolitik that a similar attempt to reinforce the existing political order in Asia could prove fruitful, Mao's revolutionary rhetoric notwithstanding. Through an affirmation of the status quo and agreements on controlled contacts between societies, Bahr recognized an opportunity to "normalize" the Cold War in Asia. Beginning in March 1967 the Chinese Foreign Ministry had given numerous signals that it desired this very kind of conservative political framework for improved relations with the West.[55]

In 1969 Beijing and Bonn informally joined forces to encourage American consent for what would quickly become the Asian component of detente. China and West Germany established full diplomatic relations in October 1972, a little more than six months after President Richard Nixon's dramatic meeting with Mao Zedong. Connections between the People's Republic and the Federal Republic provided the precedent for the better-known "back channels" that made Sino-American rapprochement possible.[56]

American diplomacy in Asia was consistently contradictory during the second half of the 1960s. President Lyndon Johnson gradually escalated U.S. military activities against North Vietnamese forces, including large deployments of air, land, and sea power. Simultaneously, Washington sought improved relations with North Vietnam's longtime patron, the People's Republic of China. In the eyes of American policymakers Beijing was both a "belligerent" agitator in Southeast Asia and a necessary partner in building a "more peaceful" world community.[57]

Averell Harriman, one of Washington's most experienced diplomats, observed the contradiction between "giving full support to the war in Vietnam, while at the same time making a gesture towards Red China." Harriman affirmed a growing consensus among Johnson's advisers, however, when he argued that the president had to follow this course. He explained that Washington could build international and domestic support for military activities in Southeast Asia only if it also initiated a "spectacular change in attitude towards Red China." The United States received widespread criticism for its stubborn refusal to acknowledge the authority of Mao's government, even after almost every other major state established formal relations with the People's Republic. New forms of engagement with Beijing would, according to Harriman's logic, allow America to appear less intolerant in its foreign policy.[58]

Following the advice of Harriman and others, in July 1966 the president offered his clearest public call for Sino-American reconciliation. After ritualistically affirming his determination to "make the Communists of North Vietnam stop shooting at their neighbors" and his opposition to "Communist China's policy of aggression by proxy," Johnson surprised many listeners. He advocated "reconciliation between nations that now call themselves enemies . . . Lasting peace can never come to Asia as long as the 700 million people of mainland China are isolated by their rulers from the outside world." America, he explained, wanted to break the mainland's isolation by increasing informal contacts, including exchanges of journalists, scholars, and health experts. Beijing had "rejected" most of these contacts in the past, Johnson lamented, but he promised to "persist" in opening new doors to China.[59]

American overtures to Beijing in 1966 did not get far. Convulsed by the early months of the Cultural Revolution, the Chinese ignored Johnson's conciliatory rhetoric. Mao's condemnations of Western "imperialism" and Soviet "revisionism" inspired a surge of activity directed against any meaningful relations with the allegedly corrupt external powers. In 1966 and 1967 groups of Red Guards besieged foreign diplomatic offices operated in Beijing by Great Britain, France, and even fellow communist states such as East Germany. If anything, youthful revolutionaries on the mainland used Johnson's speech to confirm their injunctions against compromise with "counterrevolutionary" forces seeking to ingratiate themselves in Chinese society.[60]

Watching the Cultural Revolution from Washington, American policy-makers were astounded by what Alfred Jenkins, a China expert on the National Security Council, called "the spectacle of the oldest civilization on earth methodically digging up its roots to the tune of raucous, uncivilized ballyhoo and bedlam." Jenkins counseled caution to avoid antagonizing China with provocative threats. Washington also had to resist the temptation to address "moderates" on the mainland with its hopes for reconciliation. American overtures would sully the reputation and imperil the safety of the most receptive figures in China. "We can hope," Jenkins wrote, "that the chaos on the mainland may continue a while, and may prove to be in our interest in the denouement . . . Meanwhile, we should try not to provide a way out for a Mao in trouble, should he sooner or later require a particularly devilish devil."[61]

Adopting Jenkins' counsel, President Johnson abandoned his inclination to seek an immediate improvement in Sino-American relations. Policymakers continued to press for expanded contacts with Beijing, but the White House put most overtures on hold. The United States would wait until a clear outcome emerged from what Walt Rostow—Johnson's special assistant for national security affairs—called "China's vaulting chaos."[62]

Through the most disruptive months of the Cultural Revolution the Chinese Foreign Ministry managed somehow to maintain limited contacts with the United States. Sino-American ambassadorial talks in Warsaw, for example, continued.[63] Despite their calls for isolation from American "imperialists," Chinese leaders continued to find diplomatic meetings "useful." Zhou Enlai also sent messages to Washington through Pakistan. He asked the nation's president, Mohammed Ayub, to tell Johnson that Mao's government would remain cautious about its commitments in Vietnam. If American forces did not threaten Chinese sovereignty, Beijing's army would refrain from combat with U.S. soldiers. Through Warsaw and Pakistan, Zhou assured Johnson that the chaos on the mainland would not create new sources of communist aggression.[64]

After the Chinese Foreign Ministry expanded its contacts with West Germany in mid-1967, direct communications between Beijing and Washington improved as well. The American ambassador in Warsaw found his Chinese counterpart more forthcoming than ever before. The frequent references to American "imperialism" made during the last two years became almost nonexistent among diplomats. This was a "significant departure from the past performance."[65]

Signs of a more conciliatory Chinese attitude toward the United States proliferated in other forums as well. In late 1968 Mao Zedong told E. F. Hill, the chairman of the Australian Communist Party, that the world had entered a period of "neither war nor revolution." Despite the belligerent rhetoric of the Cultural Revolution, the Chinese leader rejected the Marxist-Leninist argument that capitalism inevitably leads to imperialism and war. "It seems," Mao explained, "that this rule no longer works now." East German observers noted that such comments from Mao, Zhou Enlai, and other Chinese figures pointed to a new, "nonconfrontational" stand toward Washington.[66]

Officials in Hong Kong also reported that after months of Red Guard threats to the British-controlled island, Mao's government had acted decisively to protect order. In November 1967 the Chinese Foreign Ministry negotiated a series of very reasonable "understandings" with London's representatives. These included an exchange of Chinese and British prisoners, assured movement for workers from the mainland to the island, and, most important, guarantees that citizens from the two sides could engage in "proper and normal" interactions. Chinese and British authorities pledged to prevent violent activities in or near Hong Kong.[67]

London's chief negotiator observed that the representatives from the mainland operated without any "attempt to browbeat or to shout political slogans or even adopt starchy attitudes," as had been common during most of 1966 and 1967. The new professionalism of Chinese diplomats led the British to predict that after months of uncertainty "we can talk turkey with these people in the future." Like their Western counterparts, leaders in Beijing appeared intent on assuring domestic order and nurturing amicable relations with other states.[68]

In 1968 Mao confirmed his commitment to stability instead of continuous revolution when he purged many of the radicals who had recently assumed positions of authority in foreign affairs. As a consequence, the Foreign Ministry, like many other government departments, suffered from a shortage of staff. Only about 30 percent of its pre-1966 personnel remained in place. These circumstances reduced the breadth of the ministry's capabilities, but they also allowed moderates such as Zhou Enlai and Chen Yi to exert personal control over policy.[69]

Mao, Zhou, and Chen used contacts with external powers to restrain Red Guard groups that had grown too disruptive. Foreign policy moderation justified domestic moderation. In addition to the benefits of trade for a country devastated by the successive disasters of the Great Leap and the Cultural Revolution, closer foreign associations contributed to a domestic atmosphere of peace and friendship rather than violence and recrimination. Negotiations with "counterrevolutionaries" allowed Beijing to begin humanizing the enemy in Chinese eyes. A less demonic image of the United States undermined the radical anti-Americanism and xenophobia of the young Red Guards. Managing new relations with foreigners legitimized the continued authority of elderly Communist Party figures.[70]

Sino-American reconciliation grew from the work of Chinese leaders frightened by the chaos of the Cultural Revolution. Improved relations with the United States reflected a determination to pursue stability rather than risk further disruption in the name of ideological purity. As Mao's government limited the activities of radicals and bolstered the image of moderate figures, it also turned to closer relations with its most consistent Cold War enemy.

When Richard Nixon became president in January 1969, he possessed a deep understanding of American policy in China. Nixon had never visited the People's Republic, but he had come of age as a politician just as Mao's communist forces wrested control of the mainland from the Guomindang. While many of his counterparts focused their attention on the Soviet threat to Western Europe, Nixon was always drawn to Asia. As a congressman and senator from California he had strongly condemned America's postwar setbacks in China. As Eisenhower's vice president he had had little influence on policy, but he had always remained active in Asian affairs. Nixon's reputation as a rigid anticommunist hid his awareness of the importance of improved relations with China—something other than reflexive isolation—for the future of the United States.[71]

As early as October 1967 Nixon spoke of closer American contacts with Mao's government. Writing in the journal *Foreign Affairs*, he argued that "we simply cannot afford to leave China outside the family of nations, there to nurture its fantasies, cherish its hates and threaten its neighbors." Nixon elaborated: "Dealing with Red China is something like trying to cope with the more explosive ghetto elements in our own country." Carrying this analogy between the domestic and international sources of disorder forward, he explained that "in each case a potentially destructive force has to be curbed; in each case an outlaw element has to be brought within the law; in each case dialogues have to be opened; in each case aggression has to be restrained while education proceeds; and, not least, in neither case can we afford to let those now self-exiled from society stay exiled forever." Threats of violence at home and abroad required "an urgency born of necessity and a patience born of realism, moving step by calculated step" toward improved Sino-American relations.[72]

Nixon's inaugural address, delivered on 20 January 1969, marked his first move in this direction as president. In place of the muscular rhetoric about "paying any price and bearing any burden" that had punctuated Kennedy's speech eight years earlier, Nixon admitted that "we are approaching the limits of what government alone can do." Referring to Vietnam, he explained, "We are caught in war, wanting peace. We are torn by division, wanting unity."[73]

Proliferating challenges abroad and deep divisions at home made it impossible for the United States to dominate every major struggle against communist expansion. The turmoil of 1968 had left the nation in such disarray that the public's willingness to pay the costs—financial and social—of fighting the Cold War had reached a post-1945 low. "We find ourselves rich in goods," Nixon observed, "but ragged in spirit; reaching with magnificent precision for the moon, but falling into raucous discord on earth."[74]

The president emphasized cooperation with allies and adversaries for the sake of restoring stability both at home and abroad. Addressing "America's youth" and "the people of the world," Nixon argued that "we cannot learn from one another until we stop shouting at one another—until we speak quietly enough so that our words can be heard as well as our voices . . . For all our people, we will set as our goal the decent order that makes progress possible and our lives secure."[75]

Nixon did not utter a single confrontational word in his inaugural address. He trumpeted the language of "convergence" among longtime enemies despite deep ideological and strategic conflicts. Instead of deterrence and containment—core concepts of the Cold War—he emphasized compromise. "After a period of confrontation," Nixon explained, "we are entering an era of negotiation."[76]

Historians have largely neglected this inaugural address, but the leaders of China did not make the same mistake. Almost immediately Mao Zedong ordered the two largest state-run newspapers to publish the speech in its entirety.[77] Contemplating an overture of his own to the United States, Mao found Nixon's words encouraging. When he addressed a large meeting of the Chinese Communist Party three months later, the chairman sounded strikingly like the American president. He called for renewed efforts to "unite with more people" rather than pursue the "contradictions" that had provoked such violence during prior years. Instead of urging ideological purity and continuous revolution, he emphasized that "every one of us should be prudent and cautious."[78]

In the context of the Cultural Revolution this meant amnesty for alleged class enemies. The "crude and careless" behavior of the Red Guards had led

to many "mistakes." Mao ordered the release of those individuals imprisoned for following the "capitalist path." He also sounded a conciliatory
chord in his discussion of foreign affairs. Mao reaffirmed that "we should be
prepared for war year by year," but he warned that "we must not invade
others' territory." In contrast to his past enthusiasm for armed conflict, Mao
now emphasized caution. Even if invaded, he surprisingly conceded, "I am
in favor of giving up some land. China is not a small country." The chairman
proclaimed that internal unity and international peace took priority over
immediate "socialist revolution." Like Nixon, Mao was clearly backing down
from his previous belligerent rhetoric.[79]

A report that Mao commissioned from four prominent Communist officials—the "four marshals"—confirmed this conservative turn. In July 1969
they advised that "in the foreseeable future it is unlikely that U.S. imperialists and Soviet revisionists will launch a large-scale war against China, either
jointly or separately." Both of these states, the authors explained, faced "crises at home and abroad" that limited their fighting capabilities.[80]

China did not require excessive preparation for war, but it needed to remain vigilant against foreign competitors, particularly those supported by
Moscow. "The Soviet revisionists," the marshals wrote, "have made China
their main enemy, posing a more serious threat to our security than the U.S.
imperialists." The report alleged that the Kremlin's forces were "creating
tensions along the long Sino-Soviet border, concentrating troops in the border area and making military intrusions. They are creating anti-Chinese
public opinion, creating chaos on the international scene, while at the same
time forcing some Asian countries to join an anti-China ring of encircle-
ment."[81]

In response to Soviet challenges, the marshals advised that Beijing maintain China's armed strength while promoting "industrial and agricultural
production." The future security of the People's Republic required that the
nation become a "stronger economic power." For this purpose, the marshals
suggested, "We should enhance our embassies and consulates in other countries, and actively carry out diplomatic activities." Breaking out of its isolation, China would expand the "international united front of anti-imperial-
ism and anti-revisionism," also acquiring more access to foreign imports,
technology, and ideas.[82]

Coupled with China's already significant connections to West Germany
and Mao's recent turn against the Cultural Revolution, this analysis pointed
to better Sino-American relations. Nixon appeared favorably disposed to
new contacts, and Chinese leaders—especially Zhou Enlai and Chen Yi—
saw many advantages for their state. The four marshals wrote that "both

China and the United States take the Soviet Union as their enemy." Working with Washington, leaders in Beijing could balance against Soviet power on "two-fronts" while preventing the feared possibility of anti-Chinese collaboration.[83]

Chen Yi, one of the four marshals, added a personal note to the final report. He wrote that "it is necessary for us to utilize the contradiction between the United States and the Soviet Union in a strategic sense." He also called for "a breakthrough in Sino-American relations." Chen admitted that his ideas were somewhat "wild" in the context of anti-American rhetoric during the Cultural Revolution, but he recommended that state policy reflect how the "situation has changed today" for each of the great powers.[84]

Chen Yi, Zhou Enlai, and other moderate figures in the Chinese government understood that improved relations with Washington would help to stabilize international affairs and restrain radical impulses after years of chaos. The advocates of Sino-American reconciliation in Beijing sought to undermine the xenophobia and extremism of their domestic challengers by humanizing the image of their Cold War adversary. Mao's speech in April and his request for the four marshals' report gave those who wished to curtail the Cultural Revolution and end China's isolation more influence than at any time in the previous three years.[85]

In Beijing and Washington momentum began to build for reconciliation between longtime adversaries. Conciliatory gestures reflected clear strategic interests. Mao's government wanted to balance against a growing threat from the Soviet Union. The Nixon White House was desperate for Chinese assistance in ending the Vietnam War. Leaders in both states also hoped that new international openings would help to dampen domestic radicalism. After reading a report about Chinese policy debates in 1969, Nixon observed that "Mao [too] fights the educational establishment." By "educational establishment," the president referred to protesters in the United States, China, and many other states. Improved relations between governments would undercut criticisms of American "imperialism" (popular in the United States and China) and calls for "international revolution" (voiced by Chinese Red Guards and the most extreme Western demonstrators).[86]

During the summer of 1969 Sino-Soviet border tensions gained new intensity as Moscow contemplated large-scale military action against China. On 18 August 1969 Boris Davydov—a KGB agent working out of the Soviet embassy in Washington—casually asked an American official over lunch "what the U.S. would do if the Soviet Union attacked and destroyed China's nuclear installations." To the astonishment of Davydov's interlocutor—William Stearman, a special assistant to the State Department for North Vietnamese affairs—the Soviet official argued that military action against the mainland's nuclear facilities would serve U.S. interests, restraining future Chinese aggression. Similar remarks from other Soviet contacts, accompanied by military preparations near the border, confirmed that the Kremlin was serious about striking an extensive, perhaps even nuclear, blow against its communist neighbor.[87]

Soviet leaders had good reason to believe that the U.S. government would look favorably upon a preventive attack against Chinese nuclear facilities. After all, the Kennedy administration had floated similar ideas in the early 1960s. Nixon, however, was not Kennedy. Washington's political aims at the end of the decade differed markedly from those only a few years earlier.[88]

The president did not view the world in bipolar terms. He recognized that Soviet military action against China would limit U.S. leverage in Asia. It would also complicate the possibility of a dramatic breakthrough in Sino-American relations. Washington could best turn tensions among the communist states to its advantage, Henry Kissinger advised Nixon, if it refused to sanction Moscow's hegemony along the Sino-Soviet border. According to this logic, the United States could use China to play upon the Kremlin's insecurities. Continued fear of possible American collaboration with Mao's government would, the White House predicted, induce maximum Soviet flexibility on security issues in other parts of the world.[89]

Nixon adopted this approach. He told his closest advisers that Washington should tilt toward China, not the Soviet Union. American officials issued a series of public warnings against any "massive breach of international peace and security" on the Sino-Soviet border. Moscow got the message. In his next meeting with William Stearman, Boris Davydov avoided any discussion of possible Soviet military action against China.[90]

Soviet-American contacts were now circumscribed, but communications between Washington and Beijing expanded considerably.[91] In January 1970 the United States suggested that a special representative visit Beijing for high-level consultations. One month later the Chinese accepted this proposal, explaining that the visit by "a special envoy" of the president would provide a forum for "further exploration of questions of fundamental principle between China and the United States."[92]

These overtures depended upon secret channels of communication, and they justified more of the same. At a time when public unrest frequently imperiled the basic operations of government, private contacts between leaders preserved continuity. Both Richard Nixon and Zhou Enlai would later agree that confidentiality had insulated conciliatory policies against the disruptive criticisms of allies and domestic groups, especially in the West.[93]

Secret contacts also increased the stature and indispensability of particular individuals. Henry Kissinger became an international celebrity in the early 1970s—more renowned than any previous U.S. national security adviser—for his surreptitious contacts with the high and mighty. Nixon, Mao, and Zhou Enlai were already recognized around the world, but they inspired additional fascination because of their quick and unpredictable maneuvers, shrouded in secrecy. These leaders cultivated charismatic sources of authority—as Max Weber had predicted decades earlier—with a self-conscious manipulation of mystery and surprise. Stealth activities provided leaders with an unknown "magic," in Weber's terms, that made Sino-American relations a source of power and prestige for the select few who controlled the exclusive channels of communication.[94]

Events in 1970 could easily have derailed the gradual improvement in Sino-American relations if the two sides had defined their purposes in narrow strategic terms. Contrary to repeated Chinese demands that the Nixon administration reduce its military activities in Indochina, on 29 April 1970 American and South Vietnamese forces invaded the Saigon government's western neighbor, Cambodia. The operation, which included heavy B-52 bombing raids and an incursion of 31,000 American soldiers, sought to cut off North Vietnamese supply and infiltration routes.[95]

Demonstrations against this military action immediately spread across the United States. On 4 May 1970 poorly trained national guardsmen at Kent State University in Ohio fired upon a crowd of protesters, killing four unarmed students and wounding another nine. By the end of the month violent confrontations had occurred at more than seventy other schools.[96]

Mao condemned America's international and domestic "aggression." "U.S. imperialism," he argued, "looks like a huge monster," but it "is in essence a paper tiger, now in the throes of its death-bed struggle." "The Nixon government," Mao continued, "is beset with troubles internally and externally, with utter chaos at home and extreme isolation abroad." "Aggressors" and "paper tigers" were hardly candidates for friendly relations. Accordingly, the Chinese leader reaffirmed his support for anti-American forces in Indochina. He called for listeners to "unite and defeat" the United States. The fighting around Vietnam and within America offered little promise of a strategic partnership between Washington and Beijing.[97]

In contrast to the escalation of warfare in Indochina, Sino-Soviet border tensions tapered off during this period. Zhou Enlai met with Soviet premier Aleksei Kosygin in September 1969 to defuse fears of war. During three hours of discussion at the Beijing airport, the two leaders agreed to avoid military confrontations on their long frontier. They also initiated negotiations for a peaceful settlement of disputed territorial claims. In the next year Beijing and Moscow completed a new trade agreement and noticeably decreased their public criticisms of each other. China and the Soviet Union continued to harbor mutual suspicions, but their relations in 1970 grew far less antagonistic. Comparing the relative calm on the Sino-Soviet border with America's heightened military activity in Indochina, Beijing inevitably saw the United States as posing the more immediate threat.[98]

In this context, Sino-American contacts became less frequent, but they continued to operate through various confidential channels. In the summer of 1970 Beijing opened an important new line of communication with the United States in Paris. Huang Chen, China's ambassador to France, began a series of informal meetings with American military attaché Vernon Walters. Discussions through the Paris channel contributed to personal amicability between the representatives of Beijing and Washington. On a number of secret trips to the French capital in the next year, Henry Kissinger gained his first sustained and direct contact with Huang and other Chinese interlocutors.[99]

Mao Zedong and Zhou Enlai also communicated with Washington through Edgar Snow. The chairman invited the journalist to China again, as he had in 1960, for the purpose of sending a conciliatory signal to the United States. On 1 October 1970 Snow and his wife, Lois, stood beside Mao on the balcony of the Heavenly Peace Gate (Tiananmen) during the annual parade celebrating the founding of the People's Republic. According to Zhou Enlai, this unprecedented move indicated that "the door is open" for Sino-American friendship. Having used the occasion in previous years to address revolutionary Red Guards, Mao now wanted to associate himself with individuals who desired peace and coexistence. The chairman expressed his desire for mutual respect and equality between the peoples of his society and those of the United States.[100]

With Mao's encouragement, Snow recounted these sentiments in a *Life* magazine article published at the end of April 1971. Members of the U.S. government "read and re-read" Snow's text. One of Kissinger's assistants recalls that American policymakers used it as "our road map for the future."[101]

Recognizing that the White House might miss what Kissinger called the "excessive subtlety" of Snow's reception in Beijing, Zhou Enlai made China's intentions more explicit. He sent a handwritten letter to Nixon through Pakistani president Yahya Khan, declaring that China "has always been willing and has always tried to negotiate by peaceful means." "In order to discuss the subject of the vacation of Chinese territories called Taiwan," Zhou stated that "a special envoy of President Nixon's will be most welcome in Beijing."[102]

The United States and China had reached a turning point. Through Pakistan, Nixon sent a typed message to Beijing on a blank sheet of white paper, without signature. The president accepted China's invitation for a special emissary, and he explained that personal discussions should touch "on the broad range of issues which lie between the People's Republic of China and the United States, including the issue of Taiwan." The meeting would also "encompass other steps designed to improve relations and reduce tensions."[103]

During the next seven months Washington and Beijing prepared, largely through the Pakistan and Paris channels, for Henry Kissinger to visit China under a cloak of utmost secrecy. In the interim, however, Chinese leaders encouraged public anticipation of a Sino-American breakthrough. Mao and Zhou crafted images of Chinese openness in marked contrast to the isolation and fanaticism of the Cultural Revolution. Edgar Snow's very visible presence in 1970 conveyed this change in atmosphere. The chairman and his chief deputy understood that favorable publicity would encourage goodwill for the People's Republic abroad, and it would also isolate domestic radicals from those citizens buoyed by the prospect of better American relations. As China appeared less belligerent to onlookers overseas, foreign adversaries also seemed less threatening to citizens on the mainland.

The so-called Ping-Pong diplomacy of April 1971 reinforced this use of conciliatory public posturing for political purpose in China. To the surprise of almost everyone, Mao invited a group of nine young American table-tennis players, then competing in Japan, to visit the mainland. The photogenic U.S. citizens toured China along with a number of Western journalists. They created an international sensation as they posed with their Chinese counterparts for some of the most eye-catching examples of cultural friendship between the two societies since before the Cold War. *Life* magazine published a montage of photographs depicting the dedication and amicability of Chinese citizens—many in harmless-looking Red Guard uniforms, toiling in a vast and pacific mainland landscape. Overcome by the spectacle of the table-tennis players' visit, *Life* exulted: "The great wall comes down!"[104]

Kissinger, in contrast to the Ping-Pong players, traveled to China avoiding all public notice between 9 and 11 July 1971. His visit, codenamed "Polo" after the famous Italian traveler, sought to fit the emerging signs of Sino-

American friendship to specific policy purposes. In particular, the Nixon administration wanted to stabilize the international situation in Asia and use its rapprochement with Beijing to increase the president's standing at home.[105]

During Kissinger's three days of discussion with Zhou Enlai, he and his host focused on solidifying the political status quo. The United States would not abandon its close relations with Taiwan and South Vietnam, but in both cases the Nixon administration pledged to reduce its military commitments sharply and quickly. Kissinger indicated that in the United Nations and other international forums the United States would begin to recognize not only the long-denied legitimacy of Mao's government, but also its role as the representative of the Chinese people.

In return for Washington's promises of disengagement in Asia and recognition of Mao's government, Zhou indicated that Beijing would help Nixon to increase his personal standing among domestic groups and allies. Many other Western leaders—including West German chancellor Willy Brandt and the American Senate majority leader Mike Mansfield—wanted to make their own dramatic visits to China. Zhou pledged that he would not allow any other major Western figure to upstage Nixon. In addition, Beijing would curtail its public criticisms of the American president and avoid any actions that exacerbated conflict in Vietnam or the Taiwan Strait.[106]

On 15 July 1971 Washington and Beijing dramatically revealed the cooperative tenor of the secret Kissinger-Zhou meetings. The joint announcement, read to a television and radio audience in America by Nixon, explained that the president had accepted a Chinese invitation to visit the mainland before May 1972. "The meeting between the leaders of China and the United States," the statement elaborated, "is to seek the normalization of relations between the two countries and also to exchange views on questions of concern to the two sides."[107]

Kissinger comments in his memoirs that this announcement "shook the world."[108] For the first time, the governments in Washington and Beijing accepted each other publicly as equals. They committed themselves to work together for shared interests. Richard Nixon, Henry Kissinger, and Zhou Enlai stood at the center of this process, elevated as the men who had made this sea change in diplomacy possible. The Sino-American rapprochement had accomplished little of immediate substance, but it now gained an exciting momentum that, especially in the United States, isolated many opponents of the existing leadership. Nixon, Kissinger, and Zhou had displayed breathtaking initiative for conservative political purposes. Meanwhile, radical opponents remained mired in tired old rhetoric.

On the evening of 25 October 1971, after Kissinger had completed a second (this time public) visit to China, the United Nations General Assembly voted to seat the People's Republic of China and expel the Republic of China on Taiwan. After twenty-two years of American objections, Mao's government finally represented China in the United Nations. The Nixon administration had recently supported the admission of the People's Republic to the General Assembly, but it had also continued to oppose Taiwan's expulsion. The momentum of Sino-American rapprochement had, however, overtaken this position. By October 1971 both the United States and the United Nations had accepted Beijing as a legitimate great power in Asia, and as a partner against the spreading tide of disorder throughout the world. Taiwan now had to live in Beijing's shadow.[109]

After months of anticipation, on the morning of 21 February 1972 President Nixon arrived in Beijing. Zhou Enlai met the leader of the People's Republic's longtime adversary at the airport. Reversing former secretary of state John Foster Dulles' infamous refusal to shake Zhou's hand at the Geneva Conference in 1955, Nixon descended from Air Force One with an outstretched palm. The Chinese premier stared into the American president's eyes and seized Nixon's hand as an acknowledged equal. Referring to this poignant moment hours later, Zhou expressed appreciation for the reversal of Dulles' indignity. Nixon agreed that "we have broken out of the old pattern."[110]

Only three hours after the American entourage touched down in Beijing, Zhou Enlai whisked Nixon—accompanied only by Kissinger and a notetaker (Winston Lord of the National Security Council staff)—to Mao Zedong's personal study. The chairman stood with great difficulty. He shook Nixon's hand with a mix of emotional enthusiasm and physical weakness. Mao displayed what Kissinger called a "concentrated willpower" that awed his visitors.[111]

China's leader seemed to identify personally with the American president, despite the ocean of difference in their respective backgrounds. Seated in modest armchairs, surrounded by a scattering of books and hidden medical equipment, Mao told Nixon that "I voted for you during your election." He recalled reading an article predicting Nixon's victory in 1968, "when your country was in havoc."[112]

The chairman observed that China also had its share of domestic troubles. Many people had created grave difficulties for the leadership, he explained, especially in its attempts to pursue a more peaceful foreign policy. Mao referred to Lin Biao's recent attempted coup, allegedly supported by "a reactionary group which is opposed to our contact with you . . they got on an airplane and fled abroad."[113]

Nixon recognized that both he and Mao wanted to use improved Sino-American relations to stabilize the international system and restrain domestic troublemakers. He commented that he "had similar problems," especially from the "American Left." The president called upon the leaders of China and the United States to work together for the sake of eliminating "vacuums" that created disorder throughout the world.[114]

At Mao's suggestion, the two leaders pledged to keep their dealings secret. They would cooperate personally to overcome the "deadlock" that made both states, in the chairman's words, "bureaucratic in dealing with matters." Mao called his own public words about "defeating imperialism" and "establishing socialism" a "lot of big cannons." Despite all the upheaval in the name of international revolution, Mao lamented that he hadn't been able to transform China. "I've only been able to change a few places in the vicinity of Beijing," he explained. Tired and unhealthy, the chairman appeared resolved to work for order and stability, not the mirage of communist internationalism.[115]

The two leaders agreed that they shared international interests and domestic difficulties. This observation made them indispensable "friends," according to Mao. Having criticized every previous U.S. president for "gangster" behavior and excessive anticommunism, the chairman admitted that he hoped Nixon would not be "overthrown." "I like rightists," he exclaimed, contrasting their pragmatism and conservatism with the more belligerent behavior of socialists and liberals.[116]

Nixon corroborated this surprising comment from Mao. He emphasized the common experiences that connected the two leaders in the early 1970s. "I also came from a very poor family," Nixon recounted of his childhood in Whittier, California, and Mao's formative years in the Chinese province of Hunan. "History has brought us together," he continued. "The question is whether we, with different philosophies, but both with feet on the ground, and having come from the people, can make a breakthrough that will serve not just China and America, but the whole world in the years ahead . . . that is why we are here."[117]

Mao and Nixon shook hands again at the end of their hour-long conversation. The president departed from the chairman's study convinced that the leaders of the two states understood each other. Both wanted to promote order at home and stability abroad.

Nixon described the audience with the chairman as "refreshing." The moments in Mao's presence revealed that "there are many reasons why the People's Republic of China and the United States should work together." Zhou Enlai reciprocated this sentiment, commenting that "we will invariably find common ground to promote the normalization of relations between us."[118]

During their eight days in China, Nixon and Kissinger met with Zhou seven times. Only two other members of the NSC staff—Winston Lord and John Holdridge—joined the American contingent during most of these discussions. The Nixon-Zhou conversations followed the outlines of the meeting in Mao's study, but with much more detailed attention to the future of Taiwan, the Vietnam War, and the intentions of the Soviet Union. In each case, the leaders of the two states agreed to avoid provocative actions or drastic changes that would endanger their respective positions. They would cooperate to help each other find stable solutions for long-standing problems.[119]

Nixon promised to proceed with his announced disengagement from Taiwan and Vietnam. Washington's overseas withdrawals would occur gradually for the purpose of appeasing domestic critics of America's military commitments in Asia, without antagonizing hard-line anticommunists. The Chinese government would use the evidence of U.S. disengagement to strengthen its calls for unification with Taiwan and solidarity with Southeast Asian allies. Beijing would, however, refrain from embarrassing Nixon as he sought an honorable retreat.[120]

Sino-American cooperation also focused on containing the rising economic power of Japan. Memories of the Manchurian invasion, the attack on Nanjing, and World War II raised continued fears in Beijing about Japanese militarism. China's worries about a revitalized and independent government in Tokyo roughly paralleled Soviet anxieties about West Germany throughout the Cold War. Zhou and Nixon agreed that they would prevent Japan from exploiting its growing wealth to fill the "vacuums" left as the United States reduced its commitments in Vietnam, Taiwan, and perhaps even South Korea. Instead of competing for influence in Tokyo, as the interests of Realpolitik would dictate, Zhou and Nixon discussed how both could maintain "friendly" relations with Japan for the sake of encouraging "normal" development. Contradicting its public calls for the complete departure of American military influence from Asia, Beijing indicated its approval of a prolonged U.S. presence in Japan. In return, Washington would help China improve its connections with the largest capitalist economy in the region.[121]

These commitments to collaborate in containing Japan guarded the Asian status quo against disruption. They departed from the earlier American logic of using the dynamic island nation to counterbalance Communist China. As the United States reversed its Japanese favoritism, Beijing jettisoned its long-standing antipathy to any association with Tokyo. The conservative inclinations of Nixon and Zhou turned established strategy and ideology on their heads.

The joint statement approved by the leaders of China and the United States on 27 February (the "Shanghai Communiqué") embodied the efforts of the two sides to ensure future order against threatening uncertainty. The document, officially released as Nixon departed China the next day, rejected "spheres of interest" and regional "hegemony." These caveats notwithstanding, the statement affirmed the managerial role that Beijing and Washington would undertake for the future of Asia. The two sides rejected the use of force and other efforts to carry out rapid change in disputed borders between India and Pakistan, North and South Vietnam, and North and South Korea. With regard to Japan, both China and the United States emphasized the importance of friendly and democratic, rather than expansionist and unilateral, behavior in Tokyo.[122]

Most significant, Washington accepted that "the People's Republic of China is the sole legal government of China." Within this framework, Taiwan would eventually return "to the motherland." The Nixon administration made this concession that Mao's government so desperately wanted, but it rejected the use of force in pursuit of the island's "liberation." Beijing had to arrange its future with Taiwan through "peaceful" means that would not threaten stability in the region. This meant that although the People's Republic had a right to authority over the Guomindang-held territory, it could not govern Taiwan so long as local resistance threatened armed conflict.[123]

The Shanghai Communiqué created a firm basis for great-power stability in Asia and "normalization" of Sino-American relations. Less than seven years later, on 1 January 1979, China and the United States established full diplomatic relations following most of the guideposts outlined by Zhou and Nixon. At the same time, Washington severed all official ties with its long-time ally in Taiwan.[124]

Foreign policy "normalization" between China and the United States was an important part of their internal "normalization." Mao, Zhou, Nixon, Kissinger, and their successors used improved relations to limit troubling external commitments and assure international stability. At home, the gains in Sino-American rapprochement reduced the influence of inherited ideologies advocated by radical groups—the Red Guards, the New Left, and the New Right. The secret connections between Beijing and Washington insulated policy against critics. The imagery of friendship between old rivals provided a rationale for patience and order among citizens in each state.

The Sino-American rapprochement of the early 1970s did not eliminate the antagonisms born of conflicting national interests, ideological predilections, and historical experiences. Mao Zedong and Richard Nixon did not reject these differences. Quite the contrary, they accepted them and simply made them "normal" by pledging to avoid violence and disorder in their continuing competition. The threat that the Soviet Union posed for both nations made an agreement on tactical cooperation in Asia sensible to balance a common enemy. The spread of domestic chaos provided Mao and Nixon with an even greater shared difficulty. They exploited the opportunities for collusion between their states to contain disorder and bolster their standing against proliferating challengers.

Sino-American detente reflected the conservative politics of leaders running from the threatening consequences of Cold War rhetoric. Relations between China and the United States have remained uncertain since 1972, thanks, at least in part, to these shallow foundations. The two sides did not resolve long-standing strategic and ideological conflicts. Instead, they passed them on to future generations.[125]

▪ Soviet-American Detente

Relations between the United States and the Soviet Union had already reached relative stability, especially in Europe, during the decade before Nixon's visit to China. The peaceful settlement of the Cuban missile crisis and the conclusion of the Limited Test Ban Treaty marked a clear turn toward coexistence between the two nuclear superpowers. Near military parity contributed to stability, balance, and caution.

Coexistence, however, was not the same as cooperation. In the Middle East, Africa, and especially Southeast Asia, Washington and Moscow increased their challenges to each other after 1963. They frequently employed proxies to avoid the risks of direct confrontation. They supported local wars in all these areas, and expended large sums to finance domestic development along capitalist and communist lines in states—such as North and South Vietnam—that promised dubious strategic and economic benefits. Cold War competition between the United States and the Soviet Union continued, but in places unlikely to trigger nuclear armageddon.

This system of displaced superpower conflict—mostly in the so-called third world—began to come undone in the late 1960s. Instead of buttressing the respective hegemony of the strongest states, costly foreign commitments jeopardized their political standing. Resistance to military intervention, particularly in Vietnam and Czechoslovakia, motivated leaders in Washington and Moscow to curtail their competitive use of force away from home.

The U.S. government was desperate to reduce its military commitments in Asia, and most especially in Vietnam. Each day appeared to bring mounting human losses with few prospects of victory. In place of "counterinsurgency" operations, policymakers formulated the "Nixon Doctrine," which placed more of the burden of communist containment on regional powers. Washington would feed anticommunist strongmen with generous aid and equipment, but it would rely on local, not American, manpower to fight battles on the ground.[126]

The "Brezhnev Doctrine"—articulated by the Soviet leader to justify the invasion of Czechoslovakia—only temporarily hid a similar development in the Kremlin's thinking. Soviet tanks crushed the Prague Spring, but they inspired anger in many communist states. Leaders in Yugoslavia, Rumania, China, and other countries condemned the violation of Czechoslovak sovereignty. Domestic groups in Eastern Europe and the Soviet Union engaged in a series of daring protests. Most significant, morale in the Soviet and Warsaw Pact armies declined to a dangerous low point. These threatening "spillovers" convinced Brezhnev and his colleagues that they could not afford to implement the Brezhnev Doctrine again.[127]

Moscow and Washington needed to escape their difficulties through new, but still limited, forms of cooperation. The two sides remained adversaries, but they also acknowledged their interdependence. Safe Cold War competition required firm superpower authority to impose limits on the behavior of respective allies. When necessary, the United States and the Soviet Union had to collaborate to prevent local conflicts from spiraling into larger confrontations. Lyndon Johnson's undersecretary of state for political affairs, Eugene Rostow, candidly explained that he and others in Washington worried most about the international anarchy that would emerge as the authority of both superpowers began to "dissolve." "It's a nightmare situation," he warned. Anatoly Dobrynin, the Soviet ambassador to the United States, voiced Moscow's agreement with this sentiment. He also emphasized the importance of "bilateral" consultations to contain international difficulties.[128]

Washington and Moscow pursued improved relations during the late 1960s despite festering points of strategic conflict. In his last year as president, Johnson refrained from frequent criticism of the Kremlin's aggression, even after the invasion of Czechoslovakia. To the surprise of Soviet ambassador Dobrynin, Johnson continued to push for a superpower summit. When alerted that Moscow's tanks had entered Prague, the president was preoccupied not with the repression of reform, but with his plans to visit the Soviet Union "in the nearest time."[129]

The Kremlin, for its part, exerted its influence in both Hanoi and Washington to improve the prospects for a peaceful settlement of the Vietnam War. Despite the weakening effect it had on the United States, leaders in Moscow feared that a continuation of the conflict would create mounting pressures for more costly Soviet intervention. Brezhnev wanted stability in Vietnam rather than continued uncertainty. He approved a Foreign Ministry report predicting that "an end to the Vietnam conflict would undoubtedly have a positive effect on Soviet-American relations and open up new possibilities for solving certain international problems."[130]

Domestic disorder provided additional incentives for Soviet-American cooperation. More amicable relations between Moscow and Washington would reduce the overseas conflicts that encouraged internal dissent, and they would also increase the standing of leaders. Detente would create a vital new source of political stability. Policymakers within both superpowers shared an interest in drawing clear boundaries and enforcing orderly spheres of authority. Some influential figures—including McGeorge Bundy —hoped that Soviet-American detente would allow for a new focus on what he called, somewhat euphemistically, the "common problems of advanced societies."[131]

Paradoxically, the international and domestic incentives that made Soviet-American detente sensible also distracted Johnson and Brezhnev from its accomplishment. Daily crises in Vietnam, Eastern Europe, and cities throughout the world left politicians with little freedom for long-range planning. The "common problems of advanced societies" were just too overwhelming. Agreements on superpower cooperation required a period of detachment from the global shock of 1968 and a change of American leadership. In the interim, the pressures for detente continued to grow, particularly in Soviet-dominated Eastern Europe.

The urban upheavals of the 1960s left a deep imprint on Polish society. In March 1968 students and intellectuals demonstrated against what one writer called a "dictatorship of the dumb." Students from Warsaw University announced that after two centuries of German, Russian, and Soviet domination they would fight "to defend the democratic and independent traditions of the Polish nation." Popular protest movements throughout Europe, especially Czechoslovakia, inspired men and women to rise against the repressive government of Władysław Gomułka.[132]

The Polish leader, who came to power during the earlier uprisings of 1956, had offered citizens a series of promising reforms—including wage increases, rehabilitation of "internal enemies," semi-independent worker councils, and relative autonomy for the Catholic church. By the late 1960s Gomułka and his Soviet patrons had replaced these reforms with strict autarchy. To compensate for declining economic growth, the Polish Communist Party pursued a centralized plan for "selective development" that focused upon export-generating industries such as steel. Squeezing maximum productivity out of the nation's limited resources, Gomułka mobilized citizens for more work and less leisure. Individual and group freedoms became rare commodities in Polish society.[133]

The student and intellectual rebellion of 1968 only furthered Gomułka's determination to attain economic growth through an enforcement of political discipline. He manipulated popular anti-Semitism to label the demonstrators as "enemies of order" and "fifth columns" inspired by treacherous Zionist groups allegedly festering within the Polish nation. Police forces arrested thousands of dissidents, universities and factories dismissed countless critics, and many "hostile" individuals suffered public beatings.[134]

Gomułka repressed the demonstrations in 1968, but two years later he encountered much more extensive resistance. In December 1970 the Polish government raised food prices by 36 percent as part of Gomułka's plan to boost national production by reducing domestic consumption of resources. The price hikes took effect immediately—before the Christmas holiday— and they were not accompanied by wage increases or other mechanisms to support workers already struggling to survive on minimal pay. One resident of the northwestern port city Gdańsk described the horror that the latest measure of "selective development" inspired among citizens: "The coming holidays were to be the last feast before January . . . This sudden unexpected price rise in December is impossible to explain. Why before the holidays? What do they care about these few days? Why are they unnecessarily irritating people who are already anxious and worried?"[135]

From 14 through 20 December angry workers—led by the employees of the huge state-run shipyards—launched a series of strikes in Gdańsk and other Baltic coast cities. Unrest soon spread to interior areas. In Łodz, for example, female textile workers refused to work without a repeal of price increases. The work stoppages, riots, and police confrontations that convulsed Poland in the last weeks of 1970 constituted what two scholars call "the largest and most violent working-class uprising in the history of state-socialist regimes."[136]

As crowds of men and women left their factories for the streets, Polish military discipline quickly broke down. Unlike in 1968, the army and police were not arresting privileged students and allegedly "traitorous" intellectuals. Gomułka's government asked its troops to fire upon ordinary working citizens who feared that they could no longer feed their families. As early as 15 December one security officer reported that soldiers "don't want to shoot . . . they are going over to the other side." Sentiments of this kind pervaded the military. One lieutenant colonel reacted with indignation when ordered to fire upon crowds attacking a Communist Party building: "You son of a bitch, who am I going to shoot? There are women and children out there!"[137]

These circumstances marked the demise of Gomułka and his plans for "selective development." The consumer sacrifices required by state-directed investment in heavy industry had risen too high. They inspired a broad citizen revolt, and they also failed to produce promised economic growth. Under Soviet pressure to "strengthen ties with the working class," on 19 December the Polish Communist Party chose Edward Gierek as its new leader. Gomułka was forced into early retirement.

A former coal miner, Gierek pledged to reestablish stable relations between citizens and the Communist Party. He would continue to pursue economic growth through state-directed investment in heavy industry, but he would not do this at the cost of individual wages and family sustenance. Instead of "selective development," Poland would pursue a wide range of programs for *both* development and consumption. Promises of material abundance, not autarchic discipline, served as the new glue for society.[138]

In the past, Warsaw had depended primarily on Moscow for economic aid. During the early 1970s this also changed. Confronted with an economic slowdown and increasing demands throughout their empire, Soviet leaders believed that they could no longer carry the burden of supporting Poland and other ailing East European economies. A series of reforms within the East-bloc Council for Mutual Economic Assistance (CMEA) encouraged member states to seek out opportunities for trade and financial assistance in the West rather than the Soviet Union. Moscow and its allies had already begun this process by pursuing increased East-West trade during the 1960s (see Table 2 in the appendix).[139]

Under Gierek, Western loans replaced domestic sacrifice and Soviet assistance as the fuel for the Polish economy. The formerly closed state opened itself to trade and borrowing from the West. From 1970 to 1975 Polish citizens enjoyed the fastest rise in per-capita consumption among European communist societies. This increased standard of living was financed by the deepest foreign indebtedness in the Soviet bloc.[140]

Before long Poland could barely pay the interest on its loans. Annual service requirements accounted for 30 percent of the country's export income in 1975. To remain solvent each year, Gierek's government borrowed more money from the West. By 1980 Poland's annual debt servicing exceeded the total income from its exports. Only continued credit from capitalist countries allowed the communist state to keep its economy running.[141]

In retrospect, Soviet-bloc debt contributed to the economic and political bankruptcy of communism. Recurring Polish upheavals in 1976 and 1980–1982 emerged from the difficulties of servicing ballooning foreign liabilities. Loan repayment required eventual domestic sacrifices, often deeper in magnitude than those that had initially motivated leaders to look abroad for financial assistance. During the 1970s Poland and its communist neighbors lived on borrowed time.[142]

This historical judgment does not match perceptions in the immediate aftermath of the December 1970 crisis. Faced with domestic unrest and limited government resources, large loans from the capitalist states looked very attractive for leaders such as Gierek and Brezhnev. Foreign assistance allowed them to promise both economic growth and increased consumption. Workers could enjoy more meat, better housing, and additional leisure time. Economic openness, rather than enforced autarchy, assured short-term domestic stability.

With the encouragement of their governments, western banks made large loans to the Soviet bloc. During a period of slow growth rates—and recession around 1973—East European markets offered alluring opportunities for expanding exports. Foreign loans financed communist purchases of capitalist goods and, as a consequence, contributed to short-term economic stability in the United States and Western Europe. The authoritarian nature of the Soviet-bloc states made them appear safe risks for large loans. In the eyes of many bankers and government officials, undemocratic figures such as Gierek could properly discipline their societies to service heavy debt burdens.[143]

Detente, in this sense, buttressed the leadership in the Soviet bloc. Cooperating with Western officials, communist governments replaced autarchic models of development with international openness. They used foreign resources to meet rising domestic expectations. The capitalist states perceived an economic interest of their own in stabilizing the communist regimes through large loans and extensive market inroads. This arrangement could not last very long, but in the early 1970s it underpinned a period of cooperation between Cold War adversaries. President Nixon's improved relations with the Soviet Union were the most obvious fruit of East-West economic and political interdependence.

As was the case with China, Richard Nixon entered the White House possessing more firsthand knowledge of the Soviet Union than any of his immediate predecessors. During his tenure as Eisenhower's vice president he had closely observed the making of American policy toward this Cold War adversary. In July 1959 he had visited Moscow, Leningrad, Novosibirsk, Sverdlovsk, and other parts of the Soviet Union. On this trip Nixon held extensive discussions with leaders from the Kremlin, including a public debate with Nikita Khrushchev on the relative merits of capitalism and communism.[144]

When the vice president traveled to the Soviet Union in 1959 he approached his hosts from a position of strength. The United States deployed a larger nuclear arsenal than its adversary. Recent uprisings in Hungary and Poland revealed that the Soviet bloc was much more fragile than the Western alliance. Nixon could speak confidently in Moscow of his desire to "extend this [Soviet-American] competition to include the spiritual as well as the material aspects of our civilization."[145]

Ten years later, President Nixon was no longer quite so confident in his nation's capacity for spiritual and material competition. He recognized that circumstances had changed considerably in the last decade, largely to America's disadvantage. In 1969 Washington possessed more long-range bombers and nuclear submarines than Moscow. The Soviet Union, however, maintained a stockpile of 1,274 intercontinental ballistic missiles (ICBMs), compared with 1,054 under American command. Around Moscow the Soviets had also built an antiballistic missile (ABM) defense system unparalleled in the United States. War between the superpowers had long promised mutual destruction, but in the early 1970s the Kremlin deployed an arsenal with some possible advantages over American capabilities.[146]

Both superpowers confronted growing domestic dissent and resistance from former allies. The democratic societies in the West, however, appeared much more fragmented and divided than their Eastern counterparts. Citizens expressed their discontent throughout the Soviet Union, but they did not burn sections of their cities and besiege their leaders as protesters commonly did in the United States and Western Europe. The Kremlin's tyranny seemed to produce advantages in domestic discipline, as well as military capability.[147]

Shadowed by these circumstances and the escalating protests against the Vietnam War, Nixon and Kissinger believed that they had inherited a weak position for their dealings with the Soviet Union. The latter contended, in his memoirs, that while the "absolute power" of the United States had grown during the Cold War, previous policymakers had failed to grapple with the evidence that "our *relative* position was bound to decline." America had achieved what Kissinger called a "position of strength," but it suffered in bilateral relations because "our adversary, instead of negotiating, concentrated on eroding [our position] or turning our flank." According to this prognosis, the Nixon White House needed quick and creative action to avert imminent decline.[148]

Political trends gave every indication that current developments would increase Moscow's international standing at the cost of Washington's. William Hyland, one of Kissinger's close advisers on the National Security Council, recalls that the "sirens" and "continuing commotion" outside the White House made it virtually impossible for policymakers to maintain a strong and unified negotiating position with foreign visitors. With each passing day the American government confronted more violence from its own citizens. "How could the United States preserve the credibility of its foreign policy in such an atmosphere?" Hyland asked.[149]

In contrast to the more obvious chaos in the West, the Soviet Union looked strong and cohesive. This judgment grossly underestimated the internal difficulties of the communist superpower and the domestic resilience of democracy. For Nixon and Kissinger, however, the image of American weakness and Soviet strength was overpowering. It obsessed them.

From 1969 through 1971 they set out, as Kissinger has it, to rescue chance from unfavorable circumstances.[150] This meant deflecting attention from American weaknesses and connecting international issues to create new pressures for Soviet concessions. Arms control and European security had dominated the agenda for talks between the two states since the Eisenhower years. Now the White House refused to isolate these topics from the Vietnam War and relations with China. The United States demanded Soviet assistance in ending the Vietnam War before the conclusion of any arms control agreement. If Moscow was not forthcoming, Washington would seek to improve its relations with China at Soviet expense. Kissinger predicted that this strategy of "linkage" would induce a "more constructive attitude" from the Kremlin on issues of critical importance, and potential weakness, for the West.[151]

To insulate negotiations from bureaucratic and public difficulties, Kissinger opened a secret "back channel" with Soviet ambassador Anatoly Dobrynin. Meeting frequently over informal meals, the two men probed each other for areas of agreement and compromise on a wide range of topics. These discussions displayed the Soviet Union's commitment to engage the United States in meaningful deliberations, but they also showed how far both sides were from agreement on the issues most pressing to the Nixon administration. Kissinger recalls that on "about ten occasions" in 1969 alone, he "tried to enlist Soviet cooperation to help end the war in Vietnam." Dobrynin was consistently "evasive." The two states remained deadlocked on arms control and other bilateral issues that Nixon and Kissinger linked to progress on a Vietnam settlement.[152]

After two years of inconclusive discussions, the White House gained the leverage it had previously lacked in its relations with the Soviet Union. The sensation created in July 1971, when Nixon announced that Kissinger had completed a secret visit to Beijing, raised the Kremlin's fears of a Sino-American alliance against Moscow. Meeting with Kissinger for lunch in August, Dobrynin condemned China's aggressive behavior along the Soviet border and in other areas. Shaken by the recent progress in Sino-American relations, he expressed hope that Washington was not engaged in an "anti-Soviet maneuver."[153]

Nixon and Kissinger used their "China card" to reacquire the negotiating strength they had lost in the late 1960s. Relations between Washington and Beijing raised the specter that the Soviet Union would soon find itself encircled by a coalition of adversaries in both the West and the East. One internal Soviet analysis advised that Sino-American rapprochement had "threatening consequences" but was "not inevitable." Moscow could design "major obstacles" to reconciliation between China and the United States by improving its own relations with Washington.[154]

This was exactly the reaction that Nixon had hoped for. Kissinger recalls that Soviet leaders were "suddenly anxious to create the impression that more serious business could be accomplished in Moscow than in Beijing." Dobrynin sought to arrange a summit meeting between Nixon and Brezhnev before the president visited China. Turning the screws on the Kremlin, the White House accepted the idea of a Soviet-American meeting in Moscow, but Nixon made sure it occurred after his trip to Beijing.[155]

Nixon and Kissinger placed Soviet-American relations in a new strategic context. Discussions became more secret, while the range of issues was now more global. The White House exploited its triangular connections with the Soviet Union and China to compensate for weaknesses in bilateral negotiations with Moscow. Creating closer contacts with these states than they had among themselves, the United States could play one side against the other. The president demanded that both Moscow and Beijing curtail their expansionist activities or risk triggering a U.S. coalition with the other communist state.[156]

This strategy contributed, at least in part, to the settlement of the Vietnam War in January 1973. Moscow and Beijing recognized that prolonging the conflict only increased the possibility that the United States would seek an exit by allying more closely with one communist patron against the other. The Soviet Union and China had already become rivals for North Vietnam's loyalty, and this state of affairs opened the way for Nixon and Kissinger's maneuverings. To limit their risks, both Brezhnev and Mao favored negotiations between Hanoi and Washington. During the early 1960s great-power rivalries had contributed to the escalation of conflict in Southeast Asia. A decade later, detente created new pressures for foreign disengagement from the region.[157]

Most important from the perspective of the White House, Nixon and Kissinger gained political standing through their wide-ranging diplomatic contacts in the early 1970s. They appeared active and creative to an audience desperate for new initiatives in Vietnam and other areas. Without his triangular diplomacy, the president told his chief of staff, "We'd be collapsing now in Vietnam, and the Congressional resolutions on pullout would be passing." Instead, the White House exploited secret maneuvers to create "pragmatic" options. "The United States can't just stand by without trying to affect the world," Nixon asserted.[158]

The leaders of the Soviet Union found that the president's pragmatism imperiled their international status. No longer privileged as America's most important foreign counterpart, Brezhnev's standing declined as Nixon and Kissinger's rose. Almost as frightening as Sino-American collusion for the Kremlin was the prospect of Soviet irrelevance. The Moscow summit of 1972 served as a forum where both the Soviet Union and the United States attempted to solidify their respective statuses as great powers in a world that had grown more multidimensional.

Between Nixon's visit to China in February 1972 and his scheduled trip to the Soviet Union in May, North Vietnam opened a massive offensive against American-supported positions in Southeast Asia. On 30 March approximately 15,000 of Hanoi's heavily armed troops attacked South Vietnam. The invading forces pushed the South's soldiers down the long neck of the peninsula. The old imperial city of Hué—around which the armies of both sides, as well as the United States, had fought fierce battles in early 1968—was soon in jeopardy of falling under Hanoi's control.

Angered by the force of the North Vietnamese attack and fearful that the government in the South might collapse under this renewed pressure, Nixon responded with a new round of bombing raids. On 16 and 17 April American air and sea forces launched their heaviest attacks around Hanoi since the president had taken office. General Creighton Abrams, the supreme American commander in Vietnam, had requested that U.S. planes support the defense of ground positions in the South. The White House, however, ignored his advice. Nixon ordered a series of strikes designed to punish the North and to display American resolve.[159]

Despite U.S. bombing, fighting conditions in Vietnam continued to deteriorate. General Abrams sent an alarming report to Washington, indicating that soldiers defending the South had "begun to bend and in some cases to break." Abrams warned that Hué and other areas might fall under North Vietnamese control in a matter of days.[160]

Nixon took this news as a personal affront. He feared that the North Vietnamese would defeat the South before he could negotiate a deal for the honorable withdrawal of the last American soldiers and the return of prisoners of war. Hanoi's brazen attack made Nixon look as weak and ineffectual as his predecessor had during the Tet Offensive. The president now felt he had to abandon his recently acquired image as a statesman of peace, and return to his "madman" persona for the sake of frightening the North Vietnamese. He ordered Kissinger to tell Hanoi's representatives that he had "had enough." "Settle or else!" he warned.[161]

To reinforce his threat of American escalation, Nixon approved a plan to mine Haiphong. Hanoi imported more military supplies through this port, located on the Gulf of Tonkin, than any other. It was an important docking point for shipments arriving from the Soviet Union. American air strikes had already damaged four of Moscow's ships in other ports during the past month. In Haiphong, Nixon prepared to imperil additional Soviet personnel and equipment for the sake of weakening Hanoi.[162]

Kissinger expected that the leaders in Moscow would retaliate by canceling the Soviet-American summit meeting, scheduled for 22 May. Remarkably, they didn't. Events in Vietnam held far less importance for the Kremlin than the risk of closer Sino-American cooperation against the Soviet Union. Brezhnev needed a summit with the American president to restore his political standing at home and abroad. Instead of creating new tensions with the United States, he hoped to conclude a series of agreements that would stabilize the international system and eliminate the risks of triangular competition among the great powers.[163]

Nixon understood Soviet aims, and he shared a similar outlook. He traveled to Moscow intent on creating a new superpower relationship that would not change the political status quo, but make it more stable and secure. The president sought to capitalize on the benefits of his recent opening to China, building what Kissinger called a firm "structure of peace."[164]

Instead of recurring conflicts among the great powers, agreement on clear spheres of influence would ensure reduced tensions. The largest states would cooperate to limit the disruptive capabilities of small countries such as North Vietnam and Czechoslovakia. Firmly established as the legitimate hegemons in a dangerous world, leaders would avoid undermining their counterparts' control over disorderly citizens—especially naive idealists seeking broad social and political change. Nixon and Brezhnev saw this as "realistic" policy.[165]

The Moscow summit produced the first Strategic Arms Limitations Agreement (SALT I) and the ABM treaty. Together they established ceilings on future rocket construction and missile defense systems. Nixon and Brezhnev, however, gave these documents surprisingly little attention during their meetings. After all, SALT I and the ABM treaty did not actually reduce either side's nuclear arsenal; they only set relatively minor limits on later deployments. During the summit, Soviet and American leaders focused on ensuring common stability against spreading disorder. They recognized that political authority in North America, Europe, and Asia had begun to fragment. They met in hope of reducing uncertainty and uncontrolled change.[166]

In previous decades the Soviet-American rivalry had provided a simple bipolar framework for both competition and cooperation. This inherited architecture now proved inappropriate for a world in which citizens besieged their leaders, small nations challenged the influence of larger states, and China acted as an independent great power. The international environment had grown multipolar, but the United States and the Soviet Union desired the continued power and standing they had possessed in the earlier bipolar setting. What Kissinger called a new "structure of peace" would protect the benefits of order and stability for the largest states despite the fragmenting trends in world affairs. This was the conservative core of detente, and the drive behind the central accomplishment of the superpower summit.[167]

On the last day of Nixon's visit to Moscow, he and Brezhnev signed the declaration on "The Basic Principles of Relations between the United States of America and the Union of Soviet Socialist Republics." It began with a call for "mutual understanding and business-like cooperation" between the superpowers in order "to remove the threat of war" and "create conditions which promote the reduction of tensions." Instead of hostility, the two states pledged to pursue "peaceful coexistence" and to avoid any "dangerous exacerbation of their relations." Drawing on the momentum of SALT I, Moscow and Washington prepared to seek further agreements on arms control, trade, and scientific cooperation.[168]

Nixon announced that this declaration rejected formal spheres of influence for the superpowers. He called it a "landmark" turn from the "military confrontation" of the Cold War to a new period of "constructive leadership and restraint." Kissinger explained that despite the profound differences in their social systems, the United States and the Soviet Union would now "try to behave with restraint and with a maximum of creativity in bringing about a greater degree of stability and peace." The Declaration of Principles laid out what Kissinger called a "roadmap," establishing clear "rules of conduct" to govern an "age in which a cataclysm depends on the decisions of men."[169]

The language of the document and its expositors was surely promising, but it was also deeply conservative. "Restraint" and "mutual accommodation" replaced earlier calls for progressive change in the international system. In no single clause did the signatories indicate how they would work together for any purpose other than reinforcing the status quo. The document recognized the "sovereign equality of all states," but only within a framework that gave priority to the "security interests" of the superpowers. The signatories rejected formal spheres of influence, as Nixon contended, but the provisions for assured boundaries and stability legitimized the current division of authority between the East and West blocs, especially in Europe.

Instead of empowering the United Nations or some other international body to mediate disputes between states, Nixon and Brezhnev spoke of their intent to "widen the juridical basis of their mutual relations." International conflicts had become more complex and multidimensional, the two sides acknowledged, but the superpowers asserted their dominant influence in most regional confrontations. While the leaders renounced the use of force against each other, they pledged to "exert the necessary efforts so that bilateral agreements which they have concluded and multilateral treaties and agreements to which they are jointly parties are faithfully implemented." The United States and the Soviet Union would, in essence, collaborate as firemen, putting out flames of conflict around the globe.[170]

The declaration made no mention of the domestic unrest that had convulsed each of the great powers in the late 1960s. These were "internal problems," according to Kissinger, best left out of an international treaty. Claims to justice had, however, long served as central elements in both American and Soviet foreign policy. To exclude them from a general statement of principles might have been good Realpolitik, but it also sent a message that the leaders of the two superpowers wanted to insulate their activities from domestic debates about ideology and national purpose.[171]

The absence of ideals from the declaration indicated that principles would play little role in international behavior. Nixon and Brezhnev pledged to cooperate closely for the sake of global stability, confining the claims of protesters and dissidents within their respective national boundaries. Instead of containing each other through threats of force, as they had since the end of

World War II, the leaders of the United States and the Soviet Union now colluded to contain their own citizens.

The Declaration of Principles codified a Soviet-American detente that reflected newfound trust between the superpowers, born of shared domestic
and international difficulties. Through secret channels and summits, Kissinger explained to news reporters, Nixon and Brezhnev had come to understand each other better. They recognized a common interest in stability and
order, and a common danger from crusading rhetoric and unregulated disruption. Washington and Moscow laid the foundation for unprecedented
cooperation to strengthen the political status quo.[172]

▪ The "Postmodern" Legacy of Detente

Ostpolitik and Sino-American rapprochement marked the first steps toward
a conservative world order after the global disruption of 1968. Nixon's visit
to the Soviet Union was the last piece in the puzzle of detente. The leaders of
the great powers created a process that balanced threats and boosted elites—
particularly the men who made foreign policy in the United States, the Soviet Union, China, and West Germany. Detente ensured a safer status quo by
discrediting domestic and international challengers.

The strength of detente derived from the fact that it addressed the fears
and served the interests of the leaders in the largest states. Each of the great
powers gained from stability when confronted with the prospect of widespread disruption. Detente assured that the international system would operate smoothly so long as policymakers adhered to their objective "national
interests."[173]

"National interests," however, are not objective laws, but instead contested ideas. Detente's fatal weakness grew from its inability to address the
claims of citizens and small states that refused to accept the status quo because of its perceived injustice. From the day that Nixon and Brezhnev
signed the Declaration of Principles through the end of the 1970s, the leaders of the great powers suffered repeated criticism for ignoring concerns
about national self-determination, human rights, economic fairness, and racial and gender equality.[174]

Agitation around these issues had triggered the global disorder in the
1960s that initially made detente appear necessary as a source of stability.
Ironically, political leaders reacted to the criticisms of injustice voiced in
the previous decade by isolating and containing dissent, rather than by creating new sources of popular consent. Detente reflected traditional balance-
of-power considerations, but it also included a set of policies that deliber-

ately constrained domestic dynamism. Instead of eliminating the suffering and dissatisfaction inherent in the Cold War, it tried to make it all seem "normal."

Excluded from policy influence and disillusioned by the consequences of their protests, many idealistic citizens turned away from politics. The secret channels and intricate maneuverings of detente locked dissent out of government deliberations. The reformist impulses of the 1960s did not disappear, but they moved from the now largely closed world of elite policy to the less political realm of culture and community. Former radicals, like their parents, became mothers, fathers, and homeowners, but few matured with the same faith in government exhibited by earlier generations.[175]

Detente, in this sense, contributed to what many loosely call "postmodern" thought—the search for freedom *from*, rather than freedom *in*, the nation-state. Great-power politics in the early 1970s strengthened the stability of established governments while burying permanent weaknesses deep within. None of the great powers managed to mobilize its fragmented population for a united purpose or progressive policy in the next decade.[176]

Skepticism toward authority is today a global phenomenon. It is also a legacy of the circumstances and decisions inherited from the late 1960s. Leaders are no longer loved or feared. In some of the largest democracies they are ignored by as much as half of the electorate, which refrains from voting. Leaders are frequently profaned by international media that play on public distrust of politicians. In this cynical environment, we are still living with the dissent and detente of a previous generation.

CONCLUSION

The 1960s came to a close with diplomacy and domestic politics oddly frozen in place. These were the conservative consequences that, paradoxically, followed from radical social upheaval. Stability did not arise naturally during this period. It was artificially enforced by the besieged leaders of the largest states.[1]

The decade began when John Kennedy, Nikita Khrushchev, Charles de Gaulle, and Mao Zedong pursued a charismatic kind of politics. Appealing to what they recognized as widespread unease with the territorial divisions and nuclear dangers of the Cold War, these men promised an era of unprecedented achievements: Kennedy would conquer new frontiers, Khrushchev would build real-existing communism, de Gaulle would restore French *grandeur*, and Mao would guide China in a great industrial leap ahead of Europe. An expanding cohort of men and women entered universities convinced that with enlightened leadership they would change the world.

This optimism quickly soured. Youthful citizens expected too much in a world still dominated by nuclear dangers, Cold War divisions, and large bureaucratic institutions. The muscular rhetoric of charismatic leaders encouraged unrealistic hopes that far exceeded practical capabilities. This contradiction between rhetoric and capabilities explains the disjunction that emerged between public persona and private policy in each state. Leaders continued to promise their citizens more than ever before, but time and again they accepted compromises—in Berlin, Cuba, Algeria, and the aftermath of the Great Leap Forward—that rejected the aggressiveness of their rhetoric.

Vietnam was the exception that proved the rule. In this corner of Southeast Asia, John Kennedy and Lyndon Johnson believed they had to press for communist containment and economic development as proof that they really meant what they said. Vietnam appeared deceptively "safe" for the muscle flexing that charismatic leaders needed to impress young and ambitious citizens. This was hardly the first time that Americans, fearful of political and social stagnation, had displayed their "manliness" through war.[2]

Leaders in Washington did not have a monopoly on this kind of self-defeating behavior. Their counterparts in Moscow and Beijing pursued their own interventions in Vietnam. Mao also embarked on a ruinous "Cultural Revolution" that sought to purge China of the "counterrevolutionary" influences deposited on the mainland by the United States and the Soviet Union. By the end of the decade Chinese and Soviet assertiveness brought these communist states to the point of war. Leaders in both countries turned to the United States, West Germany, and other capitalist adversaries for assistance in repairing the damage of their overheated rhetoric.

Throughout this period, young men and women grew visibly more violent in nearly every society. Adopting the "language of dissent" popularized by a series of authors, students accused their elders of hypocrisy and corruption. Leaders were delegitimized by their own rhetoric. They did not conquer new frontiers, build real-existing communism, restore national *grandeur*, or achieve any great industrial leaps. Around universities, young men and women assembled to criticize and attack authorities. This was true even in the repressive communist states, where *kompanii* and Red Guard meetings became sites for organized rebellion.

By 1968 rebellion produced revolution. Young men and women took to the streets, smashing symbols of government legitimacy. In Berkeley, Washington, D.C., and other American cities mobs blocked buildings, burned streets, and fought with the state's armed police and military forces. In West Berlin and Paris students built barricades and engaged in street battles with police. In Prague men and women demonstrated for freedom and independence from Soviet intervention. In Wuhan young Red Guards seized weapons from the army and used them against their elders. This was a truly "global disruption" that threatened leaders everywhere.

Detente was a reaction to these troubling circumstances. Willy Brandt, Richard Nixon, and Leonid Brezhnev abandoned the muscular rhetoric and charismatic politics of their predecessors. Mao Zedong reincarnated himself as an opponent of the Cultural Revolution he had initially launched. Despite their ideological differences, these men colluded to stabilize their societies and preserve their authority. They refrained from challenging one another as they had throughout the Cold War. They used obsessive secrecy to insulate their activities from domestic attack. They pursued arms control and trade to furnish new resources for domestic needs. Most significant, they collaborated to bolster their respective images. The summits and agreements of the period made the leaders appear indispensable. To challenge Brandt, Nixon, Brezhnev, or Mao was to undermine new steps toward international "peace." The promise of detente became a stick with which to beat domestic critics.

In place of the charismatic politics that characterized the early part of the decade, leaders now practiced profoundly conservative politics. Detente preserved stability at the cost of progressive change. It made the sacrifices of the Cold War appear "normal," and it further isolated policymakers from their publics. In this way, detente contributed to the pervasive skepticism of our "postmodern" age.

People of all kinds are now looking beyond the boundaries of the nation-state to understand the world around them. The end of the Cold War, the Internet, and the economic turbulence of the 1990s have raised public awareness about "globalization." Environmental and human rights activism has drawn attention to common interests across cultures. Most shocking, the terrorist attacks of 11 September 2001 and the subsequent "war on terrorism" have encouraged a sense of shared danger among the members of diverse societies.

To help us comprehend what it means to think globally, scholars have begun to conceptualize history in these terms as well. By examining how states, peoples, and cultures interacted with one another in the past, we surely gain some leverage on understanding the present. To see globalization as a historic phenomenon is to recognize that the new technologies of our day are not necessarily the primary forces behind the interdependence of economies, the interpenetration of cultures, and, perhaps most worrying, the internationalization of terrorism. Studying the 1960s and detente in global terms reveals how ideas, institutions, and personalities transcended national boundaries before the Internet or the "war on terrorism."

The Cold War, more than anything else, created a remarkable conjuncture among societies in the 1960s. Nuclear dangers elicited common fears of annihilation. International competition contributed to the growth of state-run bureaucracies. This trend was especially robust in universities, which in nearly every society expanded to accommodate both a larger population of young citizens and state demands for more advanced technical training. Cold War rhetoric about capitalism and communism promoted rising expectations that, by the late 1960s, produced a common sense of disillusionment among culturally diverse men and women.

To see the period in these terms, and detente's function as counterrevolution, requires a global perspective that looks across national boundaries and within societies at the same time. It demands attention to various kinds of relationships: social, cultural, political, and diplomatic. Isolating one kind of interaction from another simply recasts the parochialism of national history over a wider geographic terrain. Understanding moments of global conjuncture such as the 1960s requires an international history that treats power as both *multicultural* and *multidimensional*. This approach involves following the interactions of ideas, institutions, and personalities at many levels. It also leads to an examination of how policies such as detente evolved from truly diverse, and often unintended, influences.

Many social reforms grew out of the 1960s, especially with regard to race and gender relations in the United States and Western Europe. These accomplishments, however, pale in comparison with the extensive ambitions voiced by reformers at the time. Poverty, despite the writings of John Kenneth Galbraith and Michael Harrington, remains prevalent on city streets and in rural communities throughout the wealthiest nations. The gap between the richest and poorest states also remains large, and has probably grown since the 1960s.[3]

Communism has collapsed in the Soviet Union and Eastern Europe, but citizens in many societies are still deprived of an effective political voice. They suffer from the kind of isolation that angered dissidents and protesters decades earlier. Unrepresentative international bodies such as the European Union and the World Trade Organization worsen this "democratic deficit," even in the most democratic states. Demonstrations against these international institutions have evoked images somewhat similar to those of the 1960s: young men and women marching, organized groups staging sit-ins, and mobs vandalizing city streets.[4]

Detente constrained political and economic reform in the last quarter of the twentieth century. Cooperation among the leaders of the largest states discouraged creative policymaking and risk-taking. Quite the contrary, triangular diplomacy and Ostpolitik emphasized political predictability. Extensive coordination among a tiny group of men excluded most advocates of change. Political institutions, as a consequence, grew more rigid. Boundaries for authority, both national and international, were also fortified.

The history of globalization is, in this sense, intimately connected with detente. International institutions continue to embody the conservative inclinations of leaders. They are generally opaque, elitist, and dominated by the largest states. They have important public influence, but they remain creatures of national governments. Detente protected a state-centered world and forestalled hopes for the creation of truly independent international authorities.

The excesses of the 1960s discredited political idealism. As a consequence, many societies suffer from what one writer calls "diminishing expectations."

"Personal preoccupations" have replaced collective engagement and common purpose. Christopher Lasch has defined this as the "culture of narcissism" that emerged from the "turmoil of the sixties" and continues to characterize a world in which politics lack popular meaning. "Having no hope of improving their lives in any of the ways that matter," Lasch has written, "people have convinced themselves that what matters is . . . to live for yourself, not for your predecessors or posterity." Detente encouraged narcissism among leaders and citizens, especially in Europe and the United States.[5]

This narcissism has infected relations among states and societies. Since the 1960s leaders have generally failed to build popular consensus for their foreign policies. Even after 11 September 2001 government deliberations have remained highly centralized and secretive. President George W. Bush and his counterparts in Europe, the Middle East, and other regions have spoken of a "moral crusade," but they have done little to engage citizens on fundamental issues. No leader has seriously asked his or her constituents to think about why people turn to terrorism. Nor has any figure of authority articulated a vision for how citizens can cooperate to improve global conditions. Most troubling, governments have deployed force at home and abroad with the worthy intention of preventing future terrorism, but also with little public discussion about infringements on individual liberties. Like their predecessors in the late 1960s, leaders have protected stability at the cost of liberty.

Terrorist threats might justify this calculation. It is, however, a decision that requires public discussion, not elite dictate. The history of the 1960s and detente warns that stability without consensus prohibits progress. Anger and resentment fester, moving from traditional institutions to other, often more belligerent, venues. To some extent, this process has encouraged bursts of "home-grown" violence in Europe and North America since the early 1970s. It has also produced militant behavior among men and women, frequently from the Arab world, who feel dispossessed by globalization. Although many of the claims articulated by terrorists are illegitimate, we must take seriously their alienation from the processes of economic growth, political democratization, and cultural recognition. The anger that fuels terrorism has deep roots in past policies, both domestic and international, that have excluded many people from a personal stake in the existing order.

Moralistic rhetoric and isolated policymaking, though sometimes necessary, will not reintegrate the dispossessed into a world of global markets, democratizing states, and Hollywood movies. Combining force with consensus-building efforts, both at home and abroad, appears much more likely to turn people away from terrorism. Residents of different societies need not agree on all issues to recognize that they share a common fate. They need not enjoy similar lifestyles to understand that they benefit from peaceful trade and cooperation. The leaders of the largest states must work to show, in actions and in words, that their foreign policies reflect the concerns of international citizens, not just national constituents or national "interests."

Building consensus, of course, is difficult and sometimes impossible. It can also inspire violent counterreactions. That said, alternative approaches to stability without consensus are far worse. Detente failed to satisfy citizens, it prolonged Cold War sacrifices, and it created festering resentments. Contemporary policies that advocate isolated decisionmaking appear little better. Foreign policy is also social policy. We will never build a better world until leaders and citizens recognize this simple truism and work together in the use of force and the pursuit of peace.

APPENDIX

NOTES

SOURCES

INDEX

APPENDIX:

TABLES AND FIGURES

Table 1. Student enrollments in higher education

Year	United States	West Germany	France	Great Britain	Soviet Union	China
1955	2,812,000	133,884	152,246	85,200	1,800,000	292,000
1960	3,789,000	203,335	216,426	107,700	2,400,000	961,623
1965	5,921,000	279,345	368,154	168,600	3,900,000	674,436
1970	8,581,000	386,244	602,712	228,000	4,500,000	47,800

Sources: United States: U.S. Department of Health, Education and Welfare, *Projections of Educational Statistics to 1975–76* (Washington, D.C., 1966), 5, 102; idem, *Projections of Educational Statistics to 1980–81* (Washington, D.C., 1972), 23, 158. West Germany: *Statistisches Jahrbuch für die Bundesrepublik Deutschland* (Stuttgart, 1956–1971), 1956: 91; 1961: 106; 1966: 102; 1971: 81; Hansgert Peisert and Gerhild Framhein, *Systems of Education: Federal Republic of Germany* (New York, 1978), 14; Hedwig Rudolph and Rudolf Husemann, *Hochschulpolitik zwischen Expansion und Restriktion: Ein Vergleich der Entwicklung in der Bundesrepublik Deutschland und der Deutschen Demokratischen Republik* (Frankfurt, 1984), 134. France: Pierre Bourdieu et Jean Claude Passeron, *Les héritiers: Les étudiants et la culture* (Paris, 1964), 120–121; Jürgen Schriewer, *Die Französischen Universitäten, 1945–68* (Bad Heilbrunn, 1972), 561; Alain Bienaymé, *Systems of Higher Education: France* (New York, 1978), 4–5; H. D. Lewis, *The French Educational System* (London, 1985), 101. Great Britain: W. A. C. Stewart, *Higher Education in Postwar Britain* (London, 1989), 268, 271–272. Soviet Union: Mervyn Matthews, *Education in the Soviet Union: Policies and Institutions since Stalin* (London, 1982), 206; Seymour M. Rosen, *Higher Education in the USSR: Curriculums, Schools, and Statistics* (Washington, D.C., 1963), 100; S. Frederick Starr, "New Communications Technologies and Civil Society," in *Science and the Soviet Social Order,* ed. Loren R. Graham (Cambridge, Mass., 1990), 31. People's Republic of China: Suzanne Pepper, *Radicalism and Education Reform in 20th-Century China: The Search for an Ideal Developmental Model* (New York, 1996), 198, 285–86, 416; Ruth Hayhoe, *China's Universities, 1895–1995: A Century of Cultural Conflict* (New York, 1996), 96.

Table 2. East-West trade (in millions of dollars)

Year	Soviet bloc imports	Soviet bloc exports
1961	2,140	2,204
1971	6,904	6,749
1975	25,819	17,627

Note: "East" = CMEA; "West" = OECD.

Source: Robert V. Roosa, Armin Gutowski, and Michiya Matsukawa, *East-West Trade at a Crossroads: Economic Relations with the Soviet Union and Eastern Europe* (New York, 1982), 14–15.

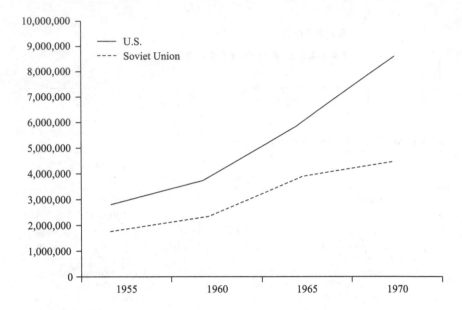

Figure 1. Higher education enrollment in the United States and the
Soviet Union, 1955–1970

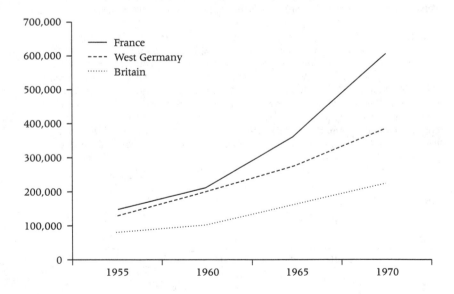

Figure 2. Higher education enrollment in West Germany, France, and
Great Britain, 1955–1970

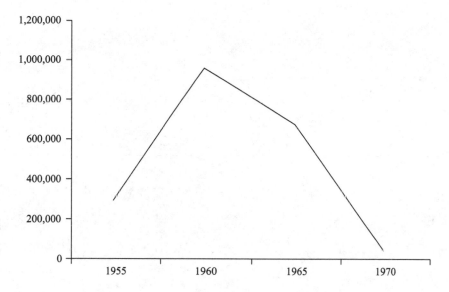

Figure 3. Higher education enrollment in the People's Republic of China, 1955–1970

NOTES

The following abbreviations are used in the notes.

AAPBD	*Akten zur Auswärtigen Politik der Bundesrepublik Deutschland* (Munich, 1994–2000)
AN	Archives Nationales, Paris, France
BA	Bundesarchiv, Koblenz, Germany
CWIHPB	*Cold War International History Project Bulletin*
DzD	*Dokumente zur Deutschlandpolitik* (Frankfurt, 1967–1987)
FFM	Archives du Ministère des Affaires Etrangères, Paris, France
FRUS	*Foreign Relations of the United States* (Washington, D.C., 1977–2001)
JFKL	John F. Kennedy Presidential Library, Boston, Massachusetts
LBJL	Lyndon B. Johnson Presidential Library, Austin, Texas
LC	Library of Congress, Manuscript Reading Room, Washington, D.C.
LNC	Charles de Gaulle, *Lettres, Notes, et Carnets*, 3 vols. (Paris, 1986–87)
NA	U.S. National Archives, College Park, Maryland
NSA	National Security Archive, George Washington University, Washington, D.C.
NSC	National Securitty Council
NSF	National Security File
PA/AA	Politisches Archiv des Auswärtigen Amts, Bonn, Germany
POF	President's Office File
PPP: DDE	*Public Papers of the Presidents: Dwight D. Eisenhower* (Washington, D.C., 1954–1961)
PPP: JFK	*Public Papers of the Presidents: John F. Kennedy* (Washington, D.C., 1962–1964)
PPP: LBJ	*Public Papers of the Presidents: Lyndon B. Johnson* (Washington, D.C., 1964–1969)
PPP: RN	*Public Papers of the Presidents: Richard Nixon* (Washington, D.C., 1970–1974)
PRO	Public Records Office, Kew, England
RFE/RL	Records of Radio Free Europe/Radio Liberty, Open Society Archives, Central European University, Budapest, Hungary
SM	Seeley Mudd Manuscript Library, Princeton, New Jersey
UPC	Underground Press Collection, Hoover Institution Library, Stanford, California
YUL	Yale University Library, Manuscripts and Archives

INTRODUCTION

1. See John Lewis Gaddis, *The Long Peace: Inquiries into the History of the Cold War* (New York, 1987), 215–245.

2. Wang Shaoguang, *Failure of Charisma: The Cultural Revolution in Wuhan* (New York, 1995), 157–60; Simon Leys, *The Chairman's New Clothes: Mao and the Cultural Revolution*, trans. Carol Appleyard and Patrick Goode (New York, 1977), 79–80; "Mao's Talks at Three Meetings with Comrades Chang Ch'un-ch'iao and Yau Wen-yüan," in *Chairman Mao Talks to the People: Talks and Letters, 1956–1971*, trans. John Chinnery and Tieyun, ed. Stuart Schram (New York, 1974), 277–279; editorial, *People's Daily (Renmin ribao)*, 6 November 1967, reprinted and translated in *Mao Papers: Anthology and Bibliography*, ed. Jerome Chen (New York, 1970), 149.

3. Jean Lacouture, *De Gaulle: The Ruler, 1945–1970*, trans. Alan Sheridan (New York, 1991), 548–549; Jacques Massu, *Baden 68* (Paris, 1983), 87–92; François Flohic, *Souvenirs d'Outre-Gaulle* (Paris, 1979), 176–183.

4. Speech by Willy Brandt at Conference of Non-Nuclear States, Genf, 3 September 1968, box 288, Papers of Egon Bahr, Archive of the Social Democratic Party, Friedrich-Ebert-Stiftung, Bonn, Germany.

5. CIA report, "Restless Youth," September 1968, Folder: Youth and Student Movements, box 13, Files of Walt Rostow, NSF, LBJL; Harry McPherson, Oral History, interview 5, tape 2: 14, LBJL.

6. Richard Nixon, "Inaugural Address," 20 January 1969, in *PPP: RN*, 1969: 1–4. For Nixon's uses of the phrase "war at home" see Michael S. Sherry, *In the Shadow of War: The United States since the 1930s* (New Haven, 1995), 292–307.

7. KGB memorandum to the Council of Ministers of the Soviet Union, 5 November 1968, in *Istoricheski arhiv* 1 (1994), 176–193; Dmitri Volkogonov, *Sem' Vozhdey: Galeria liderov SSSR v dvukh knigakh* (Moscow, 1995), 2: 33–34.

8. See Henry Kissinger, *White House Years* (Boston, 1979), 191–194; idem, *Diplomacy* (New York, 1994), 703–761; Anatoly Dobrynin, *In Confidence: Moscow's Ambassador to America's Six Cold War Presidents* (New York, 1995), 191–264; Raymond L. Garthoff, *Détente and Confrontation: American-Soviet Relations from Nixon to Reagan*, rev. ed. (Washington, D.C., 1994), 57–73; Gaddis, *The Long Peace*, 215–245; idem, *Strategies of Containment: A Critical Appraisal of Postwar American National Security Policy* (New York, 1982), 274–308; Marc Trachtenberg, *A Constructed Peace: The Making of the European Settlement, 1945–1963* (Princeton, 1999), 379–402.

1. THE STRAINS OF NUCLEAR DESTRUCTION

1. See Bernard Brodie, "War in the Atomic Age," in *The Absolute Weapon: Atomic Power and World Order*, ed. Brodie (New York, 1946), 21–69.

2. On the political objectives of war, see the classic text: Carl von Clausewitz, *On War*, trans. and ed. Michael Howard and Peter Paret (Princeton, 1984), 86–99, 585–593.

3. See John Lewis Gaddis, *The Long Peace: Inquiries into the History of the Cold War* (New York, 1987), 215–245; idem, *We Now Know: Rethinking Cold War History* (Oxford, 1997), 278–280; Marc Trachtenberg, *A Constructed Peace: The Making of the European Settlement, 1945–1963* (Princeton, 1999), 379–402; Anders Stephanson, "The United States," in *The Origins of the Cold War in Europe: International Perspectives*, ed. David Reynolds (New Haven, 1994), 23–51.

4. Eisenhower, "Address before the UN General Assembly on Peaceful Uses of Atomic Energy," 8 December 1953, in *PPP: DDE*, 1953: 817.

5. Robert A. Divine, *Blowing on the Wind: The Nuclear Test Ban Debate, 1954–1960* (New York, 1978), 3–18.

6. Memorandum of Discussion at the 190th Meeting of the NSC, 25 March 1954, *FRUS* 1952–54, 2 (pt. 1): 642; Eisenhower to Winston Churchill, 19 March 1954, in *The Churchill-Eisenhower Correspondence, 1953–1955*, ed. Peter G. Boyle (Chapel Hill, 1990), 125.

7. Quoted in Robert Bowie and Richard Immerman, *Waging Peace: How Eisenhower Shaped an Enduring Cold War Strategy* (New York, 1998), 49.

8. Gaddis, *We Now Know*, 230.

9. See Divine, *Blowing on the Wind*, 36–83; Lawrence S. Wittner, *Resisting the Bomb: A History of the World Nuclear Disarmament Movement, 1954–1970* (Stanford, 1997), 51–59, 125–159, 246–264.

10. Account of Dulles' remarks in Memorandum of Discussion from the NSC Meeting, 6 May 1954, *FRUS* 1952–54, 2 (pt. 2): 1428.

11. Quoted in John S. D. Eisenhower, *Strictly Personal* (Garden City, N.Y., 1974), 176.

12. Eisenhower, "Statement on Disarmament Presented at the Geneva Conference," 21 July 1955, in *PPP: DDE*, 1955: 715. Eisenhower did not use the term *open skies* in his public statement.

13. Bowie and Immerman, *Waging Peace*, 222–241; Albert Wohlstetter, "The Delicate Balance of Terror," *Foreign Affairs* 37 (January 1959): 211–234.

14. Bowie and Immerman, *Waging Peace*, 187–189.

15. Gary John Tocchet, "September Thaw: Khrushchev's Visit to America, 1959" (Ph.D. diss., Stanford University, 1995); Jeremi Suri, "America's Search for a Technological Solution to the Arms Race: The Surprise Attack Conference of 1958 and a Challenge for Eisenhower Revisionists," *Diplomatic History* 21 (Summer 1997): 417–451.

16. Bowie and Immerman, *Waging Peace*, 43–45. For a broader analysis of American thought regarding "national security," see Michael J. Hogan, *A Cross of Iron: Harry S. Truman and the Origins of the National Security State, 1945–54* (New York, 1998), 1–22, 366–418; Aaron L. Friedberg, *In the Shadow of the Garrison State: America's Anti-Statism and Its Cold War Grand Strategy* (Princeton, 2000), 9–80.

17. John Lewis Gaddis, *Strategies of Containment: A Critical Appraisal of Postwar American National Security Policy* (New York, 1982), 129–136.

18. Fred Kaplan, *The Wizards of Armageddon* (New York, 1983), 125–173; Gregg Herken, *Counsels of War* (New York, 1987), 88–134.

19. Robert Cutler to John Foster Dulles, 7 April 1958, *FRUS* 1958–60, 3: 66–68. See also Paper by Cutler, 1 May 1958, ibid., 78.

20. See Dean Acheson, *Power and Diplomacy* (Cambridge, Mass., 1958), 1–28; Henry Kissinger, *Nuclear Weapons and Foreign Policy* (Garden City, N.Y., 1958), 145–166; Maxwell Taylor, *The Uncertain Trumpet* (New York, 1960), 130–180; Herman Kahn, *On Thermonuclear War* (Princeton, 1960), 96–116; Robert Divine, *The Sputnik Challenge* (New York, 1993), 77–96, 175–184. For data on the size of the U.S. and Soviet nuclear arsenals see the Web site of the National Resources Defense Council: www.nrdc.org/nrdc/nrdcpro/nudb.

21. Memorandum of Discussion at the 375th Meeting of the NSC, 7 August 1958, *FRUS* 1958–60, 3: 132–135; David Alan Rosenberg, "The Origins of Overkill: Nuclear Weapons and American Strategy," in *The National Security: Its Theory and Practice, 1945–1960*, ed. Norman Graebner (New York, 1986), 160–178.

22. Eisenhower, quoted in Marc Trachtenberg, *History and Strategy* (Princeton, 1991), 214. See also Campbell Craig, *Destroying the Village: Eisenhower and Thermonuclear War* (New York, 1998), 78–107; Gaddis, *We Now Know*, 239–244.

23. David L. Snead, *The Gaither Committee, Eisenhower, and the Cold War* (Columbus, 1999), 119–128; Kaplan, *The Wizards of Armageddon*, 125–143.

24. Wohlstetter, "The Delicate Balance of Terror," 230.

25. The official title of the Surprise Attack Conference was "The Conference of Experts for the Study of Possible Measures Which Might Be Helpful in Preventing Surprise Attack and for the Preparation of a Report thereon to Governments." Delegates from the participating nations—the United States, Great Britain, France, Canada, Italy, the Soviet Union, Poland, Czechoslovakia, Romania, and Albania—met in Geneva, Switzerland, from 10 November to 18 December 1958. See Suri, "America's Search for a Technological Solution," 421–425.

26. Eisenhower, "Farewell Radio and Television Address to the American People," 17 January 1961, in *PPP: DDE*, 1960–61: 1035–40; National Resources Defense Council, "Table of Global Nuclear Stockpiles, 1945–1996," http://www.nrdc.org/nrdc/nrdcpro/nudb; Gaddis, *Strategies of Containment*, 359; Wohlstetter, "The Delicate Balance of Terror," 213–222, 231–234; Taylor, *The Uncertain Trumpet*, 130–180; Kissinger, *Nuclear Weapons and Foreign Policy*, 145–166.

27. George F. Kennan, *Russia, the Atom, and the West* (New York, 1958), 51, 55, 95.

28. Eisenhower, "Farewell Radio and Television Address," 1037–38.

29. Lloyd Gardner, *Pay Any Price: Lyndon Johnson and the Wars for Vietnam* (Chicago, 1995), 24–39; Kennedy, "Commencement Address at Yale University," 11 June 1962, in *PPP: JFK*, 1962: 470–475.

30. For Kennedy's use of the phrase "way of life," see "Radio and Television Report to the American People on the Berlin Crisis," 25 July 1961, in *PPP: JFK*, 1961: 533–540; "Address on the First Anniversary of the Alliance for Progress," 13 March 1962, in *PPP: JFK*, 1962: 220–224.

31. Arthur M. Schlesinger Jr., *The Vital Center: The Politics of Freedom* (Boston, 1949), 161, 245; idem, "The Shape of National Politics to Come," 12 May 1959, folder 280, box 216, Papers of Chester Bowles, YUL (hereafter Bowles Papers); Dean Acheson's notes from the president's call on Justice (Felix) Frankfurter, 26 July 1962, folder 148, box 12, Papers of Dean Acheson, YUL (hereafter Acheson Papers).

32. Walt Rostow, Oral History, 1964, 149, JFKL; David Halberstam, *The Best and the Brightest* (New York, 1972).

33. Roger Hilsman, Oral History, 14 August 1970, 28, JFKL. Hilsman served in the Kennedy administration as director of the State Department's Bureau of Intelligence and Research, and later as assistant secretary of state for Far Eastern affairs.

34. "Address of Senator John F. Kennedy Accepting the Democratic Party Nomination for the Presidency of the U.S., Los Angeles," 15 July 1960, www.jfklibrary.org/j071560.htm; Arthur Schlesinger Jr. to Chester Bowles, 18 August 1959, folder 280, box 216, Bowles Papers. See Frederick Jackson Turner's famous essay "The Significance of the Frontier in American History," in *Annual Report of the American Historical Association for the Year 1893* (Washington, D.C., 1894). Turner's essay is reprinted in John Mack Faragher, ed., *Rereading Frederick Jackson Turner* (New York, 1994), 31–60. On Kennedy's invocation of a mythic, regenerative "wild west" in his new frontier rhetoric, see Richard Slotkin, *Gunfighter Nation: The Myth of the Frontier in Twentieth-Century America* (New York, 1992), 489–504.

35. Kennedy, "Special Message to the Congress on Urgent National Needs," 25 May 1961, in *PPP: JFK*, 1961: 396–406.

36. Ibid., 403, 406.

37. Kennedy, "Address at Rice University," 12 September 1962, in *PPP: JFK*, 1962: 668–671. See also Michael Sherry, *In the Shadow of War: The United States since the 1930s* (New Ha-

ven, 1995), 237–241; Walter McDougall, . . . *The Heavens and the Earth: A Political History of the Space Age* (New York, 1985), 307–360.

38. Robert S. McNamara with Brian VanDeMark, *In Retrospect: The Tragedy and Lessons of Vietnam* (New York, 1995), 14.

39. McGeorge Bundy, *Danger and Survival: Choices about the Bomb in the First Fifty Years* (New York, 1988), 334–351.

40. McNamara to Kennedy, 10 May 1961, *FRUS* 1961–63, 8: 79–81. Francis Gavin explains that the term *flexible response* was rarely defined explicitly or applied consistently; "The Myth of Flexible Response: United States Strategy in Europe during the 1960s," *International History Review* 23 (December 2001): 847–875.

41. Paul Nitze to Theodore Sorenson, 9 October 1961, folder 2, box 83, Papers of Paul Nitze, LC (hereafter Nitze Papers).

42. NSC 68, 7 April 1950, *FRUS* 1950, 1: 235–292.

43. Nitze to Sorenson, 9 October 1961.

44. See Draft Memorandum from McNamara to President Johnson, 19 December 1963, *FRUS* 1961–63, 8: 565–587; Gaddis, *Strategies of Containment*, 198–273; Trachtenberg, *A Constructed Peace*, 286–297. American military spending did increase in nominal terms from 1960 through 1966, but it declined as a percentage of the gross national product during this period.

45. Walter W. Heller, *New Dimensions of Political Economy* (Cambridge, Mass., 1966), 28–29, 36; idem, "Kennedy Economics Revisited," in *Economics in the Public Service: Papers in Honor of Walter W. Heller*, ed. Joseph A. Pechman and N. J. Simler (New York, 1982), 238–239.

46. Heller, *New Dimensions of Political Economy*, 28, 36; Kennedy, "Commencement Address at Yale University," 11 June 1962, in *PPP: JFK*, 1962: 473, 475.

47. Herbert Stein observes that American presidents since Franklin Roosevelt had adopted various ideas about fiscal spending to stimulate the economy. Kennedy's policies—especially the tax cut enacted in 1964—marked the triumph of what Stein calls a long evolving "fiscal revolution in America." This sea change in economic thought was tempered, Stein writes, by continuing (though less popular) calls for balanced budgets in the 1960s. Fiscal conservatism would, of course, regain its hold over policymakers in the 1990s. See Herbert Stein, *The Fiscal Revolution in America: Policy in Pursuit of Reality*, 2d rev. ed. (Washington, D.C., 1996), 372–468. See also Gaddis, *Strategies of Containment*, 204, 226–228; Diane Kunz, *Butter and Guns: America's Cold War Economic Diplomacy* (New York, 1997), 103–108; Francis J. Gavin, "Gold, Dollars, and Power: The Politics of the U.S. Balance of Payments, 1958–1971" (Ph.D. diss., University of Pennsylvania, 1997), 12–13.

48. Heller, *New Dimensions of Political Economy*, 71–79.

49. Report to Kennedy by the Task Force on Foreign Economic Policy, 31 December 1960, box 213, Papers of George Ball, SM; quotations from pp. R-6 and 62–63.

50. Nick Cullather, "Development? It's History," *Diplomatic History* 24 (Fall 2000): 641.

51. W. W. Rostow, *The Stages of Economic Growth: A Non-Communist Manifesto* (1960; reprint, New York, 1990), 4–16, 36–58, 162–164. See also Michael E. Latham, *Modernization as Ideology: American Social Science and "Nation Building" in the Kennedy Era* (Chapel Hill, 2000), 30–46, 69–108, 151–207; D. Michael Shafer, *Deadly Paradigms: The Failure of U.S. Counterinsurgency Policy* (Princeton, 1988), 48–132, 240–275; Robert J. McMahon, *The Cold War on the Periphery: The United States, India, and Pakistan* (New York, 1994), 273; Andrew J. Rotter, *Comrades at Odds: The United States and India, 1947–1964* (Ithaca, 2000), 108–115.

52. "A Program of Action to Prevent Communist Domination of South Vietnam," 1 May 1961 (submitted to the president on 3 May 1961), *FRUS* 1961–63, 1: 104–105.

53. Kennedy, handwritten note, no date, folder: Germany, Security 1/61–6/61, box 117, POF, JFKL.

54. Trachtenberg, *A Constructed Peace*, 293–297. Trachtenberg minimizes Kennedy's anxieties about the nuclear choices he might have to make.

55. Position Paper: Progress toward a Viable World Order, 26 May 1961, folder: USSR–Vienna Meeting, Background Documents, 1953–61 (G–Q), box 126, POF, JFKL.

56. Memorandum of Conversation between Kennedy and Khrushchev, 4 June 1961, 10:15 A.M., folder: USSR—Vienna Meeting, Memos of Conversations 6/61 (I); Position Paper: Progress toward a Viable World Order, 26 May 1961, folder: USSR—Vienna Meeting, Background Documents, 1953–61 (G–Q), box 126, POF, JFKL.

57. Report of the Four-Power Working Group on Germany including Berlin, 10 February 1961, folder: Germany, Security, 1/61–6/61, box 117, POF, JFKL.

58. Quoted in Michael Beschloss, *The Crisis Years: Kennedy and Khrushchev, 1960–1963* (New York, 1991), 278.

59. John Ausland, "Inter-relationship between Unrest in East Germany and/or East Berlin and Possible Allied Military Operations Designed to Induce the Soviet Union to Re-open Access to Berlin," 8 April 1963, folder: Berlin—Arms Stockpile, box 1, Record Group 59, 250/62/34/03—Files of the Deputy Under Secretary for Political Affairs, NA. See also Ausland to U.S. East Germany Working Group, 22 December 1961, ibid.

60. Trachtenberg, *A Constructed Peace*, 379–402.

61. See ibid.; Gaddis, *We Now Know*, 149–151.

62. James F. Tent, *The Free University of Berlin: A Political History* (Bloomington, 1988), 278; David E. Murphy, Sergei A. Kondrashev, and George Bailey, *Battleground Berlin: CIA vs. KGB in the Cold War* (New Haven, 1997), 3–50, 103–304.

63. Tent, *The Free University of Berlin*, 279–281; Alexandra Richie, *Faust's Metropolis: A History of Berlin* (New York, 1998), 770–778.

64. Egon Bahr, draft message to West German President Theodor Heuss, 11 July 1962, box 44A, Papers of Egon Bahr, Archive of the Social Democratic Party, Friedrich-Ebert-Stiftung, Bonn, Germany (hereafter Bahr Papers); Bahr to Mr. Ronald T. Schuster (president of Hunter College), 21 October 1961, box 44B, Bahr Papers. See also Bahr to Willy Brandt, 11 November 1961, ibid. The American government received many reports of declining morale in West Germany after the construction of the Berlin Wall. See American Embassy, Bonn, to Washington, 20 September 1962, folder: Germany, General 9/62; American Embassy, Bonn, to Washington, 5 October 1962, folder: Germany, General 10/1/62–10/14/62, both box 76, NSF, JFKL.

65. See Secretary of State Dean Rusk's comments in Memorandum of Conference with Kennedy and Congressional Leaders, 21 February 1962, *FRUS* 1961–63, 14: 837–839; Kennedy's comments in Memorandum of Conversation with Alexei Adzhubei [Khrushchev's son-in-law] and Georgi Bolshakov, 31 January 1962, ibid., 780–784.

66. According to opinion polls, the number of West German citizens who rated reunification as a priority rose from 19 percent in August 1961 to 47 percent in January 1965. Among respondents aged sixteen to twenty-nine, reunification rated as a priority for 50 percent. See "Der Wunsch der Deutschen nach Wiedervereinigung," 14 June 1965; "Probleme der deutschen Wiedervereinigung," 28 June 1965; "Katechismus zur deutschen Frage," 12 January 1966, all IIA1, band 1, PA/AA; "Die deutsche Frage," 20 March 1965; "Stand der Deutschland-Frage," 1965, IIA1, band 5, PA/AA.

67. Hans-Peter Schwarz, *Adenauer: Der Staatsmann, 1952–1967* (Stuttgart, 1991), 670.

68. See Adenauer to the State Secretary, 9 December 1960, III/50, Papers of Konrad Adenauer, Stiftung Bundeskanzler-Adenauer-Haus, Rhöndorf, Germany (hereafter Adenauer Papers); Adenauer's address at the Tutzing Protestant Academy (uncorrected manuscript), 19 July 1963, 02.31, 1963/band 1, Reden, Interviews, Aufsätze; and Adenauer's speech at the Free University, West Berlin, 5 December 1958, 16.25, 1958/band 2, Adenauer Papers.

69. Adenauer's address at Tutzing Protestant Academy (uncorrected manuscript), 19 July 1963; Adenauer to Khrushchev, 8 January 1960, III/1; Adenauer's speech before the Christian-Social collegiate group at the University of Cologne, 15 February 1960, 16.27 1960, band 1, all Adenauer Papers.

70. Adenauer's 5 March 1962 interview with *Le Monde*, reprinted in *DzD*, 8: 218–221. See also Adenauer's comments in the account of his discussion with Henry Kissinger, 16 February 1962, III/60; and Adenauer to Charles de Gaulle, 20 November 1962, III/3a, Adenauer Papers.

71. Adenauer's 5 March 1962 interview with *Le Monde*, *DzD*, 8: 221. See also Adenauer's note, 20 December 1960, III/50; and Adenauer's discussion with British ambassador Frank Roberts, 21 February 1963, III/78, Adenauer Papers.

72. Adenauer's 5 March 1962 interview with *Le Monde*, *DzD*, 8: 221. See also the account of Adenauer's interview with the German Press Agency, 14 March 1962, *DzD*, 8: 251–253.

73. See Charles de Gaulle to Adenauer, 20 September 1962, III/3a; de Gaulle to Adenauer, 23 August 1963, III/3a; Adenauer's discussion with Frank Roberts, 21 February 1963, III/78, all Adenauer Papers; Schwarz, *Adenauer*, 750–751.

74. See the account of the discussion between Adenauer and de Gaulle, 21–22 September 1963, III/79, Adenauer Papers. See also Schwarz, *Adenauer*, 758–761, 810–826; Maurice Vaïsse, *La grandeur: Politique étrangère du général de Gaulle, 1958–1969* (Paris, 1998), 162–263.

75. Horst Osterheld to Adenauer, 12 November 1962; and Talking Points for the Negotiations in Washington, November 1962, III/61, Adenauer Papers; David Klein to McGeorge Bundy, 12 November 1962, folder: Germany, General 11/62, box 76 (Temporary), NSF, JFKL; paper given by Karl Carstens to Bill Tyler, November 1962, ibid. For the best secondary account of this proposal see Klaus Gotto, "Adenauers Deutschland- und Ostpolitik, 1954–1963," in *Adenauer Studien*, ed. Rudolf Morsey und Konrad Repgen, vol. 3 (Mainz, 1974), 70–75.

76. Adenauer and Carstens presented their proposal for a ten-year freeze in the Central European status quo to Kennedy on 14 November 1962. According to the American notes from this meeting, the president commented that "we could live with this." See Memorandum of Conversation between Adenauer and Kennedy, 14 November 1962, 4:30 P.M., *FRUS 1961–63*, 15: 433–443.

77. Kennedy, "Remarks at Rudolph Wilde Platz, West Berlin," 26 June 1963, in *PPP: JFK, 1963*: 524–525; "Address at the Free University of Berlin," 26 June 1963, ibid., 527, 529. Kennedy inadvertently misspoke during his first speech. Instead of the intended "I am a Berliner," his words translated as "I am a jelly donut." Kennedy should have said "Ich bin Berliner."

78. Adenauer renewed his requests for independent West German control of nuclear warheads—tactical, and perhaps even strategic—in order to strengthen deterrence against limited Soviet aggression in Central Europe. See the account of Adenauer's discussion with

Kennedy, 14 November 1962 (morning), III/61, Adenauer Papers. Adenauer's request for tactical nuclear weapons and Kennedy's firm rejection do not appear in the American notes from this conversation. See Memorandum of Conversation between Adenauer and Kennedy, 14 November 1962, 11 A.M., *FRUS* 1961–63, 15: 427–433.

79. Trachtenberg, *A Constructed Peace,* 379–398.

80. Adenauer to de Gaulle, 22 November 1961, III/3a; and Discussion between Adenauer and Henry Kissinger, 16 February 1962, III/60, Adenauer Papers; Wilhelm Grewe, Oral History, 2 November 1966, p. 9, JFKL; Schwarz, *Adenauer,* 730–745.

81. Adenauer to de Gaulle, 22 November 1961, III/3a, Adenauer Papers; Heinrich Krone diary, 18 August 1963, in Morsey and Repgen, *Adenauer Studien,* 179–181; Schwarz, *Adenauer,* 727–729.

82. Adenauer's address at Tutzing Protestant Academy (uncorrected manuscript), 19 July 1963.

83. Nikita Khrushchev, *Khrushchev Remembers,* trans. and ed. Strobe Talbott (Boston, 1970), 32.

84. *Khrushchev Remembers,* 23; Khrushchev's speech at the Sixth Polish United Workers' Party Central Committee Plenum, Warsaw, 20 March 1956, trans. L. W. Gluchowski, *CWIHPB* 10 (March 1998): 46. For a recent English edition of Zola's novel see Emile Zola, *Germinal,* trans. Leonard Tancock (London, 1954). Zola originally published his novel in France in 1885.

85. See Robert C. Tucker, *Stalin in Power: The Revolution from Above, 1928–1941* (New York, 1990), 4.

86. Zola, *Germinal,* 170–171.

87. *Khrushchev Remembers,* 27, 34, 42–44, 50–63.

88. Khrushchev's speech at Polish United Workers' Party Central Committee Plenum, 20 March 1956, 48–49.

89. Khrushchev, Special Report to the Twentieth Congress of the Communist Party of the Soviet Union, 24–25 February 1956, trans. U.S. State Department, reprinted in *Khrushchev Remembers,* 564.

90. Ibid., 612–613.

91. Khrushchev, *Report Delivered at the Twenty-second Congress of the Communist Party of the Soviet Union, 18 October 1961,* trans. Soviet Novosti Press Agency (London, 1961), 23, 50.

92. Khrushchev, Memorandum to the Central Committee of the Communist Party of the Soviet Union Presidium, 8 December 1959, *CWIHPB* 8–9 (Winter 1996–97): 418; idem, Report delivered at Twenty-second Congress of the Communist Party, 46.

93. On the failures of Khrushchev's industrial and agricultural reforms see Alec Nove, *An Economic History of the USSR* (New York, 1982), 329–341, 356–370; Geoffrey Hosking, *The First Socialist Society: A History of the Soviet Union from Within* (Cambridge, Mass., 1993), 356–362.

94. Matthew Evangelista, "'Why Keep Such an Army?': Khrushchev's Troop Reductions," Cold War International History Project Working Paper 19 (Washington, D.C., 1997), 4–6; Khrushchev, Memorandum to Central Committee, 8 December 1959, 419.

95. See Vladislav Zubok, "Khrushchev's 1960 Troop Cut: New Russian Evidence," *CWIHPB* 8–9 (Winter 1996–97): 417.

96. See Note on the discussion between Khrushchev and Walter Ulbricht, Moscow, 26 February 1962, *CWIHPB* 11 (Winter 1998): 224–226; Gaddis, *We Now Know,* 248–257.

97. Walter Ulbricht's speech to the Moscow Conference of Secretaries of the Central

Committees of the Communist Workers' Parties, 3–5 August 1961, reprinted and translated in Hope Harrison, "Ulbricht and the Concrete 'Rose': New Archival Evidence on the Dynamics of Soviet-East German Relations and the Berlin Crisis, 1958–1961," Cold War International History Project Working Paper 5 (Washington, D.C., 1993), app. H. See also William Glenn Gray, "The Hallstein Doctrine: West Germany's Global Campaign to Isolate East Germany, 1949–1969" (Ph.D. diss., Yale University, 1999), 155–162.

98. See Harrison, "Ulbricht and the Concrete 'Rose,'" 50; Vladislav Zubok and Constantine Pleshakov, *Inside the Kremlin's Cold War: From Stalin to Khrushchev* (Cambridge, Mass., 1996), 256.

99. Speaking in Hot Springs, Virginia, on 21 October 1961, Deputy Secretary of Defense Roswell Gilpatric explained that "we have a second strike capability which is at least as extensive as what the Soviets can deliver by striking first. Therefore, we are confident that the Soviets will not provoke a major nuclear conflict"; address by Gilpatric, reprinted in U.S. Arms Control and Disarmament Agency, *Documents on Disarmament, 1961* (Washington, D.C., 1962), 545.

100. On West Germany see Alan Milward, *The European Rescue of the Nation State* (Berkeley, 1992), 134–167, 407–421; Schwarz, *Adenauer*, 385–401; Trachtenberg, *A Constructed Peace*, 146–200. On East Germany see Note on discussion between Khrushchev and Ulbricht, 26 February 1962, 224–226; Charles S. Maier, *Dissolution: The Crisis of Communism and the End of East Germany* (Princeton, 1997), 3–107.

101. See, for example, Khrushchev's letter to Kennedy, 28 September 1962, *FRUS* 1961–63, 6: 157.

102. See Adenauer's speech to the Christian Democratic Union Party rally in Siegen, 2 July 1958, 16.25 1958/band II; and Adenauer's discussion with Kennedy, 14 November 1962 (morning), III/61, Adenauer Papers; William Trimble (minister-counselor to the American embassy in Bonn), diary entries for 24 and 28 February 1958, folder: Germany—Diary, 1958, box 9, William C. Trimble Papers, SM; Trimble to Fletcher Warren, 10 April 1957, folder: Chronological File, Official, April–June 1957, box 2, ibid.; Henry Kissinger to McGeorge Bundy, 1 June 1961, and enclosed summary of meeting with Minister of Defense Franz-Josef Strauss, 10 May 1961, folder: Kissinger, Henry A., 6/1/61–8/28/62, box 31, POF, JFKL; Trachtenberg, *A Constructed Peace*, 146–200.

103. Gaddis, *We Now Know*, 140; Message from Khrushchev to Kennedy, 11 December 1962, *FRUS* 1961–63, 6: 230.

104. See Chen Jian and Yang Kuisong, "Chinese Politics and the Collapse of the Sino-Soviet Alliance," in *Brothers in Arms: The Rise and Fall of the Sino-Soviet Alliance, 1945–1963*, ed. Odd Arne Westad (Stanford, 1998), 259–277; Zubok and Pleshakov, *Inside the Kremlin's Cold War*, 220–229.

105. See Odd Arne Westad, "The Sino-Soviet Alliance and the United States," in idem, *Brothers in Arms*, 175–176.

106. See M. Y. Prozumenschikov, "The Sino-Indian Conflict, the Cuban Missile Crisis, and the Sino-Soviet Split, October 1962: New Evidence from the Russian Archives," *CWIHPB* 8–9 (Winter 1996–97): 251–257.

107. See *Khrushchev Remembers*, 472–475; Zubok and Pleshakov, *Inside the Kremlin's Cold War*, 229–231.

108. Mikhail Suslov, draft report "on the [October 1959] trip of the Soviet party-governmental delegation to the PRC [People's Republic of China]," 18 December 1959, *CWIHPB* 8–9 (Winter 1996–97): 261.

109. See letter from the Communist Party of the Soviet Union to the Chinese Communist Party, 27 September 1958, *CWIHPB* 6–7 (Winter 1995–96): 226–227; Vladislav Zubok, "Khrushchev's Nuclear Promise to Beijing during the 1958 Crisis," ibid., 219, 226.

110. *Khrushchev Remembers,* 467–470.

111. On Khrushchev's overblown rhetoric and his alliance difficulties see Gaddis, *We Now Know,* 234–259.

112. Soviet Embassy in Beijing to PRC Ministry of Foreign Affairs, 18 July 1960, *CWIHPB* 8–9 (Winter 1996–97): 249–250. Roderick MacFarquhar notes that Khrushchev did support the Chinese position in the 1962 Sino-Indian War, but almost exclusively through confidential diplomatic channels. See *The Origins of the Cultural Revolution,* vol. 3 (New York, 1997), 312–314.

113. On this general point see Paul Kennedy, *Strategy and Diplomacy, 1870–1945: Eight Studies* (London, 1983), 13–39.

114. Zubok and Pleshakov, *Inside the Kremlin's Cold War,* 192.

115. Marc Trachtenberg provides evidence that in 1961 and early 1962 Kennedy seriously contemplated American capabilities for a nuclear first strike. Trachtenberg does not provide evidence, however, that Kennedy considered implementing these potential capabilities. See Trachtenberg, *A Constructed Peace,* 293–295.

116. On American considerations of preemptive and preventive nuclear strikes in the 1950s see Trachtenberg, *History and Strategy,* 100–152; Rosenberg, "The Origins of Overkill," 150–155.

117. Trachtenberg, *History and Strategy,* 146–152; idem, *A Constructed Peace,* 295–297.

118. See Gaddis, *The Long Peace,* 196–203; Suri, "America's Search for a Technological Solution," 423–424.

119. *Khrushchev Remembers,* 493.

120. On "Operation Mongoose" see Memorandum from the Chief of Operations, Operation Mongoose (Edward Lansdale), to the Special Group (Augmented), 8 August 1962, Attachment on Covert Activities, 7 August 1962, *FRUS 1961–63,* 10: 901; Thomas G. Paterson, *Contesting Castro: The United States and the Triumph of the Cuban Revolution* (New York, 1994), 258–262. On "Lantphibex-62" see Aleksandr Fursenko and Timothy Naftali, *"One Hell of a Gamble": The Secret History of the Cuban Missile Crisis* (New York, 1997), 166–167; James Hershberg, "Before 'The Missiles of October': Did Kennedy Plan a Military Strike against Cuba?" in *The Cuban Missile Crisis Revisited,* ed. James A. Nathan (New York, 1992), 237–280.

121. *Khrushchev Remembers,* 493–494. See also Fursenko and Naftali, *"One Hell of a Gamble,"* 170–183; Barton J. Bernstein, "Reconsidering the Missile Crisis: Dealing with the Problems of the American Jupiters in Turkey," in Nathan, *The Cuban Missile Crisis Revisited,* 55–129.

122. Khrushchev to Kennedy, 28 October 1962, *FRUS 1961–63,* 6: 183; Castro to Khrushchev, 31 October 1962, in James Blight, Bruce Allyn, and David Welch, *Cuba on the Brink* (New York, 1993), 489.

123. Philip Nash, *The Other Missiles of October: Eisenhower, Kennedy, and the Jupiters, 1957–1963* (Chapel Hill, 1997), 92–116, 151–171; Philip Zelikow, "American Policy and Cuba, 1961–1963," *Diplomatic History* 24 (Spring 2000): 329–331.

124. Khrushchev to Kennedy, undated (November 1962); Khrushchev to Kennedy, 14 November 1962; Khrushchev to Kennedy, 11 December 1962, *FRUS 1961–63,* 6: 208, 212, 229–230.

125. Joseph Conrad, *Heart of Darkness* (1899), ed. Robert Kimbrough (New York, 1988), 68.

126. See, for example, the audio transcripts of the Executive Committee from 9:45 A.M., 19 October 1962, and 10:00 A.M., 26 October 1962, in Ernest May and Philip Zelikow, eds., *The Kennedy Tapes: Inside the White House during the Cuban Missile Crisis* (Cambridge, Mass., 1997), 176, 439–471.

127. Kennedy, "Commencement Address at American University," 10 June 1963, in *PPP: JFK*, 1963: 462.

128. Khrushchev to Kennedy, 27 July 1963, *FRUS* 1961–63, 6: 301–302.

129. Ibid., 302; text of Khrushchev's 2 July 1963 speech in East Berlin, folder: Test Ban Treaty Background 2, box 540, Papers of W. Averell Harriman, LC; Memorandum of Conversation between Anatoly Dobrynin and Llewellyn Thompson, 10 September 1963, *FRUS* 1961–63, 6: 306.

130. See Khrushchev to Castro, 30 October 1962, in Blight, Allyn, and Welch, *Cuba on the Brink*, 485–488; MacFarquhar, *Origins of the Cultural Revolution*, 3: 318–323.

2. POLITICAL CONSTRAINTS AND PERSONAL CHARISMA

1. See Max Weber. *Economy and Society: An Outline of Interpretive Sociology*. ed. Guenther Roth and Claus Wittich, 3 vols. (New York, 1968), 1: 246–254; Reinhard Bendix, *Max Weber: An Intellectual Portrait* (Garden City, N.Y., 1960), 310–320. The "routinized" limits on political change were not an entirely new problem in the 1960s. Alexis de Tocqueville, for example, recognized that the extraordinary expansion of central control over local administration in the eighteenth century—through the French monarch's *intendants*—restricted the ability of reform-minded officials to address popular demands. Similarly, Max Weber criticized the rapidly expanding state bureaucracy of late Wilhelmine Germany for smothering reform initiatives originating among National Liberals and Social Democrats in Parliament. See Alexis de Tocqueville, *L'Ancien Régime et la Révolution* (Paris, 1952), 99–190; Bendix, *Max Weber*, 432–449.

2. On the sources of nationalism in "imagination," "will," and "memory"—all of which contradict the "ordinary" experience of daily politics—see Benedict Anderson, *Imagined Communities: Reflections on the Origin and Spread of Nationalism*, rev. ed. (London, 1991), 37–46, 163–206; Eric Hobsbawm, "Mass-Producing Traditions: Europe, 1870–1914," in *The Invention of Tradition*, ed. Eric Hobsbawm and Terence Ranger (Cambridge, 1983), 263–307; George L. Mosse, *The Nationalization of the Masses: Political Symbolism and Mass Movements in Germany from the Napoleonic Wars through the Third Reich* (New York, 1975), 1–20; Jeffrey Herf, *Divided Memory: The Nazi Past in the Two Germanys* (Cambridge, Mass., 1997), 1–12, 373–394.

3. Max Weber defined charisma as "a certain quality of an individual personality by virtue of which he is considered extraordinary and treated as endowed with supernatural, superhuman, or at least specifically exceptional powers or qualities. These are such as are not accessible to the ordinary person, but are regarded as of divine origin or as exemplary, and on the basis of them the individual concerned is treated as a 'leader.' In primitive circumstances this peculiar kind of quality is thought of as resting on magical powers, whether of prophets, persons with a reputation for therapeutic or legal wisdom, leaders in the hunt, or heroes in war"; *Economy and Society*, 1: 241. The literature on the sources, meanings, and consequences of charisma is enormous. My use of the concept reflects the influence of

ibid., esp. 241–245; Bendix, *Max Weber*, 302–310; Edward Shils, "Charisma, Order, and Status," *American Sociological Review* 30 (April 1965): 199–213; S. N. Eisenstadt, "Charisma and Institution Building: Max Weber and Modern Sociology," in *Max Weber: On Charisma and Institution Building*, ed. Eisenstadt (Chicago, 1968), ix–lvi; Clifford Geertz, "Centers, Kings, and Charisma: Reflections on the Symbolics of Power," in *Rites of Power: Symbolism, Ritual, and Politics since the Middle Ages*, ed. Sean Wilentz (Philadelphia, 1985), 13–38; Peter Lassman, "The Rule of Man over Man: Politics, Power, and Legitimation," in *The Cambridge Companion to Weber*, ed. Stephen Turner (New York, 2000), 94–95.

4. Charles de Gaulle to Philippe de Gaulle, 22 January 1961, in *LNC*, 1961–63: 27.

5. Charles de Gaulle, *Mémoires de guerre*, 3 vols. (Paris, 1954–1959), 3: 240.

6. Claude Mauriac, quoted in Jean Lacouture, *De Gaulle: The Ruler, 1945–1970*, trans. Alan Sheridan (New York, 1991), 24.

7. Ibid., 29, 97–104.

8. Charles de Gaulle to Philippe de Gaulle, 4 June 1961, in *LNC*, 1961–63: 94.

9. In the 21 October 1945 elections the Communists and Socialists received 26.1 and 24.6 percent of the vote respectively. The Radicals received 9.3 percent of the vote. Outside the political left, the Republicans and the Conservatives received 25.6 and 14.4 percent of the vote respectively.

10. Weber, *Economy and Society*, 1: 217–223; Bendix, *Max Weber*, 382–449; Lacouture, *De Gaulle*, 113, 122.

11. Lacouture, *De Gaulle*, 123–124.

12. William Hitchcock, *France Restored: Cold War Diplomacy and the Quest for Leadership in Europe, 1944–1954* (Chapel Hill, 1998), 29–40.

13. Gabrielle Hecht, *The Radiance of France: Nuclear Power and National Identity after World War II* (Cambridge, Mass., 1998), 58–90; Bertrand Goldschmidt, *Les rivalités atomiques, 1939–1966* (Paris, 1967), 177–234; Marcel Duval, "Pierre Guillaumat et l'arme atomique," and Georges-Henri Soutou, "Pierre Guillaumat, le CEA et le nucléaire civil," in *Pierre Guillaumat: La passion des grands projets industriels*, ed. Georges-Henri Soutou and Alain Beltran (Paris, 1995), 41–47, 97–124; Jacques Hymans, "Reaching for the Big One: Oppositional Nationalism and the Bomb in the French Fourth Republic," paper presented at the American Political Science Association conference, September 1998.

14. Avner Cohen, *Israel and the Bomb* (New York, 1998), 17–21, 49–60; Pierre Péan, *Les deux bombes: Comment la France a "donné" la bombe à Israël et à l'Irak* (Paris, 1982), 77–121.

15. Hitchcock, *France Restored*, 116–132, 169–202.

16. See Note from de Gaulle, 8 January 1960, folder: 1960, box CM7, Papers of Maurice Couve de Murville, Archives of Contemporary History, National Foundation for the Study of Political Science, Paris, France (hereafter Couve Papers).

17. See de Gaulle to Maurice Couve de Murville, 1 August 1960, in *LNC*, 1958–60: 383–384.

18. See Irwin M. Wall, *France, the United States, and the Algerian War* (Berkeley, 2001), 9–98; Matthew Connelly, "The Algerian War for Independence: An International History" (Ph.D. diss., Yale University, 1997), 250–272.

19. See Maurice Vaïsse, *La grandeur: Politique étrangère du général de Gaulle, 1958–69* (Paris, 1998), 671–680; Wall, *France, United States, and Algerian War*, 192–228, 260–268. Wall is far more critical of de Gaulle's foreign policy than Vaïsse.

20. De Gaulle to General Ely, 17 January 1959, in *LNC*, 1958–60: 183–184; Charles de Gaulle to Philippe de Gaulle, 14 February 1960, ibid., 330. In January 1961 75 percent of

the voters in France and 70 percent of the voters in Algeria approved the call for Algerian "self-determination."

21. Matthew Connelly offers a different interpretation, focusing on the decline of France's international standing—especially in the third world—as a consequence of the Algerian War; "The Algerian War for Independence," 387–453. Irwin Wall points to a decline in France's standing in Europe and the United States; *France, United States, and Algerian War,* 229–259.

22. Charles de Gaulle to Philippe de Gaulle, 19 July 1960, in *LNC,* 1958–1960: 379; Charles de Gaulle to Harold Macmillan, 25 April 1959, ibid., 217–218.

23. Note for Hervé Alphand, 10 December 1958, ibid., 147–148; de Gaulle to Dwight Eisenhower, 17 September 1958, ibid., 82–84; de Gaulle to Raymond Aron, 9 December 1963, in *LNC,* 1961–63: 400.

24. De Gaulle to General Lavaud, 4 February 1960, in *LNC,* 1958–60: 326.

25. Charles de Gaulle to Philippe de Gaulle, 14 February 1960, ibid., 330–331; de Gaulle to Eisenhower, 24 November 1959, ibid., 283–284; Memorandum of Conversation between Kennedy and de Gaulle, 1 June 1961, 3:30 P.M., folder: France, Security 1961 (d), box 116a, POF, JFKL.

26. McGeorge Bundy to President Kennedy, 7 May 1962, folder: France, Security 1962, box 116a, POF, JFKL.

27. Charles de Gaulle to Philippe de Gaulle, 6 November 1960, in *LNC,* 1958–60, 406; same to same, 18 May 1960, ibid., 358–359; Vaïsse, *La grandeur,* 34–52.

28. De Gaulle to Couve de Murville, 5 October 1960, in *LNC,* 1958–60: 401; Announcement, October 1959, ibid., 262; de Gaulle to Khrushchev, 12 August 1960, ibid., 391–392.

29. Charles de Gaulle to Philippe de Gaulle, 18 May 1960; and de Gaulle to Eisenhower, 19 May 1960, ibid., 358–360.

30. De Gaulle to Macmillan, 25 April 1959, ibid., 217–218; de Gaulle to Macmillan, 29 August 1961, in *LNC,* 1961–63: 132.

31. Hugo Young, *This Blessed Plot: Britain and Europe from Churchill to Blair* (London, 1998), 118–130; Geir Lundestad, *"Empire" by Integration: The United States and European Integration, 1945–1997* (Oxford, 1998), 51–57.

32. De Gaulle's note on the organization of Europe, 30 July 1960, in *LNC,* 1958–60: 382–83.

33. Charles de Gaulle to Philippe de Gaulle, 4 June 1961, in *LNC,* 1961–63: 93; de Gaulle to Adenauer, 22 September 1960, in *LNC,* 1958–1960: 396.

34. De Gaulle's notes on Europe, 17 July 1961, in *LNC,* 1961–63: 107–108.

35. On de Gaulle's derisive use of the term *Anglo-Saxons* in another context, see de Gaulle to Couve de Murville, 14 April 1962, ibid., 230. For evidence that the Kennedy administration offered France limited nuclear assistance in 1962–63 see Hervé Alphand to Couve de Murville, 1 June 1962; Alphand to Couve de Murville, 9 November 1962, folder 1962, box CM7, Couve Papers. See also Georges-Henri Soutou, *L'alliance incertaine: Les rapports politico-stratégiques franco-allemands, 1954–1996* (Paris, 1996), 154–156.

36. De Gaulle's press conference, 14 January 1963, in de Gaulle, *Discours et Messages,* vol. 4: *August 1962–December 1965* (Paris, 1970), 69; idem, *Mémoires d'espoir: Le renouveau, 1958–1962* (Paris, 1970), 200; Jean Monnet to Konrad Adenauer, 21 November 1960, folder 1960, box CM7, Couve Papers.

37. Account of the discussions between de Gaulle and Adenauer, 14 September 1958, III/3a, Papers of Konrad Adenauer, Stiftung Bundeskanzler-Adenauer-Haus, Rhöndorf,

Germany (hereafter Adenauer Papers); de Gaulle to Adenauer, 15 October 1958, in *LNC,* 1958–60: 109–10; same to same, 9 March 1961 and 24 March 1962, in *LNC,* 1961–63: 54–55, 221–222.

38. Vaïsse, *La grandeur,* 258–259.

39. John J. McCloy to Konrad Adenauer, 4 February 1963, folder 3, box GY1, Papers of John J. McCloy, Amherst College Archives and Special Collections. See also Dean Acheson to Konrad Adenauer, 19 January 1963, III/1, Adenauer Papers.

40. McGeorge Bundy, Draft Memorandum for the President, 30 January 1963, folder: France, "The U.S. and de Gaulle," 1/30/63, box 116a, POF, JFKL.

41. Hans-Peter Schwarz, *Adenauer: Der Staatsmann, 1952–1967* (Stuttgart, 1991), 768.

42. Ibid., 810–826; Horst Osterheld, *"Ich gehe nicht leichten Herzens . . .": Adenauers letzte Kanzlerjahre, ein dokumentarischer Bericht* (Mainz, 1986), 194–270.

43. McGeorge Bundy, Draft Memorandum for the President, 30 January 1963, folder: France, "The U.S. and de Gaulle," 1/30/63, box 116a, POF, JFKL; George Ball to President Kennedy, 20 June 1963, folder: De Gaulle, box 213, George Ball Papers, SM.

44. See Khrushchev to Kennedy, 27 July 1963; and Memorandum of Conversation between Anatoly Dobrynin and Llewellyn Thompson, 10 September 1963, *FRUS* 1961–63, 6: 301–302, 306–307; Marc Trachtenberg, *A Constructed Peace: The Making of the European Settlement, 1945–1963* (Princeton, 1999), 382–398; Gordon H. Chang, *Friends and Enemies: The United States, China, and the Soviet Union, 1948–1972* (Stanford, 1990), 233–252.

45. De Gaulle to Kennedy, 4 August 1963, in *LNC,* 1961–63: 356–358.

46. De Gaulle, Note, 11 September 1963, ibid., 371.

47. De Gaulle, Note, 27 October 1963, ibid., 382–383.

48. De Gaulle, Note, ca. 25 November 1960, in *LNC,* 1958–60: 413.

49. Jonathan Spence, *The Search for Modern China* (New York, 1990), 516–517.

50. Conversation between Stalin and Mao, 16 December 1949, *CWIHPB* 6–7 (Winter 1995–96): 5–6; Conversation between Stalin and Mao, 22 January 1950, ibid., 8–9. On Mao's reliance upon Soviet assistance during the 1930s see Michael M. Sheng, *Battling Western Imperialism: Mao, Stalin, and the United States* (Princeton, 1997), 15–50.

51. Conversation between Stalin and Mao, 16 December 1949; Conversation between Stalin and Mao, 22 January 1950, *CWIHPB* 6–7 (Winter 1995–96): 6, 9; Chen Jian, *China's Road to the Korean War: The Making of the Sino-American Confrontation* (New York, 1994), 9–30, 92–209; John Lewis Gaddis, *We Now Know: Rethinking Cold War History* (Oxford, 1997), 66–84; William Stueck, *Rethinking the Korean War* (Princeton, 2002), 87–117.

52. Harry Harding, *Organizing China: The Problem of Bureaucracy, 1949–1976* (Stanford, 1981), 32–70.

53. Roderick MacFarquhar, *The Origins of the Cultural Revolution,* 3 vols. (New York, 1974–1997), 1: 28.

54. Ibid., 31–32.

55. Ibid., 87 and 87n.

56. Ibid., 87; Timothy Cheek, *Propaganda and Culture in Mao's China: Deng Tuo and the Intelligentsia* (Oxford, 1997), 171–172.

57. See MacFarquhar, *Origins of the Cultural Revolution,* 1: 86–91; Harding, *Organizing China,* 87–115.

58. See Vladislav Zubok and Constantine Pleshakov, *Inside the Kremlin's Cold War: From Stalin to Khrushchev* (Cambridge, Mass., 1996), 186–187.

59. Harding, *Organizing China,* 134–135.

60. MacFarquhar, *Origins of the Cultural Revolution*, 1: 52.

61. Ibid., 169–176; Chen Jian, *Mao's China and the Cold War* (Chapel Hill, 2001), 145–162.

62. Mao Zedong, "On the Correct Handling of Contradictions among the People (Speaking Notes)," 27 February 1957, in *The Secret Speeches of Chairman Mao: From the Hundred Flowers to the Great Leap Forward,* ed. Roderick MacFarquhar, Timothy Cheek, and Eugene Wu (Cambridge, Mass., 1989), 146, 175, 165. These speaking notes from Mao's speech differ in significant ways from the official version of the speech published in the *People's Daily* on 19 June 1957. On the discrepancies between the original and published versions of the speech see Michael Schoenhals, "Original Contradictions—On the Unrevised Text of Mao Zedong's 'On the Correct Handling of Contradictions among the People," *Australian Journal of Chinese Affairs* 16 (July 1986): 99–112.

63. Mao, "On Correct Handling (Speaking Notes)," 154, 167, 174–77. On Mao's early anarchism see Arif Dirlik, *The Origins of Chinese Communism* (New York, 1989), 4–54.

64. Mao, "On Correct Handling (Speaking Notes)," 133.

65. Ibid., 142. These passages about CCP-sponsored violence did not appear in the published version of Mao's speech.

66. Ibid., 170–173.

67. Ibid., 141, 177–178.

68. These quotations come from an official transcript of Mao Zedong's speech at a meeting of the representatives of the Communist and Workers' parties of twelve socialist countries, Moscow, 14 November 1957, translated in Michael Schoenhals, "Mao Zedong: Speeches at the 1957 'Moscow Conference,'" *Journal of Communist Studies* 2 (June 1986) 112–114.

69. Mao Zedong, Speech at a meeting of the representatives of sixty-four Communist and Workers' parties, 18 November 1957, ibid., 118.

70. Mao Zedong, Talks at the Beidaihe Conference (draft transcript), 19 August 1958, in MacFarquhar, Cheek, and Wu, *Secret Speeches of Chairman Mao*, 406.

71. Mao Zedong, Talks at the Beidaihe Conference (draft transcript), 21 August 1958 (morning), ibid., 412.

72. MacFarquhar, *Origins of the Cultural Revolution*, 2: 84.

73. Mao, Talks at the Beidaihe Conference (draft transcript), 19 August 1958, 410.

74. Mao, Talks at the Beidaihe Conference (draft transcript), 21 August 1958 (morning), 411; MacFarquhar, *Origins of the Cultural Revolution*, 2: 88–90.

75. Mao, Talks at the Beidaihe Conference (draft transcript), 30 August 1958 (morning), 434.

76. Ibid., 435.

77. David Bachman, *Bureaucracy, Economy, and Leadership in China: The Institutional Origins of the Great Leap Forward* (New York, 1991), 96–132, 157–190; idem, "Chinese Bureaucratic Politics and the Origins of the Great Leap Forward," *Journal of Contemporary China* 9 (Summer 1995): 35–55. For the use of government-ordered terror during the Great Leap see Jasper Becker, *Hungry Ghosts: Mao's Secret Famine* (New York, 1996), 99–111, 183–197.

78. For the quotation from Mao see Talks at the Beidaihe Conference (draft transcript), 19 August 1958, 406. The description of China's "tumble into nightmare" comes from Jonathan Spence, *Mao Zedong* (New York, 1999), 148.

79. Becker, *Hungry Ghosts*, 85; MacFarquhar, *Origins of the Cultural Revolution*, 2: 328.

80. MacFarquhar, *Origins of the Cultural Revolution*, 2: 327–328.

81. Ibid., 329–330; 3: 2.

82. Becker, *Hungry Ghosts,* 83–96, 255–74; MacFarquhar, *Origins of the Cultural Revolution,* 2: 332–336, 3: 4–6.

83. MacFarquhar, *Origins of the Cultural Revolution,* 3: 29.

84. Ibid., 34–65.

85. Account of a discussion with Comrade Liu Shaoqi, 8 February 1961, FBS 363/15322; Account of a discussion between Ambassador Wandel and Comrade Zhou Enlai, FBS 363/15321, Papers of Walter Ulbricht, Archives for the German Democratic Republic and the Archives for the Parties and Mass Organizations of the German Democratic Republic, Berlin-Lichterfelde, Germany.

86. Kenneth T. Young, *Negotiating with the Chinese Communists: The United States Experience, 1953–1967* (New York, 1968), 3–22, 47–59.

87. Edgar Faure, "Reconnaissance de la Chine," *Espoir* 1 (September 1972): 20–21; idem, *The Serpent and the Tortoise: Problems of the New China,* trans. Lovett F. Edwards (London, 1957), 3–51; idem, *Mémoires* (Paris, 1984), 2: 655; Maurice Couve de Murville, "Le sens d'un acte," *Espoir* 1 (September 1972): 14–15; idem, *Une politique étrangère, 1958–1969* (Paris, 1971), 125–127.

88. Chester Bowles, "Current Thoughts," 1 May 1962, folder 156, box 392, Chester Bowles Diaries, Chester Bowles Papers, YUL; Bowles to President, 6 February and 27 June 1962, folder: China, Security, 1962–1963, box 113a, POF, JFKL; Chester Bowles, "The 'China Problem' Reconsidered," *Foreign Affairs* 38 (April 1960): 476–486; Faure, *The Serpent and the Tortoise,* 197–205; Edmond Jouve, "Les préliminaires et le communiqué du 27 janvier 1964," in *L'établissement de relations diplomatiques entre la France et la Chine populaire* (Paris, 1995), 11–13.

89. Roger Hilsman to Walter P. McConaughy, 7 July 1961, folder: China, General, 7/15/61–7/24/61, box 22, NSF, JFKL; American Embassy, Taipei, to American Embassy, Warsaw, 19 September 1962, folder: China Cables, 9/5/62–10/15/62, box 25a, NSF, JFKL.

90. CIA, "The Signs of Chinese Communist Friendliness," 17 July 1961, folder: China, General, 7/15/61–7/24/61, box 22, NSF, JFKL; Franz Schurmann, "Letter from Hong Kong," 28 May 1961. Arthur Schlesinger Jr. forwarded a copy of Schurmann's letter to Walt Rostow on 12 June 1961; folder: China, General, 5/1/61–6/12/61, box 22, NSF, JFKL. See also Yawei Liu, "The United States According to Mao Zedong: Chinese-American Relations, 1893–1976" (Ph.D. diss., Emory University, 1996), 371–375. Edgar Snow—the famous author of a book profiling the courageous CCP "Long March" across China in 1934–35—also reported on Mao's personal interest in improved relations with the United States. Mao reportedly commented to Snow that he wanted to swim in the Mississippi and Potomac Rivers before he grew too old. See Edgar Snow to Walter Lippmann, 10 May 1961, folder 1970, box 103, Walter Lippmann Papers, YUL; Liu, "The United States According to Mao Zedong," 372–373.

91. Hilsman to McConaughy, 7 July 1961, folder: China, General, 7/15/61–7/24/61, box 22, NSF, JFKL.

92. De Gaulle to Eisenhower, 26 October 1959, in *LNC,* 1958–60: 275–277.

93. Qiang Zhai, *China and the Vietnam Wars, 1950–1975* (Chapel Hill, 2000), 46–49, 82.

94. De Gaulle to Edgar Faure, 9 October 1963, folder 1963, box CM8, Couve Papers; Discussion between de Gaulle and Lester Pearson, Prime Minister of Canada, 15 January 1964, folder 2, box CM9, ibid.; Instructions for Edgar Faure, 26 September 1963, in *LNC,* 1961–63: 374–375.

95. Instructions for Faure, 26 September 1963, in *LNC,* 1961–63: 374–375; Discussion

between de Gaulle and Pearson, 15 January 1964, folder 2, box CM9, Couve Papers; Report on de Gaulle's meeting with the Chinese Ambassador, Huang Chen, 19 June 1964, Series: Asia, 1956–67, Subseries: China, vol. 527, FFM.

96. Faure to de Gaulle, 7 November 1963, folder 1963, box CM8, Couve Papers. See also the account of Zhou Enlai's comments, 2 November 1963, ibid.; Faure, "Reconnaissance de la Chine," 23–25.

97. See Instructions for Mr. Paye, 11 May 1964, Series: Asia, 1956–67, Subseries: China, vol. 527, FFM; de Gaulle, Note, 6 February 1964, in *LNC,* 1964–66: 32. On the secret French-Chinese discussions, see de Gaulle's instructions for Jacques de Beaumarchais, December 1963, folder 1963, box CM8, Couve Papers. The published version of this document is dated to the end of January; *LNC,* 1964–66: 29–31.

98. De Gaulle to Chiang Kai-shek, 15 January 1964, in *LNC,* 1964–66: 22–23.

99. See, for example, Albert Ravenholt, "Red China's Food Crisis," January 1961, folder: China, General 1/20/61–2/19/61, box 21, NSF, JFKL; CIA Report to Walt Rostow, 18 May 1961, folder: China, General, 5/1/61–6/12/61, box 22, NSF, JFKL.

100. CIA Report to Rostow, 18 May 1961.

101. Ravenholt's report "Red China's Food Crisis" was distributed publicly by the American Universities Field Staff Reports Service.

102. Vaïsse, *La grandeur,* 520–521.

103. Ibid.

104. See Chang, *Friends and Enemies,* 203–227; Marc J. Selverstone, "'All Roads Lead to Moscow': The United States, Great Britain, and the Communist Monolith" (Ph.D. diss., Ohio University, 2000).

105. Discussion between André Malraux and Zhou Enlai in Beijing, 2 August 1965, Series: Asia, 1956–67, Subseries: China, vol. 532, FFM; Meeting between André Malraux and Mao Zedong, 3 August 1965, ibid.

106. Discussion between André Malraux and Chen Yi, 23 July 1965, ibid.

107. John Wilson Lewis and Xue Litai, *China Builds the Bomb* (Stanford, 1988), 35–39, 60–72.

108. Mao Zedong to Khrushchev, 6 June 1963, quoted in Shu Guang Zhang, "Between 'Paper' and 'Real Tigers': Mao's View of Nuclear Weapons," in *Cold War Statesmen Confront the Bomb: Nuclear Diplomacy since 1945,* ed. John Lewis Gaddis, Philip Gordon, Ernest May, and Jonathan Rosenberg (Oxford, 1999), 211.

109. Statement by the People's Republic of China Government, 16 October 1964, in Lewis and Xue, *China Builds the Bomb,* 241–243.

110. See the Council on Foreign Relations Advisory Group on the Implications for the U.S. of a Chinese Communist Nuclear Capability, 23 May 1963, vol. 102, box 255, Records of the Council on Foreign Relations, Records of Groups, SM; McGeorge Bundy, Memorandum for the Record, 15 September 1964, folder: "Memos for the President, Volume 6," box 2, NSF-NSC Staff Files, LBJL; Robert Komer to McGeorge Bundy, 18 September 1964, *FRUS* 1964–68, 30: 96–99; G. W. Rathjens, "Destruction of Chinese Nuclear Weapons Capabilities," U.S. Arms Control and Disarmament Agency, 14 December 1964, NSA; William Burr and Jeffrey T. Richelson, "Whether to 'Strangle the Baby in the Cradle': The United States and the Chinese Nuclear Program, 1960–1964," *International Security* 25 (Winter 2000/01): 54–99.

111. Notes, 8 February and 17 February 1966, Series: Asia, 1956–67, Subseries: China, vol. 533, FFM.

112. On the French role in encouraging American intervention in Indochina, see Mark

Lawrence, "Selling Vietnam: The European Colonial Powers and the Origins of the American Commitment to Vietnam, 1944–1950" (Ph.D. diss., Yale University, 1998); Wall, *United States and Postwar France*, 233–262.

113. Meeting between de Gaulle and the CCP Ambassador, 16 May 1966, Series: Asia, 1956–67, Subseries: China, vol. 533, FFM. See also Fredrik Logevall, *Choosing War: The Lost Chance for Peace and the Escalation of War in Vietnam* (Berkeley, 1999), 2–4, 44–48.

114. Vaïsse, *La grandeur*, 381–386.

115. Discussion between Couve de Murville and Huang Chen, 12 May 1966, Series: Asia, 1956–67, Subseries: China, vol. 533, FFM.

116. Hannah Arendt, *On Revolution* (New York, 1963), 21, 217.

117. See François Furet, *Penser la Révolution française* (Paris, 1978), 13–130; idem, *Le passé d'une illusion: Essai sur l'idée communiste au vingtième siècle* (Paris, 1995), 17–48.

118. Lucien Paye to the French Ministry of Foreign Affairs, 16 July 1964, Series: Asia, 1956–67, Subseries: China, vol. 527, FFM.

119. Marilyn A. Levine, *The Found Generation: Chinese Communists in Europe during the Twenties* (Seattle, 1993), 64–202.

120. Mao Zedong to Josef Stalin, 26 April 1948, quoted in Sheng, *Battling Western Imperialism*, 165. See also Gaddis, *We Now Know*, 62–70, 77–82.

121. Zhai, *China and the Vietnam Wars*, 10, 212–213.

122. Address by Chen Yi, 14 July 1964, Series: Asia, 1956–67, Subseries: China, vol. 527, FFM.

123. Lucien Paye to the French Foreign Ministry, 9 July 1966, Series: Asia, 1956–67, Subseries: China, vol. 533, FFM.

124. Mao Zedong, Talk at the Central Work Conference, 25 October 1966, in *Chairman Mao Talks to the People: Talks and Letters, 1956–71*, trans. John Chinnery and Tieyun, ed. Stuart Schram (New York, 1974), 270–274; Resolutions of the Eleventh Plenum of the Central Committee of the CCP—the Sixteen Articles, 8 August 1966, in *Mao Papers: Anthology and Bibliography*, ed. Jerome Ch'en (New York, 1970), 117, 123–124.

125. Resolutions of the Eleventh Plenum of the Central Committee of the CCP, in Ch'en, *Mao Papers*, 125–126.

126. Zhou Enlai, letter to Capital University Red Guard Revolutionary Rebel Headquarters, 27 September 1966, in *China's Cultural Revolution, 1966–1969: Not a Dinner Party*, ed. Michael Schoenhals (Armonk, N.Y., 1996), 27.

127. Mao Zedong, Notes on the Report of Further Improving the Army's Agricultural Work by the Rear Service Department of the Military Commission, 7 May 1966, in Ch'en, *Mao Papers*, 103–105.

128. Meeting between André Malraux and Mao Zedong, 3 August 1965, Series: Asia, 1956–67, Subseries: China, vol. 532, FFM.

129. *People's Daily*, 30 August 1967, in Ch'en, *Mao Papers*, 145.

130. Chen Yi, "Ode to Jean-Jacques Rousseau," folder: 1965, Box: CM8, Couve Papers. According to the archival files, Couve de Murville received a French version of this poem in 1965.

131. Editorial, *People's Daily*, 6 November 1967, in Che'en, *Mao Papers*, 149; Lin Biao's Political Report, *People's Daily*, 15 April 1969, ibid., 159. Rousseau's writings influenced a number of radical intellectuals in China during the late nineteenth and early twentieth centuries. When many of these Chinese thinkers and their followers joined the Communist party, Rousseau's ideas fused with Marxist doctrine. Early communists such as Zhou

Enlai and Chen Yi never abandoned their attachment to Rousseau's thought. On Rousseau's influence in China see Spence, *The Search for Modern China*, 259, 303. On the debate concerning Rousseau's works in early twentieth-century China see Benjamin Schwartz, *In Search of Wealth and Power: Yen Fu and the West* (Cambridge, Mass, 1964), 220–222.

132. Report of the discussion between Mao Zedong and Maurice Couve de Murville, 14 October 1970, folder 2, box CM10, Couve Papers.

133. De Gaulle, draft political manifesto, late 1966, in *LNC*, 1966–69: 48–54.

134. De Gaulle to Marie-Agnès Cailliau, 12 May 1967, ibid., 106; De Gaulle to Georges Pompidou, 12 February 1967, ibid., 75.

135. Lucien Paye to the French Foreign Ministry, 9 July 1966, Series: Asia, 1956–67, Subseries: China, vol. 533, FFM; Note, 20 January 1967, ibid., vol. 536; Paye to the French Foreign Ministry, 31 January 1967, ibid.

136. Paye to the French Foreign Ministry, 14 July 1967, ibid. vol. 537.

137. Shils, "Charisma, Order, and Status," 213.

3. THE LANGUAGE OF DISSENT

1. On the "youth boom" see Arthur Marwick, *The Sixties: Cultural Revolution in Britain, France, Italy, and the United States, c.1958–c.1974* (Oxford, 1998), 45. For demographic data see *Statistical Abstract of the United States* (Washington, D.C., 1965–1981), 1965: 23; 1981: 26; B. P. Pockney, *Soviet Statistics since 1950* (New York, 1991), 33–34; B. R. Mitchell, *International Historical Statistics: Europe, 1750–1993*, 4th ed. (New York, 1998), 4, 8, 20–22, 42–43; *Statistical Yearbook of China* (Hong Kong, 1981–1987), 1981: 94; 1986: 80.

2. On comparative generational experiences see Karl Mannheim, *Essays on the Sociology of Knowledge*, ed. Paul Kecskemeti (London, 1952), 286–320; Robert Wohl, *The Generation of 1914* (Cambridge, Mass, 1979), 203–237.

3. On the early language of student dissent and its relation to both the civil rights and nuclear disarmament movements see Abe Peck, *Uncovering the Sixties: The Life and Times of the Underground Press* (New York, 1985), 19–40; Maurice Isserman and Michael Kazin, *America Divided: The Civil War of the 1960s* (New York, 2000), 23–45; Michael Kazin, *The Populist Persuasion: An American History* (New York, 1995), 199–200; Maurice Isserman, *If I Had a Hammer: The Death of the Old Left and the Birth of the New Left* (Urbana, 1987), 127–169; Clayborne Carson, *In Struggle: SNCC and the Black Awakening of the 1960s* (Cambridge, Mass, 1981), 9–211; William H. Chafe, *Civilities and Civil Rights: Greensboro, North Carolina, and the Black Struggle for Freedom* (New York, 1980), 16–214; Lawrence S. Wittner, *Resisting the Bomb: A History of the World Nuclear Disarmament Movement, 1954–1970* (Stanford, 1997), 41–60.

4. Robert A. Divine, *The Sputnik Challenge* (New York, 1993), 162–166. By later standards, the amount of loan and fellowship money included in the 1958 act was relatively small.

5. See Paul Josephson, *New Atlantis Revisited: Akademgorodok, The Siberian City of Science* (Princeton, 1997), 9–30.

6. C. P. Snow, *The Two Cultures* (Cambridge, 1993), 1–21, 41–51. This text is based on lectures that Snow delivered at Cambridge University on 7 May 1959.

7. Conant to Eisenhower, 23 February 1959, folder: G—Correspondence, 1957–64, box 129, Personal Papers of James B. Conant, Harvard University Archives—Nathan Pusey Library, Cambridge, Mass. (hereafter Conant Papers). See also James Killian to Conant,

25 November 1959, folder: K—Correspondence, 1957–1964, box 131, ibid.; James G. Hershberg, *James B. Conant: Harvard to Hiroshima and the Making of the Nuclear Age* (New York, 1993), 208–390, 687–705.

8. James B. Conant, *Slums and Suburbs: A Commentary on Schools in Metropolitan Areas* (New York, 1961), 88–109, 144–147; Frank B. Berry (deputy assistant secretary of defense) to Conant, 1 February 1962; Berry to Conant, 15 March 1962; Conant to Berry, 20 March 1962, folder: B—Personal File in New York, box 127, Conant Papers.

9. Conant to Frank Bowles, 14 February 1963, folder: B—Personal File in New York, box 127, Conant Papers. See also Conant, *Slums and Suburbs*, 88–96; Nicholas Lemann, *The Big Test: The Secret History of the American Meritocracy* (New York, 1999), 42–122.

10. James B. Conant, *Shaping Educational Policy* (New York, 1964), 2–8, 109–134.

11. Conant to Bernard Baruch, 9 May 1963, folder: B—Personal File in New York, box 127, Conant Papers.

12. Conant, "Grußwort zum Neuen Jahr," December 1963, folder: December 1963, box 134, Conant Papers; Conant to Clark Kerr (president of the University of California at Berkeley), 7 October 1963, folder: October 1963, ibid.

13. Suzanne Pepper, *Radicalism and Education Reform in 20th-Century China: The Search for an Ideal Developmental Model* (New York, 1996), 278–351. Mao violently reversed this meritocratic model during the late 1960s; ibid., 352–380.

14. Modern "industrial society," according to French sociologist Raymond Aron, created ever-greater separation between the "public work" of society and the "private life" of the family. Along these lines, higher education became a distinct part of society's "public work." See Raymond Aron, *Dix-huit leçons sur la société industrielle* (Paris, 1962), 97–117.

15. Definitions of "higher education" differed among societies during the 1960s. In the United States this term referred to the colleges and universities across the nation. In West Germany and Great Britain, however, an extensive system of "polytechnical" schools existed, providing a more preprofessional experience for students than did traditional universities. In addition to sizable universities in many major cities, the Soviet government financed a large number of specialized institutes that in some cases supplemented, and in other cases substituted for, university education. The structure and attendance in virtually all educational institutions on mainland China changed considerably, and sometimes in contradictory directions, during the 1960s. Despite these convulsions, colleges and universities in major cities remained the fundamental institutions for "higher education" in China. By the end of the decade, however, the shortened curriculums and military governance of many Chinese universities made these institutions appear very different from their Western counterparts.

The historian must remain conscious of these comparative differences in higher education while also paying heed to important similarities across societies. Most important for my analysis, higher education during the 1960s required that a growing cohort of young men and women (usually between eighteen and twenty-five years of age) spend an extended period away from home, living and studying with other citizens of similar age. How and what students studied differed considerably, but almost all institutions of higher education shared a few characteristics: They allowed students to communicate with other young citizens in large numbers. They exposed students—often informally—to heretical ideas. They also provided a common space for group organization.

16. The statistics on student enrollments come from the following published sources. United States: U.S. Department of Health, Education and Welfare, *Projections of Educational*

Statistics to 1975–76 (Washington, D.C., 1966), 5, 102; idem, *Projections of Educational Statistics to 1980–81* (Washington, D.C., 1972), 23, 158. West Germany: *Statistisches Jahrbuch für die Bundesrepublik Deutschland* (Stuttgart, 1956–1971), 1956: 91; 1961: 106; 1966: 102; 1971: 81; Hansgert Peisert and Gerhild Framhein, *Systems of Education: Federal Republic of Germany* (New York, 1978), 14; Hedwig Rudolph and Rudolf Husemann, *Hochschulpolitik zwischen Expansion und Restriktion: Ein Vergleich der Entwicklung in der Bundesrepublik Deutschland und der Deutschen Demokratischen Republik* (Frankfurt, 1984), 134. France: Pierre Bourdieu et Jean Claude Passeron, *Les héritiers: Les étudiants et la culture* (Paris, 1964), 120–121; Jürgen Schriewer, *Die Französischen Universitäten, 1945–68* (Bad Heilbrunn, 1972), 561; Alain Bienaymé, *Systems of Higher Education: France* (New York, 1978), 4–5; H. D. Lewis, *The French Educational System* (London, 1985), 101. Great Britain: W. A. C. Stewart, *Higher Education in Postwar Britain* (London, 1989), 268, 271–272. Soviet Union: Mervyn Matthews, *Education in the Soviet Union: Policies and Institutions since Stalin* (London, 1982), 206; Seymour M. Rosen, *Higher Education in the USSR: Curriculums, Schools, and Statistics* (Washington, D.C., 1963), 100; S. Frederick Starr, "New Communications Technologies and Civil Society," in *Science and the Soviet Social Order,* ed. Loren R. Graham (Cambridge, Mass., 1990), 31. People's Republic of China: Pepper, *Radicalism and Education Reform,* 198, 285–86, 416; Ruth Hayhoe, *China's Universities, 1895–1995: A Century of Cultural Conflict* (New York, 1996), 96.

17. Antonio Gramsci, *Selections from the Prison Notebooks,* trans. and ed. Quintin Hoare and Geoffrey Nowell Smith (New York, 1971), 5–23.

18. Marwick, *The Sixties,* 80–95.

19. Alexis de Tocqueville, *L'Ancien Régime et la Révolution* (Paris, 1952), 226–231.

20. See Charles Tilly, *From Mobilization to Revolution* (Reading, Mass., 1978), 52–97; Mancur Olson, *The Logic of Collective Action* (Cambridge, Mass., 1965), 5–65.

21. Robert Darnton, "An Early Information Society: News and Media in Eighteenth Century Paris," *American Historical Review* 105 (February 2000): 14; idem, *The Forbidden Best-Sellers of Pre-Revolutionary France* (New York, 1995), 181–197, 224–231, 240–246. I am not arguing that language creates reality, but instead that it frames and deeply conditions human behavior. In this sense, my use of discourse theory draws more upon Clifford Geertz than upon Michel Foucault. I find Foucault's writing brilliant and provocative, but I remain uncomfortable with his willingness to make discourse almost a complete substitute for material reality. As I see it, language conditions but does *not* determine human behavior. See Clifford Geertz, *The Interpretation of Cultures* (New York, 1973), 193–233; Michel Foucault, *The Archaeology of Knowledge,* trans. A. M. Sheridan Smith (New York, 1972), 3–76.

22. See Darnton, *Forbidden Best-Sellers,* 22–24, 60–82, 137–166, 211–216; idem, *The Literary Underground of the Old Regime* (Cambridge, Mass., 1982), 1–40, 199–208.

23. Daniel Bell, *The End of Ideology: On the Exhaustion of Political Ideas in the Fifties* (Glencoe, Ill., 1960), 370, 373.

24. Ibid., 373, 363–368, 375.

25. On the geopolitical "settlement" of the early 1960s see Marc Trachtenberg, *A Constructed Peace: The Making of the European Settlement, 1945–1963* (Princeton, 1999), 352, 379–402.

26. John Kenneth Galbraith, *The Affluent Society* (Boston, 1958), 122.

27. Ibid., 355.

28. Ibid., 327.

29. Michael Harrington, "Our Fifty Million Poor: Forgotten Men of the Affluent Society," *Commentary* 28 (July 1959): 19–27; idem, *The Other America: Poverty in the United States* (1962; reprint, New York, 1993), esp. 190–196. See also idem, "Slums, Old and New," *Commentary* 30 (August 1960): 118–124. Harrington noted that various studies of poverty differed in their assessments of what the U.S. Bureau of Labor called the annual budget for the "minimum maintenance" of a family of four. "There is no point in getting involved in an endless methodological controversy over the precise point at which a family becomes impoverished," Harrington explained; "somewhere between 20 and 25 percent of the American people are poor. They have inadequate housing, medicine, food, and opportunity"; *The Other America*, 192–193.

30. Harrington, *The Other America*, 9, 12.

31. Ibid., 12.

32. Ibid., 14–18, 158.

33. Ibid., 13.

34. John Kenneth Galbraith, "Challenges of a Changing World," 11 November 1958, folder: "Challenges of a Changing World," box 98, Papers of John Kenneth Galbraith, JFKL.

35. For discussions of the often-overlooked conservative sources of social criticism in America see Alan Brinkley, "The Problem of American Conservatism," *American Historical Review* 99 (April 1994): 409–429; Jonathan Schoenwald, *A Time for Choosing: The Rise of Modern American Conservatism* (New York, 2001), 14–34; Rick Perlstein, *Before the Storm: Barry Goldwater and the Unmaking of the American Consensus* (New York, 2001), 3–16; George H. Nash, *The Conservative Intellectual Movement in America since 1945* (New York, 1976).

36. William F. Buckley Jr., *Up from Liberalism* (New York, 1959), 194, 196.

37. Ibid., 114–115. On the founding of the *National Review* see Perlstein, *Before the Storm*, 70–76; John B. Judis, *William F. Buckley, Jr.: Patron Saint of the Conservatives* (New York, 1990), 114–127.

38. Buckley, *Up from Liberalism*, 102–112; Buckley to James Burnham, 11 October 1960, folder: Interoffice Memos (1960), box 10, Papers of William F. Buckley Jr., YUL (hereafter Buckley Papers). See also Frank S. Meyer to Buckley et al., 10 May 1960, ibid.

39. The New Left has inspired a rich historical literature, but until recently the New Right has received less serious attention. On the New Left see Kirkpatrick Sale, *SDS* (New York, 1973); Todd Gitlin, *The Sixties: Years of Hope, Days of Rage* (New York, 1987); James Miller, *"Democracy Is in the Streets": From Port Huron to the Siege of Chicago* (Cambridge, Mass., 1987); Doug Rossinow, *The Politics of Authenticity: Liberalism, Christianity, and the New Left in America* (New York, 1998). On the New Right, see John A. Andrew III, *The Other Side of the Sixties: Young Americans for Freedom and the Rise of Conservative Politics* (New Brunswick, N.J., 1997); Rebecca Klatch, *A Generation Divided: The New Left, the New Right, and the 1960s* (Berkeley, 1999); Matthew Dallek, *The Right Moment: Ronald Reagan's First Victory and the Decisive Turning Point in American Politics* (New York, 2000); Lisa McGirr, *Suburban Warriors: The Origins of the New American Right* (Princeton, 2001); Perlstein, *Before the Storm*; Schoenwald, *A Time for Choosing*.

40. Barry Goldwater, *The Conscience of a Conservative* (Shepherdsville, Ky., 1960), 90. L. Brent Bozell, a longtime acquaintance of Buckley, wrote the text for *Conscience of a Conservative*. Clarence Manion, a conservative political activist, arranged for the publication and distribution of the book. See Perlstein, *Before the Storm*, 43–68.

41. Goldwater, *The Conscience of a Conservative*, 110–111, 118.

42. "A Statement of First Principles by the Sharon Conference," 11 September 1960, folder: Young Americans for Freedom (1960), box 12, Buckley Papers. For a list of the students who attended the founding YAF meeting in Sharon, Connecticut, see Attendees, Sharon Conference, 10–11 September 1960, ibid. See also Andrew, *The Other Side of the Sixties*, 76–101, 187–203; Perlstein, *Before the Storm*, 69–95, 471–487.

43. Dan T. Carter, *The Politics of Rage: George Wallace, the Origins of the New Conservatism, and the Transformation of American Politics* (New York, 1995), 195–225, 294–370, 465–468; Kazin, *The Populist Persuasion*, 222–242.

44. McGirr, *Suburban Warriors*, 111–146, 187–216; Dallek, *The Right Moment*, 62–80.

45. A large literature has grown around the contradictions between America's Cold War rhetoric and the experience of domestic racism. See Mary L. Dudziak, *Cold War Civil Rights: Race and the Image of American Democracy* (Princeton, 2000), 115–202; Brenda Gayle Plummer, *Rising Wind: Black Americans and U.S. Foreign Affairs, 1935–1960* (Chapel Hill, 1996), 217–297, 327–328; Thomas Borstelmann, *The Cold War and the Color Line: American Race Relations in the Global Arena* (Cambridge, Mass., 2001), 85–221; Penny Von Eschen, *Race against Empire: Black Americans and Anticolonialism, 1937–1957* (Ithaca, 1997), 7–95.

46. Students for a Democratic Society: Constitution (as amended by the National Convention, 12–13 June 1959), series 1, reel 1, folder 1, SDS Collection, Wisconsin Historical Society, Madison (hereafter SDS Papers). See also "Is There a Significant Place for the White Southerner in the Integration Struggle?" (a discussion paper for consideration at the Student Conference in Chapel Hill, North Carolina, 4–6 May 1962), series 1, reel 1, folder 4, SDS Papers; Tom Hayden to SDS, 4–6 May 1962, ibid.

47. SDS Port Huron Statement, 16 June 1962, 46–47, series 1, reel 1, folder 6, SDS Papers. The SDS Port Huron Statement is reprinted in Miller, *Democracy Is in the Streets*, 329–374.

48. Quoted in Carson, *In Struggle*, 10.

49. See, for example, reporters' focus on the upcoming presidential election, Soviet threats, *and race relations* at the president's news conference of 16 March 1960; *PPP: DDE, 1960–61*: 293–302.

50. Martin Luther King Jr., "Facing the Challenge of a New Age," address before the First Annual Institute on Non-Violence and Social Change, Montgomery, Alabama, December 1956; reprinted in James Melvin Washington, ed., *A Testament of Hope: The Essential Writings and Speeches of Martin Luther King, Jr.* (San Francisco, 1986), 136.

51. Martin Luther King Jr., "The Rising Tide of Racial Consciousness," speech to the National Urban League, 1960; reprinted in ibid., 146.

52. SDS Port Huron Statement, 16 June 1962, 1. See also Tom Hayden, *Reunion: A Memoir* (New York, 1988), 73–102; Miller, *"Democracy Is in the Streets,"* 141–54.

53. See Michael Scammell, *Solzhenitsyn: A Biography* (New York, 1984), 112–143. The acronym GULAG stood for the State Ministry of the Camps (Gosudarstvennoye Upravleniye Lageryov).

54. Aleksandr Solzhenitsyn, *One Day in the Life of Ivan Denisovich*, trans. H. T. Willetts (New York, 1991). Solzhenitsyn initially published his novella in *Novy Mir* 11 (November 1962). The text for *Ivan Denisovich* differs slightly among Russian editions (especially those published in the 1960s) and Western translations. In all cases, however, the textual differences are minor. I have relied on the Willetts translation, which is faithful to the 1973 French edition. Having analyzed the different versions of *Ivan Denisovich*, one scholar identifies the 1973 edition as "basically the original text." See Gary Kern, "Solzhenitsyn's Self-

Censorship: The Canonical Text of Odin Den' Ivana Denisovicha," *Slavic and East European Journal* 20 (Winter 1976): 421–436.

55. Solzhenitsyn, *One Day in the Life of Ivan Denisovich*, 67.

56. Ibid., 178, 32.

57. Ibid., 175.

58. Ibid., 75.

59. See Amir Weiner, "In the Long Shadow of War: The Second World War and the Soviet and Post-Soviet World," *Diplomatic History* 25 (Summer 2001): 443–456; Vojtech Mastny, *The Cold War and Soviet Insecurity: The Stalin Years* (New York, 1996), 23–29.

60. Solzhenitsyn, *One Day in the Life of Ivan Denisovich*, 44, 83.

61. Zhores A. Medvedev, *Ten Years after Ivan Denisovich*, trans. Hilary Steinberg (New York, 1973), 4–12, 30–38, 57–67; idem, *The Rise and Fall of T. D. Lysenko*, trans. I. Michael Lerner (New York, 1969).

62. Gregori Baklanov, quoted in Cornelia Gerstenmaier, *The Voices of the Silent*, trans. Susan Hecker (New York, 1972), 67.

63. *Samizdat* is short for *samsebyaizdat*, literally "to publish oneself."

64. Ludmilla Alexeyeva and Paul Goldberg, *The Thaw Generation: Coming of Age in the Post-Stalin Era* (Pittsburgh, 1990), 83.

65. Ibid., 84.

66. Ibid., 97–101.

67. Ibid., 104.

68. François Furet, *Le passé d'une illusion: Essai sur l'idée communiste au vingtième siècle* (Paris, 1995), 17–48, 547–572.

69. See Sheila Fitzpatrick, *Stalin's Peasants: Resistance and Survival in the Russian Village after Collectivization* (New York, 1994), 5–16; idem, *Everyday Stalinism: Ordinary Life in Extraordinary Times* (New York, 1999), 132–136, 182–187.

70. See Vladimir Bukovsky, *To Build a Castle: My Life as a Dissenter*, trans. Michael Scammell (New York, 1979), 195–222.

71. See M. Mondich, "The Orthodox Treatment of the Problem of Fathers and Sons," 3 September 1964, Radio Liberty Analysis, box 80-1-497, fond 300, RFE/RL; "K Probleme Molodezhi v SSSR," 6 February 1962, Report from the Institute for the Study of the USSR, Munich, ibid.

72. Ivan Turgenev, *Fathers and Sons* (1862), trans. Michael R. Katz (New York, 1994), 19, 35, 38.

73. Ibid., 36.

74. Isaiah Berlin, "Fathers and Children: Turgenev and the Liberal Predicament," in *Russian Thinkers* (New York: Penguin, 1978), 279.

75. Ibid., 300.

76. Ibid., 300–301.

77. "Where Do Skeptics Come From in the USSR?" 5 September 1963, Radio Liberty Analysis, box 80-1-497, fond 300, RFE/RL.

78. "Molodezh Sovetskovo Soyuza," 5–6 November 1962, Institute for the Study of the USSR, Munich; and "Komsomol and Youth," 19 April 1963, ibid.; "Problema podrostkov i perestroika roboti komsomola," 13 October 1965; and "The Interests and Aspirations of Soviet Youth," 3 November 1965, box 80-1-496, fond 300, RFE/RL; "Which Books Are Popular among Soviet Youth," 13 October 1964, box 80–1–497, ibid.

79. Alexeyeva and Goldberg, *The Thaw Generation*, 100–101; "Soviet Student Film Producers in Revolt," 15 September 1961; and "'Rebel' Poets in Saratov University," 29 May 1961, box 80-1-853, fond 300, RFE/RL; "A Representative of the Soviet 'Lost Generation,'" 1 August 1962; and "Is There a 'Lost Generation' in the USSR," 16 April 1963, box 80–1–497, ibid.; M. Mondich, "Apolitichina li Sovetskaya Molodezh," 23 July 1965; and "Paplov on Western Ideology's Influence over Soviet Youth," 1 September 1966, box 80-1-496, ibid.; "A Student's Open Defense of Abstract Art," 23 February 1961, box 80-1-853, ibid.; "The Concept of Heroism Revisited," 29 June 1965, box 80-1-496, ibid.

80. Nina Rozwadowska-Janowska and Piotr Nowicki, eds., *NYET!—i Konformisti: Obrazi Sovetskovo Iskysstva 50-x do 80-x godov* (Warsaw, 1994), 99, 102; *Kommunist* 1 (1963).

81. Alexeyeva and Goldberg, *The Thaw Generation*, 104. See also "Skepticism with a Chuckle," 11 September 1963, box 80-1-497, fond 300, RFE/RL.

82. *Komsomolskaya Pravda*, 27 April and 20 August 1961; "No Work for Graduates," 23 May 1962, box 80-1-853, fond 300, RFE/RL; "Molodezh yhodit iz kolhozov v goroda," 1 December 1964, box 80-1-497, ibid.

83. *Komsomolskaya Pravda*, 7 June 1962.

84. Mary Gale Mazur, "A Man of His Times: Wu Han, the Historian" (Ph.D. diss., University of Chicago, 1993), 108–117, 123–135.

85. Wu Han to Hu Shi, 30 January 1932, quoted in ibid., 202–203.

86. Ibid., 567–572.

87. Wu Han, *Hai Jui's Dismissal*, in *The Heresy of Wu Han: His Play "Hai Jui's Dismissal" and Its Role in China's Cultural Revolution*, trans. and ed. Clive Ansley (Toronto, 1971), 76.

88. This area is now part of Changshu province.

89. Wu Han, *Hai Jui's Dismissal*, 16, 21–27.

90. Ibid., 35, 39, 45, 57, 59.

91. Ibid., 79.

92. Wu Han's introduction to the play, ibid., 10.

93. Ibid., 65.

94. Ibid., 26.

95. Ibid., 63. On "local knowledge" see Clifford Geertz, *Local Knowledge: Further Essays in Intepretive Anthropology* (New York, 1983), 3–16, 73–93, 167–234; James C. Scott, *Seeing like a State: How Certain Schemes to Improve the Human Condition Have Failed* (New Haven, 1998), 309–341.

96. Wu Han, *Hai Jui's Dismissal*, 9. On Peng Dehuai's criticisms of Mao and the Great Leap see Roderick MacFarquhar, *The Origins of the Cultural Revolution*, 3 vols. (New York, 1983), 2: 187–251. On the evident connections between Hai Jui and Peng Dehuai see Jonathan D. Spence, *The Search for Modern China* (New York, 1990), 599–600; Merle Goldman, "The Unique 'Blooming and Contending' of 1961–62," *China Quarterly* 37 (January–March 1969): 74.

97. See Spence, *The Search for Modern China*, 600–601; MacFarquhar, *Origins of the Cultural Revolution*, 3: 252–254.

98. Deng Tuo, "The Kingly Way and the Tyrannical Way," *Beijing wanbao* (Beijing Evening News) 25 February 1962, trans. Timothy Cheek in *Chinese Law and Government* 16 (Winter 1983–84): 67. This is one of a series of short columns that Deng Tuo published as the "Evening Chats at Yanshan." See Timothy Cheek, *Propaganda and Culture in Mao's China: Deng Tuo and the Intelligentsia* (Oxford, 1997), 215–277.

99. On the paper's circulation see MacFarquhar, *Origins of the Cultural Revolution*, 3: 250.

100. Goldman, "The Unique 'Blooming and Contending' of 1961–62," 60. See also idem, *China's Intellectuals: Advise and Dissent* (Cambridge, Mass., 1981), 16–88.

101. MacFarquhar, *Origins of the Cultural Revolution*, 3: 253.

102. This quotation comes from an article published by Yao Wenyuan in the *People's Daily*, 11 May 1966, trans. Timothy Cheek in *Chinese Law and Government* 16 (Winter 1983–84): 81. See also Lars Ragvald, *Yao Wenyuan as a Literary Critic and Theorist: The Emergence of Chinese Zhdanovism* (Stockholm, 1978), 104–161; MacFarquhar, *Origins of the Cultural Revolution*, 3: 254–258; James R. Pusey, *Wu Han: Attacking the Present through the Past* (Cambridge, Mass., 1969), 49–69.

103. See Jonathan Spence, *Mao Zedong* (New York, 1999), 159–165; MacFarquhar, *Origins of the Cultural Revolution*, 3: 410–460; Li Zhisui, *The Private Life of Chairman Mao: The Memoirs of Mao's Personal Physician*, trans. Tai Hung-Chao (New York, 1994), 416–421.

104. In December 1966, for example, two separate groups of Red Guards seized the offices of Shanghai's party newspaper, the *Liberation Daily*. Like most participants in the Cultural Revolution, the two student factions articulated a deep enmity toward the local members of the government. The Red Guards forced the mayor of Shanghai, Cao Diqiu, to "confess" that the troubles at the offices of the *Liberation Daily* resulted from the "bourgeois reactionary line" of the city's administrators. Cao affirmed that the government and the Communist Party would learn from the "proletarian and revolutionary" behavior of the rebels. See Lynn T. White III, *Policies of Chaos: The Organizational Causes of Violence in China's Cultural Revolution* (Princeton, 1989), 238–240. On the importance of factional divisions among the Red Guards during the Cultural Revolution see Anita Chen, "Dispelling Misconceptions about the Red Guard Movement: The Necessity to Re-examine Cultural Revolution Factionalism and Periodization," *Journal of Contemporary China* 1 (September 1992): 61–85; Stanley Rosen, *Red Guard Factionalism and the Cultural Revolution in Guangzhou (Canton)* (Boulder, 1982), 101–146.

105. *People's Daily*, 26 December 1966, quoted in White, *Policies of Chaos*, 235.

106. Quoted in Anita Chan, *Children of Mao: Personality Development and Political Activism in the Red Guard Generation* (Seattle, 1985), 144.

107. The *Little Red Book* of assorted quotations from Chairman Mao was organized in approximately 300 pages under thirty-three wide-ranging topic headings (e.g., "Socialism and Communism," "Imperialism and All Reactionaries Are Paper Tigers," "Self-Reliance and Arduous Struggle," "Youth"). The *Little Red Book* provided ubiquitous and malleable ammunition for Red Guard attacks on established figures. Lin Biao—defense minister and member of the infamous Cultural Revolution "Gang of Four" until his failed coup against Mao in 1971—first ordered the creation of the *Little Red Book* for army indoctrination in 1964. For an English translation of the *Little Red Book* see *Quotations from Chairman Mao Tsetung* (Peking, 1972). On Lin Biao's role in the creation of the *Little Red Book* see Spence, *Mao Zedong*, 157–158.

108. Mao Zedong, Talk to Leaders of the Center, 21 July 1966, in *Chairman Mao Talks to the People: Talks and Letters, 1956–1971*, trans. John Chinnery and Tieyun, ed. Stuart Schram (New York, 1974), 254.

109. Mao Zedong, "Notes on Comrade Ch'en Cheng-jen's Report on His 'Squatting Point,'" 29 January 1965, in *Mao Papers: Anthology and Bibliography*, ed. Jerome Ch'en (New York, 1970), 99–100.

110. Mao Zedong, Speech at a Meeting with Regional Secretaries and Members of the Cultural Revolutionary Group, 22 July 1966, in Schram, *Chairman Mao Talks to the People*, 257.

111. Wu Han, *Hai Jui's Dismissal*, 45.

112. See Goldman, *China's Intellectuals*, 64.

113. Wu Han disappeared during the Cultural Revolution, never to be seen in public again. Deng Tuo committed suicide in 1966. Liao Mosha miraculously survived the Cultural Revolution.

114. Rolf Wiggershaus, *The Frankfurt School: Its History, Theories, and Political Significance*, trans. Michael Robertson (Cambridge, Mass, 1994), 127–380, 408–445.

115. Herbert Marcuse, *One-Dimensional Man: Studies in the Ideology of Advanced Industrial Society* (1964; reprint, Boston, 1991), xlviii.

116. Herbert Marcuse, *Soviet Marxism: A Critical Analysis* (New York, 1958), 169–170; idem, *Eros and Civilization: A Philosophical Inquiry into Freud* (1955; reprint, Boston, 1966), 21–54.

117. See C. Wright Mills, *The Power Elite* (New York, 1956), 3–29, 269–361; Milovan Djilas, *The New Class: An Analysis of the Communist System* (1957; reprint, New York, 1985), 37–69.

118. Peck, *Uncovering the Sixties*, 38–39. On the reading habits of student activists see "References of Interest," series 1, reel 1, folder 10, SDS Papers; Gretchen Dutschke, *Rudi Dutschke: Eine Biographie* (Cologne, 1996), 37–47; Wiggershaus, *The Frankfurt School*, 609–636; Hayden, *Reunion*, 77–81; Gitlin, *The Sixties*, 11–44, 246–247.

119. Marcuse, *One-Dimensional Man*, 17–18, 21, 146, 153, 159.

120. Ibid., 34–55, 244.

121. Ibid., 193.

122. Ibid., 189–91, 245. Marcuse also used the term *technological fetishism* to update Marx's concept of the "fetishism of the commodity"; ibid., 235; Karl Marx, *Capital* (1867), trans. Ben Fowkes, 2 vols. (New York, 1990), 1: 163–177.

123. Marcuse, *One-Dimensional Man*, 170–194.

124. Ibid., 251.

125. Ibid., 220–221; Marcuse, *Eros and Civilization*, 197–221.

126. Marcuse, *One-Dimensional Man*, 220–221; idem, *An Essay on Liberation* (Boston, 1969), 89–90.

127. Marcuse, *One-Dimensional Man*, 56–83; idem, *An Essay on Liberation*, 23–48. Marcuse's 1922 doctoral dissertation, "Der deutsche Künstlerroman" (The German Artist-Novel), had included a discussion of the works of Goethe and Thomas Mann (then a relatively young writer). See Douglas Kellner, *Herbert Marcuse and the Crisis of Marxism* (London, 1984), 18–32.

128. Marcuse, *One-Dimensional Man*, 57; idem, *An Essay on Liberation*, 23–48.

129. Herbert Marcuse, "Postscript 1968," in Robert Paul Wolff, Barrington Moore Jr., and Herbert Marcuse, *A Critique of Pure Tolerance* (Boston, 1969), 120–123.

130. Herbert Marcuse, "Political Preface 1966," in *Eros and Civilization*, xvii.

131. Ibid., xix.

132. See Wiggershaus, *The Frankfurt School*, 622–624.

133. Rudi Dutschke, "Mallet, Marcuse 'Formierte Gesellschaft' und politische Praxis der Linken hier und anderswo," 1965; idem, "Diskussionsbeitrag," 25 April 1965; Rudi

Dutschke and Horst Kurnitzky to Herbert Marcuse, 26 December 1967, all reprinted in *Frankfurter Schule und Studentenbewegung: Von der Flaschenpost zum Molotowcocktail, 1946– 1995,* ed. Wolfgang Kraushaar, 3 vols. (Hamburg, 1998), 2: 186–188, 190–193, 329–330.

134. Gitlin, *The Sixties,* 246.

135. On the synthetic sources of Beatles music and the group's almost indescribable popularity during the 1960s, see Hunter Davies, *The Beatles,* 2d rev. ed. (New York, 1996), 104, 180–206.

136. Marshall Berman, review of *One-Dimensional Man, Partisan Review* 31 (Fall 1964): 617.

137. Marcuse, *An Essay on Liberation,* viii, 86, 88.

138. Ibid., 85.

139. Ibid., 85–86.

140. Ibid., 89.

141. CIA, "Restless Youth," September 1968, folder: Youth and Student Movements, box 13, Files of Walt W. Rostow, NSF, LBJL.

4. THE ILLIBERAL CONSEQUENCES OF LIBERAL EMPIRE

1. For some examples from the voluminous literature on the "democratic peace" see Michael Doyle, "Kant, Liberal Legacies, and Foreign Affairs (Part I)," *Philosophy and Public Affairs,* 12 (Summer 1983): 213–224; idem, "Liberalism and World Politics," *American Political Science Review* 80 (December 1986): 1155–56, 1164; Bruce Russett, *Grasping the Democratic Peace: Principles for a Post-Cold War World,* 2d ed. (Princeton, 1995); John M. Owen IV, *Liberal Peace, Liberal War: American Politics and International Security* (Ithaca, 1997). For criticisms of the "democratic peace" literature see John Mearsheimer, *The Tragedy of Great Power Politics* (New York, 2001); Kenneth Waltz, "The Emerging Structure of International Politics," *International Security* 18 (Fall 1993): 44–79; Christopher Layne, "Kant or Cant: The Myth of the Democratic Peace," *International Security* 19 (Fall 1994): 5–49; David E. Spiro, "The Insignificance of the Liberal Peace," ibid., 50–86.

2. Doyle, "Liberalism and World Politics," 1156, 1161; Owen, *Liberal Peace, Liberal War,* 22–63.

3. Doyle, "Liberalism and World Politics," 1154–55; Edward W. Said, *Culture and Imperialism* (New York, 1993), xxiii–xxvi, 282–303; James C. Scott, *Seeing like a State: How Certain Schemes to Improve the Human Condition Have Failed* (New Haven, 1998), 262–306.

4. See William Appleman Williams, *The Tragedy of American Diplomacy* (1959; reprint, New York, 1972), 13–16, 38, 88; Walter LaFeber, *The New Empire: An Interpretation of American Expansion, 1860–1898* (Ithaca, 1963), 62–101; Michael H. Hunt, *Ideology and U.S. Foreign Policy* (New Haven, 1987), 19–45.

5. Walter McDougall, *Promised Land, Crusader State: The American Encounter with the World since 1776* (Boston, 1997), 203–222; Frank Ninkovich, *The Wilsonian Century: U.S. Foreign Policy since 1900* (Chicago, 1999), 53–77, 121–144, 205–214.

6. Douglas J. Macdonald, *Adventures in Chaos: American Intervention for Reform in the Third World* (Cambridge, Mass., 1992), 29–73, 249–253; Michael Latham, *Modernization as Ideology: American Social Science and "Nation-Building" in the Kennedy Era* (Chapel Hill, 2000), 69–108; D. Michael Shafer, *Deadly Paradigms: The Failure of U.S. Counterinsurgency Policy* (Princeton, 1988), 96–102.

7. Department of State, Round Table Discussion, 6 October 1949, quoted in Andrew Rotter, *The Path to Vietnam: Origins of the American Commitment to Southeast Asia* (Ithaca, 1987), 116.

8. See de Gaulle's conversation with Chinese ambassador Huang Chen, 19 June 1964, Series: Asia, 1956–67, Subseries: China, vol. 527, FFM; de Gaulle to Lyndon Johnson, 10 June 1964 and 5 February 1966, in *LNC*, 1964–66: 69–70, 249–250.

9. See Ronald Aronson, "The Movement and Its Critics," *Studies on the Left* 6 (January–February 1966): 3–19; Robert Wolfe, "American Imperialism and the Peace Movement," *Studies on the Left* 6 (May–June 1966): 28–43; Charles DeBenedetti with Charles Chatfield, *An American Ordeal: The Antiwar Movement of the Vietnam Era* (Syracuse, 1990), 103–138. On the criticisms voiced by America's allies see Fredrik Logevall, *Choosing War: The Lost Chance for Peace and the Escalation of War in Vietnam* (Berkeley, 1999), 149–153.

10. Qiang Zhai, *China and the Vietnam Wars, 1950–1975* (Chapel Hill, 2000), 122–215; Ilya Gaiduk, *The Soviet Union and the Vietnam War* (Chicago, 1996), 156–170, 215–245; Chen Jian, "China's Involvement in the Vietnam War, 1964–69," *China Quarterly* 142 (June 1995): 380–385.

11. The literature on the U.S. role in the Vietnam War is enormous—more than any mortal can master. Two particularly thorough overviews of this literature are Robert Divine, "Vietnam Reconsidered," *Diplomatic History* 12 (Winter 1988): 79–93; and Gary Hess, "The Unending Debate: Historians and the Vietnam War," *Diplomatic History* 18 (Spring 1994): 239–264. Some important recent studies are not included in these overviews: Marilyn Young, *The Vietnam Wars, 1945–1990* (New York, 1991); Lloyd Gardner, *Pay Any Price: Lyndon Johnson and the Wars for Vietnam* (Chicago, 1995); Michael Sherry, *In the Shadow of War: The United States since the 1930s* (New Haven, 1995), 237–336; Robert Buzzanco, *Masters of War: Military Dissent and Politics in the Vietnam Era* (New York, 1996); Michael H. Hunt, *Lyndon Johnson's War: America's Cold War Crusade in Vietnam, 1945–1968* (New York, 1996); Edwin Moïse, *Tonkin Gulf and the Escalation of the Vietnam War* (Chapel Hill, 1996); Timothy Lomperis, *From People's War to People's Rule: Insurgency, Intervention, and the Lessons of Vietnam* (Chapel Hill, 1996); Robert Schulzinger, *A Time for War: The United States and Vietnam, 1941–1975* (New York, 1997); H. R. McMaster, *Dereliction of Duty: Lyndon Johnson, Robert McNamara, the Joint Chiefs of Staff, and the Lies That Led to Vietnam* (New York, 1997); Robert Dallek, *Flawed Giant: Lyndon Johnson and His Times, 1961–1973* (New York, 1998); Logevall, *Choosing War;* David Kaiser, *American Tragedy: Kennedy, Johnson, and the Origins of the Vietnam War* (Cambridge, Mass., 2000).

12. See William Duiker, *Ho Chi Minh* (New York, 2000), 62–261; Jean Lacouture, *Ho Chi Minh: A Political Biography*, trans. Peter Wiles (New York, 1968), 17–70; Mark Philip Bradley, *Imagining Vietnam and America: The Making of Postcolonial Vietnam, 1919–1950* (Chapel Hill, 2000), 107–133; George McT. Kahin, *Intervention: How America Became Involved in Vietnam* (New York, 1986), 13–15.

13. Marshall to Jefferson Caffery (American ambassador to France), 3 February 1947, *FRUS 1947*, 6: 68.

14. Melvyn Leffler, *A Preponderance of Power: National Security, the Truman Administration, and the Cold War* (Stanford, 1992), 380–383; John Lewis Gaddis, *The Long Peace: Inquiries into the History of the Cold War* (New York, 1987), 101–103; William Stueck, *The Korean War: An International History* (Princeton, 1995), 31–41; Chen Jian, *China's Road to the Korean War: The Making of the Sino-American Confrontation* (New York, 1994), 102–106, 125–135.

15. For a sample of contemporary "realist" criticisms of American policy in Vietnam see Hans Morgenthau, *Vietnam and the United States* (Washington, D.C., 1965), preface and 25–42; Ronald Steel, *Walter Lippmann and the American Century* (Boston, 1980), 557–572.

16. Zhai, *China and the Vietnam Wars*, 45–49; David L. Anderson, *Trapped by Success: The Eisenhower Administration and Vietnam, 1953–1961* (New York, 1991), 23.

17. See the text of the Final Declaration, 21 July 1954, in James Cable, *The Geneva Conference of 1954 on Indochina* (London, 1986), 146–148. The United States did not sign the Final Declaration, but it pledged to adhere to the agreements.

18. Zhai, *China and the Vietnam Wars*, 70–73.

19. Anderson, *Trapped by Success*, 91–119; Schulzinger, *A Time for War*, 82–86.

20. Anderson, *Trapped by Success*, 136.

21. Sherry, *In the Shadow of War*, 250.

22. On the public pressures for political and social change and their connection to foreign policy, see McGeorge Bundy to Kennedy 16 May 1963, folder: Bundy, McGeorge—A Study of Attitudes toward Cold War Issues, 5/16/63, box 62a, POF, JFKL; Frank Ninkovich, *Modernity and Power: A History of the Domino Theory in the Twentieth Century* (Chicago, 1994), 248, 267–275. Hamilton Fish Armstrong, the editor of *Foreign Affairs* and a close acquaintance of McGeorge Bundy, commented on the ideological pressures influencing U.S. policy in Vietnam; Washington, D.C., 20 February 1962, folder 1962, box 103, Hamilton Fish Armstrong Diaries, SM. For analysis of public ambivalence regarding Vietnam see Logevall, *Choosing War*, 281–292; John Mueller, *War, Presidents, and Public Opinion* (New York, 1973), 42–167.

23. This is the general message of Robert McNamara's memoirs. He refuses to criticize the aims and intentions of the Kennedy administration. The United States, he writes, "fought in Vietnam for eight years for what it believed to be good and honest reasons . . . administrations of both parties sought to protect our security, prevent the spread of totalitarian Communism, and promote individual freedom and political democracy." According to McNamara's argument the problem was not the mission, but the location. Robert S. McNamara with Brian VanDeMark, *In Retrospect: The Tragedy and Lessons of Vietnam* (New York, 1995), xvi, 319–335.

24. Robert K. Brigham, *Guerrilla Diplomacy: The NLF's Foreign Relations and the Viet Nam War* (Ithaca, 1999), 3, 10–11.

25. Ibid., 153–154; Zhai, *China and the Vietnam Wars*, 137; Gaiduk, *Soviet Union and the Vietnam War*, 10–11, 47.

26. Brigham, *Guerrilla Diplomacy*, 15–39, 130–131; Duiker, *Ho Chi Minh*, 524–527.

27. Edward Lansdale to Secretary of Defense and Deputy Secretary of Defense, 17 January 1961, folder: Memoranda, 1958–1961, box 42, Papers of Edward G. Lansdale, Hoover Institution Archives, Stanford, Calif. (hereafter Lansdale Papers); Lansdale, "A Program of Action to Prevent Communist Domination of South Vietnam" 6 May 1961, folder: Declassified Documents (from box 6, folder 4), box 95, Lansdale Papers; Lansdale, Basic Counterinsurgency Plan for Viet-Nam, Saigon, 4 January 1961, *FRUS* 1961–63, 1: 1–12; Summary Record of a Meeting, The White House, 28 January 1961, ibid., 13–15; Memorandum from the President's Deputy Special Assistant for National Security Affairs (Rostow) to the President's Special Assistant for National Security Affairs (Bundy), 30 January 1961, ibid., 16–19; Walt Rostow, Oral History, 21 March 1969, 63–64, LBJL; Anderson, *Trapped by Success*, 196.

28. Richard H. Shultz Jr., *The Secret War against Hanoi: Kennedy's and Johnson's Use of Spies, Saboteurs, and Covert Warriors in North Vietnam* (New York, 1999), 16–40; Lawrence Freedman, *Kennedy's Wars: Berlin, Cuba, Laos, and Vietnam* (New York, 2000), 287–292.

29. See Latham, *Modernization as Ideology*, 21–68; Shafer, *Deadly Paradigms*, 48–103; Douglas Blaufarb, *The Counterinsurgency Era: U.S. Doctrine and Performance* (New York, 1977), 52–88.

30. W. W. Rostow, *The Stages of Economic Growth: A Non-Communist Manifesto*, 3d ed. (Cambridge, 1990), 58.

31. Ibid., 70–71.

32. "A Program of Action to Prevent Communist Domination of South Vietnam," 1 May 1961 (submitted to the president on 3 May 1961), *FRUS* 1961–63, 1: 93–115. See also Shafer, *Deadly Paradigms*, 116–127.

33. National Security Action Memorandum Number 124, 18 January 1962, *FRUS* 1961–63, 2: 48–50; McNamara to Kennedy, 2 January and 2 February 1962, ibid., 1–3, 71–72; Paul Frederick Cecil, *Herbicidal Warfare: The RANCH HAND Project in Vietnam* (New York, 1986), 21–152.

34. Roger Hilsman, "A Strategic Concept for South Vietnam," 2 February 1962, *FRUS* 1961–63, 2: 73–90.

35. Ibid.

36. Ibid., 83–84.

37. Latham, *Modernization as Ideology*, 187; Young, *The Vietnam Wars*, 86.

38. Hilsman to Maxwell Taylor, 31 March 1962, *FRUS* 1961–63, 2: 244–246; Schulzinger, *A Time for War*, 122–123.

39. An American marine colonel used a similar phrase later in the war; Schulzinger, *A Time for War*, 262.

40. Hilsman to Rusk, 19 September 1963, *FRUS* 1961–63, 4: 269–271; Kahin, *Intervention*, 148–153; Brigham, *Guerrilla Diplomacy*, 13.

41. Latham, *Modernization as Ideology*, 202–207; Gardner, *Pay Any Price*, 40–64.

42. Memorandum of a Meeting, White House Situation Room, 3 October 1963, *FRUS* 1961–63, 4: 356–357.

43. Telegram from the Embassy in Vietnam (Lodge) to the Department of State, 28 October 1963, *FRUS* 1961–63, 4: 442–446.

44. Lodge to McGeorge Bundy, 25 October 1963, ibid., 434–436; Bundy to Lodge, 25 October 1963, ibid., 437.

45. Memorandum of a Conference with the President, 29 October 1963, 4:20 P.M., *FRUS* 1961–63, 4: 468–471.

46. Ibid., 471; Memorandum of a Conversation with the President, 29 October 1963, 6:00 P.M., ibid., 472; Bundy to Lodge, 30 October 1963, ibid., 500–502.

47. Lodge to Department of State, 1 November 1963, ibid., 513.

48. Ibid.

49. Military Assistance Command, Vietnam (Harkins), to Joint Chiefs of Staff, 2 November 1963, ibid., 528–531. Harkins initially opposed the coup. See Harkins to Maxwell Taylor, 30 October 1963, ibid., 479–482.

50. Quotation from Maxwell Taylor, *Swords and Plowshares* (New York, 1972), 301. See also McNamara, *In Retrospect*, 84–85; Arthur M. Schlesinger Jr., *A Thousand Days: John F. Kennedy in the White House* (New York, 1965), 909–910.

51. Kennedy to Lodge, 6 November 1963, *FRUS* 1961–63, 4: 579–580.

52. McNamara, *In Retrospect*, 90.

53. Robert Dallek, *Lone Star Rising: Lyndon Johnson and His Times, 1908–1960* (New York, 1991), 126; idem, *Flawed Giant*, 23–24.

54. Dallek, *Lone Star Rising*, 77, 125–156.

55. Barbara Jordan, Oral History, 28 March 1984, 4–8, LBJL; Roy Wilkins, Oral History, 1 April 1969, 23–24, LBJL. Also see Harry McPherson, Oral History, 9 April 1969, interview 5, tape 2: 14, LBJL.

56. Dallek, *Flawed Giant*, 8–15, 44–46.

57. Ibid., 15–16.

58. Paper presented by the vice president, undated (ca. May 1961), *FRUS* 1961–63, 1: 150; Roy Wilkins, Oral History, 6–7, LBJL.

59. Dallek, *Lone Star Rising*, 324.

60. Gardner, *Pay Any Price*, 52. Created by Congress on 18 May 1933, the TVA constructed dams, under direct federal control, along the Tennessee River. The hydroelectric power produced by the dams fed the energy needs of more than seven states and, in the words of one historian, brought "jobs, investment, and the promise of prosperity to a sprawling area that had stagnated since the Civil War"; David Kennedy, *Freedom from Fear: The American People in Depression and War, 1929–1945* (New York, 1999), 148.

61. Paper presented by the vice president, undated (ca. May 1961), 150–151; Dallek, *Flawed Giant*, 83.

62. Johnson, "Special Message to Congress: 'The American Promise,'" 15 March 1965, in *PP: LBJ*, 1965, 1: 281–287.

63. Johnson, "Address at Johns Hopkins University: 'Peace without Conquest,'" 7 April 1965, ibid., 394–399.

64. Ibid., 396.

65. Ibid., 396–397.

66. Ibid., 397.

67. Ibid., 398.

68. Ibid., 398–399.

69. A number of scholars have pointed to Johnson's anxieties about members of the political right and the American military who advocated a massive expansion of the war in Vietnam. I do not believe these anxieties were really critical in Johnson's thinking. For a different view see Brian VanDeMark, *Into the Quagmire: Lyndon Johnson and the Escalation of the Vietnam War* (New York, 1991), 216–217; George C. Herring, *LBJ and Vietnam: A Different Kind of War* (Austin, 1994), 25–62.

70. For a similar analysis see Gardner, *Pay Any Price*, 89–126.

71. On the curtailment of New Deal reforms after 1937 see Alan Brinkley, *The End of Reform: New Deal Liberalism in Recession and War* (New York, 1995), 15–174.

72. I transcribed this conversation from the original audio recording. See President Johnson's Telephone Conversation with Senator Richard Russell, 27 May 1964, 10:55 A.M., citations 3519–21, tape WH6405.10, Recordings of Telephone Conversations, White House Series, LBJL. In my transcriptions I have tried to retain the distinctive southern pronunciation of the speakers. The Johnson White House produced a secret and incomplete transcript of this and other conversations; Transcripts of Telephone Conversations, White House Series, May 1964 (no. 3 of 3), LBJL.

73. Johnson's Telephone Conversation with Russell, 27 May 1964.

74. Ibid. See Mike Mansfield to Johnson, 6 January and 1 February 1964, folder: McGeorge Bundy, 11/63–2/64, vol. 1 (1 of 2), box 1, NSF—Memos to the President, LBJL; George Ball to Dean Rusk, 31 May 1964; and Ball, "How Valid Are the Assumptions Underlying Our Viet-Nam Policies?" 5 October 1964, box 213, George Ball Papers, SM.

75. Johnson's Telephone Conversation with McGeorge Bundy, 27 May 1964, 11:24 A.M., citation 3522, tape WH6405.10, Recordings of Telephone Conversations, White House Series, LBJL; Johnson's Telephone Conversation with Russell, 27 May 1964.

76. Johnson's Telephone Conversation with Adlai Stevenson, 27 May 1964, 10:50 A.M., citation 3518, tape WH6405.10, Recordings of Telephone Conversations, White House Series, LBJL.

77. Ibid.; Johnson's Telephone Conversation with Attorney General Robert Kennedy, 28 May 1964, 11:45 A.M., citations 3539–40, tape WH6405.11, Recordings of Telephone Conversations, White House Series, LBJL; McGeorge Bundy to Johnson, 25 May 1964, folder: McGeorge Bundy, 4/1–30/64, vol. 3, box 1, NSF—Memos to the President, LBJL; Shultz, *The Secret War against Hanoi*, 37–40, 78–127; Kahin, *Intervention*, 205.

78. Johnson's Telephone Conversation with Robert McNamara, 30 July 1964, 10:12 A.M., citation 4421, tape WH6407.19, Recordings of Telephone Conversations, White House Series, LBJL; Memorandum from McNamara to the President, 13 March 1964, folder: McGeorge Bundy, 3/1–31/64 (1 of 2), box 1, NSF—Memos to the President, LBJL; Bundy to Johnson, 25 May 1964, folder: McGeorge Bundy, 4/1–30/64, vol. 3, box 1, NSF—Memos to the President, LBJL. See also Herring, *LBJ and Vietnam*, 1–24.

79. Johnson's Telephone Conversation with Russell, 27 May 1964; Johnson's Telephone Conversation with McGeorge Bundy, 27 May 1964.

80. McNamara to the President, 13 March 1964, folder: McGeorge Bundy, 3/1–31/64 (1 of 2), box 1, NSF—Memos to the President, LBJL; Henry Cabot Lodge to Washington, 20 February 1964, folder: McGeorge Bundy, 3/1–31/64 (2 of 2), box 1, NSF—Memos to the President, LBJL.

81. See Schulzinger, *A Time for War*, 144. This argument is at the core of William Appleman Williams' classic work, *The Tragedy of American Diplomacy*, esp. 59–89.

82. William P. Bundy, untitled and unpublished manuscript (last revised 18 March 1972), chap. 16, Papers of William Bundy, LBJL.

83. Ibid., chap. 1; Logevall, *Choosing War*, 154–192.

84. The North Vietnamese and the Chinese claimed that the area within twelve miles of the coast was restricted "national" water. The United States refused to recognize this claim, allowing only three miles of "national" waters offshore. See Moïse, *Tonkin Gulf and Escalation of Vietnam War*, 50–93; Shultz, *The Secret War against Hanoi*, 174–192.

85. See Johnson's Telephone Conversation with McNamara, 3 August 1964, 1:21 P.M., citation 4639; Johnson's Telephone Conversation with McNamara, 4 August 1964, 9:43 A.M., citation 4658-a, Transcripts of Telephone Conversations, White House Series, August 1964 (1 of 4), LBJL.

86. Moïse, *Tonkin Gulf and Escalation of Vietnam War*, 97–105; Logevall, *Choosing War*, 198–203. For evidence that Johnson and McNamara expected a second North Vietnamese attack in the Gulf of Tonkin, see Johnson's Telephone Conversation with McNamara, 4 August 1964, 9:43 A.M.

87. Johnson's Telephone Conversation with Senator George Smathers, 3 August 1964,

8:40 P.M., citation 4654, Transcripts of Telephone Conversations, White House Series, August 1964 (1 of 4), LBJL.

88. See Moïse, *Tonkin Gulf and Escalation of Vietnam War*, 106–207.

89. Notes Taken at Leadership Meeting on 4 August 1964, folder: 4 August 1964 Leadership Breakfast, box 1, Meeting Notes File, LBJL; Johnson's Telephone Conversation with McNamara, 4 August 1964, 10:53 A.M., citation 4662a, Transcripts of Telephone Conversations, White House Series, August 1964 (1 of 4), LBJL; Johnson's Telephone Conversation with Congressman George Mahon, 4 August 1964, 8:38 P.M., citation 4700a, Transcripts of Telephone Conversations, White House Series, August 1964 (2 of 4), LBJL.

90. Notes Taken at Leadership Meeting on 4 August 1964.

91. See Moïse, *Tonkin Gulf and Escalation of Vietnam War*, 221–225.

92. Johnson's Telephone Conversation with Barry Goldwater, 4 August 1964, 10:06 P.M., citation 4715a, Transcripts of Telephone Conversations, White House Series, August 1964 (2 of 4), LBJL.

93. Schulzinger, *A Time for War*, 152.

94. Moïse, *Tonkin Gulf and Escalation of Vietnam War*, 247–250.

95. During late 1964 the NLF increased the frequency of its raids against South Vietnamese and American installations, including a Christmas Eve attack on a U.S. officers' billet in Saigon. Maxwell Taylor—then American ambassador to South Vietnam—called for air strikes against the North. Again, the president refused as he had since August. Schulzinger, *A Time for War*, 169–170; William P. Bundy manuscript, chap. 1.

96. McGeorge Bundy to the President, 7 February 1965, folder: McGeorge Bundy, 1/1–2/28/65, vol. 18 (1 of 2), box 2, NSF—Memos to the President, LBJL.

97. Ibid.; McGeorge Bundy, A Policy of Sustained Reprisal (annex to 7 February 1965 memo), ibid.

98. Telegram from Johnson to Maxwell Taylor, 8 February 1965, folder: McGeorge Bundy, 1/1–2/28/65, ibid.; John McCone's notes from the Meeting of the NSC, 8 February 1965, *FRUS* 1964–68, 2: 192–197; John McCone's Memorandum for the Record, 10 February 1965, ibid., 220–225; Telegram from the Department of State to the Embassy in Vietnam, 13 February 1965, ibid., 263–265; VanDeMark, *Into the Quagmire*, 61–71.

99. McGeorge Bundy to the President, 16 February 1965, folder: McGeorge Bundy, 1/1–2/28/65, vol. 18 (1 of 2), box 2, NSF—Memos to the President, LBJL; John McCone, Memorandum for the Record, 8 February 1965, *FRUS* 1964–68, 2: 195.

100. See Editorial Note, *FRUS* 1964–68, 2: 390; Logevall, *Choosing War*, 333–374.

101. McGeorge Bundy to the President, 6 March 1965, folder: McGeorge Bundy, March—4/14/65, vol. 9 (2 of 2), box 3, NSF—Memos to the President, LBJL; Memorandum from the Office of Current Intelligence to John McCone, 23 February 1965, *FRUS* 1964–68, 2: 359–361; Memorandum from the Director of the U.S. Information Agency to Johnson, 24 February 1965, ibid., 363–365; John McCone, Memorandum for the Record of Discussion with President Johnson, 25 February 1965, ibid., 372–373; Telegram from the Embassy in Vietnam to the Department of State, 7 March 1965, ibid., 408–411; Commander of the American Military Assistance Command (William Westmoreland) to the Chairman of the JCS (General Earle Wheeler), 6 March 1965, ibid., 400–401; McGeorge Bundy's summary of McNamara's remarks in a private discussion, Memorandum for the Record, 18 March 1965, ibid., 458–460.

102. McGeorge Bundy, Key Elements of Discussion, 1 April 1965, folder: McGeorge

Bundy, March—4/14/65, vol. 9 (1 of 2), NSF—Memos to the President, LBJL; VanDeMark, *Into the Quagmire*, 109–113.

103. Memorandum for the President on Southeast Asia Economic Development Planning, 1 April 1965; and McGeorge Bundy to the President, 14 April 1965, folder: McGeorge Bundy, March—4/14/65, vol. 9 (1 of 2), NSF—Memos to the President, LBJL.

104. VanDeMark, *Into the Quagmire*, 105; Brigham, *Guerrilla Diplomacy*, 40–74; Zhai, *China and the Vietnam Wars*, 130–175; Gaiduk, *Soviet Union and Vietnam War*, 35–72.

105. Meeting Notes from Johnson, Rusk, McNamara, Bundy, Ball, Valenti, 17 December 1965, folder: December 17, 1965—9:41 A.M., box 1, Meeting Notes File, LBJL.

106. Diane Kunz, *Butter and Guns: America's Cold War Economic Diplomacy* (New York, 1997), 108–119, 155–179; Jeremy Richard Fielding, "The Currency of Power: Anglo-American Economic Diplomacy and the Making of British Foreign Policy, 1964–1968" (Ph.D. diss., Yale University, 1999), 289–413.

107. Meeting Notes from Johnson, Rusk, McNamara, Moyers, et al., 26 February 1966, folder: February 26, 1966—1:05 P.M., box 1, Meeting Notes File, LBJL.

108. Notes from the President's Meeting with McNamara, 12 July 1967, folder: July 12, 1967, box 1, Tom Johnson's Notes of Meetings, LBJL; Schulzinger, *A Time for War*, 217.

109. Notes of the President's Activities during the Detroit Crisis, 24 July 1967, folder: July 24, 1967—11:25 A.M., box 1, Tom Johnson's Notes of Meetings, LBJL; Notes of the President's Meeting with Rusk, McNamara, et al., 21 November 1967, folder: November 21, 1967—8:30 A.M., box 1, Tom Johnson's Notes of Meetings, LBJL. On the urban riots in 1967 see "Final Report of Cyrus R. Vance, Special Assistant to the Secretary of Defense, Concerning the Detroit Riots, July 23 through August 2, 1967," included with Cyrus R. Vance, Oral Histories, 3 November 1969—9 March 1970, LBJL; Thomas J. Sugrue, *The Origins of the Urban Crisis: Race and Inequality in Postwar Detroit* (Princeton, 1996), 259–268; Sidney Fine, *Violence in the Model City: The Cavanagh Administration, Race Relations, and the Detroit Riot of 1967* (Ann Arbor, 1989), 155–301; Tom Hayden, *Rebellion in Newark: Official Violence and Ghetto Response* (New York, 1967), 9–61.

110. Notes of the President's Meeting with Rusk, McNamara, Rostow, Helms, and George Christian, 3 October 1967, folder: October 3, 1967—6:10 P.M., box 1, Tom Johnson's Notes of Meetings, LBJL; Notes of the President's Meeting with Rusk, McNamara, et al., 21 November 1967.

111. Bunker to Rusk, 28 January 1968, folder: January 31, 1968—8:40 A.M., box 2, Tom Johnson's Notes of Meetings, LBJL; Schulzinger, *A Time for War*, 258.

112. Schulzinger, *A Time for War*, 259.

113. Ronald Spector, *After Tet: The Bloodiest Year in Vietnam* (New York, 1993), 117–183, 202–241, 279–294, 312; Lewis Sorley, *A Better War: The Unexamined Victories and Final Tragedy of America's Last Years in Vietnam* (New York, 1999), 31–96.

114. Seymour Hersh, *My Lai 4: A Report on the Massacre and Its Aftermath* (New York, 1970), 44–75; Spector, *After Tet*, 203–204. According to Vietnamese sources, 504 civilians died in My Lai on 16 March 1968. David L. Anderson, ed., *Facing My Lai: Moving beyond the Massacre* (Lawrence, Kans., 1998), 3–4. Anderson's numbers are higher than those given by Hersh and Spector.

115. Chester J. Pach Jr., "Tet on TV: U.S. Nightly News Reporting and Presidential Policy Making," in *1968: The World Transformed*, ed. Carole Fink, Philipp Gassert, and Detlef

Junker (New York, 1998), 55–56, 65–67; Robert V. Daniels, *Year of the Heroic Guerrilla* (New York, 1989), 235–47.

116. See Daniels, *Year of the Heroic Guerrilla*, 235–247; Arif Dirlik, "The Third World," in Fink, Gassert, and Junker, *1968*, 295–317.

117. Harry McPherson, Oral History, interview 5, tape 2: 14, LBJL.

5. THE GLOBAL DISRUPTION OF 1968

1. John Lewis Gaddis, *The Long Peace: Inquiries into the History of the Cold War* (New York, 1987), 215–245. On the youth challenges to the "long peace" see Charles DeBenedetti with Charles Chatfield, *An American Ordeal: The Antiwar Movement of the Vietnam Era* (Syracuse, 1990), 217; Arthur Marwick, *The Sixties: Cultural Revolution in Britain, France, Italy, and the United States, c. 1958–c.1974* (New York, 1998), 584–586.

2. Francis Fukuyama uses "great disruption" to describe the breakdown in social order among the "developed" countries between the mid-1960s and the 1990s. Fukuyama attributes this crossnational phenomenon to the shift from an "industrial era" of factory production to an "information age" of knowledge-based work. Old bonds of family and community declined during this period of transition, according to Fukuyama. My analysis agrees with Fukuyama's on the nature of the crossnational social breakdown, beginning in the 1960s. I, however, draw closer connections between domestic disorder and great-power politics during the period. I also provide a more specific comparative and international historical narrative. See Francis Fukuyama, *The Great Disruption: Human Nature and the Reconstitution of Social Order* (New York, 1999), esp. 3–139.

3. On the historical patterns of revolutionary upheaval, see Crane Brinton, *The Anatomy of Revolution* (New York, 1938), 244–302; Barrington Moore Jr., *Social Origins of Dictatorship and Democracy: Lord and Peasant in the Making of the Modern World* (Boston, 1966), 453–508; Theda Skocpol, *States and Social Revolutions: A Comparative Analysis of France, Russia, and China* (New York, 1979), 161–293. A literature on transnational social movements is beginning to emerge. See Gerd-Rainer Horn and Padraic Kenney, eds., *Transnational Moments of Change: European Society, 1945, 1968, 1989* (St. Martin's, forthcoming).

4. For a classic account of how "rising expectations" can contribute to popular revolution during a period of reform see Alexis de Tocqueville, *L'Ancien Régime et la Révolution* (Paris, 1952), 226–231. See also Marwick, *The Sixties*, 247–287, 359–403.

5. Max Weber defined "legitimacy" as "voluntary compliance" with an authority deemed "valid"; *Economy and Society: An Outline of Interpretive Sociology*, ed. Guenther Roth and Claus Wittich (New York, 1968), 1: 212–301. Walter Lippmann was one of the first writers to use the phrase "manufacture of consent" for the manipulation of public opinion; Walter Lippmann, *Public Opinion* (New York, 1922), 248. More recently, Edward Herman and Noam Chomsky have used the phrase in *Manufacturing Consent: The Political Economy of the Mass Media* (New York, 1988), 1–35.

6. Clark Kerr, the school's titular leader between 1959 and 1967, aptly described the campus as a "multiversity"—an empire with responsibilities that exceeded the model of a small teaching college from which it had grown. Kerr, *The Uses of the University* (Cambridge, Mass, 1972, based on lectures delivered in 1963), 1–45.

7. W. J. Rorabaugh, *Berkeley at War: The 1960s* (New York, 1989), 4–7, 173, 181.

8. David Lance Goines, *The Free Speech Movement: Coming of Age in the 1960s* (Berkeley, 1993), 103–395.

9. Rorabaugh, *Berkeley at War*, 31.

10. Ibid., 33–38; Goines, *The Free Speech Movement*, 430–444.

11. On the University of Michigan teach-in see James Miller, *"Democracy Is in the Streets": From Port Huron to the Siege of Chicago* (Cambridge, Mass, 1987), 229. Students at Berkeley and other elite universities were statistically *unlikely* to serve in Vietnam. Most received education deferments or found other means of avoiding combat service. Christian Appy shows that during a period when the college-educated population ballooned, 80 percent of the men drafted to serve in Vietnam had no more than a high school education. The vast majority of Americans who fought (and died) in Southeast Asia between 1965 and 1973 came from working-class backgrounds with little wealth or education. Christian G. Appy, *Working-Class War: American Combat Soldiers and Vietnam* (Chapel Hill, 1993), 17–43.

12. DeBenedetti, *An American Ordeal*, 111–112; Todd Gitlin, *The Sixties: Years of Hope, Days of Rage* (New York, 1987), 177–188.

13. Gerard J. DeGroot, "'Left, Left, Left!': The Vietnam Day Committee, 1965–66," in *Student Protest: The Sixties and After*, ed. DeGroot (New York, 1998), 85–99. DeGroot emphasizes the shortcomings and the radicalism of the Vietnam Day Committee.

14. Rorabaugh, *Berkeley at War*, 106.

15. *Berkeley Barb*, 13 August 1965, reel 1, UPC. On the founding of the *Berkeley Barb* see Abe Peck, *Uncovering the Sixties: The Life and Times of the Underground Press* (New York, 1985), 29–32; Laurence Leamer, *The Paper Revolutionaries: The Rise of the Underground Press* (New York, 1972), 30–33; Arthur Seeger, *The Berkeley Barb: Social Control of an Underground Newsroom* (New York, 1983), 11–17.

16. On the astonishing growth of the paper see Seeger, *The Berkeley Barb*, 12–13.

17. *Berkeley Barb*, 15 April 1966, reel 1, UPC.

18. *Berkeley Barb*, 28 July–3 August 1967, reel 2, UPC.

19. "Resistance Grows on Day of Terror," *Berkeley Barb*, 20–26 October 1967, reel 2, UPC. See also Rorabaugh, *Berkeley at War*, 117–118; DeBenedetti, *An American Ordeal*, 196.

20. DeBenedetti, *An American Ordeal*, 196–198; Robert McNamara with Brian VanDeMark, *In Retrospect: The Tragedy and Lessons of Vietnam* (New York, 1995), 303–305.

21. "The Berkeley Style Wins on Both Coasts," *Berkeley Barb*, 27 October–2 November 1967, reel 2, UPC. See also "Pentagon Protesters in Victory Mood," ibid.

22. "The Berkeley Style Wins on Both Coasts," *Berkeley Barb*, 27 October–2 November 1967; and "Day the Campus Shook," *Berkeley Barb*, 1–7 December 1967, reel 2, UPC.

23. See DeBenedetti, *An American Ordeal*, 27–138; Maurice Isserman, *If I Had a Hammer: The Death of the Old Left and the Birth of the New Left* (Urbana, 1987), 127–169; Lawrence Wittner, *Resisting the Bomb: A History of the World Nuclear Disarmament Movement, 1954–1970* (Stanford, 1997), 51–60. Other, more violent traditions also contributed to the civil rights and youth movements of the 1960s. See Timothy B. Tyson, *Radio Free Dixie: Robert F. Williams and the Roots of Black Power* (Chapel Hill, 1999), 189–219, 291, 308.

24. *Berkeley Barb*, 9–15 February 1968, reel 5, UPC. See also Michael Sherry, *In the Shadow of War: The United States since the 1930s* (New Haven, 1995), 283–307.

25. On Che's death see Jon Lee Anderson, *Che Guevara: A Revolutionary Life* (New York, 1997), 701–743. On the American government's efforts to provide military support and intelligence for Che's capture, see Peter Kornbluh, ed., "The Death of Che Guevara: Declassified," National Security Archive Electronic Briefing Book 5, http://www.gwu./edu/~nsarchiv.

26. Todd Gitlin, "Che Lives. Che Dies," *Berkeley Barb*, 24–30 November 1967, reel 2,

UPC. On the idolization of Che Guevara and other "guerrillas" in the student movement see Gitlin, *The Sixties*, 263–282; Maurice Isserman, "You Don't Need a Weatherman but a Postman Can Be Helpful," in *Give Peace a Chance: Exploring the Vietnam Antiwar Movement*, ed. Melvin Small and William D. Hoover (Syracuse, 1992), 28–34.

27. Rorabaugh, *Berkeley at War*, 120.

28. The *Black Panther* newspaper employed militant rhetoric and a call to arms among African Americans in the cause of self-defense. The front page of one issue asked: "What is the essential difference between the man on the bottom and the pigs on top? The Gun. If the brother had had his piece with him, it is obvious that the pigs would have had to deal with him in a different way. And the brother may have gotten something down—that is, if he knew how to shoot straight. Guns Baby Guns"; *Black Panther*, 20 July 1967, reel 257, UPC.

29. See the Black Panther list of demands and beliefs, *Black Panther*, 16 March 1968, reel 257, UPC. Until 1968 African Americans bore a disproportionate burden of the Vietnam War. Their rate of military service and combat death exceeded their proportion of the general population. African Americans accounted for 11 percent of the general population, but they suffered 20 percent of the combat deaths during the early years of the Vietnam War. Largely as a result of the criticisms raised by Martin Luther King Jr., the Black Panthers, and others, after 1968 the rate of military service for African Americans became more commensurate with their proportion of the general population. See Appy, *Working-Class War*, 19–22.

30. Rorabaugh, *Berkeley at War*, 76–86.

31. "Ten days that shook the university" (last part of a series), *Berkeley Barb*, 16–22 February 1968, reel 5, UPC.

32. Maurice Isserman and Michael Kazin, *America Divided: The Civil War of the 1960s* (New York, 2000), 227.

33. Clayborne Carson, *In Struggle: SNCC and the Black Awakening of the 1960s* (Cambridge, Mass., 1981), 215–303.

34. See Vojtech Mastny's essay, "Planning for the Unplannable," and the translated text of "Plan of Actions of the Czechoslovak People's Army for War Period" (1964), in "Taking Lyon on the Ninth Day: The 1964 Warsaw Pact Plan for a Nuclear War in Europe and Related Documents," Parallel History Project on NATO and the Warsaw Pact, www.isn.ethz.ch/php.

35. James F. Tent, *The Free University of Berlin: A Political History* (Bloomington, Ind., 1988), 1–176.

36. Ibid., 195–320.

37. Alexandra Richie, *Faust's Metropolis: A History of Berlin* (New York, 1998), 770–778.

38. Jürgen Habermas, "Student Protest in the Federal Republic of Germany," in *Toward a Rational Society: Student Protest, Science, and Politics*, trans. Jeremy J. Shapiro (Boston, 1970), 15, 18. Habermas originally delivered this lecture in November 1967.

39. "Protest!" ca. November–December 1966, folder: Berlin, 1966–67, box 87, German Subject Collection, Hoover Institution Archives, Stanford, Calif. (hereafter German Collection). See also Rolf Uesseler, *Die 68er: APO, Marx, und freie Liebe* (Munich, 1998), 192–207; Gerhard Bauss, *Die Studentenbewegung der sechziger Jahre* (Cologne, 1977), 34–41.

40. Tent, *The Free University of Berlin*, 321–322; Richie, *Faust's Metropolis*, 779. American writers often confuse the Socialist German Student Union (Sozialistische Deutsche Studentenbund) with Students for a Democratic Society in the United States. Both used the

initials SDS. The two groups were very different in origin, and they never created significant organizational ties. The Socialist German Student Union, initially formed in September 1946, remained closely associated with the Social Democratic Party in West Germany until 1960. From 1960 through 1970 the Socialist German Student Union acted as an independent group, growing progressively more radical in its criticism of the established West German parties. Torn by internal disputes, the Socialist German Student Union dissolved itself in 1970. Students for a Democratic Society, in contrast, emerged only in 1959–60 and without any party affiliation. It had no explicit socialist tradition, and it began as a moderate organization committed to "participatory democracy," civil rights, and nuclear disarmament. During the 1960s Students for a Democratic Society grew more extreme in its criticism of established political institutions. The organization moved far to the ideological left—the "New Left"—but it never embraced socialist traditions in the way that the German student group did. Students for a Democratic Society also disbanded in the early 1970s, torn by internal strife. On the history of the Socialist German Student Union see Jürgen Briem, *Der SDS: Die Geschichte des bedeutendsten Studentenverbandes der BRD seit 1945* (Frankfurt, 1976). On the history of Students for a Democratic Society see Kirkpatrick Sale, *SDS* (New York, 1973).

41. The Manifesto of the NPD (1965), reprinted in Ivor Montagu, *Germany's New Nazis* (London, 1967), 127–131. See also Fred Richards, *Die NPD: Alternative oder Wiederkehr?* (Munich, 1967), 126–129; David Nagle, *The National Democratic Party: Right Radicalism in the Federal Republic of Germany* (Berkeley, 1970), 35–122.

42. Manifesto of the NPD, 128–131; Patrick Moreau, *Les héritiers du IIIe Reich: L'extrême droite allemands de 1945 à nos jours* (Paris, 1994), 7–14, 76–94.

43. See "Akademisches Proletariat?" folder: Berlin 1966–67, box 87, German Collection; Uesseler, *Die 68er*, 65–84; "Stand der Deutschlandfrage," 24 May 1965, band 5, IIA1—80.00, PA/AA; Klaus Hildebrand, *Von Erhard zur Großen Koalition, 1963–1969* (Stuttgart, 1984), 202–218, 283–301, 365–383.

44. See Telegram from Secretary of State Dean Rusk to the Department of State, 14 December 1965, FRUS 1964–68, 13: 283–284.

45. Student announcement, ca. 1967, folder: Berlin, 1967, box 87, German Collection.

46. Richie, *Faust's Metropolis*, 779.

47. Kennedy, Remarks in the Rudolph Wilde Platz, Berlin, 26 June 1963, in *PPP: JFK*, 1963: 524–525; Address at the Free University of Berlin, 26 June 1963, ibid., 526–529.

48. Tent, *The Free University of Berlin*, 322; "11 Seized in Berlin in a Reported Plot to Kill Humphrey," *New York Times*, 6 April 1967. For the text of Humphrey's speech see *Department of State Bulletin* 56 (1 May 1967): 680–681.

49. Summary Notes of the 569th Meeting of the National Security Council, 3 May 1967, *FRUS 1964–68*, 13: 572–573.

50. Tent, *The Free University of Berlin*, 322–323.

51. See the account of the conversation between Chancellor Kiesinger and Shah Reza Pahlavi, 28 May 1967, in *AAPBD, 1967*, 2: 797–808; Memorandum from State Secretary Rolf Lahr, 4 January 1967, AAPBD, 1967, 1: 19–22.

52. Tent, *The Free University of Berlin*, 323.

53. See James A. Bill, *The Eagle and the Lion: The Tragedy of American-Iranian Relations* (New Haven, 1988), 141–176.

54. "Warum Wir demonstrieren," in "Dokumente des 2. Juni 1967 und der Zeit danach," folder: Berlin, 1967, box 87, German Collection.

55. Ibid.

56. See the eyewitness accounts in the German newsweekly *Der Spiegel,* 12 June 1967. See also Uesseler, *Die 68er,* 244–255; Tent, *The Free University of Berlin,* 323–324.

57. See *Der Spiegel,* 12 June 1967.

58. Ibid.; Heinrich Albertz, "Sicherheit und Ordnung müssen gewährleistet bleiben," in "Dokumente des 2. Juni 1967 und der Zeit danach."

59. Public demand, in "Dokumente des 2. Juni 1967 und der Zeit danach."

60. Conversation between Chancellor Kiesinger and Iranian Ambassador Malek, 15 June 1967, in *AAPBD,* 1967, 2: 911–917.

61. Rudi Dutschke interview in *Der Spiegel,* 10 July 1967. See also idem, "Mallet, Marcuse 'Formierte Gesellschaft' und politische Praxis der Linken hier und anderswo" (1965), in *Frankfurter Schule und Studentenbewegung: Von der Flaschenpost zum Molotowcocktail, 1946–1995,* 3 vols., ed. Wolfgang Kraushaar (Hamburg, 1998), 2: 186–187.

62. Dutschke interview in *Der Spiegel,* 10 July 1967. See also Dutschke's discussion with Ernst Bloch in Rudi Dutschke, *Mein langer Marsch: Reden, Schriften, und Tagebücher aus zwanzig Jahren* (Hamburg, 1980), 80–87; Ingo Cornils, "'The Struggle Continues': Rudi Dutschke's Long March," in DeGroot, *Student Protest,* 104–106.

63. "Akademisches Proletariat?" ca. late 1967, folder: Berlin, 1966–67, box 87, German Collection; Rudi Dutschke, "Professor Habermas, Ihr begriffloser Objektivismus erschlägt das zu emanzipierende Subjekt" (9 June 1967), in Kraushaar, *Frankfurter Schule und Studentenbewegung,* 2: 251–253; Rolf Wiggershaus, *The Frankfurt School: Its History, Theories, and Political Significance,* trans. Michael Robertson (Cambridge, Mass., 1994), 617–619. Radical students formed a parallel "Critical University," offering their own ad hoc courses. See "Kritische Universität: Provisorisches Verzeichnis," winter semester 1967–68, folder: Berlin, 1967, box 87, German Collection.

64. Rudi Dutschke's diary entry for 17 June 1967, in *Mein langer Marsch,* 70; Cornils, "'The Struggle Continues,'" 110–112.

65. Dutschke, "Rebellion der Studenten" (1968), in *Mein langer Marsch,* 68–69.

66. Ibid.

67. Dutschke diary, January 1968, in *Mein langer Marsch,* 122; See also ibid., 71–72; Announcement of the International Vietnam Conference, West Berlin, 17–18 February 1968, folder: Berlin, 1968, box 88, German Collection; Bauss, *Die Studentenbewegung der sechziger Jahre,* 95.

68. See the open letter to the government of Poland, 12 March 1968, folder: Berlin, 1968, box 88, German Collection; Report from the Rector of the Free University, ibid., box 87.

69. See "Freunde und Genossen!" 11 April 1968, folder: Berlin, 1968, box 88, German Collection; *Aktuell* 1 (12 April 1968), folder: Periodicals, *Aktuell*—Berlin, box 86, German Collection; Report from the Rector of the Free University.

70. See Stefan Aust, *Der Baader Meinhof Komplex* (Hamburg, 1985), 103–320; A. D. Moses, "The State and the Student Movement in West Germany, 1967–77," in DeGroot, *Student Protest,* 144–149.

71. Carson, *In Struggle,* 215–264; Dan T. Carter, *The Politics of Rage: George Wallace, the Origins of the New Conservatism, and the Transformation of American Politics* (New York, 1995), 294–370; David J. Garrow, *Bearing the Cross: Martin Luther King, Jr., and the Southern Christian Leadership Conference* (New York, 1986), 527–624.

72. John Morton Blum, *Years of Discord: American Politics and Society, 1961–1974* (New York, 1991), 301.

73. See Report of the President's Task Force on the Los Angeles Riots, 11–15 August 1965 (report dated 17 September 1965), folder: President's Task Force Report, box 129, Papers of Ramsey Clark, LBJL; Final Report of Cyrus R. Vance (Special Assistant to the Secretary of Defense) Concerning the Detroit Riots, 23 July–2 August 1967, attached to Cyrus Vance, Oral History, 3 November 1969, LBJL; Thomas J. Sugrue, *The Origins of the Urban Crisis: Race and Inequality in Postwar Detroit* (Princeton, 1996), 231–271; Garrow, *Bearing the Cross*, 577–602.

74. Ibid., 610–622.

75. Ibid., 621.

76. Gerald Posner, *Killing the Dream: James Earl Ray and the Assassination of Martin Luther King, Jr.* (New York, 1998), 3–250.

77. Garrow, *Bearing the Cross*, 612.

78. On public reactions to John F. Kennedy's assassination see William Manchester, *The Death of a President, November 20–November 25, 1963* (New York, 1967), 497–500; Arthur M. Schlesinger Jr., *A Thousand Days: John F. Kennedy in the White House* (Boston, 1965), 935–940.

79. Isserman and Kazin, *America Divided*, 228.

80. Ben W. Gilbert and the staff of the *Washington Post, Ten Blocks from the White House: Anatomy of the Washington Riots of 1968* (New York, 1968), 16.

81. Ibid., 26.

82. Ibid., 36–37.

83. Ibid., 30, 36–37.

84. Ibid., 103–119; Isserman and Kazin, *America Divided*, 227–228.

85. Gilbert, *Ten Blocks from the White House*, 32, 105, 119.

86. *Report of the National Advisory Commission on Civil Disorders* (New York, 1968), 1.

87. Allen Matusow, *The Unraveling of America: A History of Liberalism in the 1960s* (New York, 1984), 367–373.

88. In September 1968 the CIA reported that "there are, in fact, striking parallels between the situation today and the conditions of cynicism, despair, and disposition toward violence which existed after World War I and which later helped produce Fascism and National Socialism . . . Many sociologists and psychologists believe that industrial societies are disjunctive, that they tend to aggravate conflict between generations. If this is so, there is a likelihood that dissidence will worsen and that its base will broaden"; CIA Report, "Restless Youth," September 1968, folder: Youth and Student Movements, box 13, Files of Walt W. Rostow, NSF, LBJL.

89. De Gaulle to Marie-Agnès Cailliau, 12 May 1967, in *LNC*, 1966–1969: 106; de Gaulle to Pompidou 12 February 1967, ibid., 74–75. See also François Flohic, *Souvenirs d'Outre-Gaulle* (Paris, 1979), 172.

90. "La Tempête Revolutionnaire de Mai," *Servir le peuple*, 21 January 1969, AJ/78/34, AN; "La Commune n'est pas morte," n.d., AJ/78/35, AN.

91. "Verités revolutionnaires," Nanterre, n.d., doc. 1215, microfiche 49, Les tracts de mai 1968, 4-Lb61–600 (1968), French National Library, François Mitterrand location, Paris (hereafter Les tracts de mai). See also "Mai 1968," Nanterre, doc. 1202, microfiche 48, ibid.; "Verités revolutionnaires: Lexique revolutionnaire," Nanterre, 24 October 1968, doc. 1214, microfiche 49, ibid.

92. On the so-called Fouchet Plan for reform in French education, see the speech by Christian Fouchet, minister of national education, 18 May 1965, 870191/0001, Center for Contemporary Archives, Fontainebleau, France.

93. Ronald Fraser et al., *1968: A Student Generation in Revolt* (London, 1988), 163; Marwick, *The Sixties*, 559. Fraser's book contains a remarkable collection of oral history interviews conducted mainly in 1984 and 1985.

94. Student tract, quoted in Daniel Cohn-Bendit and Gabriel Cohn-Bendit, *Obsolete Communism: The Left Wing Alternative*, trans. Arnold Pomerans (New York, 1968), 49–50. See also Fraser et al., *1968*, 163.

95. "Et la Liberté?" doc. 6870, microfiche 274, Les tracts de mai; Cohn-Bendit and Cohn-Bendit, *Obsolete Communism*, 51–57; Alain Touraine, *Le mouvement de mai ou le Communisme utopique* (Paris, 1968), 114–125; Fraser et al., *1968*, 164.

96. Marwick, *The Sixties*, 607.

97. "Les impératifs actuels de l'Action revolutionnaire," May 1968, Sorbonne, doc. 1406, microfiche 57; "Manifeste du Comité pour le developpement de l'action dans les organismes d'étude et de recherches en sciences économiques et en sciences humaines," May 1968, Sorbonne, doc. 1418, microfiche 58; Dossier du Comité d'action revolutionnaire de la Sorbonne, May 1968, doc. 1406, microfiche 56, all Les tracts de mai.

98. "Mouvement Occident," doc. 6833; "Que veut Occident?" 20 May 1968, doc. 6835; "Occident," doc. 6841; "Ni Gaulliste, Ni Communiste," doc. 6842, all microfiche 273, Les tracts de mai.

99. Fraser, *1968*, 178.

100. Marwick, *The Sixties*, 606.

101. Cohn-Bendit and Cohn-Bendit, *Obsolete Communism*, 58.

102. "La Commune n'est pas morte," Nanterre, AJ/78/35, AN; Leaflet from the Action Committee, Sorbonne, doc. 1485, microfiche 60, Les tracts de mai; Marwick, *The Sixties*, 607–608.

103. Report of the student commission, "Université et société," doc. 1656, microfiche 68, Les tracts de mai.

104. "Les impératifs actuels de l'Action revolutionnaire"; Victor Hugo, *Les misérables*, trans. Charles E. Wilbour (New York, 1997).

105. Fraser, *1968*, 179.

106. Ibid., 183.

107. Lucien Rioux and René Backmann, *L'explosion de mai: 11 mai 1968, Histoire complète des "événements"* (Paris, 1968), 196; Jean Lacouture, *De Gaulle: The Ruler, 1945–1970*, trans. Alan Sheridan (New York, 1991), 530.

108. Fraser, *1968*, 187–188.

109. Lacouture, *De Gaulle*, 532.

110. "Le 13 mai au soir," Sorbonne, doc. 1404, microfiche 56, Les tracts de mai.

111. "L'éducation nationale: Revue hebdomadaire d'information pédagogique," 30 May 1968, AJ/78/34, AN.

112. Lacouture, *De Gaulle*, 535, 538, 542; Georges Pompidou, *Pour rétablir une vérité* (Paris, 1982), 190–191.

113. Maurice Grimaud, *En mai, fais ce qu'il te plaît: Le préfet de police de mai 68 parle* (Paris, 1977), 19; Marwick, *The Sixties*, 612–613.

114. Pompidou, *Pour rétablir une vérité*, 184–192. Pompidou disregarded this order and attempted to negotiate with the students as well.

115. Lacouture, *De Gaulle*, 544–548; Pompidou, *Pour rétablir une vérité*, 192–193.

116. Lacouture, *De Gaulle*, 548.

117. Ibid., 548–549; Jacques Massu, *Baden 68* (Paris, 1983), 87–92; Flohic, *Souvenirs d'Outre-Gaulle*, 176–183.

118. Massu, *Baden 68*, 90.

119. De Gaulle, Radio Address, 30 May 1968, in *Discours et messages* (Paris, 1970), 5: 292–293.

120. Marwick, *The Sixties*, 615–617.

121. Lacouture, *De Gaulle*, 560; Marwick, *The Sixties*, 616–617.

122. See "Verités revolutionnaires," November 1968, Nanterre, doc. 1215, microfiche 49, Les tracts de mai; *Lutte Ouvrière*, 10 July 1968, AJ/78/34, AN; *La cause du peuple*, November 1968, AJ/78/33, AN.

123. Marwick, *The Sixties*, 617–618.

124. Lacouture, *De Gaulle*, 575.

125. H. Gordon Skilling, *Czechoslovakia's Interrupted Revolution* (Princeton, 1976), 32–42.

126. Excerpts from Václav Havel's and Ludvík Vaculík's speeches at the Fourth Czechoslovak Writers' Congress, 27–29 June 1967, in *The Prague Spring 1968: A National Security Archive Documents Reader*, trans. Mark Kramer, Joy Moss, and Ruth Tosek, ed. Jaromír Navrátil et al. (Budapest, 1998), 9–10.

127. Resolution of the September 1967 Central Committee Plenum of the Communist Party of Czechoslovakia, in Navrátil et al., *The Prague Spring 1968*, 12; Skilling, *Czechoslovakia's Interrupted Revolution*, 45–46.

128. See the reflections of Soviet general Aleksandr Mayorov, interviewed in Miklós Kun, *Prague Spring—Prague Fall: Blank Spots of 1968*, trans. Hajnal Csatorday (Budapest, 1999), 139; Vladimir V. Kusin, *Political Grouping in the Czechoslovak Reform Movement* (New York, 1972), 123–126; Skilling, *Czechoslovakia's Interrupted Revolution*, 72–77.

129. Excerpts from Milan Kundera's speech at the Fourth Czechoslovak Writers' Congress, in Navrátil et al., *The Prague Spring 1968*, 8–9.

130. Galia Golan, *The Czechoslovak Reform Movement: Communism in Crisis, 1962–1968* (New York, 1971), 261–262; Paul Berman, *A Tale of Two Utopias: The Political Journey of the Generation of 1968* (New York, 1996), 195–253.

131. Betty Friedan, *The Feminine Mystique* (1963; reprint, New York, 1983); Daniel Horowitz, *Betty Friedan and the Making of the Feminine Mystique* (Amherst, 1998), 197–223.

132. Friedan to Mudr Hanus Papousek, Prague, 7 December 1967, folder 917, box 26, Papers of Betty Friedan, Arthur and Elizabeth Schlesinger Library, Radcliffe Institute, Cambridge, Mass. See also Friedan to Annika Baude, 7 November 1967, ibid.; *Czechoslovak Woman* 3 (1968), published by the Czechoslovak Union of Women, in folder 921, box 26, ibid.

133. Skilling, *Czechoslovakia's Interrupted Revolution*, 79–80.

134. Ibid., 80.

135. "Unrest among Prague Students," Radio Free Europe Research Report, 28 November 1967, file 300, subfile 30, box 30/1/313, RFE/RL. See also Kusin, *Political Grouping in Czechoslovak Reform Movement*, 136–137.

136. Skilling, *Czechoslovakia's Interrupted Revolution*, 80–82.

137. "Unrest among Prague Students"; Golan, *The Czechoslovak Reform Movement*, 264–265.

138. Telegram from the U.S. Embassy in Czechoslovakia to the Department of State, 2 December 1967, *FRUS* 1964–68, 17: 180–182.

139. Skilling, *Czechoslovakia's Interrupted Revolution*, 166.

140. Ibid., 166–168.

141. János Kádár's report to the Hungarian Socialist Workers' Party Politburo of a

telephone conversation with Leonid Brezhnev, 13 December 1967, in Navrátil et al., *The Prague Spring 1968*, 20–22.

142. Ibid.

143. Remarks by Leonid Brezhnev at a Meeting of Communist Party Officials, Prague, 9 December 1967, ibid., 18–19; Andrei Aleksandrov-Agentov, *Ot Kollontai do Gorbacheva: Vospominaniya diplomata, sovetnika A. A. Gromyko, promoshchnika L. I. Brezhneva, Yu. V. Andropova, K. U. Chernenko, M. S. Gorbachev* (Moscow, 1994), 145–147.

144. Resolution of the Communist Party of Czechoslovakia's Central Committee Plenum, 5 January 1968; and Alexander Dubček's Speech Marking the 20th Anniversary of Czechoslovakia's "February Revolution," 22 February 1968, in Navrátil et al., *The Prague Spring 1968*, 34–36, 51–54.

145. Ibid., 53.

146. Ibid., 52.

147. Ibid.; Kieran Williams, *The Prague Spring and Its Aftermath: Czechoslovak Politics, 1968–1970* (New York, 1997), 14–25.

148. The Action Program of the Communist Party of Czechoslovakia, 10 April 1968, in Navrátil et al., *The Prague Spring 1968*, 92–95.

149. Stenographic Account of the Meeting of the Warsaw Pact states 23 March 1968, ibid., 64–72. Gomułka referred to the popular revolution in Hungary during 1956 and the Warsaw Pact invasion that followed. See Johanna Granville, *The First Domino: Hungary and the USSR in 1956* (College Station, 2001).

150. Brezhnev to Dubček, 11 April 1968, in Navrátil et al., *The Prague Spring 1968*, 98–100.

151. Ibid., 99.

152. Kusin, *Intellectual Origins of the Prague Spring*, 1–18, 140–142; Skilling, *Czechoslovakia's Interrupted Revolution*, 217–224, 827–852; Williams, *Prague Spring and Its aftermath*, 3–28.

153. Ludvík Vaculík, "Two Thousand Words," 27 June 1968, in Navrátil et al., *The Prague Spring 1968*, 177–181.

154. Ibid., 178, 180–181.

155. Ibid., 180–181.

156. Ibid., 179, 181.

157. Skilling, *Czechoslovakia's Interrupted Revolution*, 277–279; Miklós Kun's interview with Ludvík Vaculík in Kun, *Prague Spring—Prague Fall*, 204–208.

158. Skilling, *Czechoslovakia's Interrupted Revolution*, 277.

159. Letter from the Soviet Politburo, 4 July 1968, in Navrátil et al., *The Prague Spring 1968*, 194–198.

160. Ibid., 194.

161. Ibid., 195, 197.

162. Transcript of the Warsaw Meeting, 14–15 July 1968, ibid., 212–233. See also Dmitri Volkogonov, *Sem' Vozhdey: Galeria liderov SSSR v dvukh knigakh*, 2 vols. (Moscow, 1995), 2: 41–42.

163. Letter from the leaders of the Soviet Union, Poland, East Germany, Hungary, and Bulgaria to the Central Committee of the Communist Party of Czechoslovakia, 15 July 1968, in Navrátil et al., *The Prague Spring 1968*, 234–238. On Soviet fears of a "spillover" from the Prague Spring in other parts of the Eastern bloc, see Mark Kramer, "The Czechoslovak Crisis and the Brezhnev Doctrine," in *1968: The World Transformed*, ed. Carole Fink, Philipp Gassert, and Detlef Junker (New York, 1998), 141–145.

164. Transcript of Brezhnev's Telephone Conversation with Dubček, 13 August 1968, in Navrátil et al., *The Prague Spring 1968*, 345–356.

165. Ibid., 350. On the politicization of the Czechoslovak military during 1968 and the popularity of the Prague Spring reforms among many officers, see Condoleezza Rice, *The Soviet Union and the Czechoslovak Army, 1948–1983* (Princeton, 1984), 111–156. See also the reflections of Soviet general Aleksandr Mayorov, interviewed in Kun, *Prague Spring—Prague Fall*, 139–40.

166. Williams, *Prague Spring and Its Aftermath*, 112–125; Kramer, "Czechoslovak Crisis and Brezhnev Doctrine," 151–156.

167. Report by Kirill Mazurov, 21 August 1968, in Navrátil et al., *The Prague Spring 1968*, 452.

168. Tad Szulc, *Czechoslovakia since World War II* (New York, 1971), 390–394.

169. Skilling, *Czechoslovakia's Interrupted Revolution*, 769; Szulc, *Czechoslovakia since World War II*, 417–418.

170. Speech by Nicolae Ceauşescu, 21 August 1968, in *Winter in Prague: Documents on Czechoslovak Communism in Crisis*, ed. Robin Alison Remington (Cambridge, Mass., 1969), 359–361.

171. Resolution Adopted by the Central Committee of the League of Communists of Yugoslavia, 23 August 1968, ibid., 361–367.

172. "Total Bankruptcy of Soviet Modern Revisionism," 23 August 1968, reprinted from the *Beijing Review* 11, 23 August 1968, ibid., 326–328. See also Gordon H. Chang, *Friends and Enemies: The United States, China, and the Soviet Union, 1948–1972* (Stanford, 1990), 386–387.

173. For a firsthand account of the Red Square demonstration see Natalia Gorbanevskaya, *Red Square at Noon*, trans. Alexander Lieven (London, 1972), 27–41. On the Polish student and intellectual protests of 1968 see Jerzy Eisler, "March 1968 in Poland," in Fink, Gassert, and Junker, *1968*, 237–251.

174. KGB memorandum presented in the Central Committee of the Communist Party of the Soviet Union, 5 November 1968, reprinted in *Istoricheskii arhiv* 1 (1994): 176–193; V. Grishin to the Central Committee of the Communist Party of the Soviet Union, 21 and 22 August 1968, in Navrátil et al., *The Prague Spring 1968*, 453–455; "Three Years of Reactions in the Soviet Union to the 1968 Invasion of Czechoslovakia," 16 August 1971, file 300, subfile 80, box 80/1/1028, RFE/RL; Skilling, *Czechoslovakia's Interrupted Revolution*, 753–754; John Bushnell, *Moscow Graffiti: Language and Subculture* (Winchester, Mass., 1990), 205–233.

175. Williams, *Prague Spring and Its aftermath*, 144–191, 226–253; Kramer, "Czechoslovak Crisis and Brezhnev Doctrine," 158–159; Rice, *Soviet Union and Czechoslovak Army*, 157–196.

176. Gale Stokes, *The Walls Came Tumbling Down: The Collapse of Communism in Eastern Europe* (New York, 1993), 12–45; Williams, *Prague Spring and Its aftermath*, 251–253; Matthew J. Ouimet, "All That Custom Has Divided: National Interest and the Secret Demise of the Brezhnev Doctrine, 1968–1981" (Ph.D. diss., University of Washington, 1997), 115–133.

177. Radical students in France and other countries spoke of China as the "red base of the worldwide proletarian revolution." Protesters in Europe pledged to "defend" China against both U.S. and Soviet aggression. See "Contre la sainte alliance réactionnaire, défense de la Chine rouge" 1969, AJ/78/35, AN. See the Unofficial Enunciation of the "Brezhnev Doctrine," 26 September 1968, in Navrátil et al., *The Prague Spring 1968*, 502–

503. For an extended discussion of the Brezhnev Doctrine, see Ouimet, "All That Custom Has Divided," 136–143.

178. Quotation from *La cause du peuple: Journal communiste révolutionnaire proletarian* 1 (November 1968), AJ/78/33, AN.

179. Wang Shaoguang, *Failure of Charisma: The Cultural Revolution in Wuhan* (New York, 1995), 148–149; Lynn T. White, *Policies of Chaos: The Organizational Causes of Violence in China's Cultural Revolution* (Princeton, 1989), 221–305; Stanley Rosen, *Red Guard Factionalism and the Cultural Revolution in Guangzhou (Canton)*, (Boulder, 1982), 95–245; Chien Yu-Shen, *China's Fading Revolution: Army Dissent and Military Divisions, 1967–68* (Hong Kong, 1969), 1–57.

180. Mao's former physician, Dr. Li Zhisui, reports that Mao "did not feel safe" during the Cultural Revolution. Mao's security guards worried about his personal safety as Red Guard violence escalated, including attacks on the Communist Party residences at Zhongnanhai. Li Zhisui, *The Private Life of Chairman Mao*, trans. Tai Hung-chao (New York, 1994), 478, 490–491.

181. Quotation from "Whither China?" dated 6 January 1968, trans. in Klaus Mehnert, *Peking and the New Left: At Home and Abroad* (Berkeley, 1969), 82–100. See also Mehnert's analysis in ibid., 11–72. The "Hunan Provincial Proletarian Revolutionary Great Alliance Committee" referred to itself with the Chinese abbreviation *Sheng-wu-lian*—the three characters for "province," "proletariat," and "alliance." On the "May 16 Corps" see ibid., 26–27.

182. Ibid., 86, 93, 96–100.

183. Chien, *China's Fading Revolution*, 1–3; Jonathan D. Spence, *The Search for Modern China* (New York, 1990), 610–611.

184. Mao and Zhou embarked on an "inspection" tour together in Wuhan, but the chairman's presence was kept secret; Wang, *Failure of Charisma*, 149.

185. Excerpts from Minoru Shibata's account of the "Wuhan Incident" in Chien, *China's Fading Revolution*, 235–238. See also Wang, *Failure of Charisma*, 149–157.

186. Wang, *Failure of Charisma*, 157–160; Simon Leys, *The Chairman's New Clothes: Mao and the Cultural Revolution*, trans. Carol Appleyard and Patrick Goode (New York, 1977), 79–80.

187. Leys, *The Chairman's New Clothes*, 80.

188. "Whither China?" in Mehnert, *Peking and the New Left*, 90; Wang, *Failure of Charisma*, 161–163.

189. For an example of direct military intervention in village politics see Anita Chan, Richard Madsen, and Jonathan Unger, *Chen Village under Mao and Deng*, 2d ed. (Berkeley, 1992), 129–133. See also Chien, *China's Fading Revolution*, 9–57.

190. Mao's Talks at Three Meetings with Comrades Chang Ch'un-ch'iao and Yau Wen-yüan, in *Chairman Mao Talks to the People: Talks and Letters, 1956–1971*, trans. John Chinnery and Tieyun, ed. Stuart Schram (New York, 1974), 277–279. See also editorial, *People's Daily*, 6 November 1967, reprinted and translated in *Mao Papers: Anthology and Bibliography*, ed. Jerome Chen (New York, 1970), 149.

191. Leys, *The Chairman's New Clothes*, 106–107.

192. Editorial, *People's Daily*, 1 March 1968, in Chen, *Mao Papers*, 152; editorial, *People's Daily*, 7 August 1968, ibid., 155.

193. Editorial, *People's Daily*, 3 August 1967, ibid., 143; Mao, "The Workers Come and Take Over," August 1968, in Mehnert, *Peking and the New Left*, 140; "Scientific and Tech-

nological Training," 21 July 1968, British Broadcasting Corporation Monitoring Service, Summary of World Broadcasts, Part 3, the Far East, reprinted in Chen, *Mao Papers*, 154.

194. Leys, *The Chairman's New Clothes*, 129.

195. Thomas P. Bernstein, *Up to the Mountains and Down to the Villages: The Transfer of Youth from Urban to Rural China* (New Haven, 1977), 21–32, 68–96, 198–238; Chan, Madsen, and Unger, *Chen Village under Mao and Deng*, 9–12, 104–111.

196. *People's Daily*, 12 and 14 September and 23 December 1968, in Chen, *Mao Papers*, 156–157.

197. Leys, *The Chairman's New Clothes*, 157–162.

198. Mehnert, *Peking and the New Left*, 66–67. Chinese criticisms of Che received little publicity in Europe and North America.

199. Ibid., 67–69.

200. William H. Whyte Jr., *The Organization Man* (New York, 1956), 3–59, 392–404. The movie *The Man in the Gray Flannel Suit*, based on Sloan Wilson's 1955 best-selling novel, appeared in movie theaters in 1956. On the symbolic relevance of the film see Emily S. Rosenberg, "'Foreign Affairs' after World War II: Connecting Sexual and International Politics," *Diplomatic History* 18 (Winter 1994): 59–70. For a sample of the internationally popular music lyrics from the late 1960s listen to "Revolution I," in *The Beatles* (first released in 1968); John Lennon, "Power to the People," in *The John Lennon Collection* (first released in 1971). The Beatles' song "Revolution I" sympathized with demonstrators, but it was ambivalent about the prospects for changing the world through protest: "We all want to change the world . . . if you go carrying pictures of Chairman Mao, ain't gonna make it with anyone anyhow . . . you know it's gonna be alright."

6. THE DIPLOMACY AND DOMESTIC POLITICS OF DETENTE

1. See John Lewis Gaddis, "Rescuing Choice from Circumstance: The Statecraft of Henry Kissinger," in *The Diplomats, 1939–1979*, ed. Gordon A. Craig and Francis L. Loewenheim (Princeton, 1994), 564–592; Walter Isaacson, *Kissinger: A Biography* (New York, 1992), 66, 761.

2. See Theodore Roszak, *The Making of a Counter Culture: Reflections on the Technocratic Society and Youthful Opposition* (Garden City, N.Y., 1969), 42–83; Ludmilla Alexeyeva and Paul Goldberg, *The Thaw Generation: Coming of Age in the Post-Stalin Era* (Pittsburgh, 1990), 83–104; John Bushnell, *Moscow Graffiti: Language and Subculture* (Boston, 1990), 67–171; Martin King Whyte, "Urban Life in the People's Republic," in *The Cambridge History of China*, ed. Rodrick MacFarquhar and John King Fairbank (New York, 1991), 15: 727–728.

3. See Robert D. Putnam, *Bowling Alone: The Collapse and Revival of American Community* (New York, 2000), 15–47, 93–115; Francis Fukuyama, *The Great Disruption: Human Nature and the Reconstitution of Social Order* (New York, 1999), 15–60, 87–91, 112–126. Public civility is very difficult to measure in closed societies such as the Soviet Union and China. Case studies, however, appear to confirm the trends in social fragmentation and isolation traced in the Western states during this period. Anita Chan, Richard Madsen, and Jonathan Unger describe the disaffection among young men and women who were part of the "sent-down" group of Chinese youths moved to the countryside during the Cultural Revolution. Many of them later fled to Hong Kong, Western Europe, and the United States. See *Chen Village under Mao and Deng*, 2d ed. (Berkeley, 1992), 226–235, 252–255. Studies of public disaffection in the Soviet Union after the late 1960s include Richard Stites, *Russian Popular*

Culture: Entertainment and Society since 1900 (New York, 1992), 154–177; and Bushnell, *Moscow Graffiti,* 67–171.

4. On "countercultural" and "antipolitical" behavior see Roszak, *The Making of a Counter Culture,* xi–xiv, 1–83; Todd Gitlin, *The Sixties: Years of Hope, Days of Rage* (New York, 1987), 203–206, 353–361; Arthur Marwick, *The Sixties: Cultural Revolution in Britain, France, Italy, and the United States, c. 1958–c. 1974* (New York, 1998), 801–806; Gale Stokes, *The Walls Came Tumbling Down: The Collapse of Communism in Eastern Europe* (New York, 1993), 12–45; Suzanne Berger, "Politics and Antipolitics in Western Europe in the Seventies," *Daedalus* 108 (Winter 1979): 27–50.

5. Raymond Garthoff, *Détente and Confrontation: American-Soviet Relations from Nixon to Reagan,* rev. ed. (Washington, D.C., 1994); John Lewis Gaddis, *Strategies of Containment: A Critical Appraisal of Postwar American National Security Policy* (New York, 1982), 274–344; idem, *The Long Peace: Inquiries into the History of the Cold War* (New York: 1987), 215–245; Keith L. Nelson, *The Making of Détente: Soviet-American Relations in the Shadow of Vietnam* (Baltimore, 1995). The most influential memoirs from the period include Henry Kissinger, *White House Years* (Boston, 1979); idem, *Years of Upheaval* (Boston, 1982); Richard Nixon, *RN: The Memoirs of Richard Nixon* (New York, 1978); Gerard Smith, *Doubletalk: The Story of the First Strategic Arms Limitation Talks* (Garden City, N.Y., 1980); Willy Brandt, *People and Politics: The Years 1960–1975,* trans. J. Maxwell Brownjohn (Boston, 1976); Egon Bahr, *Zu meiner Zeit* (Munich, 1996).

6. See Aleksandr Solzhenitsyn, *The Mortal Danger: How Misconceptions about Russia Imperil America,* trans. Michael Nicholson and Alexis Klimoff (New York, 1980), 37–53; Mikhail Heller and Aleksandr Nekrich, *Utopia in Power: The History of the Soviet Union from 1917 to the Present,* trans. Phyllis B. Carlos (London, 1986), 650.

7. Willy Brandt's speech at the Tutzing Christian Academy, 15 July 1963, *DzD,* 9: 567. See also Brandt's speech at Harvard University, 2 October 1962, *DzD,* 8: 1151–55.

8. Brandt's speech at Tutzing Christian Academy, 566–571.

9. Egon Bahr's speech at the Tutzing Christian Academy, 15 July 1963, *DzD,* 9: 573.

10. Ibid., 575.

11. Bahr to Brandt, 4 April 1963, box 49B, Papers of Egon Bahr, Archive of the Social Democratic Party, Friedrich-Ebert-Stiftung, Bonn, Germany (hereafter Bahr Papers).

12. Draft of Bahr's speech at the University of Hamburg, 1 June 1964, box 348, Bahr Papers.

13. Ibid.

14. "Die Bemühungen der deutschen Regierung und ihrer Verbündeten um die Einheit Deutschlands, 1955–1965," IIA1, band 75, PA/AA. See also the press release from the West German radio information service, 25 March 1964, B2, band 155, PA/AA.

15. From 1960 to 1965 trade between East and West Germany grew by approximately 20 percent. See "Zweiter Bericht über den Interzonenhandel," March 1966, B137/3664, BA; "Die Bemühungen der deutschen Regierung und ihrer Verbündeten um die Einheit Deutschlands, 1955–1965," IIA1, band 75, PA/AA; Robert Mark Spaulding, *Osthandel and Ostpolitik: German Foreign Trade Policies in Eastern Europe from Bismarck to Adenauer* (Providence, 1997), 453–458, 488.

16. Lyndon Johnson, Remarks in New York City Before the National Conference of Editorial Writers, 7 October 1966, in *PPP: LBJ,* 1966: 1128. On Johnson's distraction from European affairs and his difficult relations with America's West European allies, particularly West Germany and France, see Egon Bahr's memorandum, 27 October 1966, box 352,

Bahr Papers; Frank Costigliola, "Lyndon B. Johnson, Germany, and the 'End of the Cold War,'" and Nancy Bernkopf Tucker, "Lyndon Johnson: A Final Reckoning," in *Lyndon Johnson Confronts the World: American Foreign Policy, 1963–1968*, ed. Warren I. Cohen and Nancy Bernkopf Tucker (New York, 1994), 173–210, 314–318. Thomas Alan Schwartz rejects the conventional wisdom on Johnson's distraction from Europe. He argues that Johnson's European policies accomplished quite a lot: holding a troubled NATO alliance together after France's withdrawal, pressing for ratification of the Nuclear Non-Proliferation Treaty, beginning negotiations for a readjustment of financial and military burdens in Western Europe, and encouraging the early steps toward improved East-West relations. See Schwartz, *In the Shadow of Vietnam: Lyndon Johnson and Europe* (Cambridge, Mass., 2003). Schwartz makes a strong, but ultimately unpersuasive, argument. If Johnson cared so much about European policy, why did it take him until October 1966 to articulate a vision for "building bridges" across the continent? Why did it take him until June 1967 to arrange a poorly prepared meeting with Soviet leader Aleksei Kosygin? Unlike any of his predecessors, Johnson gave Europe far less attention than Southeast Asia. His accomplishments in Europe, though significant, were consistently overshadowed—even among Washington's closest allies—by growing frustration with America's policies in Vietnam. On 18 December 1968, for instance, Egon Bahr wrote that the West German government must act more independently of U.S. leadership not only in Europe but in Asia, for the purpose of brokering an end to the Vietnam War and encouraging worldwide support for Ostpolitik. American foreign policy had become more of a problem than a solution for the needs of West European allies; Egon Bahr's memorandum, 18 December 1968, in *AAPBD*, 1968, 2: 1613–17. Members of Harold Wilson's government in Great Britain had a similar point of view; George Brown, White Paper for the Cabinet, Review of Foreign Policy, 23 February 1968, CAB 129/136, PRO.

17. See the brief prepared by the West German Foreign Ministry for discussions with French leaders, 24 May 1965; and Brief for West German-French consultations, 13–14 January 1967, IIA6, band 167, PA/AA.

18. Peace Note of the Federal Republic of Germany, 29 March 1966, in *Politics and Government in Germany, 1944–1994: Basic Documents*, ed. Carl-Christoph Schweitzer et al. (Providence, 1995), 128.

19. "Die Bemühungen der deutschen Regierung und ihrer Verbündeten um die Einheit Deutschlands, 1955–1965," IIA1, band 75, PA/AA. Some scholars criticize the 1966 Peace Note for not proposing anything new. The Peace Note acknowledged that Bonn had to pursue an active Ostpolitik, but it continued to deny the legitimacy of the East German government. See Peter Bender, *Neue Ostpolitik: Vom Mauerbau bis zum Moskauer Vertrag* (Munich, 1986), 112–115; William E. Griffith, *The Ostpolitik of the Federal Republic of Germany* (Cambridge, Mass., 1978), 127–128.

20. The Declaration of the Grand Coalition Government, 13 December 1966, in Schweitzer et al., *Politics and Government in Germany*, 130. See also the new chancellor Kurt-Georg Kiesinger's speech in the Bundestag, 13 December 1966, B136/6787, BA; Klaus Hildebrand, *Von Erhard zur Großen Koalition, 1963–1969* (Stuttgart, 1984), 323–339.

21. Memorandum from Bahr, 21 April 1968, box 389, Bahr Papers; Draft for a speech to the nuclear disarmament conference, 28 August 1968, box 288, ibid.; "Gesamtdeutsche Kontakte/Jugend, Studenten," 6 February 1969, B137/2294, BA.

22. Bahr draft article for *Christ und Welt*, February 1965, box 9B, Bahr Papers.

23. On Brandt and Bahr's frustrations with the Grand Coalition see Bahr memoran-

dum, 27 October 1966, box 352, Bahr Papers; Bahr to Brandt, 4 January 1967, ibid.; "Aktuelle aussenpolitische Probleme," 1969, box 310, ibid.

24. Bahr to Brandt, 15 November 1966, box 352, ibid.

25. A number of officials made this point to the West German government at the time. See Dr. Kassel to the Ministry for All-German Questions, 6 February 1969, B137/2291, BA; Memorandum from a meeting with the Catholic student community in Halle, 19 July 1969, B137/2295, BA.

26. Speech by Willy Brandt at the Conference of Non-Nuclear States in Genf, 3 September 1968, box 288, Bahr Papers.

27. See draft answer to the Soviet-Berlin Communiqué of 6 January 1968, box 310, Bahr Papers.

28. Report on the student meeting in East Berlin, 18–19 January 1969; Report from the meeting of students from Dresden, Munich (and Aachen) in East Berlin, 17–20 January 1969; Report from the Berlin meeting with our friends from Karl-Marx City, 4–5 January 1969; Memorandum from a meeting with the Catholic student community in Halle, 19 July 1969, all B137/2295, BA.

29. Report from the meeting of students from Dresden, Munich (and Aachen) in East Berlin, 17–20 January 1969; Report from the meeting in East Berlin 15 February 1969; and Report from the meeting between students of South Halle and Cologne in Leipzig, 14 March 1969, B137/2295, BA; Report on the trip to East Berlin, 23–27 June 1968; and Report from the meeting in Berlin, 19–22 September 1968, B137/2291, BA.

30. Arnulf Baring, *Machtwechsel: Die Ära Brandt-Scheel* (Stuttgart, 1982), 396–403; Karl Dietrich Bracher, Wolfgang Jäger, and Werner Link, *Republik im Wandel, 1969–1974: Die Ära Brandt* (Stuttgart, 1986), 54–67; Clay Clemens, *Reluctant Realists: The Christian Democrats and West German Ostpolitik* (Durham, N.C., 1989), 59–66.

31. Timothy Garton Ash, *In Europe's Name: Germany and the Divided Continent* (New York, 1993), 69.

32. Bahr, *Zu meiner Zeit*, 297.

33. Bahr to Henry Kissinger, 19 November 1969, box 439, Bahr Papers.

34. Account of a discussion between Bahr and Kissinger, 17 August 1970; and Horst Ehmke's account of his discussion with Kissinger, Martin Hillenbrand, Helmut Sonnenfeldt, and Rolf Pauls, 21 December 1970, box 439, Bahr Papers.

35. See the acknowledgment of this fact in the discussion between Bahr and Kissinger, 17 August 1970.

36. M. E. Sarotte, *Dealing with the Devil: East Germany, Détente, and Ostpolitik, 1969–1973* (Chapel Hill, 2001), 54–56.

37. Ibid., 65–111.

38. Treaty Between the Federal Republic of Germany and the Union of Soviet Socialist Republics, 12 August 1970, in Schweitzer et al., *Politics and Government in Germany*, 131–132.

39. Letter on German Unity, 12 August 1970, ibid., 132.

40. Treaty Between the Federal Republic of Germany and the Union of Soviet Socialist Republics, 12 August 1970, 131. See also Sarotte, *Dealing with the Devil*, 67–71.

41. Bahr quoted in Garton Ash, *In Europe's Name*, 72. Mary Sarotte observes that the ranks of the repressive East German secret police (the Staatssicherheitspolizei, commonly known as the "Stasi") grew during the period of Ostpolitik; *Dealing with the Devil*, 54.

42. Treaty between the Federal Republic of Germany and the People's Republic of Poland, 7 December 1970; Treaty on the Basis of Relations between the Federal Republic of

Germany and the German Democratic Republic ("Basic Treaty"), 26 May 1972; Treaty between the Federal Republic of Germany and the Czechoslovak Socialist Republic, 11 December 1973, in Schweitzer et al., *Politics and Government in Germany*, 62–63, 133–134, 136–137.

43. The Four-Power Agreement on Berlin, 3 September 1971; Agreement between the Government of the Federal Republic of Germany and the Government of the German Democratic Republic on Transit Traffic of Civilian Persons and Goods between the Federal Republic of Germany and Berlin (West), 17 December 1971, ibid., 33–34, 36. See also Sarotte, *Dealing with the Devil*, 113–134.

44. Griffith, *Ostpolitik*, 234.

45. See Record of a meeting between Chinese Ambassador Wang Kuochuan and General Peter Florin, 8 June 1962; and Record of a conversation with Chinese Ambassador Chang Haifung, 9 September 1965, FBS 363/15321, Papers of Walter Ulbricht, Stiftung Archiv der Parteien und Massenorganisationen der DDR im Bundesarchiv (SAPMO), Berlin-Lichterfelde, Germany (hereafter Ulbricht Papers); Pierre Prosper Cerles, Beijing, to Paris, 23 May 1967, Series: Europe, 1961–1970, Subseries: Federal Republic of Germany, vol. 1579, FFM.

46. Kuo-kang Shao, *Zhou Enlai and the Foundations of Chinese Foreign Policy* (New York, 1996), 277–279; Ilya Gaiduk, *The Soviet Union and the Vietnam War* (Chicago, 1996), 223–226.

47. The Rumanian ambassador to France, Dr. Dimitriu, conveyed an initial message from Beijing to Etienne Manac'h, the long-serving director of Asian affairs in the French Foreign Ministry. Paris maintained full diplomatic relations with China at this time, but communications between the two countries had become somewhat strained since the beginning of the Cultural Revolution. Beijing relied upon its closer connections with Rumania to transmit important messages in confidence. Etienne Manac'h Note, 17 March 1967, Series: Europe, 1961–1970, Subseries: Federal Republic of Germany, vol. 1579, FFM. Dimitriu and Manac'h became the hubs for a line of discreet diplomatic communications that began in Beijing and ended in Bonn. This was the Sino–West German counterpart to the Federal Republic's secret interactions with the Soviet Union and East Germany at the time. Mao's government improbably opened this channel without any prompting from West Germany or France.

48. Memorandum from Alexander Böker, 11 April 1967, in *AAPBD*, 1968, 1: 293, n. 1. Böker conveyed the Chinese message to then West German foreign minister Willy Brandt. On 16 April 1967 Brandt jotted a handwritten note that indicated both his excitement and his caution with regard to China. "Do not ignore this," he wrote Böker. "Treat this very carefully. Initially only in view of trade representation." See ibid.

49. Memorandum from Klaus Schütz, 19 May 1967, in *AAPBD*, 1967, 2: 754–755. Fei Yiming was an editor at *Dagong Bao*, a procommunist newspaper published in Hong Kong. Chinese scholar Xue Litai has confirmed that Fei Yiming maintained direct contacts with Zhou Enlai and frequently served as his informal envoy to foreign leaders; interview with Xue Litai, 10 August 2000, Stanford University.

50. Memorandum from Klaus Schütz, 19 May 1967. For evidence of deterioration in Sino–East German relations see Ambassador Hegen to Walter Ulbricht et al., 1 February 1967, FBS 363/15322, Ulbricht Papers; Jean-Louis Toffin to Maurice Couve de Murville, 5 November 1968, Series: Europe, 1961–1970, Subseries: Federal Republic of Germany, vol. 1579, FFM.

51. Memorandum from Klaus Schütz, 19 May 1967.

52. Ibid.

53. Memorandum from Georg Duckwitz, 10 June 1968, in *AAPBD*, 1968, 1: 686–688; Memorandum from Ulrich Sahm, 5 July 1968, *AAPBD*, 1968, 2: 845–847; François Seydoux to Paris, 11 March 1968; and Note, 19 May 1969, Series: Europe, 1961–1970, Subseries: Federal Republic of Germany, vol. 1579, FFM.

54. Memorandum from Egon Bahr, 18 December 1968, *AAPBD*, 1968, 2: 1613–17; François Seydoux to Paris, 17 March 1970, Series: Europe, 1961–1970, Subseries: Federal Republic of Germany, vol. 1579, FFM.

55. Memorandum from Egon Bahr, 18 December 1968.

56. Brandt, *People and Politics,* 420–424.

57. Memorandum from James C. Thomson Jr. to Bill Moyers, 15 March 1966, *FRUS* 1964–68, 30: 274–275.

58. Memorandum from Averell Harriman to Bill Moyers, 3 June 1966, ibid., 318–319. For similar opinions from other Johnson advisers see Memorandum from Robert Komer to President Johnson, 19 April 1966, ibid., 285–286; Memorandum from James C. Thomson Jr. to Walt Rostow, 4 August 1966, ibid., 364–366; "Communist China: A Long Range Study," Prepared by the Special State-Defense Study Group, June 1966, ibid., 332–343. Of all Johnson's advisers, Secretary of State Dean Rusk was the most wary of establishing improved relations with Beijing. See Memorandum from Rusk to President Johnson, 22 February 1968, ibid., 645–650.

59. Lyndon Johnson, "Remarks to the American Alumni Council: Asian Policy" 12 July 1966, in *PPP: LBJ*, 1966: 718–722. See also Johnson's News Conference, 20 July 1966, ibid., 744–751; Dean Rusk to all Diplomatic and Consular Posts, Guidance for Discussion of Communist China, 17 January 1967, folder: POL 1 CHICOM-US, box 1974, State Department Central Files, RG 59, NA.

60. On the night of 22 August 1967 a mob of Chinese Red Guards attacked and burned the British consulate in Beijing. For a firsthand account of this event see D. C. Hopson to George Brown, 8 September 1967, PREM 13/1966, PRO. In late January 1967 a large group of Red Guards began a series of demonstrations around the French embassy in Beijing, shouting through loudspeakers at all hours of the day and night, restricting the movement of the ambassador, and threatening to attack the embassy grounds; Lucien Paye to Paris, 31 January 1967; and Paye to Maurice Couve de Murville, 16 June 1967, Series: Asia, 1956–1967, Subseries: China, vol. 536, FFM; Note, 4 July 1967, ibid., vol. 537. For an account of Red Guard attacks on East German diplomatic offices see Hegen to Ulbricht et al., 1 February 1967, FBS 363/15322, Ulbricht Papers.

61. Alfred Jenkins to Walt Rostow, 16 September 1966, *FRUS* 1964–68, 30: 388–389.

62. Walt Rostow to President Johnson, 9 January 1967, ibid., 499–500. On America's discreet overtures for improved Sino-American contacts after July 1966 see James C. Thomson Jr. to Walt Rostow, 4 August 1966, ibid., 364–366; Action Memorandum from William Bundy et al. to Dean Rusk, 1 December 1966, ibid., 471–475; William Bundy to Rusk, 30 December 1966, ibid., 492–494.

63. Ambassadorial talks between American and Chinese representatives in Warsaw began on 15 September 1958 and continued intermittently through 1970. See Kenneth T. Young, *Negotiating with the Chinese Communists: The United States Experience, 1953–67* (New York, 1968), 161–298.

64. Telegram from the Embassy in Poland to the Department of State, 7 September 1966, *FRUS* 1964–68, 30: 383–386; Memorandum by the CIA Board of National Estimates,

23 September 1966, ibid., 401; Telegram from the Embassy in Poland to the Department of State, 25 January 1967, ibid., 509–512; Shao, *Zhou Enlai and Chinese Foreign Policy,* 196–197.

65. Telegram from the Embassy in Poland to the Department of State 8 January 1968, *FRUS* 1964–68, 30: 630–632; Letter from Ambassador John Gronouski to Rusk, 11 January 1968, ibid., 632–634.

66. Conversation between Mao Zedong and E. F. Hill, 28 November 1968, *CWIHPB* 11 (Winter 1998): 161; Winzer to Ulbricht et al., December 1968, FBS 363/15322, Ulbricht Papers.

67. D. Trench, Hong Kong, to Commonwealth Office, 26 and 25 November 1967, FCO 21/210, PRO. The Chinese government did not show the same restraint in Macao. On this island—under a Portuguese colonial governor—Beijing helped to orchestrate continual demonstrations and riots. Faced with an ultimatum from the mainland in April 1968, Lisbon's representative ceded most authority over commerce and immigration in Macao to Chinese authorities. See "The Portuguese Capitulation in Macao," ca. April 1968, FCO 21/233, PRO.

68. E. T. Davies, Hong Kong, to R. Whitney, Beijing, 15 December 1967, FCO 21/210, PRO. See also "The Cultural Revolution: Spring 1968," FCO 21/25, PRO; Handwritten diary of British foreign minister Michael Stewart, 13 May 1968, No. 8/1/5, Papers of Michael Stewart, Churchill Archives Center, Churchill College, Cambridge.

69. Barbara Barnouin and Yu Changgen, *Chinese Foreign Policy during the Cultural Revolution* (London, 1998), 63–65; Shao, *Zhou Enlai and the Foundations of Chinese Foreign Policy,* 197–199.

70. For a similar analysis of Mao's motives see Chen Jian, *Mao's China and the Cold War* (Chapel Hill, 2001), 238–276.

71. Nixon recounted his extensive experience with Asian affairs in July 1969, during his whirlwind trip through the region; Richard Nixon, Informal Remarks in Guam with Newsmen, 25 July 1969, in *PPP: RN,* 1969: 544–555. See also William Bundy, *A Tangled Web: The Making of Foreign Policy in the Nixon Presidency* (New York, 1998), 4–13. Jeffrey Kimball observes that while Nixon adopted belligerent anticommunist positions on the war in Vietnam, he displayed much more flexibility in his reflections on Sino-American relations before entering the White House; *Nixon's Vietnam War* (Lawrence, Kans., 1998), 32–39.

72. Richard M. Nixon, "Asia after Viet Nam," *Foreign Affairs* 46 (October 1967): 111–125.

73. Richard Nixon, "Inaugural Address," 20 January 1969, in *PPP: RN,* 1969: 1–4.

74. Ibid., 2.

75. Ibid., 1–2.

76. Ibid., 3.

77. See Mao Zedong's comments on an article by a commentator of *Renmin ribao* and *Hongqi,* January 1969, *CWIHPB* 11 (Winter 1998): 161. The text of Nixon's inaugural address appeared in the *People's Daily* and *Red Flag.*

78. Mao Zedong's Speech at the First Plenary Session of the CCP's Ninth Central Committee, 28 April 1969, *CWIHPB* 11 (Winter 1998): 163–165.

79. Ibid., 163–164.

80. Report by Four Chinese Marshals to the Central Committee, "A Preliminary Evaluation of the War Situation," 11 July 1969, ibid., 166–168. This document is also reprinted

in Barnouin and Changgen, *Chinese Foreign Policy during the Cultural Revolution*, 139–142. The authors of the report were Chen Yi, Ye Jianying, Nie Rongzhen, and Xu Xiangqian. They received the title "marshal" for their military service on behalf of the CCP. For background on the reports of the four marshals see Chen, *Mao's China and the Cold War*, 245–249.

81. Report by Four Chinese Marshals, 166–167.

82. Ibid., 168.

83. Ibid., 167. See also the follow-up "Report by Four Chinese Marshals to the CCP Central Committee," 17 September 1969, *CWIHPB* 11 (Winter 1998): 170.

84. "Further Thoughts by Marshal Chen Yi on Sino-American Relations," *CWIHPB* 11 (Winter 1998): 170–171.

85. Roderick MacFarquhar, "The Succession to Mao and the End of Maoism," in MacFarquhar and Fairbank, *Cambridge History of China*, 15: 320–323; Chen, *Mao's China and the Cold War*, 249–276.

86. Nixon quoted in Kissinger, *White House Years*, 176–177.

87. Memorandum of Conversation, William Stearman and Boris Davydov, 18 August 1969, folder: Political Affairs and Relations, 3/1/69, box 1973, POL CHICOM-US, RG 59, Central Files, NA; Department of State Telegram to the American Embassy, Hong Kong, et al., 21 August 1969, folder: Political Affairs and Relations, 2/1/69, box 1974, POL 1 CHICOM-USSR, RG 59, Central Files, NA. See also Kissinger, *White House Years*, 183–186; Allen Whiting, "Sino-American Détente," *China Quarterly* 82 (June 1980): 336. Viktor Gobarev claims that Moscow intentionally leaked the possibility of a military strike against China in order to intimidate Beijing; "Soviet Policy toward China: Developing Nuclear Weapons, 1949–1969," *Journal of Slavic Military Studies* 12 (December 1999): 46–47.

88. In the early 1960s the U.S. government seriously considered a preventive strike against China's nascent nuclear facilities. See William Burr and Jeffrey T. Richelson, "Whether to 'Strangle the Baby in the Cradle': The United States and the Chinese Nuclear Program, 1960–1964," *International Security* 25 (Winter 2000/01): 54–99; Gordon H. Chang, "JFK, China, and the Bomb," *Journal of American History* 74 (March 1988): 1287–1310.

89. Kissinger, *White House Years*, 179. For an earlier anticipation of this argument see the notes from a State Department discussion, including Marshall Green, John Holdridge, and others, 21 June 1969, folder: POL 32-1 CHICOM-USSR, 6/1/69, box 1975, RG 59, Central Files, NA.

90. Memorandum of Conversation, William Stearman and Boris Davydov 10 November 1969, folder: Political Affairs and Relations, 10/1/69, box 1974, POL 1 CHICOM-USSR, RG 59, Central Files, NA; Kissinger, *White House Years*, 182–184.

91. On 12 December 1969 Nixon prohibited members of his administration from discussing Sino-American contacts with Soviet representatives; Henry Kissinger to William Rogers, 12 December 1969; and Kissinger to Theodore L. Eliot, 15 December 1969, folder: Political Affairs and Relations, 3/1/69, box 1973, POL CHICOM-US, RG 59, Central Files, NA.

92. Telegram from Department of State, 11 December 1969, ibid.; American Embassy, Warsaw, to Department of State, 24 January 1970, folder: POL CHICOM-US, 1/15/70, box 2187, RG 59, Central Files, NA; American Embassy, Warsaw, to Department of State, 21 February 1970, folder: POL CHICOM-US, 2/5/70, box 2188, ibid.

93. Memorandum of Conversation between Richard Nixon, William Rogers, Henry Kissinger, Zhou Enlai, Yeh Chien-ying, Li Hsien-nien, et al., 21 February 1972, Beijing;

Memorandum of Conversation between Nixon, Kissinger, Zhou Enlai, et al., 22 February 1972, Beijing. These and other top-secret documents from Nixon's February 1972 visit to Beijing are available from "Record of Historic Nixon-Zhou Enlai Talks in February 1972 Now Declassified," NSA, http://www.gwu.edu/~nsarchiv/nsa/publications/DOC_readers/kissinger/nixzhou (hereafter Nixon-Zhou Talks).

94. See Walter Isaacson's humorous chapter on Kissinger as celebrity, *Kissinger*, 355–370. On charismatic imagemaking see Max Weber, *Economy and Society: An Outline of Interpretive Sociology*, 3 vols., ed. Guenther Roth and Claus Wittich (New York, 1968), 1: 241–245; Reinhard Bendix, *Max Weber: An Intellectual Portrait* (Garden City, N.Y., 1960), 302–310.

95. Kimball, *Nixon's Vietnam War*, 210–211; William Shawcross, *Sideshow: Kissinger, Nixon, and the Destruction of Cambodia* (New York, 1979), 128–149.

96. Kimball, *Nixon's Vietnam War*, 215–216; Bundy, *A Tangled Web*, 155–164.

97. Mao's Statement on Cambodia, 20 May 1970, in *Sino-American Relations, 1949–1971*, ed. Roderick MacFarquhar (New York, 1972), 248–249.

98. Soviet Report on 11 September 1969 Kosygin-Zhou Meeting, *CWIHPB* 6–7 (Winter 1995–96): 191–193. On the improvement in Sino-Soviet relations during 1970 and calls for a new "united front" against American imperialism, see John W. Garver, *China's Decision for Rapprochement with the United States, 1968–1971* (Boulder, 1982), 84–107; Gaiduk, *Soviet Union and Vietnam War*, 228–229.

99. Vernon Walters, *Silent Missions* (Garden City, N.Y., 1978), 523–550; John Holdridge, *Crossing the Divide: An Insider's Account of Normalization of U.S.-China Relations* (Lanham, Md., 1997), 39–40.

100. Edgar Snow, *The Long Revolution* (New York, 1972), 3–12, 171–173, 181–183.

101. Edgar Snow, "A Conversation with Mao Tse-Tung," *Life* 70 (30 April 1971): 46–48. This article is reprinted in idem, *The Long Revolution*, 167–176. On the reaction in the U.S. government see Holdridge, *Crossing the Divide*, 49.

102. Kissinger, *White House Years*, 701.

103. Ibid., 702.

104. Snow, "A Conversation with Mao Tse-Tung." Zhou Enlai later told Nixon that "the decision to invite the American table tennis team to China was made by Chairman Mao personally"; Memorandum of Conversation between Nixon, Kissinger, Zhou, et al., 21 February 1972, Nixon-Zhou Talks.

105. Kissinger, *White House Years*, 733–736.

106. Memorandums of Conversations between Henry Kissinger, Zhou Enlai, et al., 9 July 1971, 10 July 1971 afternoon, 10 July 1971 evening, 11 July 1971, reprinted in William Burr, ed., "The Beijing-Washington Back Channel and Henry Kissinger's Secret Trip to China," NSA Electronic Briefing Book 66, http://www.gwu.edu/~nsarchiv/NSAEBB/NSAEBB66. See also Kissinger, *White House Years*, 747–753; Holdridge, *Crossing the Divide*, 42, 50–63; Patrick Tyler, *A Great Wall: Six Presidents and China* (New York, 1999), 94–102.

107. Nixon, Remarks to the Nation Announcing Acceptance of an Invitation to Visit the People's Republic of China, 15 July 1971, in *PPP: RN, 1971*: 819–820.

108. Kissinger, *White House Years*, 755.

109. Kissinger to Nixon, 14 July 1971, in Burr, "The Beijing-Washington Back Channel." See also Kissinger, *White House Years*, 770–774, 784–787.

110. Memorandum of Conversation between Nixon, Kissinger, Zhou, et al., 21 February 1972, Nixon-Zhou Talks.

111. Kissinger, *White House Years*, 1058. See Nixon's account of his nearly identical im-

pression, *RN*, 560–564. A little more than a month before Nixon's arrival in Beijing, Mao Zedong—now seventy-eight years old—suffered from what his doctor diagnosed as congestive heart failure. See Li Zhisui, *The Private Life of Chairman Mao: The Memoirs of Mao's Personal Physician*, trans. Tai Hung-chao (New York, 1994), 548.

112. Memorandum of Conversation between Mao Zedong, Zhou Enlai, Wang Hairong, Tang Wensheng, Richard Nixon, Henry Kissinger, and Winston Lord, 21 February 1972, Mao's Residence, Beijing. This memo, based on the notes taken by Winston Lord, is reprinted in Jeffrey T. Richelson, ed., "China and the United States: From Hostility to Engagement, 1960–1998," NSA Electronic Briefing Book 18, http://www.gwu.edu/~nsarchiv/NSAEBB/NSAEBB19. The document is also reprinted in William Burr, ed., *The Kissinger Transcripts: Top Secret Talks with Beijing and Moscow* (New York, 1998), 59–65.

113. Ibid. In April 1969 the Ninth Congress of the Chinese Communist Party made Lin Biao Mao's designated successor. Lin was particularly popular among radical Red Guard groups. After attempting to launch a coup against Mao, Lin died on 13 September 1971 when his plane, fleeing the mainland for sanctuary in the Soviet Union, mysteriously crashed in Mongolia. In 1972 Zhou Enlai labeled Lin a "renegade and traitor." See Jonathan D. Spence, *The Search for Modern China* (New York, 1990), 617.

114. Memorandum of Conversation between Mao Zedong, Zhou Enlai, Wang Hairong, Tang Wensheng, Richard Nixon, Henry Kissinger, and Winston Lord, 21 February 1972, Mao's Residence, Beijing.

115. Ibid.

116. Ibid.

117. Ibid. Mao's family actually enjoyed modest prosperity during his childhood. The family farm occupied three acres, which, one historian writes, "was enough to support a family if well managed." See Jonathan Spence, *Mao Zedong* (New York, 1999), 3.

118. Memorandum of Conversation between Nixon, Kissinger, Zhou, et al., 21 February 1972, Nixon-Zhou Talks.

119. For the most explicit statements of this kind from both sides, see Memorandum of Conversation between Nixon, Kissinger, Zhou, et. al., 26 February 1972; and Memorandum of Conversation between Nixon, Kissinger, Zhou, et. al., 28 February 1972, Nixon-Zhou Talks.

120. See Memorandum of Conversation between Nixon, Kissinger, Zhou, et al., 22 February 1972; Conversation between Nixon, Kissinger, Zhou, et al., 24 February 1972, Nixon-Zhou Talks.

121. See Memorandum of Conversation between Nixon, Kissinger, Zhou, et al., 22 February 1972; Memorandum of Conversation between Nixon, Kissinger, Zhou, et al., 24 February 1972, Nixon-Zhou Talks.

122. Joint Communiqué issued by the People's Republic of China and the United States of America, 28 February 1972, Shanghai, reprinted in Kissinger, *White House Years*, 1490–92.

123. Ibid.

124. See Tyler, *A Great Wall*, 273–275.

125. Richard H. Solomon, "The China Factor in America's Foreign Relations: Perceptions and Policy Choices," in *The China Factor: Sino-American Relations and the Global Scene*, ed. Solomon (Englewood Cliffs, 1981), 5–14; Tyler, *A Great Wall*, 427–428.

126. Speaking to reporters in Guam on 25 July 1969, Nixon explained that the United States would continue to aid its allies overseas but would "reduce American involvement"

in future regional conflicts. While the Nixon administration expanded American bombing efforts throughout Southeast Asia between 1969 and 1970, it remained consistent in its determination to reduce U.S. troop commitments in the area. During his first three years in office, the president decreased the number of American soldiers deployed in Indochina by 80 percent. The Nixon Doctrine also curtailed military operations close to the Chinese border. In late 1969, for example, the U.S. Navy terminated its destroyer patrols in the Taiwan Strait, first begun at the outbreak of the Korean War. See Nixon, Informal Remarks in Guam, 25 July 1969, in *PPP: RN*, 1969: 548, 554; Annual Foreign Policy Report, 18 February 1970, in *PPP: RN*, 1970: 118–119; Gaddis, *Strategies of Containment*, 298–299; Kimball, *Nixon's Vietnam War*, 131–137, 193–212.

127. Matthew J. Ouimet, "All That Custom Has Divided: National Interest and the Secret Demise of the Brezhnev Doctrine, 1968–1981" (Ph.D. diss., University of Washington, 1997), 115–136, 209–211; Mark Kramer, "Ukraine and the Soviet-Czechoslovak Crisis of 1968 (Part 1): New Evidence from the Diary of Petro Shelest," *CWIHPB* 10 (March 1998): 234–47; idem, "The Czechoslovak Crisis and the Brezhnev Doctrine," in *1968: The World Transformed*, ed. Carole Fink, Philipp Gassert, and Detlef Junker (New York, 1998), 141–145, 156–171.

128. Eugene Rostow, Oral History, 2 December 1968, 24, LBJL; Memorandum of Conversation between Anatoly Dobrynin, Dean Rusk, and Llewellyn Thompson, 23 August 1968, *FRUS* 1964–68, 17: 254–257; Walt Rostow to President Johnson, 31 August 1968, ibid., 263–264; Anatoly Dobrynin, *In Confidence: Moscow's Ambassador to America's Six Cold War Presidents, 1962–1986* (New York, 1995), 156–158.

129. Summary of Meeting between President Johnson, Walt Rostow, and Soviet Ambassador Dobrynin, 20 August 1968, *FRUS* 1964–68, 17: 236–241; Notes of Cabinet Meeting, 22 August 1968, ibid., 248–249; Dobrynin, *In Confidence*, 177–186.

130. Quotation from Soviet Foreign Ministry Memorandum, partially reprinted in Dobrynin, *In Confidence*, 157. Dobrynin reports that in 1967 and 1968 this document "served as the basis for Soviet foreign policy toward the United States"; ibid., 156–158, 185–186. See also Gaiduk, *Soviet Union and Vietnam War*, 156–193. During the June 1967 meetings between President Johnson and Aleksei Kosygin (chairman of the Soviet Council of Ministers), Moscow's representative attempted to help mediate an end to the Vietnam War; Memorandum of Conversation between Johnson and Kosygin, 23 June 1967, 3:44–4:35 P.M., *FRUS* 1964–68, 14: 531–536.

131. Memorandum of Conversation between McGeorge Bundy and Anatoly Dobrynin, 26 April 1968, ibid., 643–46; Walt Rostow to President Johnson, 31 August 1968, ibid., 17: 263–265; Schwartz, *In the Shadow of Vietnam*, chap. 5.

132. Stefan Kisielewski quoted in Jerzy Eisler, "March 1968 in Poland," in Fink, Gassert, and Junker, *1968*, 245; Text presented to students gathering on the campus of Warsaw University, 8 March 1968, in Peter Raina, *Political Opposition in Poland, 1954–1977* (London, 1978), 126.

133. Grzegorz Ekiert and Jan Kubik, *Rebellious Civil Society: Popular Protest and Democratic Consolidation in Poland, 1989–1993* (Ann Arbor, 1999), 26–31; Keith John Lepak, *Prelude to Solidarity: Poland and the Politics of the Gierek Regime* (New York, 1988), 37; Roman Laba, *The Roots of Solidarity: A Political Sociology of Poland's Working-Class Democratization* (Princeton, 1991), 15–17; Wlodzimierz Brus, "1966 to 1975: Normalization to Conflict," in *The Economic History of Eastern Europe, 1919–1975*, ed. M. C. Kaser (Oxford, 1986), 194–197.

134. Eisler, "March 1968 in Poland," 238–241, 248–251; David Ost, *Solidarity and the Politics of Anti-Politics: Opposition and Reform in Poland since 1968* (Philadelphia, 1990), 49–53.

135. Stanislaw Michel quoted in Laba, *The Roots of Solidarity*, 20.

136. Ekiert and Kubik, *Rebellious Civil Society*, 35.

137. Laba, *The Roots of Solidarity*, 34, 61.

138. Timothy Garton Ash refers to this as Gierek's "great leap"; *The Polish Revolution: Solidarity, 1980–82* (London, 1983), 13–17.

139. Robert V. Roosa, Armin Gutowski, and Michiya Matsukawa, *East-West Trade at a Crossroads: Economic Relations with the Soviet Union and Eastern Europe* (New York, 1982), 14–15. In January 1949 the Soviet Union, Bulgaria, Hungary, Poland, Rumania, and Czechoslovakia formed the CMEA. East Germany entered the CMEA in September 1950. On the CMEA reforms of the 1960s see Randall W. Stone, *Satellites and Commissars: Strategy and Conflict in the Politics of Soviet-Bloc Trade* (Princeton, 1996), 33–39.

140. Between 1970 and 1975 Polish hard-currency debt rose from $1.1 billion to $7.7 billion. During this period the total hard-currency debt of the Soviet bloc grew from $7 billion to $29 billion. By 1980 Soviet-bloc debt ballooned to $62.9 billion. See Benjamin J. Cohen, *In Whose Interest? International Banking and American Foreign Policy* (New Haven, 1986), 181. On the growth in Polish per-capita personal consumption see Cal Clark and John M. Echols III, "Developed Socialism and Consumption Policies in the Soviet Bloc: An Empirical Evaluation," in *Developed Socialism in the Soviet Bloc: Political Theory and Political Reality*, ed. Jim Seroka and Maurice D. Simon (Boulder, 1982), 165.

141. Cohen, *In Whose Interest?* 182.

142. Garton Ash, *The Polish Revolution*, 17–28; Lepak, *Prelude to Solidarity*, 144–164.

143. Arthur Burns, chairman of the Federal Reserve, wrote President Nixon that the United States "faces an entirely new economic problem—one that our nation has never before had to face: namely, an inflation feeding on itself at a time of substantial unemployment." During a series of trips to the Soviet bloc, Burns offered a partial solution to American economic difficulties through increased trade with the communist states; large Western loans to the Soviet bloc would reduce inflation in the United States and finance more job-creating American exports. See Burns to Nixon, 22 June 1971, folder: Nixon, Richard—Outgoing, 199-6/1971, box N1, Arthur Burns Papers, Gerald R. Ford Presidential Library, Ann Arbor, Michigan; Burns to Winston Lord, 11 April 1974, folder: State Department, January–September 1974, box B97, ibid.

144. Richard Nixon, *Six Crises* (Garden City, N.Y., 1962), 235–291; Walter Hixson, *Parting the Curtain: Propaganda, Culture, and the Cold War, 1945–1961* (New York, 1997), 176–183.

145. Quoted in Stephen Ambrose, *Nixon* (New York, 1987), 1: 526.

146. See the data on nuclear weapons stockpiles provided by the National Resources Defense Council, www.nrdc.org. See also Melvin Small, *The Presidency of Richard Nixon* (Lawrence, Kans., 1999), 109–110; David Holloway, *The Soviet Union and the Arms Race*, 2d ed. (New Haven, 1984), 87–88.

147. On the evidence of declining American power in the late 1960s see George Herring, "Tet and the Crisis of Hegemony," in Fink, Gassert, and Junker, *1968*, 31–53; Paul Kennedy, *The Rise and Fall of the Great Powers: Economic Change and Military Conflict from 1500 to 2000* (New York, 1987), 413–437; Robert M. Collins, "The Economic Crisis of 1968 and the Waning of the 'American Century,'" *American Historical Review* 101 (April 1996): 396–422.

148. Kissinger, *White House Years*, 62. See also Gaddis, "Rescuing Choice from Circumstance," 564–592; Isaacson, *Kissinger*, 66, 761.

149. William Hyland, *Mortal Rivals: Superpower Relations from Nixon to Reagan* (New York, 1987), 19.

150. Kissinger, *White House Years*, 54; Gaddis, "Rescuing Choice from Circumstance," 572–575.

151. Notes from Conversation between Michael Palliser and Henry Kissinger, 19 December 1968, PREM 13/2097, PRO; Kissinger, *White House Years*, 129–138; Gaddis, *Strategies of Containment*, 289–305.

152. Dobrynin, *In Confidence*, 198–208; Kissinger, *White House Years*, 138–147.

153. Memorandum of Conversation between Kissinger and Dobrynin, 17 August 1971, in Burr, *The Kissinger Transcripts*, 45.

154. The quotations come from a report written by Georgi Arbatov, then director of the Soviet Union's Institute for the Study of the United States and Canada, cited in Garthoff, *Détente and Confrontation*, 273.

155. Kissinger, *White House Years*, 766–767.

156. Garthoff, *Détente and Confrontation*, 277–278.

157. Zhai, *China and the Vietnam Wars*, 193–208; Gaiduk, *Soviet Union and Vietnam War*, 244–250; Dobrynin, *In Confidence*, 243–250, 260–264; Garthoff, *Détente and Confrontation*, 281–294. William Bundy argues that Moscow and Beijing did not contribute to a settlement in Vietnam, but rather "stood aside" as Washington and Hanoi negotiated; *A Tangled Web*, 371. I would argue that "standing aside" created strong pressures for Hanoi to complete a settlement. Hanoi recognized that without a settlement it might lose its foreign support.

158. H. R. Haldeman, diary entries for 17 and 19 July 1971, *The Haldeman Diaries: Inside the Nixon White House* (New York, 1995), 389, 391.

159. Kimball, *Nixon's Vietnam War*, 302, 305.

160. Lewis Sorley, *Thunderbolt: From the Battle of the Bulge to Vietnam and Beyond: General Creighton Abrams and the Army of His Times* (New York, 1992), 322; Bundy, *A Tangled Web*, 315.

161. Quotation from Nixon, *RN*, 594. See also Kimball, *Nixon's Vietnam War*, 312.

162. Bundy, *A Tangled Web*, 316–318; Kimball, *Nixon's Vietnam War*, 307, 311–316.

163. Dobrynin, *In Confidence*, 246–249; Garthoff, *Détente and Confrontation*, 290–292.

164. Kissinger, *White House Years*, 1252–57; idem, *Diplomacy* (New York, 1994), 761.

165. Kissinger, *White House Years*, 1252–57.

166. On the limited scope of SALT I and the ABM treaty see Hyland, *Mortal Rivals*, 54–55.

167. The accounts offered by Henry Kissinger and Anatoly Dobrynin confirm this analysis, with a less critical tone; Kissinger, *White House Years*, 1252–57; Dobrynin, *In Confidence*, 251–257.

168. "Basic Principles of Relations between the United States of America and the Union of Soviet Socialist Republics," 29 May 1972, *U.S. Department of State Bulletin* 66 (26 June 1972): 898–899.

169. Nixon, "The Moscow Summit: New Opportunities in U.S.-Soviet Relations," 1 June 1972, speech delivered before a joint session of Congress, ibid., 855–859; Kissinger, News Conference, 29 May 1972, ibid, 890–897.

170. "Basic Principles of Relations between United States and Union of Soviet Socialist Republics."

171. Kissinger, News Conference, 29 May 1972, 892. The literature on the role of moral and political values in foreign policy is enormous. For two representative works see Michael H. Hunt, *Ideology and U.S. Foreign Policy* (New Haven, 1987), 1–18, 125–170; Vladislav Zubok and Constantine Pleshakov, *Inside the Kremlin's Cold War: From Stalin to Khrushchev* (Cambridge, Mass., 1996), 1–8.

172. Kissinger, News Conference, 29 May 1972, 896.

173. See Kissinger, *White House Years,* 1252–57; idem, *Diplomacy,* 56–77, 703–761.

174. See Kissinger, News Conference, 29 May 1972, 892, 896; Garthoff, *Détente and Confrontation,* 1144–46. On the subjective qualities of "national interest," see Frank Ninkovich, "Interests and Discourse in Diplomatic History," *Diplomatic History* 13 (Spring 1989): 135–161; Anders Stephanson, *Kennan and the Art of Foreign Policy* (Cambridge, Mass., 1989), 176–207; Gaddis, *Strategies of Containment,* 288.

175. On the transformation of political protest into cultural dissent see Barbara Epstein, *Political Protest and Cultural Revolution: Nonviolent Direct Action in the 1970s and 1980s* (Berkeley, 1991), 21–57. A number of scholars have documented the precipitous decline of public trust in government since the 1960s. Authors differ in their assessments of the causes and implications, but they almost universally agree that citizens throughout North America, Europe, and Asia have expressed much more dissatisfaction with their governments since the years of detente. See Ronald Inglehart, *The Silent Revolution: Changing Values and Political Styles among Western Publics* (Princeton, 1977), 3–71; Dieter Fuchs and Hans-Dieter Klingemann, "Citizens and the State: A Relationship Transformed," in *Citizens and the State,* ed. Fuchs and Klingemann (Oxford, 1995), 419–443; Robert D. Putnam, Susan J. Pharr, and Russell J. Dalton, "What's Troubling the Trilateral Democracies?" in *Disaffected Democracies: What's Troubling the Trilateral Countries,* ed. Susan J. Pharr and Robert D. Putnam (Princeton, 2000), 3–27; Joseph S. Nye Jr., "The Decline of Confidence in Government," and Gary Orren, "Fall From Grace: The Public's Loss of Faith in Government," in *Why People Don't Trust Government,* ed. Joseph S. Nye Jr., Philip D. Zelikow, and David King (Cambridge, Mass., 1997), 1–18, 77–107.

176. "Postmodern" thinkers seem to share a revulsion toward "modern" projects for centralized, state-directed social reform. They also tend to view great-power politics as inherently repressive and corrupt. I believe that these common elements of thought reflect the anger and frustration born of the protests in the late 1960s and the subsequent workings of detente. My attempt to historicize postmodernism draws on Hans Bertens, *The Idea of the Postmodern: A History* (New York, 1995), 3–52; Martin Jay, *Downcast Eyes: The Denigration of Vision in Twentieth-Century French Thought* (Berkeley, 1993), 329–594; Jürgen Habermas, *The Philosophical Discourse of Modernity: Twelve Lectures,* trans. Frederick G. Lawrence (Cambridge, Mass., 1987), 161–293; James C. Scott, *Seeing like a State: How Certain Schemes to Improve the Human Condition Have Failed* (New Haven, 1998), 87–179, 309–357.

CONCLUSION

1. Historians have made similar arguments about the periods following World Wars I and II. See Arno J. Mayer, *Politics and Diplomacy of Peacemaking: Containment and Counterrevolution at Versailles, 1918–1919* (New York, 1967), 3–30; Charles S. Maier, *Recasting Bourgeois Europe: Stabilization in France, Germany, and Italy in the Decade after World War I* (Princeton,

1988), 481–594; idem, *In Search of Stability: Explorations in Historical Political Economy* (Cambridge, 1987), 261–273.

2. See Kristin L. Hoganson, *Fighting for American Manhood: How Gender Politics Provoked the Spanish-American and Philippine-American Wars* (New Haven, 1998); Emily S. Rosenberg, *Financial Missionaries to the World: The Politics and Culture of Dollar Diplomacy, 1900–1930* (Cambridge, Mass., 1999); John Milton Cooper Jr., *The Warrior and the Priest: Woodrow Wilson and Theodore Roosevelt* (Cambridge, Mass., 1983).

3. See Arthur Marwick, *The Sixties: Cultural Revolution in Britain, France, Italy, and the United States, c. 1958–c. 1974* (Oxford, 1998), 801–806; William Julius Wilson, *The Truly Disadvantaged: The Inner City, the Underclass, and Public Policy* (Chicago, 1987), 20–62; Paul Kennedy, *Preparing for the Twenty-first Century* (New York, 1993), 193–227.

4. See Fritz W. Scharpf, *Governing in Europe: Effective and Democratic?* (Oxford, 1999), 6–42, 187–204; Philippe C. Schmitter, *How to Democratize the European Union . . . and Why Bother?* (Lanham, Md., 2000), 1–19.

5. Christopher Lasch, *The Culture of Narcissism: American Life in an Age of Diminishing Expectations* (New York, 1978), 3–7, 31–51.

SOURCES

ARCHIVAL MATERIALS

France

Archives of Contemporary History, Center for the History of Europe in the Twentieth Century, National Foundation for the Study of Politics, Paris
    Papers of Hubert Beuve-Méry
    Papers of Maurice Couve de Murville

Archives of the French Foreign Ministry, Paris
    Series: Asia, 1956–67
    Series: Europe, 1961–70

Raymond Aron Center for Political Research, School of Advanced Studies in the Social Sciences, Paris
    Papers of Raymond Aron

Center for Contemporary Archives, Fontainebleau
    Archives of the National Education Ministry

National Archives, Paris
    78 AJ 33–37: Events of May 1968
    78 AJ 52–57: Michel Quétin Collection

National Library, François Mitterrand location, Paris
    Tracts of May 1968

Germany

Chancellor Konrad Adenauer Foundation, Rhöndorf
    Papers of Konrad Adenauer

Archives of the Foreign Ministry, Bonn
    B2: Office of the State Secretary
    IIA1: Reunification
    IIA6: America
    IIA6: East-West Trade

Archives of the Social Democratic Party, Friedrich-Ebert-Stiftung, Bonn
    Papers of Egon Bahr
    Papers of Willy Brandt

National Archives, Berlin-Lichterfelde (Archives for the German Democratic Republic and Archives for the Parties and Mass Organizations of the German Democratic Republic)
    Foreign Policy Commission of the Socialist Unity Party
    Ministry of Internal Affairs

Office of Erich Honecker
Papers of Walter Ulbricht
People's Legislature

National Archives, Koblenz
B 136: Chancellor's Office
B 137: Ministry for All-German Questions
N 1174: Papers of Franz Thedieck
N 1239: Papers of Heinrich von Brentano
N 1266: Papers of Walter Hallstein
N 1351: Papers of Herbert Blankenhorn
N 1357: Papers of Karl Carstens

Great Britain

Bodleian Library, Oxford
Papers of Paul Gore-Booth

Churchill Archives Center, Churchill College, Cambridge
Papers of Archibald Fenner Brockway
Papers of A. V. Hill
Papers of Selwyn Lloyd
Papers of Michael Stewart
Papers of Patrick Gordon Walker

Public Records Office, Kew, London
CAB 128: Records of Cabinet Meetings
CAB 129: Cabinet Papers
CAB 148: Records of the Defense and Overseas Policy Committee
CO 1030: Colonial Office Papers
DEFE 4: Records of the Defense Chiefs of Staff
DEFE 10: Records of the Defense Council
FCO 7, 21, 33, 34: Foreign and Commonwealth Office Files
FO371: Foreign Office Files
HF 1: Ministry of Technology Papers
PREM 11, 13: Prime Minister's Papers

Hungary

Open Society Archives, Central European University, Budapest
Records of Radio Free Europe / Radio Liberty

Russia

Russian State Archive of Contemporary History (RGANI), Moscow
Fond 5: Soviet cultural and propaganda policies, 1953–1983
Fond 89: Politburo and Central Committee documents, 1953–1991

Russian State Archive of Socio-Political History (RGASPI), Moscow
Fond 17: Obkom (Provincial) Party affairs, 1917–1991

United States

Amherst College Archives and Special Collections
  Papers of John J. McCloy

Council on Foreign Relations Archives, New York City
  Records of Study Groups

Dwight D. Eisenhower Presidential Library, Abilene, Kansas
  Papers of John Foster Dulles
  Papers of Christian A. Herter
  Papers of the Special Assistant to the White House for Science and Technology
  Papers of the U.S. President's Science Advisory Committee
  Papers of the White House Office, Office of National Security Affairs
  Papers of the White House Office, Office of the Staff Secretary
  Ann Whitman Files

Gerald R. Ford Presidential Library, Ann Arbor, Michigan
  Henry Kissinger and Brent Scowcroft Temporary Parallel Files
  Papers of Arthur F. Burns
  White House Central Files

Harvard University Archives
  Papers of James B. Conant

Hoover Institution Archives, Stanford, California
  French Subject Collection
  German Subject Collection
  Papers of Edward G. Lansdale
  Papers of Richard Nixon

Hoover Institution Library, Stanford, California
  Underground Press Collection

Lyndon B. Johnson Presidential Library, Austin, Texas
  Meeting Notes Files
  National Security Files
  Papers of George Ball
  Papers of McGeorge Bundy
  Papers of William P. Bundy
  Papers of Tom Johnson
  Recordings of Telephone Conversations

John F. Kennedy Presidential Library, Boston, Massachusetts
  National Security Files
  Papers of John Kenneth Galbraith
  Papers of Arthur Schlesinger Jr.
  Papers of John C. Thomson Jr.
  President's Office Files

Library of Congress, Manuscript Reading Room, Washington, D.C.
  Papers of W. Averell Harriman
  Papers of the NAACP
  Papers of Paul H. Nitze

Seeley Mudd Manuscript Library, Princeton University
    Council on Foreign Relations Archive
    Papers of the ACLU
    Papers and Journals of Hamilton Fish Armstrong
    Papers of George Ball
    Papers of Jacob Beam
    Papers of Allen Dulles
    Papers of John Foster Dulles
    Papers of Freedom House–George Field
    Papers of George Kennan
    Papers of Arthur Krock
    Papers of Adlai Stevenson
    William Trimble Diaries

National Archives, College Park, Maryland
    Record Group 59, State Department Papers
    Papers of Charles Bohlen
    Nixon Presidential Materials
        National Security Files
        White House Central Files
        White House Special Files

National Security Archive, George Washington University
    Berlin Crisis Collection
    Cuban Missile Crisis Collection
    Nuclear History Collection
    Papers of Edward G. Lansdale
    Presidential Directives Collection
    United States, China, and the Bomb Collection

Radcliffe Institute, Arthur and Elizabeth Schlesinger Library, Cambridge, Massachusetts
    Papers of Betty Friedan

Sterling Memorial Library, Yale University
    Students for a Democratic Society Microfilm Collection

United States Information Agency, Washington, D.C.
    Papers of Charles Z. Wick

University of Wisconsin–Madison Archives
    Campus Disruptions Photograph Files
    Name Files
    Subject Files

Virginia Historical Society, Richmond
    David Bruce Diaries

Wisconsin Historical Society, Madison
    Michael Fellner Collection
    J. Wesley Miller Collection
    Name Files
    Gary Schulz Collection

Social Action Collection
Students for a Democratic Society Collection

Yale University Library, Manuscripts and Archives
Papers of Dean Acheson
Papers of Hanson Baldwin
Papers of Chester Bowles
Papers of William F. Buckley Jr.
Papers of Abe Fortas
Papers of Walter Lippmann

SELECTED READINGS

Alexeyeva, Ludmilla, and Paul Goldberg. *The Thaw Generation: Coming of Age in the Post-Stalin Era.* Pittsburgh: University of Pittsburgh, 1990.

Berman, Paul. *A Tale of Two Utopias: The Political Journey of the Generation of 1968.* New York: W. W. Norton, 1996.

Bundy, William. *A Tangled Web: The Making of Foreign Policy in the Nixon Presidency.* New York: Hill and Wang, 1998.

Carter, Dan T. *The Politics of Rage: George Wallace, the Origins of the New Conservatism, and the Transformation of American Politics.* New York: Simon and Schuster, 1995.

Fink, Carole, Philipp Gassert, and Detlef Junker, eds. *1968: The World Transformed.* New York: Cambridge University Press, 1998.

Gaddis, John Lewis. *Strategies of Containment: A Critical Appraisal of Postwar American National Security Policy.* New York: Oxford University Press, 1982.

Gaiduk, Ilya V. *The Soviet Union and the Vietnam War.* Chicago: Ivan R. Dee, 1996.

Gardner, Lloyd C. *Pay Any Price: Lyndon Johnson and the Wars for Vietnam.* Chicago: Ivan R. Dee, 1995.

Garthoff, Raymond L. *Détente and Confrontation: American-Soviet Relations from Nixon to Reagan.* Rev. ed. Washington, D.C.: Brookings Institution, 1994.

Gitlin, Todd. *The Sixties: Years of Hope, Days of Rage.* New York: Bantam, 1987.

Gosse, Van. *Where the Boys Are: Cuba, Cold War America, and the Making of a New Left.* New York: Verso, 1993.

Isserman, Maurice. *If I Had a Hammer: The Death of the Old Left and the Birth of the New Left.* Urbana: University of Illinois Press, 1987.

Isserman, Maurice, and Michael Kazin. *America Divided: The Civil War of the 1960s.* New York: Oxford University Press, 2000.

Kimball, Jeffrey. *Nixon's Vietnam War.* Lawrence: University Press of Kansas, 1998.

Logevall, Fredrik. *Choosing War: The Lost Chance for Peace and the Escalation of War in Vietnam.* Berkeley: University of California Press, 1999.

MacFarquhar, Roderick. *The Origins of the Cultural Revolution.* 3 vols. New York: Columbia University Press, 1974–1997.

Marwick, Arthur. *The Sixties: Cultural Revolution in Britain, France, Italy, and the United States, c. 1958–c. 1974.* Oxford: Oxford University Press, 1998.

Paterson, Thomas G. *Contesting Castro: The United States and the Triumph of the Cuban Revolution.* New York: Oxford University Press, 1994.

Rorabaugh, W. J. *Berkeley at War: The 1960s.* New York: Oxford University Press, 1989.

Sarotte, M. E. *Dealing with the Devil: East Germany, Détente, and Ostpolitik, 1969–1973.* Chapel Hill: University of North Carolina Press, 2001.

Schwarz, Hans-Peter. *Adenauer: Der Staatsmann, 1952–1967.* Stuttgart: Deutsche Verlags-Anstalt, 1991.

Schwartz, Thomas Alan. *In the Shadow of Vietnam: Lyndon Johnson and Europe.* Cambridge, Mass.: Harvard University Press, 2003.

Skilling, H. Gordon. *Czechoslovakia's Interrupted Revolution.* Princeton: Princeton University Press, 1976.

Trachtenberg, Marc. *A Constructed Peace: The Making of the European Settlement, 1945–1963.* Princeton: Princeton University Press, 1999.

Tyson, Timothy B. *Radio Free Dixie: Robert F. Williams and the Roots of Black Power.* Chapel Hill: University of North Carolina Press, 1999.

Vaïsse, Maurice. *La grandeur: Politique étrangère du général de Gaulle, 1958–1969.* Paris: Fayard, 1998.

Wang Shaoguang. *Failure of Charisma: The Cultural Revolution in Wuhan.* New York: Oxford University Press, 1995.

Williams, Kieran. *The Prague Spring and Its Aftermath: Czechoslovak politics, 1968–1970.* New York: Cambridge University Press, 1997.

Zhai, Qiang. *China and the Vietnam Wars, 1950–1975.* Chapel Hill: University of North Carolina Press, 2000.

Zubok, Vladislav, and Constantine Pleshakov. *Inside the Kremlin's Cold War: From Stalin to Khrushchev.* Cambridge, Mass.: Harvard University Press, 1996.

INDEX

ABM treaty, 256. *See also* Missiles
Abrams, Creighton, 161, 254–255
Acheson, Dean, 12–13, 57, 133
"Action Program" (Czechoslovakia), 199, 201
Adenauer, Konrad: and de Gaulle, 56–58, 60; early detente efforts by, 3, 8, 25–30, 34–35, 43, 45, 54, 216, 226, 228, 279n78; and West Berlin, 173
The Affluent Society (Galbraith), 96–97, 100
Africa, 51, 104, 132. *See also Specific African countries*
Akademgorodok (Soviet academic center), 89
Akhmatova, Anna, 109
Albertz, Heinrich, 178
Algerian War, 51–52, 57–58, 60, 73, 260
"America House" (West Berlin), 175–176
Antiballistic missile defense system. *See* Missiles
Anti-Semitism, 248
Appy, Christian, 309n11
Arbatov, Georgi, 331n154
Arendt, Hannah, 79
Arms control agreements, 3, 9–11, 14, 25–28, 251–253, 256, 261. *See also* Disarmament
Armstrong, Hamilton Fish, 302n22
Aron, Raymond, 292n14
Art (Marcuse on), 125–126
Australia, 70
Ayub, Mohammed, 230

Bachmann, Josef, 181
Bahr, Egon, 24–25, 216–226, 228
Baklanov, Gregori, 296n62
"Balance of order," 216
Ball, George, 21, 59, 151

Balzac, Honoré de, 125
Bao Dai (Vietnamese emperor), 136–137
Barzel, Rainer, 222
"The Basic Principles of Relations between the United States of America and the Union of Soviet Socialist Republics," 256–258
Bay of Pigs invasion (Cuba), 39
Beam, Jacob, 197
Beatles, 109, 127, 211
Beijing Evening News (Beijing wanbao), 118
Belgium, 78
Bell, Daniel, 94–96, 123
Ben Gurion, David, 50
Berkeley (California), 166–172, 185, 261, 309n11
Berkeley Barb, 169–171
Berlin, Isaiah, 111–112
Berlin crises, 3, 23–25, 34–35, 39, 42, 54, 173, 226, 260. *See also* Berlin Wall; East Berlin; West Berlin
Berlin Wall: construction of, 23–25, 34, 173, 178, 179; cultural exchanges across, 3, 5, 28, 173, 218, 221–223
Bikini Atoll, 9
Black Panther Party, 172, 181, 310n28
Böker, Alexander, 323n48
Bowles, Chester, 72
Bozell, Brent L., 294n40
Brandeis University, 122, 127
Brandt, Willy, 1, 24, 240, 323n48; and detente, 4–5, 8, 30, 216–226, 261
Brezhnev, Leonid, 110, 247, 250, 261; and domestic upheaval, 2, 121, 163; and East Germany, 224–225; Nixon's meeting with, 253–258; and "Prague Spring," 197–200, 202–206, 210, 212, 246. *See also* Brezhnev Doctrine

Brezhnev Doctrine, 206, 246
Buckley, William F., Jr., 99–100, 105
Bulgaria, 203, 219, 330n139
Bundy, McGeorge, 57–58, 143, 152–154, 157, 158, 247
Bundy, William, 154, 331n157
Bunker, Ellsworth, 160
Burns, Arthur, 330n143
Bush, George W., 264

Cambodia, 81, 136, 154, 157, 237
Camus, Albert, 123
Canada, 70
Cao Diqiu, 298n104
Carmichael, Stokely, 172, 183
Carstens, Karl, 28
Castro, Fidel, 39, 40, 128, 179–180
CCP (Chinese Communist Party), 61–74, 80–83, 85, 86, 208, 233
CDU. *See* Christian Democratic Union (West Germany)
CEA (Commissariat à l'Energie Atomique), 49–50, 75
Ceauşescu, Nicolae, 205
Central Intelligence Agency. *See* CIA
Chan, Anna, 319n3
Charisma: Che Guevara's, 171–172; defined, 44; de Gaulle's, 44–48, 51, 55–60, 84–87, 120, 186, 190–191, 193–194, 260; Kennedy and Khrushchev's, 260; lack of, among today's leaders, 259; as leading to disillusionment of people, 3, 15–25, 86–87, 260; Mao's, 61, 71, 80, 83–87, 120–121, 130, 237, 260; Nixon's lack of, 5; secrecy's role in maintaining, 237, 244–245; of 1960s intellectuals, 93–94; as source of authority, 44–46, 190–191, 193–194, 236–237; Stalin's, 64
Charles University (Prague), 196
Chen Yi, 72, 74, 75, 86, 231, 234–235, 326n80; and dissidents, 118; and France, 80, 81, 83, 291n131
Chiang Kai-shek, 74, 136
Chicago (Illinois), 182
China (People's Republic of): Anti-Rightist Campaign in, 93; attempts of, to transcend great-power stalemate, 3, 5, 8, 43, 44–45, 58, 74–79; detente in, 226–245; dissent in, 114–121, 130; and East Germany, 227, 229, 231; educational reform in, 91–93; and France, 3, 27, 45, 61, 67, 71, 73–87, 227, 229, 238; and Great Britain, 74–75, 229; and India, 36–38; and Korean War, 62; Mao's domestic goals for, 61–64, 67–71; Marcuse on, 127–129; nuclear arms of, 3, 75–77, 154, 215, 235–236; and overseas radicals, 210–211; political recognition of, by Western countries, 5, 74, 214, 228, 229, 240, 241, 244; "reeducation" in, 209–210; and Soviet Union, 27–28, 34–39, 41, 43, 61–67, 72, 73, 75–79, 205, 206, 227, 228, 234–238, 246, 261; and Taiwan, 62, 71, 72, 226–227, 239, 243, 244; and Tibet, 36, 62; and United States, 5, 71–73, 75, 77–79, 227, 228–245, 252–254, 258, 261; and Vietnam, 5, 73, 78, 132–134, 136, 138, 154, 159, 163, 228–230, 235, 237, 243, 254, 261; and West Germany, 226–228, 230, 261. *See also* CCP; Cultural Revolution; Great Leap Forward; Korean War; Mao Zedong; Taiwan; *Specific Chinese leaders*
Chomsky, Noam, 308n5
Christian Democratic Union (CDU—West Germany), 58, 174, 220, 222–223
Christian Social Union (West Germany), 222
Churchill, Winston, 9
CIA (Central Intelligence Agency), 2, 39, 72, 74, 129, 313n88
Civil rights movement (United States), 3, 88, 94, 102–105, 146, 148, 168, 171, 172, 181–183, 185; international dimensions of, 103–104, 126; opposition to, 101, 181. *See also* Black Panther Party
CMEA (Council for Mutual Economic Assistance), 249, 330n139
Coal and Steel Community, 50
Cohn-Bendit, Daniel, 187, 189
Cold War stalemate (between great powers): detente's normalizing of, 5, 43, 45, 59–60, 95–96, 205, 214, 224, 226, 240, 245, 255–261; Khrushchev's call for end

of, 42; and Nixon's "triangular diplomacy," 5, 235–237, 252–254; as repressing citizens, 3, 4–5, 11, 45, 92, 94–96, 99–130, 164, 177–179, 211; as restricting great powers' flexibility, 1, 5, 8, 41–43, 87; as shifting wars to Third World, 133, 245–246. *See also* Detente; Nuclear arms

Commissariat à l'Energie Atomique (CEA—France), 49–50, 75

Committee on National Defense (France), 47–48

Common Market (European), 50, 55, 56, 60. *See also* European Economic Community

Communist countries: domestic upheaval in, 64–65, 67, 105–114; lack of democracy in former, 263; opposition to, in United States, 100–102, 135; Soviet Union's retreat from allies in, 43, 249–250; Western political recognition of, 5, 34, 136, 214, 228, 229, 240, 241, 244. *See also Names of specific communist countries*

Communist Youth League (*Komsomol*), 112, 113

Conant, James, 89–91, 125

Congo, 126

Congress on Racial Equality (CORE), 104, 167–168

Conrad, Joseph, 41

The Conscience of a Conservative (Goldwater), 100–101, 294n40

Consensus, 264–265; force as demonstrating leaders' inability to achieve, 191–194, 203–206, 211–212

Cooperation. *See* Detente

CORE. *See* Congress on Racial Equality

Council for Mutual Economic Assistance (CMEA), 249, 330n139

Council of Ministers (France), 47–48

Couve de Murville, Maurice, 72, 78–79, 84, 290n130

"Critical theorists," 121–129, 179

Cronkite, Walter, 162

Cuba: and Guevara, 210; Marcuse on, 127, 128; missile crisis in, 3, 8, 38–43, 59, 156, 173, 216, 245, 260. *See also* Castro, Fidel

Cultural Revolution (China), 64, 79, 261; disillusionment following, 319n3; language of dissent leading to, 3, 114–121; Mao's encouragement of, 1, 3, 64, 65, 80–83, 85, 119–121, 128–130, 207, 210, 229, 230, 261; Mao's fleeing from, 1, 208, 318n180; Mao's suppression of, 207, 208–212, 231–235, 238, 239, 261; Marcuse on, 127–129; parallels of, with French revolutions, 81–84; as time of domestic upheaval in China, 1, 80–83, 85–86, 119–120, 130, 166, 193, 206–211, 227, 229–232, 241–242. *See also* Red Guards; Revolution

Cutler, Robert, 12

Czechoslovak Communist Party, 195, 197–204, 206

Czechoslovakia, 220, 225, 256, 330n139; "Prague Spring" in, 194–206, 210, 221, 222, 246–247, 261

Czechoslovak Union of Women, 195

Czechoslovak Union of Youth, 195

Czechoslovak Writers' Congress, 194, 200

Czech Technical College, 196

Dalai Lama, 36

Davydov, Boris, 235–236

"Declaration of the Grand Coalition" (West Germany), 220

De Gaulle, Charles: attempts of, to transcend great-power stalemate, 3, 5, 8, 43, 44–61, 73–79; charisma of, 44–48, 51, 55–60, 84–87, 120, 186, 190–191, 193–194, 260; and China, 3, 27, 45, 61, 67, 71, 73–87; and domestic upheaval in France, 1, 46, 84–85, 88, 130, 186–194, 211, 212; and Eastern European states, 219; and United States, 29; and Vietnam, 133

Democratic Republic of Vietnam. *See* North Vietnam

Demonstrations. *See* Domestic upheaval

Deng Tuo, 63, 118, 120

Deng Xiaoping, 81

De-Stalinization. *See* Stalin, Josef: later criticism of

Detente (Collaboration; Cooperation): Adenauer's early attempts at, 25–30, 34–35, 54; and balance of power considerations, 2, 23–25, 27–29, 39–43, 52–53, 77, 215–216, 250–258; de Gaulle's attempts at, 54; domestic repression as accompanying, 2, 4, 5, 23–25, 44, 177, 186, 188, 213, 216, 221–226, 231, 241–242, 256, 258–259, 261, 264, 322n41; as leading to people's political disengagement, 5, 214–215; as legitimating leaders' domestic authority, 213–215, 232, 236–237, 240, 244–245, 247, 250, 254–259, 261; as making Cold War stalemate permanent, 5, 43, 45, 59–60, 95–96, 205, 214, 224, 226, 240, 245, 255–261; as motivated by domestic upheaval, 4–5, 212, 213–260; as producing domestic upheaval, 43, 44, 258, 263–264. *See also* Non-aggression pacts; Ostpolitik

Detroit (Michigan), 160, 182

Dewey, John, 123

Diem, Ngo Dinh, 21, 136–140, 142–145, 151

Diem, Nhu, 144

Dien Bien Phu (Vietnam), 73, 135, 136

Dimitriu, Dr., 323n47

Dimona nuclear facility (Israel), 49–50

Diplomacy. *See* Foreign policy

Disarmament, 3, 54

Disillusionment: detente's role in people's, 5, 94–96, 214–215, 258–259, 263–265; political leaders' role in, 5, 105–109, 130, 163, 165, 203–206, 259, 260; in post-Cultural Revolution China, 319n3; television's role in, 102; youth's feelings of, about leaders' promises, 88, 93, 100, 104–105, 109–114, 127, 129–130, 160, 162, 165, 260–264. *See also* Domestic upheaval; Expectations

Dissent (language of), 3, 88–130, 162, 165, 167, 261. *See also* Domestic upheaval; Expectations

Dobrynin, Anatoly, 246, 252–253, 331n167

Domestic upheaval: as bringing about detente, 4–5, 212, 213–261; causes of 1960s, 1, 3–4, 43, 86–89, 93–94, 96, 100, 104–105, 109–110, 112, 129–130, 160, 162–163, 165–166, 179, 211–212, 247; detente as producing, 43, 44, 258, 263–264; against "globalization," 263; as global phenomenon in the 1960s, 1–4, 85–86, 129, 130, 162–212, 235, 261; as threatening great powers' leadership, 1–2, 4–5, 164, 166, 179, 182–183, 186–194, 196–211, 216, 220–221, 223, 224, 235–237, 245; against United States' involvement in Vietnam War, 3–4, 126, 159–161, 168–172, 181–182, 187–188, 221, 251. *See also* Disillusionment; Dissent; Force; Revolution; Youth

Dubček, Alexander, 197, 198–203, 205, 206

Duc, Thich Quang, 142

Dulles, John Foster, 10, 12, 241

Dutschke, Rudolf "Rudi," 127, 178–181

East Berlin, 39, 173, 226

East Germany (German Democratic Republic): and China, 227, 229, 231; and Czechoslovakia, 199, 203, 204; effects of Berlin Wall on, 24; political repression in, 322n41; and Rudi Dutschke, 178–179; and Soviet Union, 34–35, 38, 41, 224–225; United States' political recognition of, 214; and West Berlin, 173; and West Germany, 3, 25–30, 34–35, 181, 216–217, 221–224. *See also* East Berlin; Germany; Ulbricht, Walter; West Berlin

Educational institutions. *See* Higher education

Egypt, 49

Einstein, Albert, 9

Eisenhower, Dwight D., 53, 232, 251; criticism of, 102; economic conditions under, 96, 99; Farewell Address of, 14–15, 22, 98; nuclear arms and foreign policy under, 8–15, 20, 32–35, 38, 41; and university expansion, 89, 90; and Vietnam, 135–137, 139, 150

End of Ideology (Bell), 94–96

England. *See* Great Britain

Erhard, Ludwig, 58–60, 218–219

Ethiopia, 104

European Economic Community, 54–55. *See also* Common Market

European Union, 263

Expectations (rising): as cause of 1960s domestic upheavals, 1, 3–4, 43, 86–89, 93–94, 96, 100, 104–105, 109–110, 112, 129–130, 160, 162–163, 165–166, 179, 211–212, 247; Great Leap Forward's role in, 3, 67–71, 85; liberalism's role in, in United States, 4, 15–25, 44, 88, 91, 104–105, 129, 260; in Soviet Union, 32, 37–40. *See also* Disillusionment; Dissent; Domestic upheaval

Farmer, James, 104

Fathers and Sons (Turgenev), 110–112

Faure, Edgar, 72, 73–74

FDP (Free Democratic Party—West Germany), 26

Federal Republic of Germany. *See* West Germany

Fei Yiming, 227, 323n49

The Feminine Mystique (Friedan), 195

Fifth French Republic (1958–1969), 46, 52, 60, 85, 193

First strike considerations (in nuclear war), 13–14, 38, 235–236, 282n115

Flaubert, Gustave, 125

"Flexible response" (Kennedy's nuclear policy), 17, 18–20, 22, 277n40

Force: Black Panthers' glorification of, 172; Brezhnev's use of, in Prague, 203–206; as demonstrating leaders' inability to manufacture consent, 191–194, 203–206, 211–212; European fears about United States' willingness to use, in their defense, 12–13, 52–53; Mao's use of, 61–62, 65–66, 207–210; Stalin's use of, 31, 105–112; use of, in domestic upheavals, 4, 165–166, 174, 175, 178, 182–184, 187, 189–194, 196, 206; in Vietnam, 138–147. *See also* Cultural Revolution; Nuclear arms; Repression; *Specific wars and incidents*

Ford Foundation, 90, 91, 174

Ford Motor Company, 18

Foreign Affairs, 232

Foreign aid, 21–22, 139–142

Foreign policy: connection between domestic policy and, 98–99, 213, 264–265; domestic upheaval's impact on, 2, 3–4, 213–259; nuclear arms as a hindrance to, 7–43; popular, as shoring up weak leaders, 5; unpopular, as weakening leaders' authority, 2, 4, 39–42, 247, 260–261. *See also* Cold War stalemate; Detente; Foreign aid; Imperialism (liberal); Leaders; Nuclear arms; Secrecy; Summit meetings; *Specific wars and international crises*

Formosa. *See* Taiwan

Foucault, Michel, 293n21

Fouchet, Christian, 190

Fouchet Plan, 187

"Four marshals" (China), 234–235, 325n80

Fourth French Republic, 48–54, 58, 78

France: attempts of, to transcend great-power stalemate, 3, 5, 8, 43, 44–61, 73–79; and China, 3, 27, 45, 61, 67, 71, 73–87, 227, 229, 290n131; constitution of, 47–48, 52; domestic upheaval in, in 1960s, 1, 46, 79, 84–85, 88, 130, 186–194, 211–212, 261; and Eastern European states, 219; elections in, 46; and Great Britain, 54–56; as imperial power, 51–55, 57–58, 60, 73, 260; nuclear policy in, 49–50, 53, 54, 56, 59, 75–77, 215; revolutionary rhetoric in, 3, 45–47, 79–86; and Suez Canal crisis, 49; and Taiwan, 74; and United States, 12–13, 52–53, 56–60, 78–79; and Vietnam War, 51, 73, 78, 133–137, 163, 187; and West Germany, 27, 28, 50, 55–58, 60. *See also* De Gaulle, Charles; National Assembly; Revolution

Frankfurt (Germany), 122

Frankfurter, Felix, 16

Free Democratic Party (FDP—West Germany), 26

Free Speech Movement (Berkeley), 167–169, 171, 172

Free University (West Berlin), 28, 173–180, 185, 188

French Revolution. *See* Revolution

Friedan, Betty, 195
Friendship Treaty (Franco-German), 27, 28, 58
Fukuyama, Francis, 308n2
Furet, François, 79

Galbraith, John Kenneth, 3, 94, 96–100, 105, 123, 263
Gandhi, Mohandas, 103
Gavin, Francis, 277n40
Gdańsk (Poland), 248–249
Geertz, Clifford, 293n21
Geneva: 1954 conference in, 71, 136, 137; 1955 international meetings in, 10, 71, 241
German Democratic Republic. *See* East Germany
Germany, 121, 132, 247; possible reunification of, 23, 25, 29, 220, 225–227, 278n66. *See also* East Germany; West Germany
Germinal (Zola), 30–31
Gierek, Edward, 249–250
Gilpatric, Roswell, 281n99
Gitlin, Todd, 171–172
"Global disruption." *See* Domestic upheaval: as global phenomenon in the 1960s
"Globalization," 262–265
Gobarev, Viktor, 326n87
Goethe, Johann Wolfgang von, 125
Goldschmidt, Arthur, 147–148
Goldwater, Barry, 99, 100–102, 156
Gomułka, Władysław, 247–249
Gramsci, Antonio, 93
"Grand Coalition" (of West German political parties), 174, 220
Great Britain: and China, 74–75, 229; educational expansion in, 92; elections in, 46; and France, 54–56; and 1954 Geneva Conference, 136; as great power, 52, 67, 70, 165; nuclear arms in, 76, 215; and United States, 56. *See also* Hong Kong; Suez Canal crisis
Great Leap Forward (China), 27; criticism of, 114, 117–120; failure of, 69–72, 74, 81, 82, 115, 165, 260; as raising domestic expectations, 3, 67–71, 85; recovery from, 154, 231
Great Proletarian Cultural Revolution. *See* Cultural Revolution
"Great Refusal" (Marcuse's concept), 125–128, 179, 193
"Great Society" programs, 148–149, 159, 160
Green Berets, 141
Greensboro (North Carolina), 103
Guangzhou (China), 64, 81, 119, 207
Guevara, Ernesto "Che," 128, 171–172, 179–180, 210
Guillaumat, Pierre, 49
Gulf of Tonkin incidents, 154–157
Gulf of Tonkin Resolution, 156
Guomindang, 62, 64, 114–115, 232. *See also* Chiang Kai-shek

Habermas, Jürgen, 173–174
Hai Jui's Dismissal (Wu), 115–121
Haiphong (North Vietnam), 255
Hallstein Doctrine, 217
Harkins, Paul, 144
Harriman, W. Averell, 143, 229
Harrington, Michael, 88, 96–100, 105, 124, 130, 263
Harvard University, 90
Havel, Václav, 194–195
The Heart of Darkness (Conrad), 41
Heidegger, Martin, 123
Heller, Walter, 20
Hemingway, Ernest, 109
Herman, Edward, 308n5
Heyns, Roger, 169
Higher education: 1960s growth of, 3, 88–89, 92–93, 125, 129, 260, 269t, 270t, in China, 114, 271t, in Czechoslovakia, 195, in Germany, 222, in Soviet Union, 109–110, in United States, 166–167; as infrastructure for dissent, 88–89, 129, 292n15; reform in, 89–93; and Vietnam military service, 309n11. *See also* Dissent; Domestic upheaval; Expectations; Youth; *Specific universities and students*
Hill, E. F., 230–231
Hilsman, Roger, 16, 140–141

Hitler, Adolf, 191
Hobbes, Thomas, 124
Ho Chi Minh, 80, 81, 134–136, 138
Holdridge, John, 243
Honecker, Erich, 225
Hong Kong, 209, 231. *See also* Great Britain
Hongqi. See Red Flag
Horkheimer, Max, 122
Hotline (crisis), 42, 59
Hsü Chieh, 115–117
Huang Chen, 78–79, 238
Hué (Vietnam), 161, 254–255
Hugo, Victor, 190
Humboldt University (East Berlin), 173
Humphrey, Hubert, 176, 184
"Hunan Provincial Proletarian Revolution-
   ary Great Alliance Committee," 207
"Hundred Flowers" campaign (China), 64–
   65
Hungary, 203–204, 218–219, 330n139; do-
   mestic upheaval in, 64, 65, 67, 194
Husak, Gustav, 206
Hyland, William, 252

Imperialism (liberal), 131–162, 175, 205.
   See also Trade
India, 21, 36–38, 103, 147, 244
Indochina. *See* Vietnam War
Indonesia, 154
Intercontinental missiles. *See* Missiles
Iran, 176–178, 180
Israel, 49–50
Italy, 46, 78, 132

Japan, 132, 134, 145–146, 243–244
Jenkins, Alfred, 230
Johns Hopkins University, 149
Johnson, Lyndon B., 2, 20, 184, 191, 212;
   domestic policy of, 4, 146–149, 152,
   159–161, 171; foreign policy of, 4, 147,
   149–163, 168, 175, 219, 228–230, 246,
   260, 321n16
Jupiter missiles, 40

Kennan, George, 15
Kennedy, John F., 100; assassination of,
   145, 183; criticism of, 102, 130; and

Cuba, 39–41; domestic policies of, 20–
   22, 44; and France, 58–60, 191; "New
   Frontier" policies of, 4, 15–25, 32, 44,
   88, 91, 129, 132–134, 137, 145, 150; nuclear arms and foreign policy under, 4, 8,
   15–25, 30, 34, 41–42, 45, 56, 59, 236;
   and "space race," 17–18, 20, 22, 25, 137;
   and Vietnam, 136–148, 150, 156, 162,
   163; and West Germany, 28, 29, 60, 176
Kennedy, Robert F., 143, 153
Kent State University, 237
Kerr, Clark, 308n6
Keynes, John Maynard, 20, 21
KGB, 2, 206, 235
Khan, Yahya, 239
Khrushchev, Nikita, 88, 107, 110, 113,
   200, 203; and China, 36–38, 66, 76; and
   Cuba, 39–41; and dissent, 105, 121, 130;
   domestic goals of, 30–33, 91, 109;
   Nixon's debate with, 251; nuclear arms
   and foreign policy under, 8, 11, 22–23,
   33–45, 59, 76; on Stalin, 31–32, 64, 67,
   69, 75, 199; United States visit of, 11;
   and university expansion, 89; and West
   Germany, 25, 26
Kiesinger, Kurt Georg, 177, 178
Kimball, Jeffrey, 325n71
Kim Il Sung, 62
King, Martin Luther, Jr., 103–104, 149–
   150, 181–186, 310n29
Kissinger, Henry, 223, 236, 237, 243, 244,
   251, 255–257; secrecy used by, 5, 238–
   241, 252–253, 258
"Koba." *See* Stalin, Josef
Koestler, Arthur, 109
Kohout, Pavel, 194
Kompanii (meetings), 108–109, 111–114
Komsomol (Communist Youth League),
   112, 113
Komsomolskaya Pravda (journal), 113
Korean War, 27, 62, 71, 73, 134, 135, 152,
   162, 173. *See also* North Korea; South
   Korea
Kosygin, Aleksei, 157, 238, 321n16,
   329n130
Kriegel, František, 197
Kundera, Milan, 194, 195

Language (of dissent). *See* Dissent

Lansdale, Edward, 138–139

"Lantphibex-62," 39

Laos, 71, 72, 136, 147, 157

Lasch, Christopher, 264

Latin America, 127–128, 132, 177, 181. *See also Specific Latin American countries*

Lawrence, Ernest, 166

Leaders: charisma as source of authority for, 44–46, 190–191, 193–194, 236–237; as cultivating charisma, 3, 4, 186, 260; domestic upheavals as threat to, 1–2, 4–5, 164, 166, 179, 182–183, 186–194, 207–212, 216, 235–237, 245; importance of building public consensus by, 264–265; stable relations with foreign, as legitimating domestic authority of, 213–215, 232, 236–237, 240, 244–245, 247, 250, 254–259, 261; unpopular foreign policy as leading to weakening of, 4, 39–42, 247, 260–261. *See also* Charisma; Force; Secrecy; Summit meetings; *Specific world leaders*

Le Monde, 26, 27

Lenin, Vladimir, 106, 123, 210

Leningrad (Soviet Union), 251

Lennon, John, 211

Leviathan (Hobbes), 124

Liang Qichao, 114

Liao Masha, 118, 120

"Liberal imperialism," 131–132. *See also* Imperialism

Liberalism: discrediting of, 263–264; illiberal consequences of, 131–163, 260–261; under Kennedy, 15–25; King as exemplar of, 182–183; Mao's dislike of, 242; as raising expectations, 4, 15–25, 44, 88, 91, 104–105, 129, 260

Liberation Army Daily (China), 208

Liberation Daily (Shanghai newspaper), 298n104

Liberia, 104

Life magazine, 238, 239

Limited Nuclear Test Ban Treaty, 42, 59, 60, 75, 76, 245

Lin Biao, 242, 298n107

Lincoln Memorial (Washington, D.C.), 2

Lippmann, Walter, 308n5

Literární listy, 202

"Little Leap Forward," 62–64

Little Red Book (Mao). *See* Mao Zedong: sayings of

Litvinov, Maxim, 206

Liu Shaoqi, 65, 70–71, 81, 119

Li Zhisui, 318n180

Loan, Nguyen Ngoc, 162

Lodge, Henry Cabot, 143–145

Łód (Poland), 248

Lord, Winston, 241, 243

Louis Napoleon, 45

Lucky Dragon (ship), 9

Macao, 325n67

MacFarquhar, Roderick, 282n112

Macmillan, Harold, 54–55

Maddox (U.S. ship), 154–155

Madison, James, 99

Madsen, Richard, 319n3

Mailer, Norman, 169

Ma Lianliang, 118

Malraux, André, 82–83, 289n105

Manac'h, Etienne, 323n47

Manchuria, 243

The Man in the Gray Flannel Suit (Wilson), 319n200

Manion, Clarence, 294n40

Mann, Thomas, 125

Mansfield, Mike, 136, 151, 240

Mao Zedong, 179–180, 292n14; attempts of, to transcend great-power stalemate, 3, 5, 8, 43, 44–45, 58, 74–79; charisma of, 61, 71, 80, 83–87, 120–121, 130, 237, 260; Chinese criticism of, 114, 118–119, 130; and detente, 226–232, 238–245; domestic goals of, 61–64, 67–71, 88, 91–92, 165; as encouraging domestic upheaval, 1, 3, 64, 65, 80, 81–83, 85, 119–121, 128–130, 207, 210, 229, 230, 261; flees domestic upheaval in China, 1, 208, 318n180; and Nixon, 154, 228, 233–235, 237, 238–245, 253; sayings of, 82, 172, 179, 205, 207, 208, 210, 298n107; suppresses Cultural Revolution, 207, 208–212, 231–235, 238, 239, 261; and Taiwan crises, 35, 37; and Vietnam, 136, 163; and Wu Han, 114, 115, 117, 118

"Mao Zedong Thought." *See* Mao Zedong: sayings of

Marcuse, Herbert, 3, 89, 94, 121–130, 179, 193

Marshall, George, 135

Marshall Plan, 158

Marx, Karl, 6, 65, 123

Massu, Jacques, 192, 194

"May 16 Corps" (China), 207

Mazurov, Kirill, 204

McCain, Franklin, 103

McCloy, John J., 57

McCone, John, 143

McNamara, Robert S., 18, 143, 145, 153, 158, 160, 170, 302n23

Medvedev, Zhores, 108

Mekong River project, 148, 149, 151, 154, 158, 161

Memphis (Tennessee), 182–183

Mendès-France, Pierre, 49

Métreaux, Lilly, 190

Mill, John Stuart, 123

Mills, C. Wright, 123

Ming period (China), 114, 115, 117, 118, 120

Minh, Duong Van ("Big Minh"), 144

Les Misérables (Hugo), 190

Missiles, 56; in Cuba, 39–41; production of, 12–13, 18, 20, 34, 37, 38, 251; treaties regarding, 256. *See also* Cuba: missile crisis in; Nuclear arms

Mladá fronta, 202

Monnet, Jean, 56

Morocco, 51

Moscow (Soviet Union), 206, 251; summit meeting in, 253, 254–258. *See also* Moscow Treaty

Moscow Institute of Historical Archives, 206

Moscow Treaty, 224–225

Moyers, Bill, 159

My Lai Massacre, 161–162

Nanjing (China), 243

Nanterre University (France), 187–188

Napoleon Bonaparte, 45, 47, 83, 84

Narcissism, 264

"Nassau Summit" (1962), 56

National Advisory Commission on Civil Disorders, 185

National Assembly (France), 47, 49, 51, 85, 193

National Defense Education Act (United States), 89

National Democratic Party of Germany (NPD), 174–175, 178

National Liberation Front (South Vietnam), 78, 137–138, 140–141, 144, 153–154, 157, 161, 306n95

National Review (journal), 99, 100

National Security Council paper (NSC 68), 19

National Youth Administration (NYA), 146

"Nation-building" (in South Vietnam), 142

NATO (North Atlantic Treaty Organization), 321n16; and France, 55, 57, 60, 78; vs. Warsaw Pact countries, 34, 35, 52, 53, 59; and West Germany, 58, 175

Newark (New Jersey), 160, 182

New China News Agency, 62

New Deal, 146–152, 154, 158–159, 162

"New economics," 17, 20–22, 25

"New Frontier": rising expectations from, 4, 15–25, 32, 44, 88, 91, 129; Southeast Asia as, 132–134, 137, 145, 150

New Left: detente's impact on, 244; in France, 188; in United States, 100, 102–105, 167–168, 174, 244; in West Germany, 174

"New Look" (Eisenhower's nuclear policy), 11, 32

New Right: detente's impact on, 244; in France, 188–189; in the United States, 100, 101, 244; in West Germany, 174–175

Newton, Huey, 172

Nie Rongzhen, 326n80

Nitze, Paul, 19

Nixon, Richard, 100, 160, 238–239; on domestic upheaval, 2; foreign policy of, 5, 232–237, 240–245, 250–258, 261; lack of charisma of, 5; Mao's meeting with, 228, 240, 241–245, 253. *See also* Nixon Doctrine

Nixon Doctrine, 246, 329n126
NLF. *See* National Liberation Front (South Vietnam)
Non-aggression pacts, 42, 59. *See also* Detente
North Atlantic Council, 78
North Atlantic Treaty Organization. *See* NATO
North Korea, 62, 135, 244. *See also* Korean War
North Vietnam (Democratic Republic of Vietnam), 136, 138, 153–159, 161, 228–229, 254–256; and China, 78, 134, 154, 162, 244, 254; and Soviet Union, 134, 157, 162, 205, 247, 254. *See also* Vietnam War
"Notes from a Three-Family Village," 118
Novosibirsk (Soviet Union), 251
Novotny, Antonín, 194–199, 203
NPD (National Democratic Party of Germany), 174–175, 178
Nuclear arms: and Berkeley, 166, 167; China's, 3, 75–77, 215, 236; vs. conventional armies, 10–11, 18–19, 33; and crisis hotline, 42, 59; as deterrent to war, 8–16, 39–41; first strike considerations regarding, 13–14, 38, 235–236, 282n115; France's, 3, 49–50, 53–54, 59, 75–77, 215; Great Britain's, 76, 215; Israel's, 49–50; limits on development of, 9–10, 42; and missile production, 12–13, 18, 20, 34, 37, 38; nonproliferation efforts regarding, 77, 321n16; as producing stalemate among great powers, 2–3, 7–43, 262; Soviet Union's, 3, 7–8, 17–25, 30–43, 54, 76, 215; as symbols of national strength, 13, 32–33, 39–41, 53–54, 76–77; tests of, 9, 42, 53, 54, 59, 60, 75, 76, 154, 245; United States', 3, 7–15, 17–25, 30–43, 52–53, 76, 215; West Germany's concerns about, 25–30, 279n78. *See also* Arms control agreements; Cold War stalemate; Disarmament; Missiles

Occident (French organization), 188–189
Ochs, Phil, 169
"Ode to Jean-Jacques Rousseau" (Chen), 83

Ohnesorg, Benno, 178
One Day in the Life of Ivan Denisovich (Solzhenitsyn), 105–109, 112, 114
One-Dimensional Man (Marcuse), 122–129
"Open skies" policy, 10
"Operation Danube," 204
"Operation Mongoose," 39
Oppenheimer, Robert, 166
Orwell, George, 109
Ostpolitik, 4–5, 29, 218–228, 258, 263, 321n16. *See also* Detente
The Other America (Harringon), 97–98, 124
"Our Fifty Million Poor" (Harrington), 97

Pahlavi, Mohammed Reza (Shah), 176–178, 180
Pakistan, 147, 230, 238–239, 244
Paris Commune (1871), 45, 82, 85, 189
Paris riots (1968), 186–194, 261
Pasternak, Boris, 109
Pauling, Linus, 10
Peace. *See* Detente
"Peace Note" (West Germany), 219–220
Peng Dehuai, 117
People's Daily (Renmin ribao), 63, 118, 119, 208–210, 287n62, 325n77
People's Liberation Army (PLA—China), 82, 83, 207–208
People's Republic of China. *See* China (People's Republic of)
Peres, Shimon, 50
Philippines, 147
"Ping-Pong" diplomacy, 239
PLA (People's Liberation Army—China), 82, 83, 207–208
Pleiku (South Vietnam), 157
Poland, 230, 330n139; Communist Party in, 248; and Czechoslovakia, 199, 203, 204; domestic upheaval in, 64, 67, 247–250; international meetings in, 71, 72; and West Germany, 218, 220, 225; Workers' Party in, 31
Polaris submarine missiles, 20, 40, 56
Pol Pot, 80, 81
Pompidou, Georges, 192, 193
Port Huron Statement (SDS), 104–105
Portugal, 325n67

Postmodernism, 259, 262
"Power to the People" (song), 211
Práce, 202
Prague (Czechoslovakia), 194–206, 210, 221, 222, 246–247, 261
Presley, Elvis, 109
"A Program of Action to Prevent Communist Domination" (Kennedy task force report), 139–140
Protests. *See* Domestic upheaval
Public unrest. *See* Domestic upheaval

Qing dynasty (China), 61
Qin-Han period (China), 118

Radio Free Europe, 195
Radio Liberty, 112
Ray, James Earl, 183
Reagan, Ronald, 101–102, 172
Red Flag (Hongqi), 209, 325n77
Red Guards: detente's impact on, 244; and domestic upheaval in China, 1, 81–83, 86, 119–121, 229, 235, 298n104; factional fighting among, 206–210; Mao's restraint of, 231–235, 238. *See also* Cultural Revolution (China)
Renmin ribao. See People's Daily
Repression (domestic political): Cold War's contribution to, 3, 4–5, 11, 45, 92, 94–96, 99–130, 164, 177–179, 211; and detente, 2, 4, 5, 23–25, 44, 177, 186, 188, 213, 216, 221–226, 231, 241–242, 256, 258–259, 261, 264, 322n41. *See also* Force
Revolution: Marcuse's support for, 126, 127–129; opportunities for, 188; shared rhetoric of, in France and China, 3, 45–47, 79–86. *See also* Cultural Revolution; Domestic upheaval; Paris Commune
"Revolution" (Beatles song), 211
Rhee, Syngman, 136
Rice University, 18
Robespierre, Maximilien, 47
"Rolling Thunder" bombing program, 157–158
Roosevelt, Franklin D., 16, 89, 132, 145–146, 148, 150, 151, 277n47. *See also* New Deal

Rostow, Eugene V., 246
Rostow, Walt W., 21, 139–140, 230
Rousseau, Jean-Jacques, 83, 94, 290n131
Rubin, Jerry, 168–169
Rumania, 205, 218, 246, 330n139
Rusk, Dean, 143, 156, 160, 324n58
Russell, Bertrand, 9
Russell, Richard, 151–152, 156
"Rustication" (in China), 70–71

Sahara Desert, 53
SALT I, 256
Samizdat texts, 108–112, 114, 195, 206
San Francisco Mime Troupe, 169
Sarotte, Mary, 322n41
Satellites. *See* Missiles; Sputnik I
Savio, Mario, 168
Scheel, Walter, 223, 225, 226–228
Schlesinger, Arthur, Jr., 16, 17
Schröder, Gerhard, 218
Schurmann, Franz, 72
Schütz, Klaus, 227
Schwartz, Thomas Alan, 321n16
Schweitzer, Albert, 9–10
SDS. *See* Students for a Democratic Society
Seale, Bobby, 172
Secrecy: as leading to people's political disengagement, 5, 215, 259; as tactic used by superpowers, 5, 236–242, 244–245, 252–253, 257, 261, 264; West Germany's use of, 218, 223, 228
Sedláková, Mária, 197
Senegal, 147
Shanghai (China), 114, 119, 207, 208, 298n104
"Shanghai Communiqué," 244
Shils, Edward, 87
Sino-Soviet split. *See* China: and Soviet Union
Slovak Communist Party, 197
Slums and Suburbs (Conant), 90
Smale, Stephen, 168–169
Smathers, George, 155
SNCC. *See* Student Nonviolent Coordinating Committee
Snow, C. P., 89
Snow, Edgar, 238, 239, 288n90
Snow, Lois, 238

Social Democratic Party (SPD—West Germany), 174, 220
Socialist German Student Union, 174, 175, 310n40
Solzhenitsyn, Aleksandr, 3, 88–89, 94, 105–110, 112, 114, 121, 130; Havel's praise for, 194, 195
Sorbonne, 188–189, 191
South Africa, 104
South Korea, 62, 135, 136, 243, 244. See also Korean War
South Vietnam (State of Vietnam), 21, 136–148, 151, 153–155, 157, 161–162, 237, 240, 244, 254–255. See also National Liberation Front; Vietnam War
Southwest Texas State Teachers College, 146
Soviet Union: and China, 27–28, 34–39, 41, 43, 61–67, 72, 73, 75–79, 205, 206, 227–228, 234–238, 243, 246; and Cuba, 39–41, 43; dissent in, 105–114, 121, 130, 205–206, 251; domestic upheaval in, 1, 2, 166, 211–212, 234, 246–250; and East Germany, 34–35, 38, 224–225; educational reform in, 89, 93; Marcuse on, 122, 123; and Poland, 247–250; and "Prague Spring," 194–206, 221, 222, 246–247; purges in, 93; rising expectations in, 32, 37–40; United States' detente with, 5, 41, 58–59, 86, 235–237, 243, 245–258, 261; United States' nuclear arms negotiations with, 10–11, 14, 22–23, 42, 59–60; United States' nuclear competition with, 3, 7–25, 30–43, 54, 76, 215; and Vietnam, 5, 132–134, 136, 138, 157, 159, 163, 205, 247, 252–255, 261, 329n130; and West Berlin, 172–173; and West Germany, 25, 181, 217, 218, 223, 243, 261. See also Brezhnev, Leonid; CMEA; Cold War stalemate; KGB; Khrushchev, Nikita; Korean War; Kosygin, Aleksei; Stalin, Josef; Warsaw Pact
Špacek, Josef, 197
"Space race," 17–18, 20, 22, 25, 137
SPD (Social Democratic Party—West Germany), 174, 220

Spock, Benjamin, 169
Springer, Axel, 178
Sputnik I (satellite), 12, 67, 89
The Stages of Economic Growth (Rostow), 139
Stalin, Josef, 30, 33, 61–62, 66, 80, 191; later criticism of, 31–32, 64, 67, 69, 75, 194, 199; reign of terror under, 31–32, 105, 107, 110, 210
State of Vietnam. See South Vietnam
Stearman, William, 236
Stein, Herbert, 277n47
Stevenson, Adlai, 152–153
Stone, I. F., 169
Strategic Arms Limitations Agreements, 256
"Strategic villages" program (South Vietnam), 140–141, 145
Strauss, Franz-Josef, 35, 222
Student Nonviolent Coordinating Committee (SNCC), 103, 172, 181
Students' Executive Committee for Justice (Greensboro, North Carolina), 103
Students for a Democratic Society (SDS), 102, 104–105, 170, 171–172, 310n40
Suez Canal crisis, 12
Summit meetings: domestic importance of, 5, 261; Moscow (1972), 253, 254–258; Nassau (1962), 56; Paris (1960), 54; Sino-Soviet (1959), 36; Vienna (1961), 22–23
"Surprise Attack Conference," 14
Sverdlovsk (Soviet Union), 251
Szulc, Tad, 204

Taiwan, 147; expulsion of, from United Nations, 240, 241; and France, 74; and People's Republic of China, 62, 71, 72, 226–227, 239, 243, 244. See also Chiang Kai-shek; Guomindang; Taiwan Strait
Taiwan Strait, 27, 329n126; crises in, 3, 12, 13, 35–37, 39
Taylor, Maxwell, 143, 306n95
"Ten Point Manifesto" (NLF), 138
Terrorism, 262, 264–265
Tet offensive (Vietnam War), 161, 162, 180, 182, 255
Thadden, Adolf von, 174

Thailand, 147, 154

Thielen, Friedrich, 174

Third world: liberal imperialism toward, 131–132; Marcuse on, 126–128; superpower proxy wars in, 133, 245–246. *See also Specific third world countries and regions*

Thomas, Norman, 169

Tibet, 36, 62

Tocqueville, Alexis de, 93, 283n1

Trachtenberg, Marc, 278n54, 282n115

Trade: East-West, 3, 5, 28, 77–78, 217–219, 226–228, 231, 234, 249, 256, 261, 269t, 330n143; between Soviet Union and China, 238. *See also* Imperialism

Treaty of Friendship (Franco-German), 27, 28

"Triangular politics," 263; Adenauer's, 27, 235–237; Nixon's, 5, 235–237, 252–254

Trotsky, Leon, 123

Truman, Harry, 89, 135, 145–146, 152

Tunisia, 51

Turgenev, Ivan, 110–112

Turkey, 40

Turner, Frederick Jackson, 16

Turner Joy (U.S. ship), 155

Tutzing Christian Academy, 29, 216–218, 224

"22 March Movement," 188

"Two Thousand Words" (Vaculík), 200–202

Ulbricht, Walter, 25–26, 34, 35, 224

Unger, Jonathan, 319n3

United Nations, 34, 54, 240, 241, 257

United Nations Disarmament Commission, 54

United States: and China, 5, 71–73, 75, 77–79, 227, 228–245, 252–253, 258, 261; and Cuba, 39–40; dissent in, 96–105; domestic upheaval in, 1–4, 159–161, 166–172, 181–186, 211–212, 234, 237, 251–252, 261; educational reform in, 89–90, 93; European fears about willingness of, to defend them, 12–13, 52–53; and France, 29, 52–53, 56–60, 78–79, 191, 238; and Great Britain, 56; liberal imperialism of, 131–162, 175; Marcuse's criti-

cism of, 122–129; McCarthyism in, 93; poverty in, 96–99, 124–125, 263; propensity of, to make decisions without consulting allies, 59; protests against involvement of, in Vietnam War, 3–4, 126, 159–161, 168–172, 181–182, 187–188, 221, 251; Soviet Union's detente with, 5, 41, 58–59, 86, 235–237, 243, 245–258, 261; Soviet Union's nuclear arms negotiations with, 10–11, 14, 22–23, 42, 59, 60; Soviet Union's nuclear competition with, 3, 7–25, 30–43, 52–53, 76, 215; and Suez Canal crisis, 49; and Taiwan, 240–241, 243; Vietnam War involvement by, 4–5, 132–162, 175, 180, 219, 221, 228–230, 233, 235, 237–238, 243, 246, 251–254; and West Berlin, 173; and West Germany, 28, 29, 173, 174–175. *See also* CIA; Civil rights movement; Cold War stalemate; Korean War; Liberalism; NATO; Nuclear arms; Vietnam War; *Specific presidents*

U.S. Army, 184–185

U.S. Department of Defense, 90

U.S. Department of Labor, 97

Universities. *See* Higher education; *Specific universities*

University of California at Berkeley, 166–172, 185

University of Hamburg, 218

University of Michigan, 168

Up from Liberalism (Buckley), 99–100

Vaculík, Ludvík, 194–195, 200–202

Vaïse, Maurice, 284n19

Vienna summit meeting, 22–23

Viet Cong. *See* National Liberation Front (South Vietnam)

Viet Minh, 72

Vietnam Congress, 180

Vietnam Day Committee (Berkeley), 168–170

Vietnam War, 71, 130; and China, 5, 73, 78, 132–134, 136, 138, 154, 159, 163, 228–230, 235, 237, 243, 254, 261; class and race issues among Americans in, 309n11, 310n29; "counterinsurgency

Vietnam War *(continued)*
doctrine" in, 139–142, 145; and liberalism, 260–261; Marcuse on, 127, 128;
and Mekong River project, 148, 149,
151, 154, 158, 161; "Prague Spring" lik-
ened to, 205; protests against United
States' involvement in, 3–4, 126, 159–
161, 168–172, 181–182, 187–188, 221,
251; and Soviet Union, 5, 132–134, 136,
138, 157, 159, 163, 205, 247, 252–255,
261, 329n130; United States' involvement in, 4–5, 132–162, 175, 180, 219,
221, 228–230, 233, 235, 237–238, 243,
246, 251–254; and West Germany, 175,
180. *See also* North Vietnam; South Vietnam
Voting Rights Act, 148

Wall, Irwin M., 284n19
Wallace, George, 101, 102, 181
Walters, Vernon, 238
Wang Li, 208
Wang Pingnan, 72
War. *See* Cold War stalemate; Force; Nu-
clear arms; "War on Terrorism"; *Specific
wars*
War on Poverty program, 148–149
"War on Terrorism," 262, 264–265
Warsaw Pact, 52, 59, 175, 195, 201, 204,
206, 221, 246
Warsaw Sino-American meetings, 230
Warsaw University, 247
Washington, D.C.: anti-war demonstra-
tions in, 168–170; riots in, 183–185, 261
Washington, Walter E., 184
Watts riot (United States), 182
Weber, Max, 123, 283n1; on charisma, 44,
48, 121, 237, 283n3; on legitimacy,
308n5
Weinberg, Jacob, 168
West Berlin: Conant in, 91; domestic up-
heaval in, 172–181, 261; Kennedy in,
28, 60; possibility of reunifying, 226; So-
viet challenges to American interests in,
12, 13, 23–25, 34, 172–173. *See also*
Berlin crises; Berlin Wall; East Berlin;
Free University; West Germany

West Germany (Federal Republic of Germany), 173; and China, 226–228, 230;
Conant in, 89, 90–91; detente in, 216–
226; domestic upheaval in, 1, 5, 126–
127, 172–181, 211–212, 261; early detente efforts in, 3, 8, 25–30, 34–35, 43,
45, 54, 216, 226, 228, 279n78; and Eastern European countries, 25–30, 34–35,
219–225; effects of Berlin Wall on, 24–
25, 173; elections in, 46; fears of, about
United States' willingness to defend, 12–
13, 24–25, 52; and France, 1, 27, 28, 50,
55–58, 60; "Grand Coalition" of political
parties in, 174, 220; and Iran, 176–178;
nuclear capabilities of, 35, 279n78; as
part of European Economic Community,
54; and Soviet Union, 25, 181, 217, 218,
223, 243, 261; and United States, 28, 29,
173, 174–175. *See also* Adenauer,
Konrad; Berlin crises; Berlin Wall;
Brandt, Willy; East Berlin; Erhard, Lud-
wig; Germany; West Berlin
Westmoreland, William, 160, 161
"Whither China?" (Hunan Provincial
Committee), 207
Williams, William Appleman, 305n81
Wilson, Sloan, 319n200
Wilson, Woodrow, 132
Wohlstetter, Albert, 14
"World Association of Troglodytes," 113–
114
World Trade Organization, 263
Wu Han, 3, 89, 94, 114–121, 130
Wuhan (China), 1, 206–211, 261

Xie Fuzhi, 208
Xinjiang (China), 207
Xue Litai, 323n49
Xu Xiangquian, 326n80

Yale University, 20
Yao Wenyuan, 119
Ye Jianying, 326n80
Young Americans for Freedom (YAF),
101
Youth: and de Gaulle, 84–85, 186–194;
global upheaval by, in 1960s, 1–2, 102–

105, 112–113, 129–130, 164–212; intellectual influences on 1960s, 88–130;
numbers of, in 1960s, 3, 88–89, 91–93,
129. *See also* Disillusionment; Domestic
upheaval; Higher education
Yugoslavia, 205, 246

Zemědělské noviny, 202
Zhou Enlai, 323n49; and Cultural Revolution, 86, 208; and France, 74, 80–82,
290n131; on Great Leap Forward, 70,
71; in Hungary and Poland, 65; on Soviet and United States hegemony, 75,
234–235; and Soviet Union, 238; and
United States, 230, 231, 236–241, 243–
244
Zhukov, Georgy, 107
Zhu Yuanzhang (Ming emperor), 115, 117,
120
Zola, Emile, 30–31